ANGLO-IRISH

THE LITERARY IMAGINATION IN A HYPHENATED CULTURE

Julian Moynahan

PRINCETON UNIVERSITY PRESS • PRINCETON, NEW JERSEY

PUBLISHED BY PRINCETON UNIVERSITY PRESS, 41 WILLIAM STREET,
PRINCETON, NEW JERSEY 08540
IN THE UNITED KINGDOM: PRINCETON UNIVERSITY PRESS,
CHICHESTER, WEST SUSSEX

LIBRARY OF CONGRESS CATALOGING-IN-PUBLICATION DATA

MOYNAHAN, JULIAN, 1925–.
ANGLO-IRISH : THE LITERARY IMAGINATION
IN A HYPHENATED CULTURE / JULIAN MOYNAHAN.
P. CM.
INCLUDES BIBLIOGRAPHICAL REFERENCES (P.) AND INDEX.
ISBN 0-691-03757-4 : $24.95
1. ENGLISH LITERATURE—IRISH AUTHORS—HISTORY AND CRITICISM.
2. IRELAND—INTELLECTUAL LIFE—19TH CENTURY.
3. IRELAND—INTELLECTUAL LIFE—20TH CENTURY.
4. BRITISH—IRELAND—INTELLECTUAL LIFE.
5. IRELAND—IN LITERATURE. I. TITLE.
PR8752.M69 1994
820.9'9415'09034—DC20 94-19545

THIS BOOK HAS BEEN COMPOSED IN GALLIARD

PRINCETON UNIVERSITY PRESS BOOKS ARE
PRINTED ON ACID-FREE PAPER AND MEET THE GUIDELINES
FOR PERMANENCE AND DURABILITY OF THE COMMITTEE
ON PRODUCTION GUIDELINES FOR BOOK LONGEVITY
OF THE COUNCIL ON LIBRARY RESOURCES

PRINTED IN THE UNITED STATES OF AMERICA

1 3 5 7 9 10 8 6 4 2

IN MEMORY OF

CATHERINE MOYNAHAN RICH

1951 - 1984

CONTENTS

ACKNOWLEDGMENTS

IN WRITING this book I was aided by Guggenheim Foundation and NEH fellowships and by several grants and fellowships from the Rutgers University Research Council. I also want to thank above all Professor Joseph Frank, now of Stanford University, who in 1975, as Director of the Christian Gauss Seminars in Criticism at Princeton University, extended me the invitation to give the three lectures on Anglo-Irish writers from which this book developed.

Friendships with the Irish writers Sean O'Faolain and Benedict Kiely, and briefer acquaintanceships with Elizabeth Bowen, Patrick Kavanagh, and Frank O'Connor, by showing me how complicated a subject I was taking up, helped me, I hope, to avoid the more conventional and patriotic formulations of Irish literary culture, both in its bifurcations and in its (perhaps) underlying unity.

I am indebted to many Irish and Ireland-dwelling people, some of them academics, others artists, still others of status undetermined who showed me facets of my subject often without intending to. Among those no longer living are: T. D. Williams and Patricia Murphy, David Greene, Peter Ure, Lady Beatrice Glenavy, Siobhan Stuart, Eileen O'Faolain, Michael MacLiammoir, Roger McHugh, Owen Sheehy-Skeffington, Barbara Hayley, Terence de Vere White, and Mary M'Neese Reilly.

Among the living are: Philip Edwards, Denis Donoghue, Bill and Verette Finlay, Sean White, Maurice Harmon, Patrick Ryan, Lunia Ryan, Patrick Collins, Imogen Stuart, Ian Stuart, Andrew Carpenter, Augustine Martin, A. K. Donoghue, J. P. Donleavy, C. F. Main, Jr., Richard Murphy , Paul Muldoon, and Terence Brown.

I have been fortunate to study under great and generous teachers, especially Harry T. Levin and Richard Ellmann in Harvard graduate school, to teach with gifted and stimulating associates, especially G. Armour Craig and C. L. Barber at Amherst College, R. P. Blackmur and Laurence B. Holland at Princeton, and Richard Poirier and Thomas Edwards at Rutgers, but one's energy and thought transferences with one's students, undergraduate and graduate, numbering in the hundreds and hundreds over forty years, have been just as important.

My greatest debt of gratitude is to my wife, Elizabeth Reilly Moynahan, architect and planner, without whose prompting I should never have gone to teach in Ireland in 1963–64, where and when the first hints of my subject's design and plan were given.

Some parts of this book have appeared in different form elsewhere: In Chapter 5, I used several paragraphs discussing John Banim's *The Anglo-Irish of the Nineteenth Century* (1828) from my essay "The Image of the City in Nineteenth Century Irish Fiction," which originally appeared in *The Irish Writer and the City*, ed. Maurice Harmon (Gerrard's Crossing, Bucks.: Colin Smythe; and Totowa, N.J.: Barnes and Noble Books). In Chapter 6, I used material from my essay "The Politics of Anglo-Irish Gothic: Maturin, Le Fanu, and 'The Return of the Repressed,'" originally appearing in *Studies in Anglo-Irish Literature*, ed. Heinz Kosok (Bonn: Bouvier Verlag Herbert Grundmann, 1982). In Chapter 11, I used material from my essay "Elizabeth Bowen: Anglo-Irish Postmortem," reprinted here by permission from *Raritan: A Quarterly Review*, 9, no. 2 (1989). Copyright © 1989 by *Raritan*, 31 Mine St., New Brunswick, NJ 08903.

In Chapter 9, quotations from the unpublished diaries of Edith Somerville and Martin Ross are printed with the kind permission of Mary Kelly and the Special Collections Division of the Library of Queens University, Belfast, Northern Ireland.

In Chapter 10, poetry of W. B. Yeats, including portions of "Meditations in Time of Civil War"; "The Municipal Gallery Revisited"; "The Curse of Cromwell"; "The Tower"; "The Municipal Gallery Revisited"; and 'Under Ben Bulben" are reprinted with permission of Simon & Schuster from *The Collected Works of W. B. Yeats*, Vol. I: *The Poems*, Revised, edited by Richard J. Finneran, Copyright © 1928 by Macmillan Publishing Company, renewed 1956 by Georgie Yeats. Copyright © 1940 by Georgie Yeats, renewed 1968 by Bertha Georgie Yeats, Michael Butler Yeats, and Anne Yeats. "Upon a House Shaken by the Land Agitation" is reprinted with permission of Simon & Schuster from *The Collected Works of W. B. Yeats*, Vol. I: *The Poems*, Revised, edited by Richard J. Finneran (New York: Macmillan, 1989).

PREFACE

THE ANGLO-IRISH are gone but continue to haunt the imagination like a lost colony. One sees this in the persistence and popularity of "Big House" fiction, at a time when most surviving structures of the type have been converted into asylums and nursing homes, conference centers and guest houses, vacation homes for media stars. Some of this fiction is pastiche contrived by outsiders: for example, the New Yorker J. P. Donleavy's several farcical novels of life on Irish estates, culminating in *Leila* (1983), and the tragicomic *Troubles* (1971) by the late J. G. Farrell, an Australian. Other novels, however, including Aidan Higgins's *Langrishe Go Down* (1966), William Trevor's *Fools of Fortune* (1983) and *The Silence in the Garden* (1989), and books by M. J. Farrell (pseudonym) in her golden-years resurrection as actual Molly Keane, and by the postmodernist John Banville (*Birchwood*, 1973) are from Irish men and women who in varying degrees show filiation with the colony itself.

The word "colony" may give pause. My view is rather different from those approaches that follow Yeats in speaking of an Anglo-Irish golden age prior to the nineteenth century. This book focuses on the nineteenth century and the first half of the twentieth, describing how the Anglo-Irish "literary imagination" comes into its own just as the privileges and power of this community begin to be curtailed and what had been called an Ascendancy heads down toward an inevitable demise. Women writers (Maria Edgeworth, Somerville and Ross, Elizabeth Bowen) are a major force in the development of this literary imagination. In the move toward ending, Samuel Beckett appears as the master of the Anglo-Irish endgame, with Yeats showing the way there, and Elizabeth Bowen, on her Anglo-Irish side, contributing much to what I call the Anglo-Irish postmortem.

My view is also decidedly different from Edward W. Said's in his discussions of imperialism and colonialism as this theme applies to Ireland.[1] He assumes that colonials, except for rare individuals, are everlasting tools of the power that sent them over to occupy, settle, and dominate. I assume that an entire colony gets cut off from its extraterritorial roots, becoming as Irish as everybody else, though the cultural contribution it makes remains distinctive for as long as there are enough self-identified Anglo-Irish people on Irish ground to constitute a "critical mass."

Indeed, Said's decision to include Ireland as a sort of honorary third-world territory in his otherwise magisterial account of the imperial and cultural incursions of nineteenth- and twentieth-century white European (and American) powers on "the non-European world" (*Culture and Imperialism*, xii) is a serious miscalculation betraying his thought into a number of absurdities. In his Field Day pamphlet, *Yeats and Decolonization* (1990), Ireland is presented as an overseas (!) territory victimized by systematic British imperialism and struggling to "decolonize" itself according to ideological blueprints derived from Franz Fanon's *Wretched of the Earth* (1965) and, even more remotely, from the conference of twenty-nine Asian-African former colonies held at Bandung in Java, Indonesia, during April 1955.

Among these bizarre claims, the claim is also made that Ireland, in company with Egypt and India, Ghana and Indonesia, developed an independence movement "in the period from the First World War and concluding in the 1950s" (*Yeats and Decolonization*, 75). Movements for Irish independence, to mention only comparatively modern times, go back to the United Irish insurrections of 1798 and to Daniel O'Connell's Union Repeal movement of the 1840s, while by 1950 Ireland's nationhood, despite Partition of the northern six counties, had been secured for all of twenty-nine years.

Said also remarks that Ireland is in the pantheon of Bandung . . . "in all its suffering and greatness, because of the nationalist dynamic" (75). Out of this dynamic emerge "crucial works—Pannikar's *Asia and Western Dominance,* George Antonius's *The Arab Awakening* and the various works of the Irish Revival," not one of which is mentioned by name. Nor does Said seem aware that by 1950 Ireland, which had certainly demonstrated its sovereign independence by remaining neutral throughout the Second World War, far from continuing to wave the tattered green flag of a self-absorbed nationalism was devoting its best political efforts to securing membership in the United Nations over the resolute vetoing of its repeated applications by the U.S.S.R. Here the Inter-Party Government was only following the example of an earlier government, which in 1923 won membership for the tiny Irish Free State in the League of Nations. Small nations are attracted by large international organizations like flies to honey. The latter give the former a forum and plenty of status. Only someone entranced by the rhetoric of imperialism and colonialism would fail to see this and see also the utter irrelevance of an Arab awakening to "works" of what he chooses to call "the Irish Revival."

One cannot really argue with Said, for he knows too little of Ireland, especially about the history of its entanglements with the larger island, to provide a basis of argument. To regard the few nautical miles separating Britain and Ireland "overseas" is an illustration. Substantial portions of western Scotland lie farther from the British mainland than does Ireland. Should the Hebrides be considered colonial territory devastated by

English imperialism? How about Wales and Cornwall? How about the Isle of Man and the Orkneys?

On the issue of colonialism I want to say one last thing. The "ism" doesn't apply. Most of the writers explored in this book were offspring from a colony that was canceled and canceled itself through the Act of Union in 1800. Anglo-Irish Literature—my construction of it—begins after colonialism. We shall see these offspring—a sort of orphaned cohort—awakening to the reality of what has happened and coming to acknowledge their own unevadable—the Yeatsian adjectives are unappeasable and unpersuadable—Irish entanglements. In the process, Irish cultural identity is complicated and enriched. For about a century and a half these writers produce much of the best of Irish writing for that span of time and it is still to be called an Anglo-Irish literature. It is a hybrid literature. Hybridization is good, as Charles Darwin noted. It produces "hybrid vigor."

Beyond these matters, what is the nature of the appeal, what was the charm of the Anglo-Irish that somehow keeps them alive for us? They may answer to our contemporary feeling of being at a loss in the world, of wanting more than anything to feel at home, while knowing our fate is homelessness. The appeal is to a very strange kind of nostalgia but not the less powerful for being so strange.

ANGLO-IRISH

PROVINCIALISM GIVES US ALL THE ARTS.

—George Moore, in *Letters to John Eglinton*

ARNOLD IS WRONG ABOUT PROVINCIALISM, IF HE MEANS ANYTHING MORE THAN A PROVINCIALISM OF STYLE AND MANNER IN EXPOSITION. A CERTAIN PROVINCIALISM OF FEELING IS INVALUABLE. IT IS OF THE ESSENCE OF INDIVIDUALITY.

—Thomas Hardy, in Florence E. Hardy, *Life*

WE ARE THE PEOPLE OF BURKE; WE ARE THE PEOPLE OF GRATTAN; WE ARE THE PEOPLE OF SWIFT, THE PEOPLE OF EMMET, THE PEOPLE OF PARNELL. WE HAVE CREATED MOST OF THE MODERN LITERATURE OF THIS COUNTRY.

—W. B. Yeats, in *Senate Speeches*

THE ANGLO-IRISH ARE EMPHATICALLY, INESCAPABLY, IRISH.

—Michael Pakenham, in *New York Times Book Review*

I

PROLOGUE: "IRISH ENOUGH"

THERE is a broad definition of Anglo-Irish literature: Irish writing in English, as distinct from writing in the native Irish tongue, which, along with Welsh, Gaelic, and Breton, forms the Celtic branch of the Indo-European family of languages. Even though the phrase "Irish writing" holds considerable ambiguity, such a definition is unexceptionable for the main distinction that it draws. Other, narrower definitions will serve other purposes by drawing other, finer distinctions. Here I propose to construct several definitions, each more restricted than the previous one, until that definition best fitted to my purpose in this book as a whole has been reached. These definitions need to be challenged as soon as constructed, just as the first one was challenged on the score of ambiguity. When I have run out of challenges I should presumably have arrived at the most serviceable definition I am capable of constructing for the purposes I have in mind.

This should not be an arid exercise in classificatory or Boolean logic. The challenges are a form of reality testing with reference to a concrete field of historical and cultural inquiry bristling with problems and anomalies, most of them deriving from the centuries-prolonged English dominance in Ireland, in combination with the close physical proximity of the two island peoples. That becomes plain with the very next definition.

Anglo-Irish literature is that body of writings in English produced by the English settlers and their descendants, who begin coming into Ireland around 1167, commencing with the invasion of the Earl of Pembroke, Richard FitzGilbert de Clare, called Strongbow, and the arrival a few years later of the English and Angevin king, French-speaking Henry II. These settlers by conquest, the greater number of whom turn Protestant in the late Tudor period, are a powerful and privileged group, though always a minority in the Irish population, until they fade out of the picture after the Peace Treaty between Britain and Sinn Fein in 1922 frees most of Ireland from direct English rule.

This is a very good definition in its way, provided one makes certain things clear. To begin with, since the "Anglo" part of the designation refers no longer primarily to tongue but to place of origin, immediate or ancestral, it needs pointing out that some of the earliest "English" settlers spoke French, Welsh, and even Flemish and might have written in those languages as well as in Latin. Second, there are difficulties in assuming a more or less homogeneous and intact settler group over most of the period under survey, from the late twelfth-century invasions to the Treaty, 1167 to 1922. For instance, during the thirteenth and fourteenth centuries many descendants of the original Anglo-Norman colonists became indistinguishable from the native Irish through assimilation to the Irish language, customs and culture, and social system. At the Reformation many, though not all, of those privileged settler families failing to renounce the Catholic faith became disclassed through property attainder and other penalties. No longer the dominant class, these "Old English," as they were called, are replaced by the "New English" and the Cromwellians. These were new waves of Protestant settlers arriving in Ireland during Elizabethan and early Stuart times, in the period of the Great Rebellion (1641–52), and upon Dutch William's defeat of his father-in-law James II and the native Irish at the Boyne, Aughrim, and Limerick in the early 1690s.

Conversely, it becomes possible after the Reformation for ambitious families among the native Irish to gain access to the privileged class by renouncing their Catholic faith and swearing an oath of loyalty to the Protestant English monarch as head of government and the Established Church. This accommodation often led to intermarriage of their children with settler stock. A final anomaly occurs in the later seventeenth and early eighteenth centuries, when significant numbers of French Huguenots and Palatine Germans arrive in Ireland. Because they are Protestant, these immigrants are not subject to the severe penal restrictions under which the great mass of the Catholics are held after the Treaty of Limerick (1691), and they are rather quickly assimilated to the loyalist minority.

Evidently it is time for a new definition. Anglo-Irish literature is the writing produced by that ascendant minority in Ireland, largely but not entirely English in point of origin, that tended to be Protestant and overwhelmingly loyal to the English crown, and had its power and privileges secured by the English civil and military presence.

This definition works well for most of the eighteenth century, century of the Penal Laws, the Protestant Parliament, and the "Protestant Nation," when, in the opinion of some, including the Dublin-based Victorian historian W.E.H. Lecky (147–48) and the early twentieth century poet W. B. Yeats (*Explorations*, 345), Anglo-Ireland for the first time created a distinctive literature of its own. It was indeed distinctive, being at least until the early 1780s the product of a class that lived apart, worshipped apart, and expected to go on legislating its own rights and freedoms apart from the rest of the Irish people into the indefinite future. During this century both the Anglo-Irish Chief Justice Robinson and the Anglo-Irish Chief Chancellor Bowes distinctly laid down for the guidance of the Irish Bar "that the law does not suppose any such person to exist as an Irish Roman Catholic" (Lecky, 42). We may well wonder what sort of literature was produced in a society or class whose most accomplished jurists upheld and promulgated law based upon the assumption of the nonexistence of most inhabitants of the country.

The answer is readily available. From Congreve to Farquahar, from Swift to Goldsmith and Sheridan, mentioning only the biggest names, it was a brilliant, urbane literature, particularly distinguished in stage comedy, prose and verse satire, and in the ancillary art of parliamentary oratory. But it was not an Irish literature, or at least not Irish enough. Rather, it was an offshoot of English writing that was routinely absorbed back into the mainstream of English literary production. Typically, the Irish-born and often Irish-educated Ascendancy writers of the period left for the English capital, turning their backs upon their native place, putting their talent at the service of English culture and society. Granted that Swift, who returned from England—much against his own wishes—and wrote, occasionally, on behalf of the native Irish oppressed, complicates the picture. But a few great works—*A Modest Proposal*, *The Drapier Letters*, and a handful of descriptive and satiric poems—by one great writer do not a literature make; nor do they clear eighteenth-century Ascendancy writing as a whole from the charge that it is not "Irish enough," whatever that might mean, to constitute a significant Anglo-Irish literature for my purposes.

Literature of the Ascendancy's golden age, from the time of Queen Anne to the United Irish Risings of 1798, is certainly a sort of Anglo-Irish literature, but not the sort with which this book is concerned. Ascendancy culture was too little conscious of being involved in Irish realities and the oppressive Irish situation altogether. The Protestant Nation was not really a nation, but rather a class of colonials living a collective dream as it gathered in its picturesque parliament building on Dublin's College Green to promulgate its own privileges and immunities and, during the last part of the eighteenth century, took to debating the terms upon which it would at long last extend to the Catholics "toleration," "relief," and possibly the right to sit in its parliament.

Something shattering would have to happen to awaken the Ascendancy to reality and to show its members how they actually stood toward the English and toward their fellow-Irish before a genuine Anglo-Irish literature, reflecting on the one hand the distinctive features and traditions of this group, and on the other demonstrating its ineluctable entanglement in the full Irish situation, could get under way. The rude awakening did in fact occur in 1800, when the Dublin Parliament, coming under relentless pressure from Westminster and the English Executive in Ireland, was forced to dissolve itself, having previously voted its consent to an Act of Union between the two "kingdoms," the constitutional effect of which was to make all Irish the same and subject to the direct rule of the British government.

With these extraordinary developments the Anglo-Irish become Irish, no longer a nation apart; and if not Irish through and through, then Irish enough for a viable literature to begin. It begins in 1800, the year of the rude but salutary awakening. I have arrived at the definition which satisfies me, though it is only an outline that will take the rest of this book to fill in. Before turning to this task, I must say a further word about the phrase "Irish enough," and sketch in very broad terms of "history" the falling off of power and consequence in the Anglo-Irish community which, paradoxically, released what I am calling the Anglo-Irish literary imagination to carry out its work.

The phrase comes from Edith Somerville and Martin Ross's great Balzacian novel, *The Real Charlotte* (1894). There it describes a certain tone of voice that not everyone finds easy to recognize. Pamela Dysart, the unmarried sister of the novel's landlord hero, Christopher Dysart, uses such an intonation. In the scene where the expression is introduced Pamela has been speaking to an English Captain Cursiter, whose military unit, billeted in the district for some time, is about to leave Ireland. He has come by to say his farewells but might readily be maneuvered into a declaration of love and a marriage proposal. Pamela, however, is too scrupulous and too shy to undertake such a maneuver. That is unfortunate, for they do care for each other and, as the captain goes away, he cannot get out of his mind the sound of her voice bidding him goodbye.

She had spoken "in a soft voice that was just Irish enough for Saxons of the more ignorant sort to fail to distinguish, save in degree, between it and Mrs. Lambert's Dublin brogue" (476). Mrs. Lambert is the beautiful lower-middle class Protestant girl from North Dublin who as Francie Fitzpatrick had attracted the regard of the diffident Christopher Dysart before she threw herself away on the Dysarts' land agent, Roddie Lambert. There is yet a third young woman's voice to be heard in the novel, that of the English house guest, Miss Hope-Drummond. Doggedly and shamelessly in pursuit of matrimonial opportunities, Miss Hope-Drummond speaks in the plummy accents of late Victorian Mayfair and has the high, penetrative voice typical of her class and place of origin. Just as the ignorant Saxon auditor would hear Pamela's speech as brogue, an Irish intonation associated with lower-born city people, so would "Celts" of the more ignorant sort fail to distinguish between Pamela Dysart's and the English visitor's speaking tone of voice. Let us assume that this "soft voice," this intonation difficult to distinguish, lying between a wholly English and a wholly Irish way of speaking, is the intrinsic voice of Anglo-Irish culture after the Union, just as Pamela Dysart is assuredly a fine specimen of that culture in its autumnal phase. In these terms what follows is a try at discriminating and tracking that voice "Irish enough," from when it first becomes audible in 1800, to when it becomes a faint and ghostly whisper some century and a half later, before ceasing to sound at all.[1]

Now for the historical sketch. During the later eighteenth century the Anglo-Irish community went from strength to strength. Commercial prosperity led to the building up of Dublin and other port cities and to the design of great houses in the fine neo-classic style called Irish Georgian. Major parliamentary figures, including Flood, Curran, and Grattan, made the parliament building on College Green a debating rival of the English parliament itself. Near-revolutionary political developments, set in motion partly by the example of the American colonists' successful revolt against Britain, began with the Irish Volunteer movement in 1778 and led swiftly to the removal of English restrictions on Irish trade, the concession in 1782 of parliamentary autonomy through the repeal of Poyning's Law after three hundred and ninety-four years of subordination to the English Privy Council, and led also to a series of reform efforts, only partially carried through, aimed at curbing the influence of a few great political families such as the Beresfords, who controlled large blocs of parliamentary votes through patronage and bribery (Johnston, 99–163).

In these same years the rest of the Penal Laws still in force were repealed and Catholics, through a series of relief acts, began to enjoy civil and legal rights of a kind unknown since the Restoration period of the seventeenth century. By the Relief Bill of 1793 Catholics may vote for parliamentary candidates, though not themselves stand for election. They may bear arms, follow the professions, and become elected members of most corporations, even though, as the historian Lecky observed, "nearly every post of ambition was still reserved for Protestants" (259). By 1795, the most enlightened and substantial opinion of the day, including Edmund Burke's, Henry Grattan's, and the English Viceroy Lord Fitzwilliam's, expects full Catholic emancipation as a key to the impending settlement and reconciliation between the two communities. This will ensure the peace and prosperity of all Ireland under Dublin parliamentary rule that yet remains loyal to the English crown and guided by the spirit of the British Constitution.

Five years later the dream of reconciliation and constitutional self-rule under "devolved" powers is over. In 1800 the Dublin Parliament votes the Act of Union with Great Britain before voting itself out of existence, and on January 1, 1801, the two "kingdoms" are formally merged. This will turn out to be a disaster for two communities, both the Anglo- and native Irish. There is no real union but instead a form of direct rule by British government which, in terms of the evolution of Irish self-governent, marks a regression to before 1297, when the first somewhat representative Anglo-Irish assembly was convened at Dublin (Johnston, 164–95).

Why did this disaster occur? Various reasons have been given for the failure of the Anglo-Irish to pluck the safety of relative legislative autonomy from the nettle of a full Catholic Emancipation: there was the failure of efforts to reform the Dublin legislature, leading to passage of the Union bill through wholesale bribery and jobbing; the threatening rise of the breakaway republican movement called the United Irish, under the leadership of the northern zealot Wolfe Tone; English and Anglo-Irish fear of French revolutionary designs on Ireland; in 1798, the exceptionally violent peasant risings and their savage repression, and the French expedition into Connaught under General Humbert. Even George the Third's hatred and fear of Catholics, especially Irish ones, has been cited as a cause. Or one can follow Elizabeth Bowen in noting that "the Union was a bad deal . . . a tragedy that puts uninformed comment quite out of countenance" (*Bowen's Court*, 219). But in fact she goes further, defining the Union as a humiliation for Anglo-Ireland and quoting at length from a famous speech by the Irish lord chancellor, John Fitzgibbon, later Lord Clare, in favor of the Union and emphasizing his "superb detestable realism" (220). His words were part of the concluding debates and may well have swung the undecideds to the winning side. The Dublin Parliament, which in some sense lived for oratory, was to die by oratory as well.

Fitzgibbon's summing up plays harshly on the deepest fears of the Anglo-Irish concerning the legitimacy of their power and position in Ireland; and it cruelly exploits the anomaly noted by such foreign observers as Alexis de Toqueville (122, 124) that the Anglo-Irish are a ruling class sharing neither the religion nor the ethnicity of the people they presume to lead. The Fitzgibbon family had changed from Catholic to Protestant only a single generation before. The saturnine lord chancellor may have actually enjoyed putting the fear of God into a legislative body that must have included men who fancied themselves his social superiors for their families' having changed religions at some earlier period. He finds it easy to strike notes of menace (and almost of contempt) whose aim is to stampede the assembly into voting for immediate and irrevocable union with Britain: "What was the situation of Ireland at the revolution? And what is it at this day? The whole power and property of the country have been conferred by successive monarchs of England upon . . . three sets of English adventurers who poured into the country at the termination of three successive rebellions; confiscation is their common title; and from their first settlement they have been hemmed in on every side by the old inhabitants of the island, brooding over their discontents in sullen indignation. . . . What was the security of the English settlers for their physical existence at the revolution? And what is the security of their descendants at this day? The powerful and commanding protection of Great Britain. If by any fatality it fails, you are at the mercy of the old inhabitants of the island; and I should have hoped that samples of mercy exhibited by them in the course of the late rebellion would have taught the gentlemen who call themselves the Irish nation to reflect with sober attention on the dangers that surround them" (quoted in *Bowen's Court*, 2d ed., 220).

By "revolution" is meant the Glorious Protestant Revolution, which dismissed the Stuarts and brought William and Mary to the throne of Great Britain and Ireland in 1689. The three rebellions are O'Neill the Earl of Tyrone's at the end of the sixteenth century, the Great Rebellion at mid-seventeenth century, and the Irish uprisings in support of the deposed James II in the early 1690s. Fitzgibbon's final sentence or two raises the specter of the bloodbath, which later generations of unionists would find so serviceable in warning against cutting the ties to England.

It seems likely that the Anglo-Irish voted for the Union out of fear. Fearing a retribution by Catholics that might follow upon their full enfranchisement, they sought to sink their political identity into the larger identity of Protestant Britain's parliament, where they could never be outvoted, so they thought, by a native Irish majority. It was an act of self-betrayal. For the Anglo-Irish in voting Union did not escape their problems with the Irish Catholics. Instead, over the course of the nineteenth century they became subjects, with the other Irish, of direct and distant English rule and misrule from London. With Union then, the Anglo-Irish, far from becoming fully British, became unfortunately Irish, in the old brooding unhappy sense of the term. Of course, this did not happen all at once, nor did they realize what was happening all at once. The happening and the realization, slowly developing over time, are in great part what many of the Anglo-Irish writings examined in this book are about

A paradox of this literature, as earlier suggested, is that it flowers just when the social formation producing it enters a phase of contraction and decline. As Anglo-Irish literature "arises," the Anglo-Irish begin to go down in the world. This state of affairs is not unique in the history of literatures and of individual writers as well. The greatest writers of nineteenth-century Russia, from Lermontov and Pushkin to Turgenev, Dostoevsky, and Tolstoy, were all products of a class—the landed gentry and nobility of the provinces—which steadily declined in political and social consequence as the autocratic Czarist state became ever more centralized, bureaucratized, and policed. In American literature, there is the most brilliant period of southern writing, culminating in the fiction of Faulkner and Flannery O'Connor and the poetry of the Fugitives group, following after and reflecting upon the breakup of the Southern Agrarian social system in the wake of the Confederacy's Civil War defeat and the economic strictures and dislocations of the Reconstruction Era. Charles Dickens, James Joyce, and F. Scott Fitzgerald are just three of the many writers whose literary imaginations received powerful stimulus from their early discovery that their families were headed downward on the scales of economic security and social standing. It appears that the relation between accomplishment in literary pursuits and in the world is often inverse. The literary muse, at least in certain periods, dearly loves a loser.

But what, after all, did the Anglo-Irish lose as the nineteenth and early twentieth centuries proceeded? And how could their curtailments and setbacks appear of consequence when compared with the miseries of the native majority, who in less than a century underwent the horrors of the "Great Hunger"; mass evictions and enforced emigration of the rural populace; the rigors of the Fenian era and the Land War; the sudden disgrace and death of their legendary leader, Charles Stewart Parnell; resumption of insurrectionary violence when England's promised concession of limited Home Rule failed to materialize; and the final armed struggle for independence between 1916 and 1921? A likely answer might be "relatively little." Yet even relatively another answer suggests itself. First, much of the catastrophic history of nineteenth-century Ireland was suffered by the Anglo-Irish, right along with the peasant majority over whom they had been so long dominant. If the tenants starved in famine years, numerous landlords encountered financial ruin on famine-wracked estates, while a fair number were carried off in the fever epidemics that swept through the starving countryside. Though rural terrorists during the 1820s and 1830s, in the Fenian 1860s, and in the Land War of the 1880s were harshly suppressed and punished by the English soldiery and the loyalist police, it is also true that the prime targets of the terrorists were these very same landlords, their families, and their properties.

On a broader view, it can be seen that the curve of native fortunes for the period is a rising one. The tribulations of Fitzgibbon's "old inhabitants of the island" would end in the achievement of substantial independence and in resumed native proprietorship over much of the land that had been confiscated during the previous three centuries and more. Padraic Colum, coming to the end of his biography of Arthur Griffith, one of the founders of Sinn Fein and the first head of the Irish Free State government, cannot help sounding this note of native triumph, even though it is subdued, keeping in mind how much suffering and sacrifice had to be undergone before the descendants of the invaded Irish got back a measure of what they had always considered their own:

> National freedom is a concept that varies in different countries and covers many different sentiments. For Irish people it means a reconquest. It is a reconquest by stages, each stage leaving an emotional deposit: survival as Irish through the outlawry of the Penal days, Catholic Emancipation, destruction of feudalism through the agrarian struggle, the attainment of national consciousness through the Gaelic League and Sinn Fein. . . . The men and women in Dail Eireann, whether they voted for the Treaty or against it, had in their bones a history that [an Englishman] could never know: their grandfathers had heard for the first time in a hundred years a bell ring from a Catholic place of worship. . . . (Colum, 361)

By contrast, the curve of Anglo-Irish fortunes for the same period is irreversibly, if not always spectacularly, downward. After the Union, the Dublin parliamentarians, for so long and so brightly a force in Irish politics, culture, and society, discover they have a choice between dispersing themselves to a life of decent though uneasy obscurity on their rural estates and trying to launch new political careers in a Westminster parliament whose leaders regard most of them as provincials and natural back benchers. By 1838 the Established Church of Ireland, that backbone of Anglo-Irish Protestant culture, has lost the right to levy tithes upon the Catholic population. Previously, in 1829, the Catholic Emancipation Act provided that Catholic candidates might be nominated for, and take their seats among, the Irish parliamentary delegation at Westminster. This ends the Ascendancy political monopoly and guarantees that the small and shrinking Anglo-Irish electorate will no longer enjoy the assurance of being represented by persons of their own class and class interest. In the late 1860s the Church of Ireland is disestablished by the British parliament, while its considerable accumulations of invested wealth and real property are disendowed. Between the Gladstone Land Act of 1881 and the opening years of this century, a long series of enactments in the sphere of landlord-tenant relations drastically limit the formerly unquestioned right of the proprietor to raise rents and to evict, and force a solution to the land question that entails breaking up the system of landed estates. Thus is assured the virtual extinction of the proprietors as a distinct, privileged, and exploitative class.

These are some faint indications of the Anglo-Irish dilemma in the nineteenth century and after, in the period when the Ascendancy becomes a Descendancy. We turn now to the distinctive, haunting, and even distinguished literature the Anglo-Irish shaped as they turned losers in their lives and came to know it too.

II

MARIA EDGEWORTH (1768–1849): ORIGINATION AND A CHECKLIST

Irishness is not primarily a question of birth or blood or language; it is the condition of being involved in the Irish situation and usually of being mauled by it.
—Conor Cruise O'Brien, *Writers and Politics*

Introductory

MARIA EDGEWORTH is the true begetter of the Anglo-Irish literary line extending well into the present century. She creates its first masterpiece, *Castle Rackrent*, a narrative whose feats of impersonation and mimicry may be compared with the James Joyce of the Cyclops, Nausicaa, and Eumaeus episodes of *Ulysses*. This highly flavored and deeply unsettling tale of familial decline in an agrarian setting was probably mined by William Faulkner for *The Sound and the Fury*. The resemblance of Jason Compson to Edgeworth's grasping land agent Jason Quirk is uncannily close. Edgeworth's repertory of entropic effects and mastery of the art of declining in this book will nerve Samuel Beckett, offspring of Anglo-Irish tradition in its morbid or ending stage, to carry out his long series of fictional and dramaturgical experiments in reduction and cancellation in our own time.

Mine is a claim for Edgeworth's continuing importance surpassing the usual ones, though these are substantial enough: namely, that in her novels of Irish subject matter she first created the national and regional novel as a distinct subgenre, showing Walter Scott (*Waverley*, 2:403) and perhaps Ivan Turgenev as well (*Rackrent*, Appendix B, 118–20) how to portray a whole society through a skillful drawing and deployment of characters who are class-typical; and further, that her fiction contributes measurably to the growth of narrative realism through its innovative techniques of factual and quasi-factual documentation.

Maria Edgeworth's modern biographer Marilyn Butler makes the fullest case for the importance of her contributions to fiction as a genre

(Butler, *Maria Edgeworth*, 239–40, 485–88). On the other hand, she treats *Castle Rackrent* as something of an eccentric deviation from Edgeworth's more significant accomplishments (305–6, 352–98). It appears to mystify and partly irritate her that virtually all readers and critics have found *Castle Rackrent* Edgeworth's greatest book.

This response reflects a failure to define an essential term. Lacking a viable concept of Anglo-Irish literature and culture, yet being aware what a preposterous and thankless task it would be to try to integrate Maria Edgeworth into the native strain in Irish writing, Butler assumes she has no choice but to integrate her, as fully as possible, into English literary history. Certainly many of Edgeworth's narratives—from *Belinda* (1801) to *Vivian* (1812) to *Helen* (1834)—portraying English characters in a society of which London is the capital, fit into that history. *Castle Rackrent* does not; consequently, it must be set aside and discounted as a literary sport. In her biography Butler betrays her lack of an Anglo-Irish concept by assuming that to be Anglo-Irish and to be English are the same. Summing up the progress to maturity of Harry Ormond, the hero of *Ormond*, she remarks, "the device of introducing Ormond as a natural, unthinking Irish boy, and turning him during the course of the action into an educated Englishman, enables her to show Ireland with an intimacy she could not achieve in *Ennui* and *The Absentee*, where the narrators are both outsiders" (Butler, *Maria Edgeworth*, 386). Here her slip in attributing first-person narration to *The Absentee* is less important than the ignorance revealed of what constitutes Anglo-Irish identity: that is, the doubled or split consciousness of a unique situation, this situation entailing, on the one hand, a link with, yet removal from, English origins and English society; and on the other, a closeness to, and yet a removal or isolation from, the native Irish community.

In short, whatever Harry Ormond was while growing up, he was not a mere "Irish boy." And whatever this Protestant orphan from a settler family owning to the ducal surname of Ormond became in maturity, it could not be an "Englishman." To miss this is to miss the most interesting tensions of the tale. It is also to miss seeing how Anglo-Irish writing originating with Edgeworth differs from the earlier body of Anglo-Irish writing, often brilliant, witty, and urbane, which has already been described as a sort of gift to English letters from colonials relocating to shape literary careers in London.

Castle Rackrent is a fictional memoir of several generations of a family of landed proprietors that is narrated by Thady Quirk, an aged, unlettered peasant serving the household as steward. It was first conceived as entertainment for the family circle at Edgeworthstown, County Longford, where this family had been established since 1583, and drew on traditions and personalities in family history. English born and having lost her English mother, the fourteen-year-old Maria first came to live in her ancestral home in June 1782. It was a place with which she would develop unbreakable ties and in which her creative genius would center.

Having arrived in Ireland in the famous year of Protestant Ireland's achieving legislative independence from Britain,[1] she was joining her father, Richard Lovell Edgeworth (1744–1817). After his education in law, some years of desultory research in science and technology as a member of the midlands Lunar Society, along with Erasmus Darwin, James Watt, and Josiah Wedgewood, and several ventures as a civil engineer, he had decided to devote his remaining life to making the neglected family properties in Ireland a model of efficient and humane estate management. By 1782 Edgeworth had been married twice: first to Anna Elers of Black Burton in Oxfordshire; and after her death, to the beautiful and discipline minded Honora Sneyd of Lichfield. Now domiciled in a family home, he would be able to reassemble his offspring of the two marriages, who were scattered at various English schools and households.

It was too late to do much for Richard, Jr., the oldest son. His disposition had been spoiled and his temper rendered uncontrollable by the father's injudicious experiment of raising him on a totally permissive educational plan derived from the writings of Rousseau. This young man was soon to emigrate to South Carolina, where he died untimely in 1789. But much could be done with and for Maria, the second-oldest child. Over time Richard Lovell was to wed four wives and to sire twenty-two children, of whom Maria was the oldest to survive into the new century. She would remain unmarried, though it was not for lack of opportunity to marry. The Swedish diplomat Count Edelcrantz proposed to her during her visit to France and the Low Countries in 1802, at the time of the short-lived Peace of Amiens. By then she was already internationally known for her writings on early education. Fearing a permanent removal from home to a cold northern region, and entertaining some lingering doubts as to the count's true character, she refused the offer, but not without some hesitation and emotional distress (Butler, *Maria Edgeworth*, 192–96).

The adolescent girl began to be instructed in all phases of landlording and estate management from her very first riding out with her father as he interviewed tenants, surveyed leaseholds, and made a thorough inventory of the problems and conditions on the estate. When, after Richard Lovell's death in 1817, the inheriting son, Lovell Edgeworth, ran the property into debt, Maria took it over, sending Lovell off to England with a life income and gradually clearing the property of its encumbrances. Almost until her death in 1849, this tiny maiden half-sister, favorite aunt and literary celebrity, the correspondent and friend of Sir Walter Scott, and a guest much sought after on her rare visits to England by the best upper-class circles professing literary and scientific interests, was the manager of about six hundred acres of agricultural and village property, where several hundred souls sustained life until the great famine of 1845–48 enforced a cruel Malthusian solution of the Irish population problem in Longford as elsewhere.

Edgeworth *père* is just interesting enough himself to distract our consideration of the daughter, unless we give him some further particular notice. Eccentric and busy, he changed the basis of his educational principles from Rousseau to Locke after the debacle of his eldest son's upbringing. Under his supervision the older children at Edgeworthstown taught the newer offspring according to a "preceptorial" system employing ingenious mechanical models and toys, early instruction in reading and computation, and a method of moving from familiar objects and concepts to new knowledge by apt analogy and association (Butler, *Maria Edgeworth*, 98–105). Edgeworth himself possessed a problem-solving flair that was not quite first-rate, though Maria, if not all his offspring, believed in his great abilities to the end. At Lyons in his thirties he had spent months and a large amount of public money trying without success to divert the Rhone into a new channel. His inventions included a wooden horse that almost could climb walls; a railroad run on sail power; a heliographic signalling device, which he offered to the Dublin authorities as an early-warning system against French invasion; a fast three-wheeled carriage capable of fording deep streams; and a tracked vehicle ancestral to the modern tank. He developed a road surface superior to and prior to Macadam's (Butler, *Maria Edgeworth*, 31, 34–35). Edgeworth was a skilled magician and gifted mimic, who collected and recited stories in accurate peasant dialect. This gift for true mimicry was passed on to Maria and is important in the development of her literary talent, and, through her creative example, important to a number of later writers.

Richard Lovell Edgeworth, despite his oddities and failures, was a worthy product of the eighteenth-century Enlightenment in the English-speaking world, which produced Benjamin Franklin and the Framers of the American Constitution; such superior Anglo-Irish and British statesmen as Grattan, Fox, Burke, and the younger Pitt; and those gentleman-technologists and savants, many of them known to Edgeworth personally, whose inventions and investigations gave Britain her technological lead in the Industrial Revolution. He was also an improving landlord of a type virtually unknown in Ireland. His immediate reforms on the estate included ending donation of work and farm produce—"duty days and duty fowl"—to the landlord or his agent, offering long leases at fair rent, eliminating subletting and the subdividing of leaseholds into minute uneconomic plots, and recognizing "tenant right" (Butler, *Maria Edgeworth*, 85–87). This last recognized the tenant farmer's entitlement to recompense for his improvements to his farm over the period of his tenancy. More often in Ireland such improvements became the basis for rent increases, a practice known as "rackrenting," though any tyrannical practice in renting would be covered by the same term. He also established schools on the estate where Catholic and Protestant children were educated together, with released time for separate religious instruction.

Richard Lovell supported Catholic Emancipation, including the right of Catholic candidates to stand for the Dublin Parliament. By the mid-1790s, when sectarian feelings began to be severely polarized, in part owing to the founding of the Orange Order in 1795 and the rapid growth of terrorist secret societies organized along sectarian lines, such tolerance made Edgeworth unpopular with many of his Protestant neighbors. During the United Irish Rising and the French invasion under General Humbert in 1798, he made a point of opening the local defense forces, known as the yeomanry, to men of all faiths. For his pains he just missed being lynched that summer at Longford town on the suspicion of being a French spy (*Memoirs*, 2:115–32).

He sat in the Dublin Parliament during the debates on the Union in 1800. At first he supported the bill, but for an unusual reason: he thought that Ireland within an enlarged British realm could become a wealthy and progressive center of industry, like Yorkshire. In any case, he voted nay in order to protest the corruption and jobbery through which the majority vote was being secured (*Memoirs*, 2:133–42).

The Edgeworths were good landlords in a time of incipient Anglo-Irish decline, the characteristic signs of which were the absentee proprietor, the hard-driving estate agent, the middle man, who guaranteed the owner his full rent while achieving a fat profit for himself through various forms of rackrenting, the evicting bailiff, the cheating "gauger" (excise man) and land surveyor, and the tithe proctor, whose job it was to collect from Catholic tenants taxes to support an Established Church which had no ministry among Catholics. They stayed home, worked and studied hard, increased the profits of their holdings by astute management and rational experiment rather than by the common practice of clearing off the tenants to make grazing acreage for cattle, were tolerant in religion, and took a close, curious, and friendly interest in their tenants' lives.

In the century or so before Richard Lovell inherited his estate, several Edgeworth heirs had led disheveled lives. Their follies and dissipations were recorded in *The Black Book of Edgeworthstown*, a candid family chronicle[2] compiled by Maria's grandfather. Richard Lovell was certainly aware of this unstable rakehell strain in his heritage and had struggled to curb the violent temper he displayed from childhood on. His several marriages and many children went far to provide him with outlets for a certain warmth of temperament. His first marriage, contracted against his father's wishes, was not a success, except in its producing Maria, but the other unions were happy ones. His last wife, Frances Beaufort (1769–1865), who was a year younger than Maria, added six children to the clan and lived contentedly at Edgeworthstown for some forty-eight years after her husband's death. To her youngest half-brother, Michael Pakenham, who had entered the Indian civil service, Edgeworth addressed the last, and certainly one of the most arresting, of her works on Irish country themes, the *Tour in Connemara and The Martins of Ballinahinch* (1834). The sheer temporal scope of sibling life among the Edgeworths may be suggested by noting that Michael was forty-five years younger than his oldest half-sister.

Unlike many members of their class, the Edgeworths knew who they were, nursed no inferiority feelings toward the English gentry, and were convinced that by education and application one might become almost anything within reason. Richard Lovell was not, however, a traitor to his class, despite his fondness for proclaiming that the Irish countryman was wittier, warmer, and more intelligent than his "circumspect" or stolid English counterpart. When he felt threatened or pressed by the "lower Irish," as he did during a phase of agrarian outrages perpetrated in 1794 by a peasant secret society called the Defenders, he sounded a different note. In that year, writing to Dr. Erasmus Darwin, he even found something to be dreaded in Irish wake customs:

> By waking the bodies of their friends, the human corpse not only becomes familiar to the *sans culottes* of Ireland, but is associated with pleasure in their minds by the festivity of these nocturnal orgies. An insurrection of such people, who have been much oppressed, must be infinitely more horrid than anything that has happened in France; for no hired executioners need be sought from the prisons or the galleys. And yet the people are altogether better than in England. (*Memoirs*, 2:85)

This misunderstanding of an old custom, and the ambivalence in the final sentence, are noteworthy. Fascination with "the people," that is, the rural Catholic peasantry or tenantry, and to a lesser extent their counterparts in Irish towns and cities, emerges with the Edgeworths as an abiding concern of Anglo-Irish writing. It mingles objective curiosity with ethnic prejudice, affection with funk that may in unsettled times become terror, real familiarity with the wonder that grows from a sense of unbridgeable difference. The peasant is by turns, or even at the same time, an occasion for field research and for projected fantasy, an image of virtue and of inexplicable terror, a figure of fun and one of dignity and elevation.

A few parallels with other areas of nineteenth-century literary and social history suggest themselves: the Russian country gentleman, from Sergei Aksakov's Stepan Mikhailovich Bagrov in *Family Chronicle* to Tolstoy's Levin in *Anna Karenina*, brooding over the peasant "soul"; the drama of "race"-mingling in Mark Twain's *Pudd'nhead Wilson*; James Fenimore Cooper's depiction of the Iroquois as both wood demons and natural noblemen. Comparisons, however, must not be pressed too far. Distinctive features of the Anglo-Irish situation are the physical proximity of Britain and her dominance over all Irish classes; the religious difference between most of those who own and those who work the land; the steep disproportion of numbers between native majority and settler minority; perhaps also an informality in the daily intercourse of the proprietors with their servants and tenants that was not evident in the other instances.

Earlier in the eighteenth century, at the height of their ascendant power, the Anglo-Irish were not very interested in the Irish people, certainly not interested in their customs, subjectivity, and inwardness. Probably the penal exactions following the defeat of the Irish Jacobites precluded such an interest by denying that, at least in law, any such people as Irish Catholics existed. This interest develops toward the end of the eighteenth century and is in phase with what Lyons called the "contraction" of the Protestant Nation during the next hundred years. By the 1890s one encounters the profound absorption with the people's native language, folk and literary heritage, temperament, and character, which was so prominent in the Gaelic Language Revival and the Literary Revival.

To discover the origin of this attitude for literary purposes one must look farther back than the 1890s, even before the mid-nineteenth-century group of cultural nationalists called Young Ireland (Yeats's "Davis, Mangan, Ferguson"), to 1800, when Maria Edgeworth launched both her serious career in fiction and a sufficiently Irish Anglo-Irish literature by publishing *Castle Rackrent*.

Feats of Impersonation: *Castle Rackrent* and *Essay on Irish Bulls*

Castle Rackrent is an extended feat of impersonation or mimicry,[3] based upon real life:

> The only character drawn from the life in "Castle Rackrent" is Thady himself, the teller of the story. He was an old steward. . . . I heard him when

first I came to Ireland, and his dialect struck me, and his character, and I became so acquainted with it, that I could think and speak in it without effort: so that when, for mere amusement, without any ideas of publishing, I began to write a family history as Thady would tell it, he seemed to stand beside me and dictate and I wrote as fast as my pen would go, the characters all imaginary. (To Mrs. Stark, Sep 6, 1834; quoted in Butler, *Maria Edgeworth*, 240–41)

This steward, whose name was John Langan, focused the culture shock of the adolescent Maria upon her first coming to settle in Ireland, and Thady, the boundlessly naive, prolix, artless, sly, dissembling, and veracious tale teller, is her powerful creative response, about a decade later, to her memory of that experience. There is more to it. She uses his simplicity for some very complicated effects, works his truthfulness, along with his lying, for some inspired artistic games.

To stay with culture shock for a moment, when Sir Kit, the third Rackrent heir, brings home his new bride, an English Jewish lady he married at Bath for her fortune, and she is shown his turf stack, his extensive turf bog called Allyballycarricko'shaughlin, and his newly planted "screen" of trees, she sees only a pile of wet lumps, a dark swamp with a bizarre name, and some stunted shrubs. Not surprisingly, her response is close to hysterical, though she will prove resolute as the real horrors of her unlucky marriage to Sir Kit begin to appear. At the same time, there is a second species of culture shock in these pages and that is untraveled, uneducated Thady's dismay over Sir Kit's choice in a wife:

The bride might well be a great fortune—she was a *Jewish* by all accounts, who are famous for their great riches. I had never seen any of that tribe or nation before, and could only gather that she spoke a strange kind of English of her own, that she could not abide pork or sausages, and went neither to church nor mass.—Mercy upon his honor's poor soul, thought I, what will become of him and his, and all of us, with this heretic Blackamore at the head of Castle Rackrent estate. I never slept a wink all night for thinking of it, but before the servants I put my pipe in my mouth and kept my mind to myself; for I had a great regard for the family, and after this when strange gentlemen's servants came to the house and would begin to talk about the bride, I took care to put the best foot foremost, and passed her for a Nabob, in the kitchen, which accounted for her dark complexion, and everything. (*Rackrent*, 25–26)

He will lie then, but only out of regard for the family he serves, while his "minute prolixity" of detail and his passion for "the most minute facts relative to domestic lives"—these phrases are from the author's Preface (*Rackrent*, 1–5)—leave a strong impression of authenticity. Actually employing the authentic as an artistic and critical standard, the Preface draws a contrast between formal historical biography, where a fine or panegyrical style may be used to conceal the truth about an ill-conducted life, and the sort of informal "memoir" recited by Thady "in his vernacular idiom," where everything, including the speaker's biases, come out.

The problems in authentic narrative are with audience and reception. Edgeworth fears that to someone unacquainted with Ireland "the following Memoirs will perhaps be scarcely intelligible, or perhaps they may appear perfectly incredible." For such an "*ignorant* English reader a few notes have been subjoined by the editor." These were supplemented by a Glossary, prepared with the help of her father, that was added to the book at the last moment before publication. Otherwise, cure of ignorance was left to the memoirist, as he began his quaint account, "artlessly" went on with it, and pathetically ended it with the death of the last master he would ever serve:

> HAVING out of Friendship for the family, upon whose estate, praised be to Heaven! I and mine have lived rent free time out of mind, voluntarily undertaken to publish the Memoirs of the Rackrent Family, I think it my duty to say a few words, in the first place, concerning myself. My real name is Thady Quirk, though in the family I have been known by no other than '*honest Thady*'—after-wards, in the time of Sir Murtagh, deceased, I remember to hear them calling me '*old Thady*;' and now I'm come to 'poor Thady'—for I wear a long great coat* winter and summer, which is very handy, as I never put my hands into the sleeves, (they are as good as new), though, come Holantide next, I've had it these seven years; it holds on by a single button round my neck, cloak fashion—to look at me, you would hardly think 'poor Thady' was the father of attorney Quirk; he is a high gentleman, and never minds what poor Thady says, and having better than 1500 a year, landed estate, looks down upon poor Thady, but I wash my hands of his doings, and as I have lived so will I die, true and loyal to the family. (*Rackrent*, 7–8)

> There was none but my shister and myself left near him of all the many friends he had. The fever came and went, and came and went, and lasted five days, and the sixth he was sensible for a few minutes, and said to me, knowing me very well—'I'm in burning pain all within side of me, Thady,'—I could not speak, but my shister asked him, would he have this thing or t'other to do him good?—'No, (says he) nothing will do me good no more'—and he gave a terrible screech with the torture he was in—then again a minute's ease—'brought to this by drink (says he)—where are all the friends?—where's Judy?—Gone, hey? Aye, Sir Condy has been a fool all

his days'—said he, and there was the last word he spoke, and died. He had but a very poor funeral, after all. (*Rackrent*, 95–96)

Edgeworth's art in managing the voice and its narrative burden in these two passages is extraordinary. The opening, for all its apparent waywardness, dwelling "irrelevantly" on the coat, encapsulates the entire falling and failing action of the tale as a whole: the "landed estate" of son Jason is the Rackrent property, which he has coldly maneuvered into irretrievable debt and then seized through legal chicanery for a fraction of its real value. The asterisk following "great coat," conducting to a long footnote on the "high antiquity" of the Irish cloak or mantle, complete with citations from Spenser's "View of the Present State of Ireland" linking the Irish cloak to the garb of the Scythians, Jews, and Chaldees, would seem to pile digression on digression, except that it has the effect, quite calculated, of adding stature to the figure of Thady, making him a kind of eponym for native Irish tradition, archaic and disregarded by those who hold power in Ireland, but persisting nevertheless, into the latest time. Her note puts the cloaked figure so far back into time that Thady on one level is liberated from time, becoming archetypal. Once this transformation has occurred it does not have to be repeated. Thady will turn up again in Anglo-Irish writing, under various disguises and maskings: for example, as the ancient serving man who speaks in Yeats's late ballad "The Curse of Cromwell" and as Watt, the mad, uncomprehending, suffering servant in Samuel Beckett's novel of the same name.

The second passage narrates the death of the last Rackrent heir, Sir Condy—the name is a familiar form of Connolly—with an economy of means that is "natural" and artistic as well. The death is an agonized one and Thady's "I could not speak" is a moving understatement. One would be affected even if he had not become attached to Condy over the course of his story. The matter-of-fact last sentence returns us with a jolt to the question of a peculiar culture; for in Ireland, then and now, nothing establishes a man's reputation as effectively as the turning out for his funeral of vast numbers of friends, enemies, and strangers. It does not matter either whether the dead is Catholic or Protestant. Not Sir Connolly's dying but his poor funeral is the last disaster in the going down of the Rackrent line.

Let us return now to impersonation and mimicry, this odd gift for taking a character or a likeness so completely that "one could think and speak in it without effort," as Maria put it in her letter to Mrs. Stark. It was earlier mentioned that the father too collected and recited stories in peasant dialect entailing mimicry. Such activity for family recreation and entertaining among the landed gentry was certainly common enough. It could be a way of coping with uneasy feelings of difference and social distance from the native majority, who filled up the spaces between the widely separated and isolated demesnes. One learns from *Castle Rackrent* that the big house typically contained a "barrack room" (*Rackrent*, 49), which could be filled with beds to put up visitors from distant estates upon festive occasions such as weddings. But most of the time the family would live alone and on its own resources.

The proprietors certainly knew they were closely watched and gossiped about in the cabins, outside the chapel on Sundays and Holy Days, and at the crossroads. This not necessarily unfriendly observation and the tittle-tattle it led to would inevitably include parody and "hitting off" of the "lahdy-da" mannerisms of the landlord and his family, if only because the Irish peasant has traditionally been a master of such parody. So that Richard Lovell doing dialect stories and Maria appropriating a John Langan through her creative mimicry may be thought of as a sort of defense strategy. It entails getting one's own back and the preservation of self-identity by the "playful" takeover of an identity that is opposite and opposed.

To go a little further. While impersonation can be a way of putting someone down, or "showing someone up," it may also be a way of getting on terms of intimacy with someone one is barred from knowing well in a direct fashion, owing to social conventions and taboos; or it can be a way to discover the character of someone so different that there is no other way; or it can be all of these things at the same time. When Maria slipped into Thady's wrinkled skin and threadbare mantle she was satisfying her curiosity about and, incidentally, bringing to the world's attention, what it felt like to be native, a papist, poor, old, male, and quick to weep and to laugh. She was also escaping into a nonjudging, nonimproving sensibility through which one might bring out scandalous truth about one's class and family without becoming a traitor to one's class and family.

For the truth is that the Rackrents and Edgeworths are close kin. The Rackrent originals, "the drunken Sir Patrick, the litigious Sir Murtagh, the fighting Sir Kit and the slovenly Sir Condy" (*Rackrent*, Preface, 4–5), all exist in the *Black Book*. There, for example, we encounter "Protestant Frank" Edgeworth, who died deep in debt and a fugitive from the estate. Frank was likable but also feckless and bibulous. "After the death of his first wife, Dorothea . . . on his way to conclude a match with the daughter of the Earl of Donegal, he stayed overnight with a family called Cullum at Lisnamcan, Co. Cavan. Inopportunely he got drunk that night, and when he woke in the morning he discovered that he had been married to the unlovely Miss Dorothy Cullum—whose dowry, a rather too modest £1500, was never paid" (Butler, *Maria Edgeworth*, 15). This is Condy to the life. There is the entire ramshackle, makeshift world of the Rackrents as a matter of family scandal before it is transmuted into Maria's artful and "factual" Hibernian tale.

The Edgeworths claimed to be upset when they learned that King George III, after reading *Castle Rackrent*, said, "I know something now of my Irish subjects" (quoted in Butler, *Maria Edgeworth*, 359). For Maria in her Preface had begged the English reader to observe that these were "tales of other times," while "the manners depicted are not those of the present age." The full title—*Castle Rackrent, An Hibernian Tale, Taken from Facts, and From the Manners of the Irish Squires, Before the year 1782*—makes the same point. But the king was right. Introduction of the year 1782 was a transparent device designed to remove the present generation of the family, which had resettled in Ireland that year, from any connection with the madcap Rackrent squires. The first three inheritors, portrayed in Part One, fit very well into an eighteenth-century perspective of manners and narrative technique, but Sir Condy, whose "History" takes up the entire Part Two, separately entitled "Continuation of the Memoirs of the Rackrent Family," is much too complex and problematic a characterization for that perspective.

The truth is Edgeworth had gone deeper than manners and shown something about the gentry in their connection to each other, their tenants, and the Irish habitat which belonged not only to Ascendancy history and to the contemporary scene of 1800, but to prophecy. Sir Condy is the future even more than he is the past. From this slight novel developed the whole nineteenth- and early twentieth-century tradition of Anglo-Irish writing centered on the "big house" of the landlord class and culture as it faltered, declined, and came to ruination:

> I came on a great house in the middle of the night
> Its open lighted doorway and its windows all alight,
> And all my friends were there and made me welcome too;
> But I woke in an old ruin that the winds howled through;
> (W. B. Yeats, "The Curse of Cromwell," *The Poems*, 305)

The first part of *Castle Rackrent*, written during the middle 1790s and about ten thousand words long, carries us swiftly through three inheritors: that is, Sir Patrick, who inherited from his "cousin-german," Sir Tallyho, by changing his name from O'Shaughlin to Rackrent, and no doubt by conforming to the Established Church as well; Sir Murtagh Stopgap, whose kinship to Patrick remains unspecified; and Sir Kit, who is Murtagh's younger brother. The handling is "eighteenth century," not only in the spanking pace of the narrative but even more in the use of a ruling passion or predominant trait as the all-sufficient basis for characterization and a "just" fate for each succeeding heir.

Thus Tallyho is a passionate hunter on horseback and is killed attempting to jump his steed over a carriage that has replaced a missing gate in the estate fencing. Patrick boozes and dies of it, though he earns some local regard for having invented raspberry whiskey. Murtagh litigates with his neighbors and squeezes his tenants, working in tandem with the puritanical and acquisitive Lady Murtagh, "of the family of the Skinflints and a widow" (*Rackrent*, 12) and dies of a consumption brought on by fatigue from constant court attendance at sixteen simultaneous lawsuits. Sir Kit's is the career of Ascendancy gallantry. At first an absentee, he gambles and fortune-hunts in England until he snares the Jewish heiress at Bath. Having settled on the estate, and put his wife under lock and key for seven years, owing to her refusal to turn over her personal jewelry, he involves himself in liaisons with the daughters of neighboring landowners and is mortally wounded in a duel with the brother of one young woman over an apparent breach of promise, even though his wife is known to be living.

These careers unfold and terminate so swiftly and many of the details "taken from facts" are so eye-popping (viz. Lady Murtagh's levies upon her tenants for free yarn, work days, woolen and linen cloth, chickens, turkeys, geese, hams, honey, butter, eggs, flour, fish, and game) that certain subtleties in the rendering may be missed. Not only does Sir Tallyho lose his life in spurring his hunter at a "car" substituting for a gate, but the incident establishes the theme of stopgaps and makeshifts for the book as a whole. Out on the estate, the tenants emerge from the smoky interiors of windowless cabins with broken thatches to work with the poorest of agricultural implements in fields that are rarely limed and fertilized before planting. At the big house, the roof leaks in myriad places, the fine rooms are sparsely furnished, broken windows are stopped with rags and broken slates, and there is an old wagon at the bottom of the avenue where proper gates should be. The feckless squires are blameworthy for both sets of conditions, yet this begs the question why Irish agriculture is undercapitalized while the island's economy as a whole is overburdened with excise taxes, export quotas, and shipping charges. Maria's first novel is not out to teach, however. Broad implications are left to readers, whether of the "ignorant English" variety or not, to work out for themselves.

There is a racy strip-cartoon quality about *Castle Rackrent*, which might threaten the reader's willing suspension of disbelief had not Edgeworth ballasted the tale with an unusual amount and kind of factual documentation. Kit's locking up his wife for seven years, while continuing himself to appear in county society, is the incident that most strains credulity. But for that, she produces her most spectacular bit of fact, a footnote on Colonel M'Guire, who married in 1745 Miss Cathcart, an English heiress, and kept her locked up in his castle in Fermanagh for more than twenty years when she refused to surrender her jewels—"during which period her husband was visited by the neighboring gentry" (*Rackrent*, 30). Here Ireland becomes the place where truth and reality may be stranger than any fiction that can be created about it. Before we are through we shall see other instances of this curious reversal of the usual relations between the imagined and the real where Irish experience is in question.

The novel's Continuation, the "History of Sir Conolly Rackrent," was written a year or two after the first part. About twice as long as Part One, it focuses on a single principal character, and employs a method of relatively copious and faithful realism, opening with a genre picture of boyish life in a specific Irish village and estate, and tracing Condy's story from childhood all the way to his death in early middle age. From having seen this character merrily playing among the native Irish children in the streets of O'Shaughlin's town, visiting in the cabins of the poor, becoming a great favorite of Thady's, who says, "he was ever my white-headed boy" (39), we cannot help but feel distressed over his later deterioration and, indeed, victimization. To make matters worse, there is his having been so lucky initially, for Condy was "of a remote branch of the family: born to little or no fortune of his own" (38), was educated for the law in anticipation of his having to earn a living, and never expected to become master at the castle so soon, if at all.

Condy, once launched in adulthood, is a sort of failure artist, and his story is an inverted *Bildungsroman*. *Bildungsroman* is that narrative type, frequent in nineteenth-century fiction, which traces the development of a central character from early years to when he or she attains maturity and makes a mark on the world. With Condy, however, everything except pure temporal succession works in reverse. He comes into his own through divestiture. His career is not a shaping but an undoing. His zenith is his nadir. One recalls the time when he has lost the castle to Jason and is harboring at the Lodge, lying up in bed with "a great pain about his heart" (80). In retrospect here, one recognizes what a rich fabric of incident, character, and conflict Edgeworth has woven in the Continuation and put into the hands, the words rather, of Thady to display.

Condy's wife, the actressy and fashion-mad Isabella Moneygawl of Mount Juliet's town, has left him, suffering a bad road accident on the way back to her father's house. Jason, hearing of this accident before Condy—who never knows anything in time—has arrived with an offer of three hundred guineas in cash to buy Isabella's jointure. The jointure is a substantial interest in the estate, which will revert to Condy in the event of Isabella's death. Judy Quirk, Condy's peasant sweetheart of former days—there are strong hints she may have been his mistress—also pays a visit with her two children. This "smoke-dried" widow treats Condy with scarcely concealed flippancy and gossips unfeelingly about Isabella while cadging guineas for her "childer." When she retires to another room of the Lodge to visit with her mother, Thady's "shister," who is helping look after Condy, the old steward is scandalized to learn that Judy plans to set her cap for Jason, her own cousin, now that he owns the Rackrent estate. Thady upbraids his niece for her callousness toward "my master," until Judy's mother attacks him for his lack of loyalty toward his own family, and especially toward his son Jason. Clearly one of the things that has happened over the course of this "Hibernian Tale" is that loyalties, and perhaps identities as well, have become conflicted and problematic. Moreover, this change appears to be correlated with the shifts in the relations of power and authority that obtain between the gentry class and the common people, the great sign of that shift being Jason's seizure of the Rackrent demesne.

There is still more going on. While the Quirks "give out"[4] to each other, Condy has been closeted with two crafty operators, the gauger and the excise man. They are relieving him of his store of coins through crooked wagering, and to speed up the process they bet him a hundred guineas that he cannot drink down all the wine in a huge drinking horn that once belonged to his distinguished predecessor, the dipsomaniacal Sir Patrick. Condy rashly drinks the wine at a gulp, falls into an apoplexy, and, after lingering a little, dies the painful death we have already witnessed.

Condy is a fool and "slovenly," too, but neither term takes us to the bottom of him. One keeps recalling certain moments and scenes of his history, beginning with the boyhood time when he played and was schooled among the "mere Irish" children of the district, even having Jason, his nemesis to come, as a particular friend. There is that bizarre scene when he cannot decide whether to propose marriage to Isabella or to Judy and settles the question with a coin toss. A sheer defect of will is suggested and a total conflict of desires. The scales are in balance, yet what each holds is different. It is bodily love and liking for Judy balanced against wanting to remain loyal to his class and kind in marrying Isabella. Later on, in the elaborately staged scene where Isabella announces that she is leaving him just as his difficulties over the estate debt come to a head, he will react to her news with extraordinary mildness and generosity, offering not one word of reproach. Condy is like that, God help him. But he might not have been able to carry off this parting without breaking down had there ever been much love between them.

The most arresting scene in all of *Castle Rackrent*, and the narrative's formal climax as well, is the extended scene of Condy's dispossession by Jason, the ruthless, deceptive, and steely-willed companion of former days, whose opportunity had arisen when he became privy to the disordered affairs of the estate while acting as its manager. As it gets under way, even though Condy is the Protestant and Jason the Catholic, the scene deliberately calls up ancestral memories of the native Irish dispossession by English invasion and confiscation: "Oh Jason! Jason! how will you stand to this in the face of the county, and all who know you (says I); and what will people tink and say, when they see you living here in Castle Rackrent, and the lawful owner turned out of the seat of his ancestors, without a cabin to put his head into, or so much as a potatoe to eat?" (*Rackrent*, 77). This is close to being a ritual lament, and the scene, as it continues, keeps that character of ritual, even becoming somewhat operatic, as toasts are drunk to mark the change of ownership; the children playing in the street at the end of the avenue leading up to the castle hear of the change from Thady and set up a "willalu" or keening; and the townspeople "one and all gathered in great anger against my son Jason, and terror at the notion of his coming to be landlord over them, and they cried, No Jason! No Jason!—Sir Condy! Sir Condy! for ever! and the mob grew so great and so loud I was frightened, and made my way back to the house to warn my son to make his escape, or hide himself for fear of the consequences" (79).

What are we to make of this appalled response, the signal failure of the people to be more appreciative that one of their own has risen into the ruling class? There is a ready explanation. Jason, in some part owing to his origins, is a very hard man. The people of the estate know he will squeeze them to death, as proprietors risen from the peasantry are wont to do. Such "self-made" men know exactly how to do it, having been squeezed themselves and witnessed their relations and neighbors worked over. Whereas Condy, as all know, is a soft touch. Going further, it is likely that the people actually find it much easer to identify with Condy than with Jason, regardless of the differences of "blood," religion, and class. What they see in Condy is what they recognize in themselves, a habit and history of losing. In some ways, Anglo-Irish Sir Conolly Rackrent lives and dies quite like those earlier vassals of the medieval English king about whom he complained that after a generation or two on Irish estates they became more Irish than the Irish themselves.

After Condy's dying fall Edgeworth drops the Thady persona, appearing in the last few paragraphs as the male "editor" of these "Memoirs"

(*Rackrent*, 96–97). Here "he" shows concern as to how the impending Union with Great Britain will effect changes. The few Irish gentlemen of quality may be counted on to move away to England, but will British manufacturers cross St. George's Channel to invest in Ireland? Much will depend on the English becoming more familiar with Irish life for, until recently, "the domestic habits of no nation in Europe were less known to the English than those of their sister country" (97). Now abandoning all pretense that the milieu of the novel pertains only to the period before 1782, the editor "lays it before the English reader as a specimen of Irish manners and characters" in the present tense and time. The extensive Glossary follows.

This Glossary is less than the full commentary on *Rackrent* that George Watson, the novel's modern editor, says it is, yet it goes well beyond a mere word list. It contains four kinds of entries: 1. points of grammar and diction where Hiberno-English[5] usage differs from standard English (example: "Sir Murtagh grew mad" for "Sir Murtagh grew angry"); 2. native terms for which there are no English equivalents (example: "willalu" for the formalized Irish lament for the dead); 3. English terms that carry a different meaning in Ireland owing to differences in the two socioeconomic systems and cultures (example: "Driver—a man who is employed to drive tenants for rent; that is, to drive the cattle belonging to tenants to pound"); 4. language cited to convey to English readers knowledge about Ireland they are assumed to lack (as when a passage showing Thady's familiarity with recondite legal terms is glossed with a long entry on the remarkable legal sophistication, often accompanied by litigiousness, of the ordinary Irish person).

The Glossary is full of such overkill. Entries on the willalu, on Faery Mounts, on the wake, are nearly article length. One grasps that both Edgeworths were quite anxious about English ignorance of Ireland at this time. Perhaps they worried that most English, far from regarding Ireland as a "nation" and "sister kingdom," viewed it as a backward territory populated by quaint and uncouth natives very different from themselves. Such prejudice would be disastrous for the Irish when the country had just surrendered its somewhat representative parliament and limited sovereignty to embark on the unknown waters of a legislative union. To combat such prejudice, if it existed, the Glossary compilers, daughter and father, place themselves in a double bind, for every entry, while lessening English ignorance of Irish conditions, brings out Irish variation from the English in customs, culture, and language usage.

The last variation was the crucial one, for language was the medium through which the other differences became manifest. How the Irish use English became the subject of Maria Edgeworth's next book, which is the one work in her canon jointly authored with Richard Lovell, her father. A sort of sequel to *Rackrent*, *Essay on Irish Bulls* (1802) developed out of the work done for the *Rackrent* Glossary and from the dilemma or double bind just noted. Its main argument was that for all the common English opinion that the Irish are clumsy and illogical in using English, they often are better English speakers than the English themselves, their speech displaying more vigor and variety, greater rapidity of thought, and a superior command of image and the devices of rhetoric.

The Edgeworths did not claim that the Irish were better writers; nevertheless, since the *Essay* was written and was crammed with transcribed jokes, anecdotes, monologues, dialogues, and brief stories, all composed in a variety of accurately studied vernacular styles and idioms, it was further support for the quiet revolution on behalf of the authentic in narrative launched in *Rackrent.* Equally significant, the *Essay* contributed to the decolonializing of Irish literature in English, through its fully documented claim that the Irish use English distinctively, to express a distinctive culture and history. This process was not to be completed in a single day or by a single book. Over a century later, one finds James Joyce's Stephen Dedalus in *A Portrait of the Artist as a Young Man*, still struggling with the problem of using what he considers a borrowed or imposed tongue as he thinks about becoming a writer. There is the scene with the university prefect of studies, where Stephen is upset by the donnish English Jesuit's savoring some native English expressions that descend unaltered from the period of Chaucer and Malory (*Portrait*, 185–90). How is a provincial Irishman to insert himself into such a rich and sustained heritage? One way would be to change the terms on which the problem of becoming a creative user of English in Ireland can be stated. For this effort *Essay on Irish Bulls* might have supplied some provocative aid.

For it was and is an essay in provocation, opening in a vein of deadpan irony, admitting the full English aspersion that Irish speakers of English do indeed commit the logical blunders called bulls, then going on to show that such errors are frequent in all languages, among the most gifted and animated speakers, from the time of the classical orators onward. By the second chapter, the irony shifts gears and the Edgeworths slip into their first defense of an Irish style. After quoting an absurdly inflated sentence of polite compliment drawn form an English source, they remark: "It will, we fear, be long before the Irish emerge so far from barbarism as to write in this style" (97).

The next chapter makes distinction between verbal blunders arising from stupidity and those from a speaker's unfamiliarity with usage. They say the English will forgive a French person for mixing up gender of pronouns while an Irish speaker forced to use English in a courtroom appearance who confuses *widow* and *widower* is derided. "Among the

English, it was formerly, in law, no murder to kill a *merus hibernicus*; and it is to this day no offence against good manners to laugh at any of this species" (100). They go further, averring that "the blunders of men of all countries, except Ireland, do not affix an indelible stigma upon individual or national character" (104). The implication of a special English animus toward Ireland, a historic reluctance to forgive the Irish for being un-English, is the unhappy conclusion toward which the chapter tends.

From this point on the essay acquires a dual purpose: not only defense of the Irish handling of the English language but also vindication of the Irish national character. Thus the moral tale of little Dominick O'Reilly in Chapter Four concludes that "our Irish blunders are never blunders of the heart" (112), while the pathetic tales contributed by the "Hibernian Mendicant" in Chapter Nine show how a tragedy may result from the failure of well-meaning Irish and English people to understand one another's motives and intentions as these emerge in different native idioms. Several chapters look deeper into bulls and the relation of these logical errors to the rapidity of thought and frequent use of figurative language that typify Irish speaking.

Both these traits are illustrated with a Dublin shoeblack's court testimony, explaining how he happened to stab his fellow urchin:

> "Why, my lard, as I was going past the Royal Exchange I meets Billy. 'Billy,' says I, 'will you sky a copper?' 'Done,' says he; 'Done,' says I' and done and done's enough between jantlemen. With that I ranged them fair and even with my hook-em-snivey—up they go. 'Music!' says he 'Skull!' says I; and down they come, three brown mazards. 'By the hold! you flesh'd em,' says he. 'You lie,' says I. With that he ups with a lump of a two year old, and lets drive at me. I outs with my bread-earner, and gives it him up to Lamprey in the bread-basket." (127–28)

The shoeblack's demotic resembles the speech of the first, or belittling, speaker in the Cyclops episode of *Ulysses*. Dublin street talk, it seems, changes slowly, if at all. Richard Lovell, who found the law courts a rich lode in compiling his collections of native speech, wit, and anecdote, was the likely source of this particular specimen. Its translation into standard English, in order to compare it to "the sober slang of an English blackguard" (131) under equivalent circumstances, takes nearly three full pages of their text.

If there were still any doubt as to which speech, English or Irish, gains their support, it is cleared up in Chapter Eleven, "Irish Wit and Eloquence." Here the Edgeworths become openly partisan of Irish expressiveness. In their enthusiasm they even commit a bull: "Wild wit, invention ever new, appear in high perfection amongst even the youngest inhabitants of an Irish cottage" (139), and add a few paragraphs later, "The Irish nation, from the highest to the lowest, in daily conversation about the ordinary affairs of life, employs a superfluity of wit and metaphor which would be astonishing and unintelligible to a majority of the respectable body of English yeomen" (141). Unintelligibility, of course, has its drawbacks, especially in dealings with a nation so powerful and close by as Britain.

The final turn of the *Essay on Irish Bulls* comes in the two chapters entitled "A Bath Coach Conversation" (Twelve and Thirteen). Beginning as a conversation among Irish, Scottish, and English gentlemen who are passing the time while traveling, it soon focuses upon the particular subject of Irish public rhetoric and oratory. It is plausible that the subject should come up when one considers that a great age of public speaking in Ireland, lasting half a century or more, has just ended with the proroguing of the Dublin Parliament. The Scotchman, a rhetorician who is well versed in "tropes and figures," feels that the Irish propensity for making bulls can be understood after considering the figures of speech most favored by Irish orators:

> I will select, from the twenty chief and most moving figures of speech, only the oxymoron, as it is a favorite with Irish orators. In the oxymoron contradictions meet; in reconciling these, Irish ingenuity delights. I will further spare four out of the seven figures of less note: emphasis, enallage, and the hysteron proteron you must have; because emphasis graces Irish diction, enallage unbinds it from strict grammatical fetters, and hysteron proteron allows it sometimes to put the cart before the horse. Of the eleven grammatical figures, Ireland delights chiefly in the anti-meria, or changing one part of speech for another, and in the ellipsis or defect. Of the remaining long list of figures the Irish are particularly disposed to the epizeuxis, as 'indeed, indeed—at all, at all,' and antanaclasis, or double meaning. The tautotes, or repetition of the same thing, is, I think, full as common amongst the English. The hyperbole and catechresis are so nearly related to a bull, that I shall dwell upon them. . . . A catechresis is the boldest of any trope. *Necessity makes it borrow and employ an expression or term contrary to the thing it means to express.*

Anglo-Irish attachment to catechresis returns us to the fatal Rackrent habit of improvising makeshifts and stopgaps, except that now it is a matter of rhetoric rather than stopping a broken window with a roof slate or putting a carriage where a gate is needed.

The *Essay on Irish Bulls* reveals just how far Maria Edgeworth, with assistance from her father, was prepared to go in trying to establish Irish speaking of English, and by implication, Irish writing in English, on their own distinctive ground. Ironically, this effort comes just when the class to which the Edgeworths belong has handed over its power to legislate and its modicum of a distinct political identity to Britain. Fortunately, the effort did not end with the Edgeworths. The question of an Irish English, speech that is "Irish enough," would reappear not only in Somerville and Ross, but also in W.E.H. Lecky (147–48), in all the major figures of the Literary Revival, and most spectacularly in Joyce's Aeolus episode of *Ulysses*, which so much recalls "A Bath Coach Conversation" in its virtuoso display of the figures of rhetoric during a dialogue on Irish oratory.

Directed toward a mainly English reading audience, the *Essay* was unlikely to win many converts to the view that Irish people, "from high to low," are the better English speakers. On the other hand, any Irish reader who saw the first edition would have been annoyed that stereotypes of Irish verbal and logical blundering were being purveyed to the English reader. Once again there is the double bind inherent in the Anglo-Irish situation. In 1171, the Anglo-Norman knight Maurice Fitzgerald, besieged at Dublin by Irish forces, said to his fellow barons: "Such in truth is our lot that while we are English to the Irish, we are Irish to the English. For the one island does not detest us more than the other" (quoted in E. Curtis, 55). Things were not that bad in 1802. There is no evidence that the *Essay* was resented in either country, or that the considerable entertainment value of its bulls, jokes,and monologues, and the craft of its stories went unappreciated.[6]

Improving Landlords: *Ennui* (1809); *The Absentee* (1812); *Ormond* (1817)

A gentleman's estate should be a moral school
—Maria to Fanny Edgeworth, May 17, 1831

Marilyn Butler shows that the father was not the source of the didactic and moralizing strain in Edgeworth's fiction, which was so plainly absent from her early tour de force, *Castle Rackrent*, nor was he, apart from the work just discussed, her literary collaborator, though he did contribute two brief passages to *Ormond* and wrote short prefaces to many of her books before his death in 1817. He actually complained from time to time about her moralizing, when he felt the lesson offered was too obvious or the morality too namby-pamby. Before the daughter had acquired much experience in society to draw upon for books like *Belinda*, he shared with her his memories of society in England and in France before the Revolution. His reformist Whig ideals of progressive landlording became hers, informing the three novels about young Anglo-Irish landowners and their estates now to be considered. Yet

Richard Lovell's most significant aid to Maria's writing career was in practical matters. He acted as her agent with her publishers, was good at suggesting plot developments when she had written herself into a corner, and routinely read and corrected her drafts, performing the services of copyeditor faithfully and promptly.

When Edgeworth was writing *Ormond* during 1816, Richard Lovell was in severe pain from illness that would prove fatal. Yet he insisted on continuing to edit her chapters as they were completed. Maria rushed the novel through, hoping it would please him, even as he lay dieing, to know that she had sent the publisher another substantial narrative on which he had worked. The key word here is "worked." From that summer in 1782 when father and daughter rode the estate together, making their survey of its problems and dilapidations, theirs had been a closeness based upon shared tasks, or different tasks performed in proximity under the same roof. When her father lay dead, the novelist in deepest sorrow felt that she could never write again. This changed, of course, though she completed almost nothing during the next few years. More important, she would never write another novel about Ireland and its landlords, whether of the slovenly and gallant varieties like Condy and Kit, or of the educable and improvable kind like those depicted in *Ennui*, *The Absentee*, and *Ormond*. That subject went to the grave with the landlord she knew best, with whom she had sustained the closest working relationship.

All three of these novels are sociological works with sentimental elements, emphasizing the forming and reforming of character and the accurate representation of a whole society through a selection of type figures in typical relationships. The depicted time of the first two novels is strictly contemporaneous with their writing: namely, the years immediately following the Act of Union, when Dublin society was greatly changed by the shift of political power to Westminster, and the problem of absentee proprietorship became acute in the countryside. *Ormond* is set before the French Revolution, yet most of the ordeals of circumstance, conduct, and conscience devised for its young hero would not be very different were events occurring a full generation later. *Ennui* is the young Irish earl of Glenthorn's confession of how he contracted the upper-class neurosis called ennui while bankrupting his English fortunes through gambling and dissipation in London, only to recover psychic and moral well-being and a measure of prosperity after retreating to his Irish estate and learning the duties of a resident landlord. Slight and jejune, *Ennui* occasionally spices the moral schooling with melodramatic contrivance; there is, for example, the earl's discovery that his old peasant nurse is actually his mother. The revelation should, but does not, have any profound effect on the narrator as he continues his relentless progress toward moral maturity.

The Absentee (1812), on the other hand, is Edgeworth's best novel after *Rackrent* and deserves the classic status and wide influence it acquired in Anglo-Irish literary tradition soon after its publication. One thinks less of the very full rendering of the condition of Ireland, including Dublin, though that is very well done, than of the deep veins of realism, satire, and humor she strikes into as she depicts Regency society both in Britain and in Ireland. One of the novel's keynotes is instability and shiftiness. English society has been destabilized by the corruption and ostentation of the Court, the spread of these vices to London gentry circles, and by the strain of the war with France, which has continued, with little letup, since the mid-1790s. Irish society, including Dublin society, has been destabilized by the creation of a vacuum: officialdom takes flight to London, closely followed by the newly and shamefully created Irish peers, while there is disturbance and depression in the countryside, as the landed gentry, who used to spend more time looking after their estates, with a few winter weeks of attendance at Dublin Castle levees, now divide their time between English spas and London townhouses they can ill afford.

Almost no one is at home or where he or she should be. One example of this compulsion to shift about comes late in the book, when young Lord Colombre and Count O'Halloran search for Mr. Reynolds, Grace Nugent's grandfather, to show him compelling evidence that she is of legitimate birth. Colombre strenuously journeys in dark of night from one of the wealthy and restless old man's country houses to the next, only to be told at each house that Mr. Reynolds has moved on. When Colombre is nearly out of addresses, he learns by accident that Reynolds is back in London, having arrived there about the time Colombre began searching for him out of town. But of course the chief representatives of this compulsion to be absent are Lord and Lady Clonbrony, who let their Irish properties go to rack and ruin while attempting a social conquest of London which, though the effort may ruin them financially, can never be theirs.

We ought to despise Lady Clonbrony for her social climbing, her travesty of an upper-class "Henglish" accent, her vulgar extravagance, and her obstinate and chronic refusal to regain her senses and go home. Yet she is kind to Grace Nugent, warm-hearted under all the posing, and faithful in marriage—something that cannot be said of many "fashionables" who attend her parties without ever inviting her in return, and who deride her bad style while gluttonizing on the expensive refreshments and entertainments she provides. Equally at fault with his gambling and his running to Mr. Mordecai for ready money at a ruinous rate of interest, Lord Clonbrony at least does not attempt to put on English airs. He contributes to his wife's delinquency, however, by showing so little authority and being so acquiescent in her harebrained schemes for making a London social success. We saw this lack of authority, to an extreme, in Sir Condy. Reappearing in Lord Clonbrony, it seems a legacy of the Anglo-Irish legislative sellout.

The Absentee's fully worked design uses pleasing linkages and parallels to develop an idea of inter-involvement between contrasted national societies and cultures. Some of these devices are simple and traditional, as when Larry, the mildly comic Irish postilion attaching himself to Colombre on his Irish journey, is paralleled by English Mrs. Petito, the comic and intriguing confidential servant to Lady Dashfort and her daughter Isabel; or when a little scene involving a carter carrying household goods in the Irish countryside is paralleled later by a scene involving a goods-carrying wagoneer in the English countryside. When Colombre, just down from Oxford, begins to take in the Irish situation and come to terms with his Irish patrimony, he acquires two mature mentor figures, English Sir James Brooke, who instructs him on how Dublin society is being replenished by a new class of business and professional people, and the Irish Catholic nobleman Count O'Halloran, who teaches him about Irish antiquity and some of the immemorial traditions of native Irish culture.

A more elaborate linkage turns up between the Clonbronys in London and a couple named Raffarty in the Dublin suburbs. Mr. Raffarty, a wholesale grocer, is part of a new Irish middle class with aspirations to take part in Dublin society as it centers around the Castle. But he runs hugely into debt as Anastasia, his equally aspiring wife, sets up a showy and costly "villa" at the sea resort of Bray, complete with "a little conservatory, and a little pinery, and a little grapery, and a little aviary, and a little pheasantry, and a little dairy for show, and a little cottage for ditto, with a grotto full of shells, and a little hermitage full of earwigs, and a little ruin full of looking glass, 'to enlarge and multiply the effect of the Gothic.' But you could only put your head in, because it was just fresh painted and though there had been a fire ordered in the ruin all night, it had only smoked" (89). In the Raffarty household bad taste runs riot as untrained servants deliver ill-cooked dishes, sometimes to the table and sometimes to the guests' laps, while the grocer husband in Dublin approaches ever closer the inevitable bankruptcy that will send him and his country-bred wife flitting westward with those household goods she can cart off before the bailiffs take possession.

Of course, the Raffartys' financially suicidal social climbing matches with and parodies the Clonbronys', at the remove of Ireland and what passes in Ireland now for a business class. There is still more linkage between these couples. Anastasia, it turns out, is the sister of Lord Clonbrony's agent, "Old Nick" Garaughty, who oppresses the wretched tenants of Clonbrony town and its agricultural estate, partly to line his pockets and rise as his sister did, but also in response to frequent urgent demands from the Clonbronys for money to underwrite their London social campaigning. In this Anglo-Irish and native Irish social pyramid, where nearly everyone is misplaced except the rural tenants at the bottom, it is the bottom class that pays, and dearly, for the folly and vice of the rest.

A more subtle linkage holds between the Clonbronys and Lady Dashfort and her daughter. For much of the novel, each pair is engaged in social adventuring in the other's country. The English women, however, are genuinely vicious and are in Ireland only because they have run out their string at home. The still-attractive if shopworn Isabel, a widow, hopes that her languid posing and false reserve will seem fresh and genuine in a provincial land, at least until she can snare a new husband of means, while both count on Irish remoteness from the English capital to prevent their being exposed as the schemers and slanderers they truly are. Lord and Lady Clonbrony are in some sense a new type created by the changed political relations between the two countries, but Isabel and her mother are a very old type indeed, for English rogues and adventurers had found Ireland fair game from the earliest years of the Conquest.

There are flaws in *The Absentee*: Count O'Halloran has about as much life and reality as a cigar-store Indian, while Mordecai Lazarus is an ignorant anti-Semitic stereotype. Edgeworth's conventional, even philistine attitude about the stigma of illegitimacy turns the romance between the young principals, Lord Colombre and Grace Nugent, into an exercise in *deus ex machina* manipulation in the novel's last few chapters. Otherwise, the book is strongly plotted, full of accurate observation, and directs wit and irony at human foibles without shrillness or excessive malice. When Colombre, disguised as a Welsh mining prospector, visits the neighborhood of Clonbrony town, he spends the night in a country cottage whose occupants, besides providing harrowing details of their being "driven" by the under-agent, serve him a supper of bacon, milk, and hot potatoes on a clean wooden trencher. He observes the notched tally stick on which landlord duty days are recorded and overhears the daughter's fiancé referred to as her "bachelor." After a night's sleep in a small separate room he awakens to:

> a *fresh* morning, and there was a pleasant fire on the hearth, neatly swept up. The old woman was sitting in her chimney corner, behind a little screen of whitewashed wall, built out into the room, for the purpose of keeping those who sat at the fire from the *blast of the door*. There was a loophole in this wall, to let the light in, just at the height of a person's head, who was sitting near the chimney. The rays of the morning sun now came through it, shining across the face of the old woman, as she sat knitting. (152)

These authentic details evoke a culture, that of Irish rural life before the great famine of 1845–48, which only survived in fragments by the time Yeats and Lady Gregory, eager to discover peasant "soul," went out interviewing the people of the West about their visions and beliefs. The tally stick, like the beautiful hand-carved small wooden crosses of the Penal Era, shaped for concealment up a sleeve, survives merely in a few historical collections, while the vernacular architectural detail of the whitewashed interior partition with the aperture to let the sun through, may be lost altogether. Colombre's eye and ear register the things they do because of their strangeness and their difference from the familiar. Without choosing the role, he becomes the faithful recorder of the ways of a people with whom he can never be at one. In that respect he is Edgeworth's surrogate and embodies the paradox and the uniqueness of Anglo-Irish writing per se.

The Absentee developed from a little play that she devised for family entertainment and which Richard Lovell encouraged her to turn into prose fiction. The novel contains eminently stageable scenes and a few characters who might have come straight from the great age of English stage comedy. High comedy had been something of an Anglo-Irish monopoly, from Congreve and Farquhar at the Restoration to Goldsmith and Sheridan in the following century. The best of these characters is Mrs. Petito, the lady's servant, and her best moment—her sublime moment—comes at the London house of Mr. Reynolds. Lady Dashfort has won influence with the old man through her slanders against the St. Omars, the family of Grace Nugent's mother, and hopes to get at his money by cozening him into a marriage proposal. She sends the maid with gifts of Irish moss and cheese to keep the connection on the boil, but Mrs. Petito must wait in an anteroom until Colombre and Count O'Halloran have finished opening Mr. Reynolds's eyes at last as to the purity of Grace's mother and Lady Dashfort's malicious lies about her and the St. Omars. When the maid trips in with her gifts, she is told by the newly enlightened Reynolds to go to the devil, taking her mistress with her. Mrs. Petito shows admirable aplomb, all the more admirable considering that in an "underplot" she had entertained hopes of grabbing off the wealthy Mr. Reynolds for herself:

> "*Crimini*!" exclaimed Mrs. Petito, "what new turns are here! Well, sir, I shall tell my lady of the *metamorphoses* that have taken place, though by what magic (as I have not the honour to deal in the black art) I can't guess. But, since it seems annoying and inopportune, I shall take my *finale*, and shall thus have a verbal *P. P. C.*—as you are leaving town, it seems, for Buxton so early in the morning. My Lord Colombre, if I see rightly into a millstone, as I hope and believe I do on the present occasion, I have to

congratulate your lordship (haven't I?) upon something like a succession, or a windfall, in this *denewment.* And I beg you'll make my humble regrets acceptable to the ci-devant Miss Grace Nugent that was; and I won't *derrogate* her by any other name in the interregnum, as I am persuaded it will only be a temporary name, scarce worth assuming, except for the honour of the public adoption; and that will, I'm confident, be soon exchanged for a viscount's title, or I have no sagacity nor sympathy. I hope I don't (pray don't let me) put you to the blush, my lord."

Lord Colombre would not have let her, if he could have helped it.

"Count O'Halloran, your most obedient ! I had the honour of meeting you at Kilpatrickstown," said Mrs. Petito, backing to the door, and twitching her shawl. She stumbled, nearly fell down, over the large dog—caught at the door, and recovered herself. Hannibal rose and shook his ears. "Poor fellow! you are of my acquaintance too." She would have stroked his head; but Hannibal walked off indignant and so did she. (243–44)

Here Mrs. Petito's recovery of her frowsy dignity—a poise tested still again when she nearly falls backward over the count's Irish wolfhound Hannibal—is impressive. Her use of fractured and Anglicized French in combination with polysyllabic English words looks back to such great language manglers as Lady Wishfort and Mrs. Malaprop. Yet she gets most of the meanings right and her command of essential grammar is splendid. Considering the case made for Irish verbal gifts in *Essay on Irish Bulls*, one may wonder whether Mrs. Petito is not after all an Irishwoman in disguise.

Ormond was a try at writing an Anglo-Irish *Tom Jones*, but it fell short as Maria Edgeworth's didactic habit and moral conservatism, the latter probably strengthened by her anxiety over her father's fatal illness, got the better of her artistic instincts. The book aimed also at widening her scope of subject matter and cultural reference as it sent young Harry Ormond adventuring to "King" Corny O'Shane's demesne in the Black Islands, a remote, indeterminate location that loosely stood for an unreconstructed Gaelic and Catholic Ireland, and also sent him abroad among the gallants, easy ladies, and *philosophes* of prerevolutionary Paris.

The opening chapters followed a plan of showing a healthy, hot-tempered, yet good-hearted adolescent boy moving toward maturity and self-possession by making his own discoveries and blunders in the school of experience, including sexual experience. However, this Fielding-like approach was soon obfuscated as Harry acquired a string of moral mentors, beginning with sober Lady Annaly and her prim daughter Florence—the young lady to whom Ormond is consigned in marriage at the end—the Irish Huguenot minister Dr. Combrai, and even a sententious French abbé, in whose company the hero finds himself at evening parties in Paris drawing rooms.

This moral strait-jacketing of a lively young man is summed up in the way his taste for prose fiction changes over time. At the Black Islands, Harry comes upon a copy of *Tom Jones.* Not only does it become his favorite book, but it also determines him to "shine forth an Irish Tom Jones" (*Ormond*, 82). Lady Annaly, however, who has taken to writing him letters full of moral chiding soon heads off his enthusiasm for Fielding with a gift of works by Samuel Richardson, guiding him in the reading of *Clarissa* and, what is hard to believe, *Sir Charles Grandison.*

Her prudery and moralism in *Ormond* prevented Edgeworth from ending her novel-length explorations of Irish experience on a high note. Nevertheless, she had staked her claim as the originator of a literary tradition and would continue to influence it fundamentally over its entire course.

Conclusions about Beginnings

Anglo-Irish literature, as it takes shape in Edgeworth's originating efforts, shows some features that will guide, if not absolutely determine, the development of Anglo-Irish writing after her. One can establish a check list of characteristics, if not a paradigm. In any true Anglo-Irish work to come, one or usually several of these characteristics will appear. Only the first item is a *sine qua non.*

1. "Involvement in the Irish situation." After 1800, there is no point in trying to include writers who take themselves out of the Irish situation, by emigration or simply by avoidance of Irish subject matter. In the case of a writer who writes both England-centered and Ireland-centered works—Maria Edgeworth herself being such a writer—the latter works alone constitute that writer's contribution to the Anglo-Irish literary heritage.

2. A focus on the fortunes or misfortunes of the rural proprietors and their families in the isolated estate houses of the Irish country districts as Anglo-Irish power and authority begin their long contraction and decline.

3. A fascination, often a nervous one, with the lives of the "peasantry," that majority population of native Irish people who live surrounding and subordinate to the landlord class as family servants, large and small farming tenants, village tradespeople, poor laborers, paupers, and vagabonds.

4. Cultivation of an "attitude of research"[7] in the writer's approach to the native community and its ways. This attitude attends to the "facts" and "traits" of mere Irish social custom, folkways, oral traditions, speech patterns, and self-presentation in everyday life. It permits the Anglo-Irish writer to approach the native community without suffering disabling anxiety and without the threat of losing his or her distinct cultural, class and self-identity.

5. The isolation and separation of Anglo-Irish writing from many of its readers who are English. The strength of the position is that the writer speaks with authority of a world unknown to the reader. The weakness of the position is that the English reader may not care to know about it.

6. For all the strain and ambiguity and even the lonesomeness of the Anglo-Irish writer's position, his and her conviction that "we Irish"—this "we" to include all conditions, from high to low, settler to native, country-bred to town-bred—cultivate the English language distinctly differently from the people and the writers of Britain and may even use the language more vigorously and vividly.

Like her father, Edgeworth was uncommonly rational, practical, and unsuperstitious. She did not believe in ghosts or fairies and her letters as well as her literary publications are remarkably free of experience with the uncanny, the transcendental, and the intuitional. She does, however, report two intuitions, the first resembling a haunting, the second intensely joyful, which approach uncanniness. Both these experiences date from the period when she was just finding herself as an imaginative writer. A few lines devoted to these experiences may help us go a little deeper into her literary imagination than we have yet done. My own intuition is that any discovery one may make, however limited or speculative, will have some value for understanding writers who follow her.

The first piece of uncanniness was the haunting of her inner consciousness by the figure of Thady, who "seemed to stand beside me and dictate, and I wrote as fast as my pen would go." In Yeatsian terms, a writer just coming into her own discovers—or is discovered by—the mask or antiself through which her most authentic exploration of reality will be carried out. The speaking voice is that of a native representative of the silenced majority, who at this time have no more access to articulate literary expression in English than they have to social and economic control and political power. Yet it speaks much more of her world, and that of her ancestors, than about the submerged world of the cabins, boreens, and crossroads. So who is using whom? When one is dictated to, the dictating voice controls. Or does it? The penman, in Joycean terms, has the last word.

Maria's joyous experience occurred during the United Irish Rising of 1798 and was preceded by an experience of desolation nearly as strong. As General Humbert's French expeditionary army approached the borders of County Longford from the west, Irish guerrillas and local agrarian terrorists, seizing the opportunity to pay off old scores and to hit out at the landlords, began to raid and put to the torch the big estate houses. As these marauding bands came close, Richard Lovell decided that the family and servants must immediately evacuate Edgeworthstown House and take refuge in a town some twenty miles away, where the yeomanry and British troops afforded protection to refugees. Maria Edgeworth, then about twenty-nine, was fervently attached to her home and suffered torments as she imagined it standing open to the elements; there had not even been time to secure the doors and windows. For all she knew it had already been looted or burned out.

Thady Quirk's oddly moving account of Castle Rackrent emptied of the family, at the time when Sir Condy moved into Dublin to sit in parliament, must owe something to Maria's recollection of how she had felt about her own temporarily abandoned home in 1798: "There was a great silence . . . and I went moping from room to room, hearing the doors clap to for want of right locks, and the wind through the broken windows that the glazier never would come to mend, and the rain coming through the room and best ceilings all over the house. . . . I took myself to the servants' hall in the evening to smoke my pipe as usual, but missed the bit of talk we used to have there sadly, and ever after was content to stay in the kitchen and boil my little potatoes, and put up my bed there; and every post day I looked in the newspaper, but no news of my master" (*Rackrent*, 61).

When the emergency was over—with the surrender of Humbert's little French army, and the butchering in a bog of the "tail" of exhausted and bewildered peasants the army drew after it—the Edgeworths went home fearing the worst. The house was perfectly intact. Nothing had been stolen, damaged, or even tampered with. It was at this discovery that Maria had her intuition of overwhelming peace and joy (*Memoirs*, 2:128).

Edgeworthstown House was one of the Big Houses of Anglo-Ireland. Most of these buildings were put up between the late seventeenth and early nineteenth centuries. They were usually built four-square of quarried stone and a slate roof, in Georgian proportions and with restrained Georgian ornament, if any ornament at all. The typical structure was part plantation house, for commonly there were "offices" relating to the agricultural work of the estate located at the back, or taking up part of the bottom floor, or placed within a hollow square entered through a sturdily gated archway; part fortress, for the deeply recessed downstairs windows on all four sides were fitted with heavy inside shutters slitted for armed defense; and part family home, where the joys and disciplines of Anglo-Irish domesticity as well as a family's hopes for survival and continuance were centered. There is a pathos about these houses which, in troubled times, faced into the aroused and hostile countryside like the little square of fighting men called "the forlorn hope," shown trapped between the lines on old battle maps; and which in good times might be the pride of the district and site of its festive celebrations.

Maria Edgeworth, the great Maria who founded the line of literature this book investigates, had imagined her home to be doomed, but she discovered it had been spared. Actually, it had only been reprieved. This she may have understood in her deepest imagination, where Thady, her Mask and Daimon, spoke old family scandal and prophecy too, as fast as she could write it down.

III

WILLIAM CARLETON (1794–1869): THE NATIVE INFORMER

There's not a man in the four provinces has sich
a memory. I never head that story yet, but I could repate
it in fifty years afterwards. I could walk up any town in the
kingdom, and let me look at the signs, and I could give
them to you again just exactly as they stood.
—Carleton, "Shane Fadh's Wedding," in *Traits*

The most sporting characters among the nobility
and gentry of the country, fighting-peers, fire-eaters,
snuff-candle squires, members of the hell-fire and jockey
clubs, gaugers, gentlemen farmers, bluff yeomen, laborers,
cudgel-players, parish pugilists, men of renown within
a district of ten square miles, all jostled
each other in hurrying to see.
—Carleton, "The Dead Boxer," in *Works*

It is but just to state / For the benefit
of those who may come after him / That he
was unrivalled at / INVENTING TRUTH.
—Carleton, "Epitaph on a Liar," in *Tales and Sketches*

Introductory

WILLIAM CARLETON is the greatest imaginative writer in English to emerge from the native Irish community before James Joyce. Born a little over a century apart, the two men have much in common, beginning with their apostasy from the Catholic faith, their habit of grounding their mature literary constructions upon lived experience recollected from the period of childhood and youth, and the fact that each deliberately separated himself from the scene, society, and cultural milieu about which he was to write during most of his career. This separation is both spatial and temporal. Joyce wrote about late Victorian and Edwardian Dublin and Dubliners while living permanently abroad from 1904 onward. Until his death in 1941 he is steadily receding in time from a subject matter stationary in time. Comparably,

Carleton expressed the life of the rural peasant community during the opening years of the nineteenth century while living entirely away from the countryside, pursuing in Dublin the financially hazardous career of a professional fiction writer. This career lasted from a fairly late start in 1828 until his death in 1869. When death ended his work on the *Autobiography*—the account is broken off at the stage of early manhood—Carleton was already at the ghostly remove of sixty years from the rural scenes he evoked in all his tales and novels.

The comparison could be further pursued, except that Carleton belongs to the line of Anglo-Irish literature as I am defining it in this book, while Joyce does not. How can a writer of peasant origins who wrote of the peasantry belong to such a line? Let us hope the puzzle can be worked out without too much casuistry. A clue to the solution lies in the word "separation," as used in the previous paragraph.

Turning One's Coat and Keeping Faith

A few years before the United Irish Rebellion and the subsequent Act of Union merging the two kingdoms, William Carleton was born into the small farmer class of the Catholic peasantry in a northern part of Ireland, County Tyrone, where "planted" populations of Scottish and English Protestants during two centuries had forced most of the Catholics out of the rich bottomlands and into tenancies on barren or hilly land. Both his parents were bilingual in Irish and English at a time when the former tongue was disappearing as a written literary and record-keeping medium. Yet spoken Irish continued to support strong oral traditions in which both of Carleton's parents, his father as a storyteller, herbalist, local historian, and folklore collector, and his mother as a traditional singer and reciter of poetry, were proficient. William, the robust and petted youngest child of a large family, absorbed these traditions, songs, and stories in both tongues at the parental knee and spent much of his boyhood and youth larking about at fairs and markets, dances, rural athletic events, and wake games, being exempted almost entirely from the harsh farm labor at which most of his relatives toiled early and late. In rural society of that time such exemptions were usual for boys intended for the priesthood or, in the absence of a calling, for such "learned" occupations as teaching or clerking in an office. During substantial if irregular attendance at various village academies kept by so-called "hedge schoolmasters," young Carleton proved extra-bright at book learning. William's father was a "voteen"—that is, a peasant of exceptional, excessive, and compulsive piety. No doubt he would have been overjoyed to see his son a priest. The traditional route entailed the candidate traveling south for a period of study in the "classical academies" of Munster, followed by a local bishop's nominating him to the newly established Catholic seminary at Maynooth in Kildare.

That was not to be, even though Carleton did set out for Kerry around the age of seventeen, following the death of his father. After a couple of days' walk, during which he was fed and sheltered by kindly farmers along his route, he reached Granard, a large town not far from the estate and village of the Edgeworths. Here he put up at a small inn kept by a voteen named Grehan. For all the man's devoutness he was the first on Carleton's journey to charge him for food and lodging. In the night, Carleton dreamed of being pursued by a maddened bull intent on goring him. The next morning he turned around and went home. Here is the writer's own conclusion to this adventure, as given in the *Autobiography*:

> The notion of going to Munster originated with myself. My ambition to acquire learning, however, was not so strong as my domestic affection. On the morning of my return I felt as if I could tread upon air. Most fortunately, no one saw me until I entered the house—when my dear mother uttered an exclamation which it would be difficult to describe, and rushing to me with tottering step, fainted in my arms. (69)

In this account young Carleton returned home more like a conqueror, a veritable peasant Ulysses, than like a homesick, timid boy. Indeed, the Oedipal implications of the episode are rife, requiring little if any drawing out. It is hardly necessary to point out that the grudging innkeeper was a replication of Carleton's own late father, on his pietistic though not his fondly parental side. Carleton confesses in the *Autobiography* to feeling that his father's kind of religiosity was "senseless and superstitious" (61). Beyond the Freudian matrix there is the ecclesiastical one. The bull could represent the Church, militant and aroused. Such an interpretation has a certain plausibility in Ireland, owing to the notoriety in Irish history of Adrian's Bull, the Papal document, probably forged, conferring Ireland upon the English crown . At the very least, an equivocal attitude toward the priestly career seems to be expressed by the nightmare and by the line of action it elicited from the boy at the time.

However, his efforts at becoming a priest did not stop there. After further study locally, he took to wearing a sort of quasi-clerical garb, carried himself with preternatural dignity, and adopted a Latinate, "sesquipedalian" speaking style. All this, meant to win from his diocesan bishop the offer of a nomination to Maynooth, went for naught owing to a feud between the Carleton family's parish priest and the bishop. Visits to the famous Jesuit school at Clongowes and to Maynooth itself elicited little encouragement and no nominations. At Maynooth Carleton got into a street brawl and consorted with an Amazonian apple woman and with "Big Magee," a celebrated Irish giant who was a genius at clock-making. He began to feel himself ill-used by the Roman clergy. In light of developments to come, he was already a ticking bomb laid against the historic faith of his forefathers.

No one is sure exactly when Carleton ceased to believe in the Catholic religion, or when and how he entered the Protestant Episcopal Church of Ireland. Writing in 1869, he claimed it was his pilgrimage in 1817 to St. Patrick's Purgatory, on Station Island in Lough Derg, County Donegal, and his disgust over the superstitious practices he found there that "detached me from the Roman Catholic Church" (*Autobiography*, 92). It was in 1818, however, that he visited Clongowes and Maynooth seeking a sponsor for admission to the seminary. Perhaps the negative reaction to Station Island developed over time. While writing his memoir in 1869 he could easily have confused the order of real events with a highly imaginative recasting of events in his first published story, "The Lough Derg Pilgrim," written 1828. The actual visit to the island had come eleven years earlier.

Owing to religious differences in Ireland, changing faiths was often considered tantamount to betraying one's community and kind. In the charged political atmosphere of the 1820s, most Irish Catholics were unified under the leadership of Daniel O'Connell in the campaign for Emancipation—the winning of the right of Catholics to participate fully in the political process. Many though not all Irish Protestants opposed this. In the 1830s and 1840s the Catholic campaign, still looking to O'Connell for leadership, was for Repeal of the Union. Most Irish Protestants, along with some middle- and upper-class Catholics, were unionist. Given the linkage between differences of political outlook and religion, it is important to consider Carleton's change of faith with some care.

His conversion was sincere and proved to be permanent: Carleton died a Protestant. Gifted with no extraordinary religious sensibility, he professed the ordinary views of the church he entered: negatively, that the "errors" of Catholicism included the doctrine of exclusive salvation within the Church and that Catholic priests encouraged idolatrous and superstitious practices; positively, that the Church of Ireland was correct in professing salvation by faith alone, in its reliance on Scripture as God's revealed word, and in permitting ministers to marry.

When Carleton left the countryside about 1820, arriving in Dublin on foot and virtually penniless, he began, after some months of ragged urban bohemianism, to make his way upward through a series of employments under Protestant sponsorship. These included engagements as a private tutor, clerkships with the Sunday School Society and the Evangelical Association for Discountenancing Vice, and two out-of-town teaching jobs in Protestant parishes, both of which he quickly left. Soon he married a Dublin Protestant and settled to the responsibility of supporting a family that steadily grew to become a household of ten.

In the early nineteenth century, the temper of the Established Church was one of missionary zeal aimed at the Catholic community. It had spawned a movement called the New or "Modern" Reformation which worked to stem the tide in favor of Catholic Emancipation through anti-Catholic propaganda and by trying to win converts among the peasantry and urban poor. In 1825, Cesar Otway, a Dublin Protestant clergyman with a flair for writing and editing, founded an anti-Catholic monthly called *The Christian Examiner and Church of Ireland Magazine*. By 1828 Carleton was contributing to it his first published stories and sketches, beginning with "A Pilgrimage to St. Patrick's Purgatory," about his Lough Derg adventure. These first works of Carleton made powerful propaganda, because they gave an overwhelming impression of authenticity in their depiction of rural people, while simultaneously attacking the rural ministry of the Roman clergy. In 1830 and 1833 Carleton issued *Traits and Stories of the Irish Peasantry*, first and second series, a work of rugged genius that established him as an important writer with both Irish and English readers. *Traits and Stories* was frequently reissued with revisions, until the splendid, augmented New Edition of 1843–44 in two volumes, with illustrations by Phiz and other "Artists of Eminence" (1: title page) and with an important "Autobiographical Introduction" (1:i–xxiv). This collection also contained anti-Catholic material, although proportionately much less of it than the *Christian Examiner* pieces.

It used to be believed that most of Carleton's later revisions of his earlier work consisted of excising or softening negative presentations of the Catholic religion as his mood mellowed with age. Recent scholarship shows that this is not exactly the case (Wolff, *Carleton*, 23–53). When five of his *Christian Examiner* contributions were gathered into a book and issued along with two additional stories as *Tales of Ireland* (1834), most of the anti-Catholic passages stayed in, while a newly written author's preface rebuked the Catholic country people's "slavish" attitude toward their priests and deplored priestly prejudice against mixed marriages. The New Edition of *Traits and Stories* removes or softens some passages exhibiting bias against priests and Catholicism, but this is not the main thrust of Carleton's final revisions (Wolff, *Carleton*, 67–70). It was not until 1847, in *The Irish Agent; or, The Chronicles of Castle Cumber*, his long, ambitious novel about absentee landlords, corrupt agents, religious hypocrites, and the crimes of the Orange Order, that he presented a parish priest favorably, while turning a critical eye on his Church of Ireland counterpart. Though Carleton was by then a political conservative and unionist, he had also come under the influence of Thomas Davis's tolerant and ecumenical form of cultural nationalism. And of course by 1847 no one believed that the Established Church had a chance of converting Catholics by the route of "modern Reformation," a movement that the novel, which is set back at the opening of the nineteenth century, ridicules by name.

In 1826, Carleton sent a signed memorandum—"Points for the Right Honourable Robert Peel's Deep Consideration"—to the future British prime minister. Peel was then Home Secretary in Lord Liverpool's cabinet and had been chief secretary for Ireland from 1812 to 1816. He was also known for his opposition to the Catholic Emancipation Bill, which would finally become law in 1829. In this curious document Carleton claimed that O'Connell's Catholic Association maintained hidden connections with seditious agrarian terrorist societies such as the Ribbon Men, and that this conspiracy was abetted by the hedge schoolmasters, educated yet sometimes disaffected men who occasionally provided leadership to local Ribbon Lodges. Also privy to the plot were "a great proportionate number of the Roman Catholic clergy who are educated in Maynooth College [and who] have been and are in the habit of being connected with such flagitious combinations" (quoted in Wolff, *Carleton*, 20). A covering letter to the man charged with transmitting the memorandum to Peel contains an offer from Carleton to provide proof of his allegations (Wolff, *Carleton*, 19–22).

Though no evidence has turned up showing that Peel ever replied to Carleton's memorandum, it is still disquieting to realize that he was proposing to become an informer against his own people, in particular against the only leadership and guidance, in the form of country priests and village teachers, which the rural Catholic population possessed. Carleton had wanted to be a priest and had consorted with priests during his frustrating campaign to enter the seminary. Disliking the drunken brutality of many hedge schoolmasters, he yet had been a star pupil to several, and at one time had anticipated becoming a rural teacher himself as a second best to ordination. He had even held Ribbon membership for a brief period in late adolescence (*Autobiography*, 77–80).

Fortunately, Carleton became an informer in another, quite admirable sense of the word. With a native's intimate knowledge, a fabulous memory, and a large literary gift, he became the chronicler—the celebrant even—of Ireland's native country culture as it had somehow survived the repressions of the Penal Laws, and as it would not survive the great famine of 1845–48. He gave voice to what had been silenced through the decline in use of the native tongue and the denial of education to the rural masses during several generations; or rather, he released a myriad of voices on the far side of a silence that had been all but officially imposed. Carleton made known a world that had become unknown to the world at large and even, in some sense, to itself. One cannot imagine a task more challenging or more satisfying for a writer. After all, it appears that this peasant turncoat pretty well understood what that task was:

> With the welfare of the Irish people my heart and feelings are identified, and to this object, in all its latitude, have my pen and my knowledge of their character been directed. I found them a class unknown to literature, unknown by their own landlords, and unknown by those in whose hands much of their destiny was placed. If I became the historian of their habits and manners, their feelings, their prejudices, their superstitions and their crimes; if I have attempted to delineate their moral, religious, and physical state, it was because I saw no other person willing to undertake a task which surely must be looked upon as an important one. (*Tales of Ireland*, "Preface," x)

He sounds only a little boastful and defensive. Mostly he had done and would continue to do what he claims here. This keeping faith—literary faith—with an entire people may seem much more important in the end than William Carleton's petty crimes of priest baiting and the launching of a single memorandum indited with a poison pen.

More Ventriloquism

Maria Edgeworth in her Anglo-Irish literary debut broke through the circle of isolation imposed upon members of her privileged minority class by an inspired act of ventriloquism. Giving authentic voice to Thady Quirk, the Catholic peasant chronicler of the Rackrent dynasty in its decline and fall, she creates Anglo-Irish literature at a single stroke. In the first story of his first book, Carleton does something equivalent, yet exactly opposite. In order to begin giving voice to the silenced and unknown native condition, he puts on the mantle of the Ascendancy and speaks in what he takes to be its class accents. The book is *Father Butler* [and] *The Lough Dearg Pilgrim: Being Sketches of Irish Manners*, published in Dublin in 1829, and consisting of work reprinted from Otway's journal. Carleton's preface shows him serving his Evangelical masters: "His object was to show the moral degradation in which [the peasantry] are sunk, and the unlimited authority which their clergy, in the name of religion, exercise over them" (iii–iv). "Father Butler" carries out this rather dismal intention—up to a point. For the most part it is a wan tale, redeemed from drabness by touches of romantic nature drawing, about a youth of refinement and sensibility who is forced by his superstitious parents to become a Catholic priest when he would much prefer to marry a neighboring Protestant girl who adores him. First the lovelorn girl declines and dies, and then Father Butler does.

The narrator of this story is a landlord who happens to have come into the district quite recently. The local farm people address him as "sir" and "your honour," and gossip about him as "the gentleman who bought Squire Grame's estate an' that was lately come to live in the Castle" (12–13). He is Protestant but tolerant and shows a lively curiosity and observant eye directed at the peasants. Also he is unusual among early nineteenth-century estate owners, though certainly not unique, in being able to understand spoken Irish. As this well-intentioned newcomer wanders about, not only becoming privy to Father Butler's melancholy career but also learning about his new property and the population on it, he comes across and introduces to the reader two characters, of a type traditional to rural Ireland, who add a large measure of vitality and an exotic flavor and color to the tale.

The first is the voteen, Paddy Dimnick, a well-off farmer whose exploits of piety include a daily rosary recited high in a tree, because "the son of the Virgin Mary suffered on a tree; and don't you know also that the only prayer that was ever made on a tree was granted—that of the thief, Sir" (29), and because a tree is an excellent vantage point from which to keep "two large grey bullet eyes" (23) on his toiling field laborers. Unaware that his religious cult of the tree may be a legacy from Druidical times, Paddy likes to fault the Protestants for failing to include in *their* Bible such essential material as the Litanies to the Virgin and a full account of Purgatory. He enjoys challenging Protestants to religious debate. On such occasions his speech becomes a delirious mixture of mangled scriptural quotation, theological malapropisms, and bog Latin of the "hocus-pocus dominocus" variety. Drawn in strokes of broad satire this burlesque yet authentic figure puts life into the story whenever he appears.

The second character, the "man mountain" and pilgrim, Owen Devlin, is equally authentic:

> He was certainly above six feet high—wore a long beard, by which I judged that he wished to distinguish himself as a person set exclusively apart for religious purposes. His hat had a steeple-crown of a foot high, which made him appear of a gigantic size, and the leaf of it fell down over his shoulder, like that of a coal porter. He wore no shoes, but had on a pair of *traheens* [footless stockings] that went down to his ankles. What the color of his coat was, or whether he wore one, I could not say; for his huge body was completely enveloped in a blanket, which he had secured upon him with a leathern belt, that buckled across his middle. He had two bags upon his back, and one hanging across his breast. Under his left arm he carried a large bullock's horn, bottomed with leather, and stopped with a plug of paper—beneath which hung a tin canteen. In his left hand he bore a long

> oaken cudgel, about seven feet in length, called a *cant*, with an iron spike in the end of it; and in his right hand a string of beads, at least twice the length of Dimnick's. This colossus and Paddy went forward, bandying Irish prayers alternately. (149)

Owen Devlin is a sort of Irish *saddhu* or wandering holy man who prays incessantly while traveling in a circumscribed locale and accepting food and shelter from the charitable hands of cottagers, poor themselves in everything but faith. He is also a mountebank who peddles votive objects and medicinal nostrums at fairs and markets, an itinerant entertainer who bellows out his "rhan" or ballad of "The Blessed Scapular," which he modestly claims was jointly authored by Saints Patrick, Columcille, and Brigid; and he is probably a thief, for he gathers so much portable property into his bags that he is said to be able to pay for a son studying at the priests' college.

It is quite likely that no one much like Owen Devlin the pilgrim had appeared in English writing since the Middle Ages. He is one of the "finds" of *Father Butler*, along with his patron and crony Paddy Dimnick. Such finds make Carleton's early stories worth reading, even when they contain propaganda, for they shadow forth the greater work to follow.

The Mature Work—General Considerations

Maria Edgeworth also directly influenced William Carleton. Absentee landlords and oppressive land-grabbing agents, the latter occasionally getting their comeuppance, find their way from her fiction to his, yet this is relatively minor borrowing. The chief thing he took from her was the project of an Irish imaginative literature in English resting upon the authentic account. He would develop this possibility so far beyond her pioneering efforts that eventually she would testify that she never knew Ireland or the Irish until she came to read his fiction (Wolff, *Carleton*, 111–12). Few finer compliments have been paid by the leader of one literary generation to the leader of the next.

Carleton sometimes liked to represent himself as a literary naif, and there is truth in Benedict Kiely's remark that he took much from life and only a little from books (Kiely, 40). In the *Autobiography* he describes reading *Gil Blas* in Smollett's translation with total absorption and with so little sophistication that he mistook it for a true story. That was while he was still in the countryside, and still seeking a satisfactory alternative to becoming a priest. Le Sage's picaresque tale was one of "the books, pamphlets, odd volumes, many of these works of fiction," which might be found in the homes of unlettered Catholic families, "most carefully laid up, under the hope that some young relation might be able to read them" (*Autobiography*, 73). That is how Carleton discovered *Castle Rackrent*, the first Anglo-Irish work he ever read, while sheltering in the cabin of a farm family, near Navan in County Meath. Devouring it in a single night, he found it "inimitable" (Kiely, 44).

Several thoughts arise. It was fortunate that his first experience of Anglo-Irish writing was with an indubitable masterpiece of solid and lucid construction, whose tonal consistency was inflected with a myriad of subtleties that his native ear was best equipped to pick up. He might have first read Sydney Owenson's stagey and melodramatic *The Wild Irish Girl* (1808) with consequences for his own work difficult to predict. Whether the book was "inimitable" or not, Carleton could not have been blind, then or a few years later, to the opportunities offered him, a man of the peasantry, by Rackrent's superb deployment of the peasant as narrator and oral historian. Finally, there was the intriguing fact that this novel, so carefully aimed at the English reader, had already come to circulate among Irish people of humble condition, only a few years after its first publication in London.

Carleton went on to become initially a purveyor of anti-Catholic fictions to the circle of Reverend Otway's Protestant subscribers, and subsequently Ireland's most famous fiction writer, frequently compared with Walter Scott himself, noticed and praised at length in the great English and Scottish reviews, admired both in Britain and at home by a substantial, mainly middle-class readership. There was a lesson in this he would not have missed: sooner or later his own stories would come into the hands of the people he wrote of, and they, too, from a depth of bitter and real experience, would judge how truthfully he represented their lives. At the very least, Carleton's awareness of this fraction of his reading public should have wonderfully concentrated his search for the authentic and genuine.

Carleton wrote tales *and* novels, his best work in the shorter forms being on the whole much superior to his novels. However, the longest of his tales, notably "Going to Maynooth" and "The Poor Scholar," are actually short novels in their elaboration of incident and leisurely unfolding of story. The two finest tale collections are *Traits and Stories of the Irish Peasantry*, first series 1830, second series 1833, followed by the New Edition in two volumes dated 1843–44; and *Tales and Stories of the Irish Peasantry*, published in 1845. The latter work also carries a second title page in the first Dublin edition: *Tales and Sketches: Illustrating the Character, Useages, Traditions, Sports, and Pastimes of the Irish.* The appeal to the factual in these titles underlines the twofold nature of Carleton's task as a writer bringing a submerged and unknown world into view for the first time. He must equip his reader with enough accurate and specific knowledge for him or her to encounter an imaginative re-creation of Irish peasant life without bafflement or disbelief. We first saw this problem in *Castle Rackrent.* There the effort to inform and document began with the Preface, continued in the footnotes, and concluded in the extended commentaries of the Glossary.

Carleton met his self-elected dual responsibility—to convey "traits" and tell stories, to create literary characters and illustrate the little-known "character" of Irish peasants and their folkways or culture—in every way imaginable. Sometimes he was perfectly happy to set an imagined story side by side with a nonfictional anecdote, sketch, or essay falling into the same subject area, as he frequently did in *Tales and Sketches.* Sometimes he integrated the two functions, as in "Shane Fadh's Wedding" (*Traits*, 1:51–83), a magnificent tale of courtship and marrying, told by the bridegroom many years after his wedding day, that contains a remarkable amount of arresting detail about rural marriage far back in the Code era of the eighteenth century. "The Geography of an Irish Oath" (*Traits*, 2:1–74) yokes a nonfictional "Essay on Irish Swearing," which is mainly about the intricate evasiveness of the country people when summoned to give courtroom testimony, with an absorbing story of the rise of a poor country couple to great affluence and respect in their community, only making connection between essay and story in a final section, where the grief-stricken widower so manipulates the terms of his temperance oath that he is able to drink himself to death without technically violating his sworn word.

In "The Donagh, or the Horse-Stealers" (*Traits*, 1:381–406), the old brass and yew wood box called the donagh is certainly integral to the climax of this dark tale of rural crime, but the several thousand words of terminal footnote discussing the provenance of the box, and the reprinting of correspondence between the author and two antiquarians, are certainly not essential. Yet who would want to do without them? For his novel *Valentine M'Clutchy*, Carleton intended writing a series of "Alphabetical Appendices," modeled on the *Rackrent* Glossary. He abandoned the project while the book was in the press. One result was to strand in the text a footnote or two advising the reader to consult Appendix A on this or that recondite point of Ulster lore—except that there is no Appendix A. One would not want this any different either. Like "Printer's Devil," who appears in an asterisked footnote on the last page of *M'Clutchy*, to dispute and alter the narrator's final disposition of one of the more villainous characters—an attorney named Browbeater—the stranded footnotes sufficiently "deconstruct" the text to remind us that behind the excellent invention stands a man and not a fiction machine.

A final example: "The Lough Derg Pilgrim," Carleton's only *Christian Examiner* contribution to find a place in the definitive New Edition of *Traits and Stories*, early on gives several pages about the lake and its island retreat in excerpts from Cesar Otway's once well-known travel book, *Sketches in Ireland: Descriptive of Interesting Portions of Donegal, Cork, and Kerry* (1827). Otway was not very complimentary, describing the site as "a collection of hideous slated houses and cabins," and as "the monstrous birth of a dreary and degraded superstition, the enemy of mental cultivation, and destined to keep the human understanding in the same dark unproductive state as the moorland waste that lay outstretched around" (*Traits*, 1:238). Just before the Otway excerpt, Carleton, speaking *in propria persona*, confessed to the reader that earlier versions of the story had contained offensive passages, "which are expunged for this edition" (1:237). But the Otway diatribe is new to this edition. Here one sees the author carrying out the work of "authentication" in a wonderfully dodgy way, hoarding his Protestant propagandist cake and devouring it too.

Given his origins, his early bilingualism, and the subjects his writing focused upon, it was inevitable that Carleton would greatly extend Maria Edgeworth's researches into Hiberno-English idiom and usage. To begin with, he was not a regional dialectician. His Connaught or Munster characters speak similarly to characters in stories set in Leinster or Ulster.[1] An exception is made for the twang of the Ulster Presbyterian, which is rendered on occasion in all its "ear-piercing" distinctness. At the same time, Carleton does differentiate speech according to socioeconomic differences obtaining in the countryside. The strong farmer with his servants, herds, flax yards, and his socially ambitious wife will usually speak differently, closer to a type of standard English, than, say, the ragged Kerry laborers in "The Poor Scholar" (*Traits*, 2:257–348), who look after young Jemmy M'Evoy as he lies under a rude roadside shelter, wasting with famine fever. They speak differently and more correctly, not necessarily with greater expressiveness or command of words. When the pastor rewards with a coin one of these laborers, Paddy Dunn—"that naked, starved-looking man . . . who looks like Famine itself" (2:311), Dunn cries out, "May every hair on your honour's head become a mould-candle to light you into glory!" This carries expressiveness about as far as anyone would wish.

There is some blurring of difference at the lower end of the social scale. Small farmers, cottiers, and all but the most demoralized among the laborers and the paupers roughly come together, forming a speech community of the rural common people, who share the same religion, folk traditions, memories of a half-mythical past when the Irish were masters in their own land, and a residual familiarity with the Irish tongue; they face down daily the same ordeals and fears—of rent increases and rackrenting, land clearances and evictions, the repeated cycle of crop failure followed by famine followed by outbreaks of typhus and dysentery. At the very bottom of the scale Carleton tends to assign a particularly slovenly sort of speech to rural terrorists such as the rank and file of Ribbon Men and White Boys, and to violent criminals. In his mind, inarticulateness, violence, and conspiracy are associated.[2]

Certain people in Carleton aspire above their station, and this complicates the linguistic picture. The "bodagh" or gentleman farmer, a figure of anomaly located in uncharted social territory between the landlord class and the bulk of the peasantry, may sedulously ape the speech and bearing of his local squire. And a small farmer's son, as both the *Autobiography* and the long story "Going to Maynooth" show us, may start talking, dressing, and even eating like the parish priest.

Taken as a whole, the speech community in Carleton shows extraordinary richness and energy. One source of heightened effects is the Irish language, which he sees as particularly suited to expressing strong and tender feelings. At sorrowful partings and joyful reunions, by deathbeds and in lovemaking, his people often use emotive words and phrases drawn directly from the other tongue without translation, or else use language translating Irish idiom that expresses unbridled emotion. In "The Donagh," a father who is ordinarily brutal and neglectful cries to his mortally injured daughter, "*Acushla oge machree! Manim asthee hu!*" (1:401). The author's own note translates this as "Young pulse of my heart! My soul is within thee!" In English it may sound too extravagant to be sincere. Generally, Carleton's characters do not hold back. An unspoken assumption of the culture may be that emotion restrained is no emotion at all.

In the following passage a daughter has come into a sickroom, where her mother has just died of a sudden severe pleurisy or pneumonia. We are already on the down side of the emotional curve in a wrenching death scene, yet there is still more to come:

> "An' I'll kneel at the bed-side," said the daughter. "She was the kind mother to me and to us all; but to me in particular. 'Twas with me she took her choice to live, when they all was striving for her" . "Oh," said she, taking her mother's hand between hers, and kneeling down to kiss it, "*a Vahr dheelish*! [Sweet mother!] did we ever think to see you parting from us this way! snapped away without a minute's warning! If it was a long sickness, that you'd be calm and sinsible in; but to be hurried away into eternity and your mind dark! Oh, *Vahr dheelish*, my heart is broken to see you this way." (*Traits*, 2:53)

It is from the heart, yet it is also something of a performance. In Irish peasant culture of Carleton's time grief *is* performed. That is the point of the *keen* or *caoinne*, the formalized lamentation performed at rural funerals. In the *Autobiography*, Carleton says his mother was so gifted at keening that she was in demand at the funerals of strangers; when she lamented, the effect was so beautiful that little by little all other voices fell silent.

Other sources of verbal enrichment and high talk are the parish priest's Latinate vocabulary and sermonizing rhetoric; the apocalyptic rant, promising imminent release from the English yoke, of the "prophecy man"; the hedge schoolmaster's parody-parade of all the learned vocabularies, from mathematics and astronomy to philology and the Greek, Hebrew, and Latin classics; the traditional tricks for capturing and holding an audience used by peasant storytellers. Very rarely in Carleton's world of discourses do his top performers lack responsive listeners, whether it is a religious congregation groaning and trembling at a bog priest's sermon on the pains of Purgatory, a fair-day crowd delighted by the spiel of a traveling pedlar or "soogah," or a young girl entranced by a suitor's blandishments as the couple linger at a farm gate during the long northern summer dusk. Poor in many things, the Irish country life that Carleton's memory keeps alive was certainly not poor in speech and self-expression.

A final point about his representation of native speaking in written form. When he began to write he tried to convey peculiarities of dialect and accent by altering spelling. But as he gained experience he largely normalized his spelling and tried to suggest the Irish difference more subtly, mainly through distinctive patterns of rhythm and intonation in entire phrases, sentences, dialogue exchanges and speeches, and, of course, through a lavish use of what are called Irishisms of idiom and diction.[3] His mature technique is well shown in the following account of a poor woman on a night of storm and cold waiting in dread that something terrible has happened to her husband, whose arrival is long overdue. The speaker is Tom M'Roarkin, previously identified as a collector of local folklore and superstitions. He is supposed to be asthmatic. Here he gets through his telling without a wheeze, conveying in plain words and strongly marked rhythms how Sally M'Farland first heard the voice of the Banshee, the Death Spirit, crying in the night:

> There she lay, trembling under the light cover of the bed-clothes, for they missed Larry's coat, listening to the dreadful night that was in it, so lonely, that the very noise of the cow, in the other corner, chewing her cud, in the silence of a short calm, was a great relief to her. It was a long time before she could get a wink of sleep, for there was some uncommon weight upon her that she couldn't account for by any chance; but after she had been lying for about half an hour, she heard something that almost fairly knocked her up. It was the voice of a woman, crying and wailing in the

> greatest distress, as if all belonging to her were *under-boord.* ("Larry M'Farland's Wake," *Traits,* 1:99)

Joyce drew his fictional world from memory, but monitored Mnemosyne's reliability by checking Dublin street guides and newspapers and writing numerous Dublin correspondents for information. Carleton, too, fetched up his created world from deep wells of memory, but there were no street guides to his villages and farms, and very little of the life he re-created, apart from Ribbon and White Boy atrocities, found its way into the provincial papers. He might have gone back to Tyrone to check his recollected impressions, but he chose not to. The first visit to home territory came only in the 1850s, when the bulk of his significant work in fiction was already done. By then the countryside of his youth had been greatly changed—its teeming populations emptied through the clearances and evictions mandated when the Irish agrarian economy changed from crop cultivation on small holdings to animal grazing; reduced by the millions of famine deaths, and by the fresh diaspora to America and the British overseas colonies following the great famine of 1845–48.

Since one cannot possibly determine the accuracy of Carleton's memory by any objective standard, it is at least reassuring that he frequently expressed boundless confidence in his powers of observation and retention. The opening of Chapter 11 of the *Autobiography* amounts to a virtual *apologia pro sua vita* on this theme. After remarking that no writer ever had his opportunities for knowing the manners of the people, he says:

> Talking simply of the peasantry, there is scarcely a phase of their life with which I was not intimate. That, however, is not so much in itself . . . but not only a cultivated intellect, but strong imagination and extraordinary powers of what I may term *unconscious* observation, existed in my case. . . . My memory, too, although generally good, was then in its greatest power; it was always a memory of association. For instance, in writing a description of Irish manners, or of anything else connected with my own past experience, if I were able to remember any one particular fact or place, everything connected with it or calculated to place it distinctly before me, rushed from a thousand sources upon my memory. (128)

This seems to put Carleton as a memory adept somewhere between Wordsworth and his "spots of time" and Proust with his *madeleine.* We must not, however, ignore that on occasion he could draw the long bow, or simply be in error. His claim that "The Lough Derg Pilgrim" is as accurate and authentic as a "coloured photograph" (*Autobiography,* 91) can be challenged, as we have already seen, for his having mistaken the correct date for his change of religion. Many of his nature descriptions are exact evocations of scenes, season and weather; yet his work also contains natural description that merely reflects early nineteenth-century conventions of the visual sublime and picturesque. Carleton's work often uses material based on the recollections of his parents and other people of their generation. That is one reason it has such a lengthy backward reach into penal times. In these instances his memory has no role to perform apart from the faithful transmission of material the authenticity of which can never be established by direct testimony.

Finally, one trusts Carleton's witnessing because there is no one else to trust and because so frequently the sheer abundance, density, and *oddity* of his related detail compel belief. Here, for instance, from "The Geography of an Irish Oath," is his account of Ellish Connell as she and her husband, Peter, begin to rise in the world through shrewd enterprise at buying and selling:

> By degrees her house improved in its appearance, both inside and outside. From [selling] crockery she proceeded to herrings, then to salt, in each of which she dealt with surprising success. There was, too, such an air of bustle, activity and good-humour about her that people loved to deal with her. Her appearance was striking, if not grotesque. She was tall and strong, walked rapidly, and when engaged in fair or market disposing of her coarse merchandize was dressed in a short red petticoat, blue stockings, strong brogues, wore a blue cloak, with the hood turned up over her head, on the top of which was a man's hat fastened by a ribbon under her chin. As she thus stirred about, with a kind word and a joke for everyone, her healthy cheek in full bloom and her blue-grey eye beaming with an expression of fun and good-nature, it would be difficult to conceive a character more adapted for intercourse with a laughter-loving people. In fact she soon became a favorite, and this not the less that she was ready to meet her rivals in business with a blow as with a joke. (*Traits*, 2:23)

While noticing the phrases an editor would blue-pencil as redundant, and places where the speaker gives himself airs ("it would be difficult to conceive. . ."), one still cannot escape Ellish Connell as a substantial narrative presence implying a real existence in historical time. She is fastened down on the page as firmly as the man's hat is fastened to her head.

Carleton's fiction is full of reality stranger than fiction, the strangeness arising less from any quality of imaginative fantasy than from the fact that he is bringing into view a life which writing in English has heretofore missed. There is the Mass Green called "the Forth" in "Ned M'Keown," where the prophecy men and the voteens carry on their peculiar superstitious business, and the young people flirt and gossip on grass-covered tiers of sitting places arranged like an amphitheater, until the priest comes to celebrate mass *al fresco*, "before a plain altar of wood, covered with a little thatched shed" (*Traits*, 1:16); the "Spoileen" tent at the town fair in *Valentine M'Clutchy*, where country people who have never eaten beef or mutton in their lives gather in a mood half-abashed, half-mirthful to taste for a few pennies the spoiled mutton they imagine is the standard diet of the gentry class; and the camouflaged schoolroom in "The Hedge School" that is entered through a doorway cut into a long bank of clay; and the marital bargaining scene among peasants of the humblest condition, which Carleton gives us in "Phelim O'Toole's Courtship."

In this last example, the young woman, Peggy Donovan, must be courted in the presence of her mother and father, and her suitor must bring along his father, for that is the custom. Before the O'Tooles arrive and the sharp bargaining commences, Carleton provides an inventory-description of the one-room, sixteen- by twelve-foot cabin and its scanty furnishings, the wickerwork poultry roost inside over the only door, and the cow tethered just inside near the grain bin, whose protruding hind-quarters partially block the doorway. Carleton's description is so faithful that someone could build and furnish a model from it.[4] He next turns his eye on Peggy and her parents:

> When seven o'clock drew nigh, the inmates of the little cabin placed themselves at a clear fire; the father at one side, the mother at the other, and the daughter directly between them, knitting, for this is usually the occupation of a female on such a night. Everything in the house was clean; the floor swept; the ashes removed from the hearth; the parents in their best clothes, and the daughter also in her holiday apparel. She was a plain girl, neither remarkable for her beauty nor otherwise. Her eyes, however, were good, so were her teeth, and an anxious look, produced of course by an occasion so interesting to a female, heightened her complexion to a blush that became her. The creature had certainly made the most of her little finery. Her face shone like that of a child after a fresh scrubbing with a strong towel; her hair, carefully curled with the hot blade of a knife, had been smoothed with soap until it became lustrous by repeated polishing, and her best ribbon was tied tightly about it with a smart knot, that stood out on the side of her head with something of a coquettish air. (*Traits*, 2:224–25)

The narrator's allusions to "an occasion so interesting to a female" and to "the creature" may be patronizing, yet he is fascinated and deeply sympathetic as well. What effort does it take, moral as well as physical, to achieve a clean fire and all the rest on an earthen floor sixteen by twelve, shared with the chickens and a large ruminant animal? Carleton pulls us close into the scene, so close we can see the soapy gloss on Peggy's curls. No wonder that Maria Edgeworth testified she had never known the Irish people before getting to know them at close quarters in Carleton's books.

Like Dickens, Carleton was fascinated with crowds and with the problems mobbing poses for the art of narration as well as for public order. Dickens, as early as *Oliver Twist* and *Barnaby Rudge*, explored mob dynamics in the urban context. His somewhat older contemporary, coming to maturity just about the time the Irish countryside reached its highest population density, had only to look about him. What he saw and reflected in his fiction was sometimes hilarious, sometimes frightful, but always significant. A conservative and unionist, Carleton disliked O'Connell's Repeal politics almost as much as Maria Edgeworth did. However, like everyone else in Ireland during the 1830s and early 1840s, he could not fail to be impressed at the way O'Connell's Repeal Association shaped the rural multitude into a political force. This process reached its highest point of organization in the series of "monster" rallies held at different country places, such as the Hill of Tara, where crowds as large as half a million came together, listened to anti-Union oratory, contributed their pennies to the Repeal Fund, then dispersed to their widely scattered homes without incident.

Crowding and mobbing appear early in Carleton's work. The seedy climax of "The Lough Derg Pilgrim" comes, not in the inn or road scenes, but on the island. There the young man finds he must sleep one night three to a bed on a mattress swarming with vermin, and must spend another night standing up, praying and fasting, in a dreary chapel called "the prison," which is packed with his fellow pilgrims. Later, "Phelim O'Toole's Courtship" shows Phelim's future parents visiting a holy well, the waters of which are reputed to cure infertility, especially on the local patron saint's day. They find the shrine ringed with refreshment tents, where fiddlers and pipers are playing. At the well itself the following mad scene is in progress:

> Around the well, on bare knees, moved a body of people thickly wedged together, some praying, some screaming, some excoriating their neighbors' shins, and others dragging them out of their way by the hair of the head. Exclamations of pain from the sick or lame, thumping oaths in Irish, recriminations in broken English, and prayers in bog Latin, all rose at once to the ears of the patron saint . . . "For the sake of the Holy Virgin, keep your sharp elbows out o' my ribs."
>
> "My blessin' an' you, young man, an' do't be lanin' an me, i' you plase!"
>
> "*Damnho sherry orth, a rogarah ruah*! [Eternal perdition on you, you red rogue!] Is it my back you're brakin'?"

> "Hell pursue you, you ould sinner, can't you keep the *spike* of your crutch out o' my *stomach*! If you love me tell me so; but by the livin' farmer, I'll take no such hints as *that*!"
>
> "*I'm* a pilgrim, an' don't brake my leg upon the rock, an' my blessin' an you!"
>
> "Oh murdher sheery! my poor child 'ill be smodhered!"
>
> "My heart's curse on yoou! is it the ould cripple you're thrampin' over?"
>
> "Here, Barny, blood alive, give this purty young girl a lift, your sowl, or she'll soon be unhermost!" (*Traits*, 2:193)

Mobbing offered Carleton opportunities for rude comedy but it also created possibilities, necessities almost, for narrative experimentation. In "The Hedge School," a work marked by different sorts of linguistic experimentation and some interesting manipulation of narrative point of view, the master sits surrounded by upwards of two hundred pupils ranging in age from five or six to twenty-two. By tradition, the teacher is a polymath, a rhetorician, a show-off, a heavy drinker, a sadistic brute, and sometimes exhibits symptoms of insanity. Carleton's schoolmaster, Mat Kavanagh, qualifies on all counts, being also the leader of a terrorist band who eventually escapes hanging by abandoning his seditious principles and betraying his comrades. When Mat hears his pupils' lessons simultaneously on a dozen different subjects, while also engaging his favorites in badinage and abusing and threatening the rest, a severe problem of narrative coherence is created. Carleton solves the problem by experimenting with a multilinear prose that is somewhat analogous to musical polyphony. Beginning "Come boys, rehearse (buz, buz, buz)," and continuing for several thousand words, it ends with: "Yes, Sir." "Yes, Sir." "Yes, Sir." "I will, Sir." "And I will, Sir." "And so will I, Sir, &c. &c. &c." (*Traits*, 1:302–6). These cadential phrases mark the winding up of a sort of canon fugue in six voices, each voice standing for many besides itself. Joyce's Sirens episode in *Ulysses*, the scene in the Ormond Hotel bar that he laid out as *fuga per canonem*, has affinities with this schoolroom recitation scene of "The Hedge School."

Mob action elicits a comparable, though more limited, experiment in "The Battle of the Factions." There it is prolonged cudgel fighting among dozens of the O'Hallaghan and the O'Callaghan factions' followers, which is given a musical treatment emphasizing the percussive: "For the first twenty minutes the general harmony of this fine row might be set to music, according to a scale something like this: Whick whack—crick crack—whick whack—crick crack—&c. &c. &c. 'Here your sowl'—(crack)—there your sowl—(whack.) 'Whoo for the O'Hallaghans!'—(crack, crack, crack.) 'Hurroo for the O'Callaghans!'—(whack, whack, whack.) . . ." (*Traits*, 1:136–37). With variations, the narrative continues like this for some time. The nearest thing in modern, self-consciously experimental writing would seem to be Anglo-Irish Samuel Beckett's chorus in *Watt* for the three frogs croaking "Krakkk!" "Krek!" and "Krik!" which can actually be performed by eight voices keeping strict time (137–38).

Though he could pretend in moments of bravado that, being Irish, he enjoyed a general dust-up, Carleton certainly feared the propensity of individuals acting collectively to become infected with murderous violence and cruelty. That is what one of his best-known stories, "Wildgoose Lodge," based on an atrocity from real life in which a lynch mob of Ribbon Men burned alive a family of eight, is really about. He felt that the Irish "character," while it contained many bright lights and noble aspects, was underdeveloped and even somewhat inchoate at bottom. The cause of this underdevelopment was the broad English domination and suppression of the native Irish from far back, and, in particular, the denial of all education to the Catholic population in the Penal Era.

He discusses this in the "General Introduction" of 1842 to the new edition of *Traits and Stories*, which is specifically aimed at British readers and shows Carleton assuming a role as spokesman for his national culture and a national literature struggling to emerge. In it he does not exactly mince words:

> The Irishman was not only *not* educated, but actually punished for attempting to acquire knowledge in the first place, and in the second, punished also for the ignorance created by its absence. In other words, the penal laws rendered education criminal, and then caused the unhappy people to suffer for the crimes which proper knowledge would have prevented them from committing. It was just like depriving a man of his sight, and afterward punishing him for stumbling. (1:xviii)

Hence, and as a legacy from Penal times, passed down from parent to child, "hereditary" Irish distrust of the laws, the readiness of many Irishmen to enter into secret societies and illegal conspiracies, and the willingness of others to let the crimes of the conspirators go unreported and unpunished. The cure of these problems, Carleton goes on to say, is through the educational opportunity now becoming available; however, the maturing of the national character will take another thirty to forty years. It will also help, he thinks, if a new, responsible sort of landlord emerges, closer to an English type, who sees that his best interests and his tenants' are really the same.

Carleton does not expect that the Irish will gradually turn into Englishmen. The Irish character and temperament will always exhibit the yoking together of opposites—mirth and melancholy, realism and unbridled imagination—traits that other people, notably the British, prefer to compartmentalize. The conclusion dwells on this point, remarking that "the house of death is sure to be the merriest one in the neighborhood" (1:xxiv) at wake time, and that it is commonplace in Ireland to see religious penitents pass from severe mortifications of the flesh to such amusements as wild dancing to bagpipe and fiddle, with no sense that their behavior is incongruous or uncouth.

Carleton's Art of Story: "The clear-obscure of domestic light"

He makes out a chiaroscuro quality in peasant life, or, as he puts it, "the clear-obscure of domestic light" (*Traits*, 1:9). For instance, "*Lha Dhu*: or, The Dark Day," a tale from 1834, shapes a poignant downward flight from bright warm light into darkness and gloom. Coming in a book of stories dedicated to Wordsworth, and one of several stories detailing calamities overtaking rural young women, the collection owes something to the mood of Wordsworth's and Coleridge's *Lyrical Ballads* and to Romantic balladry altogether.

"*Lha Dhu*" opens in spring, in an idyllic northern valley, at the village of Ballydhas, where Catholics, Protestants and Presbyterians coexist in peaceful prosperity. A fair is on in the neighborhood town of Ballaghmore to which a medieval profusion of rural types, including "beggars, mendicants, and impostors" (*Works*, 2:69), are shown hastening. The scene changes to a Ballaghmore public house, where courting couples, assisted by friends, relatives, and matchmakers, are presented in different stages of cheerful negotiation.

After this bright-toned preliminary, "*Lha Dhu*" becomes a troubling account of how Hugh O'Donnell mortally injured his younger brother, Felix. Hugh struck him down with a stone when Felix, over his brother and sister's opposition, tried to leave the family farm to marry Alley Bawn Murray, a poor village girl whom he dearly loves. Brother and sister drop their opposition after Felix's grievous hurt and in guilty shame push on the marriage. The couple wed, but the mortally injured Felix dies within a month.

The story is built upon the contrast between bright beginning and somber conclusion, the "dark day" of the fratricidal assault, which should have been the glorious day bringing together two lovers, acting as a pivot. A further "darkness" comes out of the dour, unmarried older brother with his low boiling point and miserly ways. At the end of the narrative are juxtaposed the pathetic spectacle of Alley in her widow's weeds, still faithful four years later, visiting and tending Felix's grave, and the melancholia of Hugh, now a shunned recluse who will leave the remote O'Donnell farm only on essential errands, usually at night and by unfrequented ways.

In approaching Carleton's masterpiece, *Traits and Stories of the Irish Peasantry*, it should be stressed that this treasure house of rural "folkways" and stories is also a carefully planned and patterned artistic performance. In Volume 1, the quasi-Chaucerian framing narrative, centered at Ned M'Keown's crossroads shebeen, frames successively a comic folktale told by an unsuccessful entrepreneur (Ned himself); a memoir of old-fashioned courtship and marriage custom told by a widower; a cautionary tale of a peasant couple ruined through shiftlessness contributed by a historian of local traditions; and a story of faction fighting told by a schoolmaster with a mysteriously shortened arm. The device, which encourages interplay between storytellers and audience, and rivalry among narrators, is then dropped for the remainder of the two volumes. This development, freeing up the rest of the work for a variety of third- and first-person accounts, was a creative one. Carleton had much more to tell his readers about his hitherto "unknown" subject than could be gotten out either plausibly or with decorum through one local group swapping yarns at a single fireside.[5]

After the shebeen group, Volume 1 contains three substantial stories—"The Station," "The Lough Derg Pilgrim," and "The Midnight Mass"—devoted to the distinctive devotional practices of the peasantry. There is a story of rural crime, "The Donagh, or, The Horse Stealers," which is balanced in the second volume by "Wildgoose Lodge," a story about the politically motivated murder of an entire family. Similarly, the facetious comedy of "Neal Malone," the four-foot fighting tailor, which concludes Volume 1, is balanced by the comic story of "Phil Purcell, the Pig-Driver," concluding Volume 2.

Story groups shape themselves in terms of predominant yet not exclusive qualities. There are borderline instances and overlapping categories. "The Midnight Mass," which contains an attempted murder, a kidnapping, and some criminal conspiracy, could be classed with the tales of rural crime. "The Battle of the Factions" groups with "The Party Fight and Funeral" as a story about the undeclared war among localities and between various secret societies that raged in the northern districts, yet the former story, since it is narrated by the hedge schoolmaster, Pat Frayne, also groups with "The Hedge School," Carleton's long story about Mat Kavanagh, the schoolmaster of Findramore.

"Wildgoose Lodge" and "The Lianhan Shee," both in Volume 2, have strong affinities. Both are hectically Gothic in manner and both exhibit the corruption of a potential leader in the Catholic culture of rural Ireland. In "Wildgoose Lodge" it is the schoolteacher and parish clerk, Patrick Devaun, who leads the crowd astray, functioning as their "Ribbon Captain," and whipping them into a frenzy with mob oratory delivered from the altar of a remote country chapel, until the people go surging to the lodge, set it afire, and butcher those trying to escape the flames. "The Lianhan Shee" is the story of an unfrocked priest, devoting himself to good works in a poor district, who comes to be haunted by nemesis when an emaciated ex-nun turns up to complicate his new career. Evidently psychotic, she has a mysterious, shawl-covered hump on her back, which she thinks is the evil female spirit, the Lianhan Shee, directing her will and movements. But Carleton's informative note tells the reader that the same Gaelic phrase, in the usage of the country people, means "a priest's paramour" (2:96).

This story is Carleton's closest approach to a subject—sexual scandals involving priests and nuns—that was sometimes exploited in English Gothic fiction but taboo in Ireland. Both stories make much of fire, the bad priest of "The Lianhan Shee" actually burning himself to death in his own fireplace in a frenzied excess of remorse. Lest the reader find this farfetched, the author remarks in a footnote that "it is no fiction at all. It is not, I believe, more than forty, or perhaps fifty years, since a priest committed his body to the flames for the purpose of saving his soul by an incrematory sacrifice. The object of this suicide being founded on the superstitious belief, that a priest guilty of great crimes possesses the privilege of securing salvation by self-sacrifice" (2:95). This "documentation" of the "factual" basis of a bizarre fictional detail leads straight back to the story of Colonel Cathcart and his unfortunate English bride, given in a footnote of *Castle Rackrent*.

Two matched stories in the second volume are "The Geography of an Irish Oath" and "Tubber Derg; or, The Red Well." The first shows the rise to affluence and respect of Peter and Ellish Connell, mainly through their own efforts, while "Tubber Derg" details the decline from prosperity into downright beggary, through no fault of their own, of the tenant farmer Owen M'Carthy and his large family. Carleton's first version of this story, called "The Landlord and Tenant, an Authentic Story," dating from 1831, left the M'Carthys destitute and despairing, but the amplified version in the "New Edition" of *Traits* shows them making a slow, infinitely painful comeback, until they reach a degree of comfort and achieve a house nearly as good as the one they lost. This happier ending is not very believable. In the real agrarian community of Carleton's era, reprieves and second chances were as rare as rent reductions for farm leases.

Perhaps the most impressive group of stories in *Traits and Tales* are the three long tales falling together in Volume 2 which are about young country boys growing up and launching into life. This collective *bildungsroman* is comprised by "Phelim O'Toole's Courtship," "Going to Maynooth," and "The Poor Scholar." The first stands a little apart, however. It is about an ugly, amoral, irrepressible, late-arriving child born to a couple previously cursed with barrenness, who grows up to cut impish capers all over his country district, courting three women simultaneously, and ending by being transported to the Colonies for his crimes as a Ribboneer, where no doubt he is flourishing yet. "Phelim O'Toole" is Carleton's rich contribution to European rogue literature, his version of an Irish Till Eulenspiegel.

The other stories rehearse the careers of a seminarist and a priest, following the road not taken by Carleton himself when he turned back toward literature and apostasy. "Going to Maynooth" is the superior of the two. Its hero, Denis O'Shaughnessy, son of a tall, stiff-gaited small farmer known as "the walking pigeon house," is a wonderfully absurd figure as he astounds the neighbors with his verbal quibbles and pedantic disputations, takes to sitting a horse like the priest, even though he must make do with a single spur, and nearly breaks the heart of gentle Susan with pomposities about sacrificing his love for her to the glories of an ecclesiastical career. He is finally shoehorned into Maynooth through a horsetrading deal—literally—between the parish priest and the bishop that is as complicated and guileful as anything in the still-to-come Irish R. M. stories of Somerville and Ross. Distant relatives travel miles to see Denis off, including a poor old woman who gives him a live cock and two hens to lay eggs for his seminary breakfasts. Fortunately, Denis quits Maynooth shortly after arriving and returns chastened to Susan. The story ends in a joyful marriage, instead of ordination to a religious life for which the hero utterly lacks aptitude.

"The Poor Scholar" is superb on the trials of the Catholic M'Evoys in a northern district, where the Protestant farmers preempt the fertile and sheltered bottomlands, while the papists must dig in their seed potatoes on hilly barren acres swept by wind and cold rain. But when young Jemmy, on whom all his family's hopes come to rest, departs for Munster, having sworn not to return until he has been received into holy orders or died trying to attain ordination, certain compositional problems arise. Since Carleton himself had never completed the route of the "poor scholar" to the fabled academies of the southwest, his account of Jemmy's difficulties and ultimate success in Kerry relies on stereotyped characterizations and situations. However, the episode where the friendless boy falls victim to famine fever is sufficiently realized to carry conviction. Taken with one other story, these three are as close as Carleton ever came to drawing, partly in a self-satirizing vein, his own portrait of the artist as a young man. That other is "The Lough Derg Pilgrim," his "true account" in the first person of going on religious pilgrimage.

Why did Carleton include this last-mentioned work in the New Edition, since a version of it had already appeared in his first book (*Father Butler*, 201–302)? According to Barbara Hayley in an excellent study, "'The Lough Derg Pilgrim' marks a circle in Carleton's career; his first story is now included in his most significant collection. . . . In choosing it as one of the two stories that complete the collection . . . Carleton must have gauged that his English and Irish audiences would accept it, despite its still critical view of Catholic ritual" (Hayley, 355). That is true, but I would go further and maintain that the story is in some sense about the very process of electing to become a writer instead of the member of a religious order, and that is why it demanded inclusion in the collection that Carleton must have known, at least intuitively, to be his masterpiece.

The narrator first introduces himself on the family farm, hugely ambitious to perform marvels in the religious sphere on his way to becoming a cleric and comically overreaching himself in an absurd attempt to walk on water. He then sets out for Lough Derg, wearing clerical black, so that he is sometimes mistaken for a young priest by toilers in the fields along the road, even though he is barefoot. When he falls in with two elderly countrywomen in identical gray cloaks, who claim to be on the same pilgrimage to the Holy Island, they get influence over him by playing up to his vanity; then, taking advantage of a soaking rain shower, they begin to reduce his priestly pretensions by altering his garb. By the time he arrives at Petigo, the village near the lake from which trips to the island are organized, he has been pinned into one of the women's cloaks. This elicits derision from people passing. One queries, "And why, you old villain, do you drive your cub to the 'island' pinioned in such a manner—give him the use of his arms, you sinner!" The narrator comments that he must have appeared to this man, who was evidently a well-off Protestant or "heretic," as "a booby son of hers in leading strings" (1:248).

On the island, the narrator undergoes various disillusioning ordeals, which include confronting a whip-wielding priest, out of the company of his female guides. But he meets them again as he is leaving the island. The trio stick together on the homeward journey through one entire day and put up at the same inn. However, the young man awakens the next morning to discover that the women have absconded with most of his money and clothing, leaving in their place a particularly clownish hareskin cap, complete with long drooping ears and tail bobbing behind, and a dilapidated frieze jacket. The jacket he recognizes as having belonged to the woman who pinned him into her cloak. At this point he remarks, "Well, she *has* made another man of me" (1:269). He then travels homeward in his buffonish rural gear, only to be told by his parish priest amid the neighbors' general merriment, "You have fallen foul of Nell M'Cullum, the most notorious *shuler* [trickster] in the provinces: a gypsy, a fortune-teller, and a tinker's widow, but rest assured, you are not the first she has gulled—but beware the next time" (1:270).

The reverend father is of course correct according to his lights, and no doubt it was Nell M'Cullum with one of her chums. But there is another way of looking at what happened. On the road to Lough Derg and the Holy Island widely known as St. Patrick's Purgatory, Carleton met his rural muse in the guise of a fortune-telling tinker woman. Working with a collaborator and with all deliberate speed, she took him down off his clerical high horse, set him on all fours with the world he would celebrate and re-create in his fiction, put him in the way of becoming the painter of "this clear-obscure of domestic light" that is Carleton at his best, then left him to find his way home as best he could.

Carleton's other major collection is *Tales and Stories of the Irish Peasantry* (1845). This edition has a second title page calling the book *Tales and Sketches.* Consisting almost entirely of his contributions during 1840–41 to the short-lived *Irish Penny Journal*, it is a surprisingly happy work, richly illustrated by Phiz. It aims at a wide audience, primarily Irish, whom the author had reason to believe were growing up in ignorance of the strong folk traditions of their forefathers. Its subjects are traditional types—the midwife, matchmaker, storyteller (the "seanachie"), piper and fiddler, dancing master, rake—and traditional beliefs, including superstitions, which seemed on the point of disappearing. Carleton set himself temporal boundaries: "Our sketches do not go very far beyond the manners of our own times; by which we mean that we paint or record nothing that is not remembered and known by those who are now living" (5). By a sad irony, when it appeared in book form, a great number of those he is referring to were within a few years of dying in the epidemics accompanying famine, or of being forced into emigration abroad. The catastrophe about to overtake the Irish rural population makes his reprise of dying Irish traditions all the more valuable.

There are two folktales done in a slangy rural Irish demotic. "A Legend of Knockmany" relates how a cowardly giant, Finn M'Coul, managed to get around his rival, Cuchullan, without having to fight him. "The Three Wishes," a different story from one of that name in *Traits and Stories*, tells how Bill Duffy, a dissolute blacksmith, scandalizes St. Moroky and completely dumbfounds the Devil, who has thought he had an unbreakable contract with him for his soul. In eternity both heaven and hell are barred to this rogue. It is feared he will sell off the furnishings in both places. So he melts away into Will-o'-the-wisp, leading drunken travelers astray into marshes and bogs by the light of his fiery drinker's nose.

The midwife, Rose Moan, is much involved with spells and other magical practices, including "measuring the head" and "raising the spoul, or bone, of the breast" (120). These precautions prevent the fairies from substituting one of their own for the human baby during childbed. Fairies are descended from the angels who stood aside, taking no part, when Lucifer fought God on the plains of heaven. They could obliterate the human race if they chose, but they hold back because they, too, hope to be saved. Carleton shows none of the feyness of the later Celtic Revivalists as he presents country visions and beliefs. A rationalist himself, he assumes people will have visions where visions are given credence. There is no universal superstition, yet superstitiousness is universal.

His Rake, half man, half pookah, haunts the imagination. He is a chameleon, living on air and borrowings, and is "the only man that can borrow money from servant maids with a grace" (360). He spends his time seducing young women, outdancing the dancing master, and makes a figure at fairs and faction fights; yet he is also "a kind of doctor . . . and knows the use of cut-finger, robin-round-the-hedge, bugloss, ground-ivy and house-leek" (363). The Rake has a standing enmity with priests and shows an absolute indifference to his own offspring, whether illegitimate or not. Yet his greatest mystery lies in his end. He simply disappears: "He is never known to die, even by his most intimate acquaintances. . . . A space of time elapses longer than that in which he has been accustomed to reappear—he is expected by the unthinking for a while, but he comes not again" (364).

He comes not again. In the desolate, hushed, emptied-out country world of the Irish 1840s, these words describing a disappearance also write the epitaph of a culture.

Carleton as a Novelist

None of Carleton's novels reach the artistic level of his best short fiction. Part of his difficulty relates to the period in which he is attempting full-scale fiction. Romanticism had temporarily unhinged—derailed—the novel by overwhelming it with new expressive possibilities, a new politics of crisis and change, and a new expectation that any substantial story about private persons would reflect the experience of a whole society. Development in the genre, rapid in the eighteenth century, appeared to slow during the first third of the nineteenth. The path of prose fiction in

English, from Jane Austen, who had held the new revolution in sensibility at a measurable ironic distance, to the Brontë sisters and early Dickens, was strewn with wreckage, much of it Gothic. It was the age of Sir Walter Scott, whose historical fiction was certainly widely imitated by Carleton's somewhat older Anglo-Irish contemporaries, Lady Morgan (Sydney Owenson) and Charles Robert Maturin. Yet it could be argued that Scott provided a doubtful model to Irish writers surveying the home scene after Union. That was because of his preindustrial outlook. In Britain, the country experiencing the most rapid and extensive industrialization in the world, such an emphasis was constructive and restorative of a balance. In nineteenth-century Ireland, however, Great Britain's backwoods, where most of the country was an agrarian backwater, its rural populations tied to the land in a condition of near-serfdom, the Sage of Abbotsford provided no fit wisdom.

Here brief consideration of three of his most interesting and characteristic works in the genre will suffice. *Fardorougha the Miser* (1839) was his first regular novel. Its great accomplishment lies in the sustained and powerful representation of the title character, Fardorougha O'Donovan, a doting father and substantial farmer, whose habit of thrift and compulsion to fear penury turns him into an extortionate usurer. He is ashamed, his obsessive avarice struggles against his inner conviction of being unjust to those he loves, yet he is helpless in the clutches of "the famine-struck god of the miser" (*Works*, 2:194). This striking phrase reminds us that miserliness may be the characteristic vice of a rural society where eviction and crop failure are constant threats and where the economy is so starved for capital that the hoarding habit grows up almost naturally. This vice utterly conflicts with the oldest, most deep-seated peasant tradition of all—that of hospitality and openhandedness. Thus is created another of the polarities, oppositions of dark and bright, which Carleton believed make up the Irish character.

When Fardorougha is dying he mingles words of advice on saving with expressions of love for his son Connor. The old man has lost his fortune and even his farm by then—all his fear becoming a self-fulfilling prophecy—yet he cannot relinquish the unworthy one of his two consuming cares even on the brink of eternity. Carleton's representation of this conflict makes the novel memorable long after its melodramatic contrivances and elements of conventional romance have faded from a reader's mind.

Valentine M'Clutchy, the Irish Agent (1847), otherwise known as *The Irish Agent; or, The Chronicles of Castle Cumber*, oscillates uneasily between a mode of satirical burlesque which had seen its heyday in the previous century with Swift and Fielding, and a critical realism that was on the main track of where the nineteenth-century novel at its best was going. Were it not for this structural flaw it would be a great book. Even flawed, it is an important one. In it, Carleton tackles nothing less than the Problem of Ulster.

The problem, as Carleton defines it from a viewpoint sympathetic to "modern conservativism" (*M'Clutchy*, "Preface," xi–xii), stems from the politicization of religious sectarian differences in the North. Its focus is the Orange Order, an exclusively Protestant secret society founded in 1795. Members of the society were a loyal yeomanry in the United Irish Rebellion of 1798, but by 1805, the year in which the story is laid, they have become a private armed militia immune to prosecution and "unknown to the Constitution" (290). Orangemen frequently violate the civil rights of non-Protestants in and around the country town of Castle Cumber, not from any excess of misplaced patriotic zeal, but for anything they can steal during their punitive sorties. Furthermore, they take orders from individuals of the highest propertied and titled classes in Ulster. These landlords and business people, except for Squire Deaker, a reprobate with no reputation left to keep up, make a point of not appearing to have any connection with the Orange Society. Consequently, the novel, which contains much direct satire of religious hypocrisy—through its portraits of M'Slime, the "religious attorney," Darby O'Drive, the religious turncoat, and the Reverend Phineas Lucre, the worldly, gourmandizing Church of Ireland rector--is also an exposé of the strategy by which a wealthy minority exploits sectarian prejudice in the populace in order to maintain its privileges and power while appearing to abhor violence and illegality.

As a boy Carleton had seen his father threatened and humiliated and a sister forced to leave her sickbed when a band of armed Orangemen arrived at the family cottage to turn it upside down in a search for concealed arms. Such violations of personal rights were frequent in Ulster, especially during the season of Protestant commemorative holidays—the "marching season"—during July and August. If Carleton was getting even for this invasion of the family home by writing his *Irish Agent*, as it came to be called, he was also doing something more constructive in tracking Orange abuses to their source in the Ulster hierarchy of political control. Thus, although Val M'Clutchy's Orange flying squad, known as "The Bloodhounds" or "Val's Vultures," help to evict a poor village, Drum Dhu, on Christmas Day, we learn that money-hungry Lord Cumber, head landlord in the district, and a chronic absentee, is behind the eviction. By the end of the book we understand that many of the reputable gentlemen gathering in the Grand Jury Room during the Quarterly Assizes hold a large share of responsibility for the Ulster Problem.

Unhappily, Carleton has no solution except to call for a better class of landlord and the replacement of corrupt agents and middlemen like

M'Clutchy by men of principle and compassion like Mr. Henderson. The showing of dirty Orange linen in public is no guarantee that a cleanup is impending.

Perhaps the most extraordinary character in *Valentine M'Clutchy* is the gigantic parish madman Raymond na Hattha, or Raymond of the Hats, who wears numerous hats atop one another, loves roosters for their brilliant tail feathers, and is nonviolent, except when the spectacle of undeserved and unrelieved human suffering sets him raging. Raymond anticipates Stevie Verloc in Conrad's *The Secret Agent*, another mentally handicapped young man whose anguish over oppression of the innocent makes him a danger to himself and others. The conception hints at a deep despair in Carleton, a fear that oppressions practiced by a ruling group in his home province, under the cloak of religion and loyalty, will never be redressed.

The Black Prophet (1847), written in a deliberately ominous style adapted from the omen-hunting of the peasant "prophecy man," shows Carleton's response to the three years of the Great Hunger (1845–48), even though technically the story is set during the earlier historic famine of 1817. It is a study in blackness, from the beetling visage of Donnel Dhu M'Gowan, the prophecy man himself, whose hidden crimes prove just as dark as his forecasts, to the great black cloud masses, often shot through with lightning bolts, that boil in the skies during the long season of starvation and typhus,[6] to the dark beauty of Sarah, the prophet's daughter. She is full of a self-mistrust and anger that come from growing up in an unloving household. Yet she redeems her humanity by sacrificing her life to save others. The book mentions an English landowner whose Irish estate brings him an income of thirty-two thousand pounds annually—a modern equivalent would be more than a million dollars—and whose total contribution to famine relief is one hundred pounds. That is another form of blackness. There is also the black of the constant funeral processions and of mourning clothes; and behind every other instance the black blight that ruined the crops.

Throughout the novel we are shown the deaths of the young, of unknown children lying with their mother in an abandoned hut, of Sara M'Gowan, of another young woman named Peggy Murttagh, with her illegitimate baby, and of Tom Dalton, its father. It appears as if the very possibility of an Irish future is being liquidated. As a novel *The Black Prophet* has structural faults and moments of incoherence, but one cannot fail to attend and be moved by it as a *cri du coeur*. Carleton wrote no further novels of any distinction, contenting himself with potboilers such as his popular *Willie Reilly and His Dear Cooleen Bawn*. His serious work was done.

A Conclusion

Carleton certainly saw his work as following on from Maria Edgeworth's, who, he says, was the first to undertake the vindication of the Irishman at a time when he appeared as "the butt of ridicule to his neighbors" (*Traits*, 1:iv) and who, in the process, created an authentic Anglo-Irish literature that was not a colonial offshoot of English literature. But he also understood that he and she viewed Ireland with different eyes and saw different parts of the real Irish condition. These differences could be expressed by such polarities as Settler and Native, Proprietor and Tenant, Protestant and Catholic, except that he had partly compromised these distinctions by his change of religion, just as earlier Maria Edgeworth had partly compromised them in choosing a Catholic house servant of peasant origins to tell the story of Anglo-Irish planter culture as it began its long, slow decline.

They were, in a sense, hidden collaborators, even though they accomplished the main body of their work a couple of decades apart. They collaborate in laying the foundations of a literature that could testify to Irish *difference* altogether while exploring, often though not always in a tolerant spirit, the particular differences of class, sect, political program, and ethnicity which were characteristic of the country as it struggled to become master in its own house over the course of the nineteenth and early twentieth centuries.

IV

DECLENSIONS OF ANGLO-IRISH HISTORY: THE ACT OF UNION TO THE ENCUMBERED ESTATES ACTS OF 1848–49 . . . WITH A GLANCE AT A SINGULAR HEROINE

The Anglo-Irish after 1801

IT WAS NOT a good time for an ascendant class that had reached its apogee of power and brilliance in the Parliamentary Golden Age only one generation earlier. If there is truth in the aesthetic theory of "the wound and the bow,"[1] according to which creative art is a reaction to hurt and lurking inferiority feelings, then perhaps the deepest motivations of Anglo-Irish letters in this period entailed a reaction to diminished status and security, and a compensation against lowered self-esteem, collectively speaking.

Scarcely had the squibs and lampoons directed against the parliamentary sellout run their course in Dublin than there were new English squibs and lampoons ridiculing the Irish M.P.s and Union peers on their first appearances at Westminster:

> Or see him round St. James' purlieus straying
> with wondrous eyes that wealthy world surveying,
> and half his income for a garret paying.
> Or at St. Stephen's on a top bench waiting
> in fretful doze while statesmen are debating,
> unknown, unnoticed save by some pert peer,
> who thus accosts his neighbor with a sneer,
> 'Who's that, my Lord? His face I don't remember'.
> 'How could you? 'Tis a Scotch or Irish member.
> They come and go in droves but we don't know 'em.
> They should have keepers, like wild beasts, to show 'em.'
>
> (Anon., quoted in Hubert Butler, 37)

While a crew under the architect-builder James Lever, father of Charles the novelist, got busy modifying the Parliament House into a commercial bank, students just over the way at Trinity College, bastion of Anglo-Irish academic culture in Ireland and hitherto the launching pad for most Ascendancy political careers, were rumored to be transferring in droves to Oxford, Edinburgh, and Cambridge. The clergyman and Gothic novelist Charles Robert Maturin was one source of this information. Since he regularly supplemented a curate's wages by cramming Trinity aspirants, he would know. Maturin has also left us a description of Dublin from 1813, which makes the splendid city depicted in the drawings and engravings of James Malton's *Dublin Views* more like an etching of ancient urban ruins by Piranesi: "Its beauty continues . . . but it is the frightful lifeless beauty of a corpse, and the magnificent architecture of its public buildings seems like the skeleton of some gigantic frame, which the departing spirit has deserted: like the vast structure of the bones of the Behemoth, which has ceased to live for ages and around whose remains modern gazers fearfully creep and stare" (*Women*, 3:295).

Even allowing for Maturin's typical style of "sublime" exaggeration, there was certainly Anglo-Irish disarray and a power vacuum in the capital and in the rest of the country. Into this vacuum moved Daniel O'Connell, the great popular tribune and "Liberator," who, at least temporarily, shaped the fractious native majority into a disciplined force as he developed his campaign for the full political enfranchisement of Catholics, a goal actually realized in the Emancipation Act of 1829. Yet this major concession gave no breathing space for the minority. By 1830, a "tithe war" had begun, with acts of violence in the country districts when farmers resisted paying taxes levied to support the clergy. When this struggle was resolved, largely in favor of the Catholics, by the Tithe Act of 1838, O'Connell was on the point of launching his National Repeal Association, aiming at the dissolution of the Union and reconstitution of an Irish parliament.

In the year of the Monster Meetings—1843—the Anglo-Irish well understood that a group historically identified with the Union sellout and then with opposition to Catholic Emancipation would be offered little opportunity for power-sharing in an Irish legislative body reclaimed by the likes of O'Connell and his Repealers. To the young liberals and radicals clustering around Thomas Davis and *The Nation*—the "Young Ireland" group—some of whom were republicans and most of whom were eager to merge their religious and class identities in a new patriotic and ecumenical national front, this mattered not at all; but to the rest of the Anglo-Irish, the loyalist and conservative group, it mattered greatly. That is why they turned eyes of appeal to the government. In Ireland after Union that meant the Castle administration, operating from the heart of Dublin through a tentacular apparatus of bureaucrats, police, spies and informers, and British army troops.

The appeal was answered. The year 1844 saw Daniel O'Connell sentenced to a year's imprisonment for countenancing and encouraging seditious assembly. A year or so later he went to Rome to die while the Great Hunger, that watershed of modern Irish history, swallowed up Repealers and Young Irelanders alike, along with many millions of the rural population.

Yet some, including the novelist and Mayo landlord George Moore, have maintained that the Famine proved a good thing for the large landowners. According to this tough-minded Malthusian argument, the benefit came in rapidly clearing from the agricultural estates—by evictions and emigration, by hunger and fever deaths—the "uneconomic" surplus of the tenantry. In fact, the tenants did not always manage to disappear quickly enough. In 1847, Lord John Russell's Whig administration changed the Irish Poor Law so as to require that the staggering costs of famine relief in the rural districts be paid for out of estate rent collections (Woodham-Smith, 174–77, 297). The Catch-22 or Gogolian logic was that an expiring tenantry should pay for its own relief by paying its rents, which of course it could not do. Under this law, many of the proprietors were rendered bankrupt, and naturally it was the more generous in organizing famine relief on their own properties who went under in the largest numbers. The Encumbered Estates Act of 1848 merely created machinery for the disposal of the bankrupt demesnes at fire-sale prices. The new owners—English land speculators; Dublin officeholders on government sinecures; a few rich merchants, lawyers, and physicians from the larger towns; and of course the least charitable of the existing landlords, reaped the cash benefit in the disappearance of millions of peasant "dead souls" from the once densely populated and lively rural scene.

Mood and Morale

In this part of the nineteenth century, and even well before the 1840s, the Anglo-Irish tend to turn in on themselves and show low morale. The best discussion of these developments is provided by Elizabeth Bowen in *Bowen's Court*, her study of the big house of her ancestors in County Cork over about seven generations. This classic work enlarges upon family history, becoming a finely detailed and candid exploration of the planters as a class during three centuries; and yet it remains a distinguished work of art, individually styled and showing the insights and gift for irony and drama of a superb novelist. Of course, Bowen neither was the first, nor would she be the last, Anglo-Irish writer to make imaginative capital by toting up the losses and tracing the decline of her own social group in a narrative "taken from facts," many of them relating to her own family.

Like other observers of the period, she begins by describing Dublin's losing its lustre, along with its short-lived commercial prosperity, after the closing of its parliament: "The first circles of Irish fashion followed the Parliament to across the water, and envious eyes looked after them. The great failure [was] burnt into every gentleman's consciousness. If we *are*, then, no more than England's creatures, let us cash in on her smart and new monied fun. A masochistic attraction towards England—too unwilling to be love—in the Anglo-Irish began, and from now on, to be evident" (223). It was impossible that everyone should take part in this "wholesale removal of grand Ireland" to London or to Bath and other English spas. Many families simply closed up, leased out, or sold their Dublin residences and retreated to the country to cultivate private gardens and neuroses. According to Bowen, at this time on the Anglo-Irish estates began a phase of inward-turning religiosity, which looked less to the established church than "for God in one's own heart" and to worship conducted "in the fastness of the home" (Bowen, *Court*, 253). Wagons were being drawn into a circle. Thus begins that stage of Anglo-Irish experience in Ireland which Lyons called "the phase of contraction."

The religious trend inward was not uniform for all parts of the country. In the North the profession of religion continued to be highly politicized and public. But what lay behind the trend, a sense of being at fault, of ineffectuality, of puniness, and, therefore, a sense of being threatened, were surely elements contributing to Anglo-Irish malaise and introversion nearly everywhere. Bowen informs us of her relative, "Big George," Lord Kingston, who, just after the full enfranchisement of the Catholics in 1829, saw his candidate in a parliamentary by-election voted down by a thousand or more of his tenants. Upon this unexpected and unparalleled event, George immediately became incurably insane, being convinced that the tenants, who of course were doing no such thing, were marching up the avenues of his demesne, coming to tear him to pieces. She quotes from a family hymn of the period a quatrain expressing this sense of isolation and threat:

> Pilgrims here on earth, and strangers
> Dwelling in the midst of foes,
> Us and ours preserve from dangers
> In thine arms may we repose.
>
> (Bowen, *Court*, 381)

"Stranger" has always been the mere Irish code word for the English. Here, however, we have people long established in the land applying the same word to themselves.

Bad times for most people in Ireland came after 1815: when agricultural prices and the price of woven goods slumped with the winding up of the Napoleonic Wars; when small holdings began to be pressured out of existence in favor of grazing herds and flocks on large, unfenced acreage; and when Ireland was ruled by an English government whose policy was "to separate the Anglo-Irish from the Irish" so that "the menacing solidarity of 1782, the armed hope and flourishing patriotism of the Volunteers, the sense, in fact, of their Irishness in the upper classes [should] not occur again" (Bowen, *Court*, 263). Bowen also remarks, "it was difficult for England to see the native Irish as anything but aliens, and as worse, sub-human potato-eaters, worshippers of the Pope's toe. The squalor in which the Irish lived was taken to be endemic in their mentality. It would have seemed fantastic to reform their conditions. To distract the English conscience the buffoon Paddy was to come into being—the capering simians of the Cruikshank drawings" (Bowen, *Court*, 263). So much for the Edgeworths' effort in the *Essay on Irish Bulls* to show the English how clever, eloquent, and expressive the mere Irish, including the humblest, appeared to them to be.

To the Irish majority at this time, the Anglo-Irish landlords appeared to be burdensome as always, but also, in a relatively new perception, to be beside the point when it came to the struggle for fundamental rights. O'Connell, a legal advocate of genius who was deeply conservative and pacifist in his political temper, tactics, and social views, had links back through his mother's family to surviving remnants of the Irish-speaking Gaelic aristocracy of southwest Munster. He led a great mass movement, which exerted its pressure upon, and addressed its petitions to, England. Although Bowen, somewhat wistfully, makes the point that "the Duke of Wellington, the Anglo-Irish English Prime Minister" (*Court*, 266), granted Catholic Emancipation in 1829, it is more accurate to say that these rights were conceded by Wellington under pressure, because an overwhelming majority of the Irish, shaped into a disciplined, unified, nonviolent force, demanded them. When O'Connell tried to win Home Rule in the 1840s employing the same tactic of nonviolent mass action, he failed, mainly because the country was distracted by revolutionary currents presaging 1848 and because by fall of 1845 and for the next several years the ebbing energies of the masses were consumed with the fight against hunger. Nevertheless, O'Connell had taught the survivors of the famine years something they never forgot, which they passed on to succeeding generations: they were indeed the overwhelming majority of the country, poor and landless as they were, and they might yet become masters in their own land, provided they stood together and stood firm.

A Singular Heroine

The famine years offered the landlords chances for leadership and self-sacrifice, but the response was all too often a sort of moral if not a physical absenteeism. In memoirs of the period, one usually hears of the mistresses of the big houses—endlessly lading out soup from giant kettles kept simmering around the clock, visiting and nursing in the cabins and workhouse wards where fever finished off the people weakened by prolonged hunger and exposure. Among these well-born women of the Famine era, Mary Martin of Ballinahinch Castle in West Galway appears as a true heroine belonging equally to literary legend and to history.

Maria Edgeworth, who befriended her in 1833, when Mary was seventeen, and corresponded with her at intervals until 1849, called her story "a romance of real life." The two women met when Edgeworth visited the Martin Castle and wrote up her first visit to the little-known and "feudal" West in a 155-page letter to her youngest half-brother, Michael Pakenham Edgeworth, who at twenty-one was already abroad in the Indian civil service. Dating from March 1834, with extracts from later correspondence, this letter was finally published in 1950 as *A Tour in Connemara and The Martins of Ballinahinch.* It is the main source of the account that follows of an Anglo-Irish heroine and her lost world.

The Martin demesne was the largest in Ireland. Extending fifty linear miles due west from Galway city and three hundred miles around by seacoast, it comprised some of the most rugged, picturesque, and least-arable land in the island. Thomas Martin, Mary's father, ruled over it in a style Edgeworth described as feudal with qualifications: "It is not exactly a feudal state of society—but the tail of a feudal state, and in a very odd, and not poetical manner the jobbing Irish gentleman and Dublin courtier at the Castle is here and there joined up . . . with the Chieftain" (*A Tour*, 63–64).

Edgeworth arrived at Ballinahinch with an English couple, Sir Cullen and Lady Isabella Smith, after a fatiguing and dangerous coach journey, which precipitated Lady Isabella into a severe fever. Over the next three weeks, while the illness raged and what had been planned as an overnight visit extended itself, the writer became friends with the Martins and privy to a way of life she had never known. She was especially drawn to Mary, after an initial period during which she suspected, so different was she from most girls her age, that Miss Martin might be mad.

Mary Martin had never been off the estate, yet she was an expert on the life of Napoleon, whom she passionately admired, and on the plays of Aeschylus and Euripides, from which she was given to quoting lengthy extracts in the original Greek. She had "prodigious acquirements in learning," which included the Latin, Greek, French, and Hebrew languages; heraldry, metaphysics, and the history of fine arts; military tactics, civil engineering, and the art of fortification (*A Tour*, 58). Although she had memorized thousands of lines of English poetry, she had "never learned to recite or read English tolerably, but so fast and so oddly in such a Connemara accent and words so fluid, running one into the other, that at first I could not guess what language it was" (*A Tour*, 59). Outside the house Miss Martin was kindly princess of a half-barbaric principality as she rode her Connemara ponies around the immense estate, followed by her "tail" of Irish-speaking tenants, who petitioned her on various matters, and by tiny boys called "gossoons," whose job it was to carry messages in all weathers across the trackless bogland. In the drawing room, however, she was subject to moods recognizable to anyone who had seen daughters—or half-sisters—pass through adolescence. At one point Mrs. Martin said to Edgeworth about Mary, who sat sprawled on a sofa across the room, apparently wrapped in some "philosophical abstraction": "My dear, you don't understand Mary. She is living in another world and has not the least knowledge or taste or care about this world as it goes. She does not hear one word we say, and the only thing that keeps her there is you as an authoress and celebrated person. She is exceptionally curious about celebrated people, and I know would delight in talking to you about books" (*A Tour*, 57).

Sixty-three-year-old Maria did become close friends with this gifted, pedantic, proud, unworldly, and appealing young woman, who was not beautiful except for her auburn hair. And as Maria became fond of her, she began to worry about Miss Martin's future. Although the hospitality at Ballinahinch was unstinted, the castle was much dilapidated: there were broken windowpanes and leaks in the roof; splotches of damp in the ceilings and walls; and the furnishings were meager and makeshift, even in the principal rooms. Although the stables were paved in Connemara marble from the estate's own quarries, there was a severe money shortage, not only because the vast demesne was overpopulated and relatively infertile, but also because Mary's father had made over a large share of the estate income to maintain his own father at a Riviera retreat. Before the visitors resumed their journey, Mrs. Martin confessed to Edgeworth that it would be necessary for Mary to wed a very rich man if the family were to avoid financial ruin.

A year later, Mrs. Martin and Mary stopped at Edgeworthstown on their way back from London, where Miss Martin at eighteen had come out in society. Edgeworth found her still uncorrupted while her manners and accent had improved. She was interested to hear from Mrs.

Martin that Mary had impressed certain continental gentlemen of title, owing to the excellence of her French and the "Irish frankness and untutored freedom" of her bearing (*A Tour*, 82). Unfortunately, within a few months Maria learned that the London visit had led to some unpleasant consequences. A certain Count Werdinski came uninvited to Ballinahinch Castle and asked Thomas Martin for permission to court his daughter. When permission was refused, the count shook hands all around, retired to his room, attempted to shoot himself but missed, and then fell into a fit. He was removed from the house the next day in a condition of lunacy. So ended Mary's venture into the fleshpots and the marriage marts of English upper-class society.

Mrs. Martin concluded her letter reporting the Count Werdinski affair with the information that a Liverpool insurance company had assumed the debt burden of the Martin estate while leaving Thomas an income of three thousand pounds a year. In April 1838 Mary wrote Maria to report that her father was sentenced to three months in Galway gaol after a pitched battle over land boundaries between his tenants and those of a neighboring landowner named O'Flaherty. While O'Flaherty was jailed as well, it was unlikely that this development improved Miss Martin's prospects for marrying well. In the same letter she mentioned that she had written in French, for a French encyclopedia, articles on Edgeworth, Emancipation, and the Exchequer. Mary was not yet twenty-two.

The rest of the story is tragic. Between 1838 and the onset of the Famine the Martins did not get clear of their financial problems nor did Miss Martin marry. On April 23, 1847, Thomas Martin died of famine fever caught while visiting sick tenants in the Clifden workhouse. Left alone, Mary poured out her remaining resources in a vain effort to relieve the general starvation and disease. That same year she wrote a brief letter to Edgeworth reporting her decision to marry her estate agent, Arthur Gomme Bell, who agreed to adopt the Martin surname. Also in 1847, a judgment was entered in the Encumbered Estates Court that ordered the confiscation of the hugely mortgaged Martin property.

She was now landless and penniless, like the tenants to whom she had formerly played princess and ministering angel. For the next two years she and her husband lived obscurely at Brussels. There she wrote two novels, which were published but without financial success. One of them, *Julia Howard*,[2] opens with a painful death scene that is surely based on memories of her own father's death from typhus. In 1850 she emigrated with her husband to America, arriving in New York on October 29, having borne on shipboard a child that did not survive the voyage. A few days later, Mary Martin died in New York, aged thirty-four, joining in her final fate the sad multitudes of Irish people of the tenant class who made the same desperate and hopeful journey, only to perish somewhere between the old life and the new.

Without much exaggeration one can say that Mary Martin of Ballinahinch haunts the Anglo-Irish literary imagination for the rest of the century. A sentimental portrayal emphasizing her charity and her lack of luck appears in Charles Lever's *The Martins of Cro-Martin* (1853), a wildly inaccurate historical romance written during his tenure as English vice-consul at La Spezia. Yeats's early verse play *The Countess Cathleen* (1892), the first of his plays to arouse public controversy in Ireland, in some part owing to its power to deeply move the audience, draws upon her legend for its heroine, the young countess of an unspecified "olden time" who offers her soul to demons in return for money with which to buy food for her people during a great protracted "dearth." A more playful approach to the legend is made in *Through Connemara in a Governess Cart* (1903), by Edith Somerville and Martin Ross. Their trip was a deliberate retracing of Maria Edgeworth's tour of 1833 with an obligatory stop at Ballinahinch, which might have produced lachrymose sentiment from these two young women of the planter class, especially since Martin Ross, also known as Violet Martin, was Mary's blood kin. Instead, they choose to show an operation of the "folk memory" upon historical materials that is both authentic and amusing.

Strolling around the grounds of what has become a fishing hotel, they see an old woman sitting on a stone bench previously identified as "Mary Martin's seat." She is muttering to herself and smoking an old black pipe or "dudeen," which she conceals in her pocket as the young women approach her:

> It occurred to us to ask whether she remembered Mary Martin and in a moment the tears stopped.
>
> "Is it remember her?" she said, wiping her eyes on a frayed corner of her petticoat. "I remember her as well as yerself that I'm looking at."
>
> "What was she like in the face?" said my cousin in her richest brogue.
>
> "Oh musha? Ye couldn't rightly say what she was like, she was that grand! She was beautiful and white and charitable, only she had one snaggledy tooth in the front of her mouth. But what signifies that? Faith, whin she was in it the ladies of Connemara might go undher the sod. 'Twas as good for thim. And afther all they say she died as silly as ye plase down in the County Meeyo, but there's more tells me she died back in Ameriky. Oh, Glory be to God, thim was the times!"
>
> The tears began again, and she relapsed into the red petticoat. We left her there, huddled on the seat moaning and talking to herself. We could do no more for her than hope, as we looked back at her for the last time, that the pipe in her pocket had gone out. (*Connemara*, 80–81)

To be sure, most Anglo-Irish of the famine decade were neither Malthusian exploiters nor "white," self-sacrificing Connemara princesses. The worst that can be said of them is that they failed to exercise leadership in those same distressed districts where for generations they had claimed and enjoyed the status of an ascendant elite. If this group has a literary representative, it is Charles Lever, whose career spanned the middle decades of the century and who took himself and his family away from Ireland for good in 1845, just weeks before it began to be noticed that the potato plants were shrivelling and turning black. Lever wrote a whole shelf of novels and used to be mentioned in the same breath as Charles Dickens, William Thackeray, and George Eliot, who were his friends. He remains a sufficiently interesting and complicated writer on Irish and Anglo-Irish themes and problems to deserve his own chapter.

V

CHARLES LEVER (1806–72): THE ANGLO-IRISH WRITER AS DIPLOMATIC ABSENTEE, WITH A GLANCE AT JOHN BANIM

I have been an actor, a smuggler, a French officer,
an Irish refugee, a sporting character, a man of pleasure,
and a man of intrigue, and however such features may
have blended themselves into my true character,
my real part has remained undetected.
—Charles Lever, *The O'Donoghue*

How strange and how unceasing are the anomalies
of Irish life. Splendour, poverty, elevation of sentiment, savage ferocity, delicacy the most refined, barbarism the most
revolting, pass before the mind's eye in the quick
succession of the objects in a magic lantern.
—Lever, *The Knight of Gwynne*

Without being a Fenian, I have an Irishman's
hate of the Londoner.
—Lever, Letter to John Blackwood, Oct. 18, 1867

Introductory: A Chameleon of Identity

THE ACT OF UNION made moot the old constitutional argument, offered by Jonathan Swift among others (*Drapier's Letters*, 77–81), that Ireland was a kingdom of free-born Protestants in a dual system under one monarch, the English Protestant king. The result was that Anglo-Irish men and women of Charles Lever's time, when they found that they loved Ireland, could not, strictly speaking, say what it was they loved. The mere Irish knew what they loved—a native place under foreign occupation and control, which might in time become truly "a nation once again." The problem of patriotism, of a *patria*, was ever so much harder for those of the other persuasion. They did not wish to be a colony, yet they themselves, in dissolving their Protestant Parliament, had scotched the kingdom idea. And few indeed of this group, which had, after all, put down its roots in Ireland over several centuries, wanted to pretend that they were Englishmen. There was an essential bewilderment in claiming an Anglo-Irish identity then, though there really was no other identity for this group to claim.

The second son of an English architect-builder who made his Dublin career during the last gasp of the parliamentary golden age in the 1790s, and of a Kilkenny mother, most of whose male relatives were clergymen and small landowners, Charles Lever began as a fairly typical representative of the loyal, educated, rather privileged Protestant minority of the Irish capital, which was destined to undergo the disappointment of so many of its expectations in the vexed conditions of Irish life after Union. His literary gift, however, and, closely allied to it, his habit of restless fantasy entailing elaborations of self-disguise and self-reinvention, won him a measure of freedom from his Irish background and its problems. Lever is the first Dublin-born writer of any consequence before Joyce and Beckett to make most of his career on the Continent. We find him successively at Brussels, in several German city-states of the Rhine Valley, wandering in the Austrian Tyrol, in residence on the shores of Lakes Constance and Como, crossing the Austrian frontier to Bagni di Lucca, Florence, and La Spezia, and finally at Trieste, where he ended life's journey. This is only to hit the high spots. Lever was an Anglo-Irish literary émigré in an age of Anglo-Irish absenteeism. However, and this seems important, he steadfastly refused to resettle in London, though he was immensely popular with English readers, was advised to take up residence in England by his friend Thackeray, and was offered the highly paid and prestigious editorship of *Bentley's Miscellany*, a post previously filled by Charles Dickens and William Harrison Ainsworth. Furthermore, Lever's most interesting, most recoverable books are those devoted to Irish subject matter. That is why he qualifies for a place—a rather special place by virtue of his cosmopolitanism and uprootedness—in the tradition of writing with which this book is taken up.

Lever actually followed three careers. He was a physician until age thirty-six, a novelist and man of letters from his mid-twenties until his death, and a British consular officer, first at La Spezia (while actually residing in Florence during the 1850s and earlier 1860s), and then at Trieste, where he was British consul from 1867 until he died in 1872. As a physician, Lever was well qualified for that time and worked hard during the more than a decade he gave to medicine. After taking a Bachelor of Medicine at Trinity, he became a cholera officer in a remote Clare peninsula and served there during the major epidemic of 1832. He then moved to Portstewart, a sea resort and fishing village on the Ulster north coast, where he practiced general medicine and managed the local fever hospital. The last few years of his medical career were spent at Brussels, where he moved his young family after the initial success of his first novel, *Harry Lorrequer*, when it began appearing in monthly numbers. Here he practiced among the British (including Irish) colony of émigrés and at the Belgian court.

Lever kept busy as a writer, too: the shelf of his fiction is at least twice as long as Dickens's, while the number and frequency of his more-ephemeral contributions to Victorian periodicals like *Blackwood's*, *Cornhill*, and the *Dublin University Magazine* pass all reckoning. Yet Lever, who wrote rapidly, rarely revised, and habitually posted batches of his novels-in-progress to English and Irish publishers without bothering to keep a record or a copy. He often claimed to take lightly his responsibilities as an artist, although some of his apparent carelessness was probably self-doubt. In periods of depression, which became more frequent and distressing as he aged, this famous writer, whom contemporaries unfailingly described as mercurial, tended to confess having abused his talent by failing to learn even the rudiments of fictional construction and character drawing. This questioning of the seriousness of his application to literature also emerged from his stance as a gentleman. Although a close contemporary and friend of Thackeray, Dickens, Eliot, and Trollope, mid-Victorian writers responsible for transforming novel writing into the grandest of professions, Lever consistently took a different line, claiming amateur standing, maintaining that his fiction was somehow ancillary or subordinate to his position in society, to a taste for military history, especially of the Napoleonic Era, and to his gossipy interest in politics. Nevertheless, he made a great deal of money from his sustained and rapid literary production. Writing provided most of the income supporting his large family and gentlemanly life-style.

If Lever was sometimes dilatory in his consular work, it must be said that such posts were largely honorary affairs of party patronage. Certainly he busied himself collecting political rumor and fact for the diplomatic postbag, and as for the social duties of consulship—the welcoming of distinguished English visitors and joining in local fashionable society—these he carried out with enthusiasm. Indeed, society was a fourth career for the gregarious Anglo-Irishman, who had a passion for whist and dancing parties, a love of dressing up and staying up late, and an eager curiosity, abetted by his considerable facility with foreign languages, about what went on behind the scenes in the best circles of many first- and second-rank European cities. In *The O'Donoghue*, a young woman whose time has been spent schooling at a French convent and residing on a run-down demesne in remotest Munster, pays a long visit to Dublin in the care of an English family of rank and means. She discovers that "she loved society as the scene where, however glossed over by conventionalities, human passions and feelings were at work and where the power of directing or influencing others gave a stimulus to existence far higher and nobler than all the pleasures of retirement. It was life, in fact" (1:288). Here the author lends his own taste for society to the heroine, Kate O'Donoghue. The insight that the drama of society is really motivated by human passion and the power drive anticipates Henry James. In *The O'Donoghue*, too little is done with this idea. Not until his last book, *Lord Kilgobbin*, did Lever work out some of its deeper implications.

In January 1842, Lever left the medical profession by selling his Brussels practice and moved back to Dublin for what was to be three years. His reasons were several. He was accepting the prestigious and politically influential editorship of the *Dublin University Magazine*. In addition, he wanted his children to make a connection with their Irish heritage, and he needed to refresh his own knowledge of Irish scenes and subjects for future books. He also nursed political hopes, which he imagined the new Conservative viceregal administration of Lord de Gray might help him to fulfill. Lever rather fancied becoming an Irish M.P., preferably for the Trinity College constituency; and if not that, perhaps an under-secretaryship at the Castle might be forthcoming.

Little worked out according to his expectations, as little in Ireland ever does. He performed creditably at the magazine, although he claimed to find his support staff utterly incompetent. His large, comfortable house in the Dublin suburb of Templeogue became the scene of convivial entertainment for Irish writers and wits and for visiting English literary men like Thackeray. Lever enjoyed riding about the city squares and in the Phoenix Park with his stylishly turned-out children and their dogs. And he found the time for a prolonged summer tour of the Irish hinterland, which garnered him impressions to draw upon for new ventures in fiction.

On the debit side, Lever and his family were attacked by an O'Connellite mob in the streets of the capital. Polemicists of the *Nation* group, the Young Irelanders, abused him in print for his anti-Repeal political stand. In a *Nation* article of 1843, William Carleton, though himself a Conservative and anti-Repealer, launched an attack on his fellow novelist, "accusing him of every literary vice" (Downey, 1:185). At least Carleton was consistent, for as early as 1835 he had attacked Lever for literary plagiarism, a charge that has been shown to be utterly unfounded (Wolff, *Carleton*, 91–92). The final blow may have been the viceroy's indifference to his hankerings after a political role. The only plum of patronage ever offered was the position of Phoenix Park ranger. The emolument and perquisites were fifty-five pounds a year, two dressed carcasses of red deer, a tiny, rent-free house within the park, and a uniform of bright green. The job was not so much Bottom's dream as a fantasy of Leople Bloom's.

In 1845, the Levers flitted to the Continent. Charles's health immediately improved. He even found the heavy, greasy food of German inns and hostels appetizing as the family and their several servants began a vagabond existence, traveling by coach and on horseback through North Germany and the Rhineland, crossing and recrossing the Alps, fetching up eventually in Tuscany for a twenty-year stay. If the Dublin sojourn was meant to be a literary and political conquest of the writer's hometown, it had been a failure. But he may have felt it had been a success for his getting out alive with his literary powers intact. As the Levers rolled along the European highways, perhaps passing by or overtaking, amid the dust and the shouting of postilions, such touring musical virtuosi as Liszt and Dublin's own John Field, Lever may have given some little thought to the fate of his closest Irish relatives. Father James, the architect, was dead. There had been little money or real property to divide up in the estate. The slump in Dublin building construction after Union had seen to that. The older brother John, a Trinity graduate like Charles, continued as a minister of the Church of Ireland at Portumna, in remote East Galway. From recent visits to his glebe house Lever knew that John's depressions were becoming chronic and disabling. However, the sister, who had married a businessman named Baker, seemed secure. Unfortunately, within a few years Mr. Baker would desert his family, leaving behind a mountain of unpaid bills. Lever would assume these debts and the responsibility for his sister and her children for life.

The Levers arrived in Florence in fall 1847, the worst year of the continuing Irish famine. Their appearance initially caused a minor sensation, becoming a story that the novelist enjoyed recounting in later years. Mary Boyle, an Irishwoman residing in Florence during the time the Levers lived there, set down one version in her personal journal:

> He gave me a most amusing description of his entry into Florence with his three children, with whom he had performed the journey from the Tyrol on horseback. They had imbibed many of the tastes, and had adopted the greater part of the costume of the Tyrolese—such as the conical-shaped hat, with its golden cord and peacock's feathers. Altogether, his appearance with that of his youthful companions, followed by their brindled boarhound, attracted great attention as they passed slowly through the Porto San Gallo. The crowd which gathered round them were impressed by the belief that they formed part of a company of a circus or hippodrome, and Lever, in great glee, even assured me that he had been accosted on the road with a view to an engagement. (Boyle, 211)

Why this delight in being taken for what one isn't, for getting into costume and going in disguise? Was it only a flair for the theatrical, a trait that could be illustrated by many incidents in Lever's personal history from his boyhood onward? That would not explain why his fiction is so crammed with people pretending to be other people, and with characters mistaken for other characters. The virtual climax of *Harry Lorrequer* (1837), his loosely picaresque first novel, entails the young English army officer being mistaken for the composer Giacomo Meyerbeer, first by the manager of the Strasbourg opera house, then by the manager's beautiful wife, who supposedly had loved Meyerbeer some years earlier, and finally, by everyone attending the opera on that particular night. As a consequence, Lorrequer receives a standing ovation upon entering his box.

Such tricks of false or mistaken identity form the very substance of *Lorrequer*. One is reminded of certain games in which giving false leads, bluffing and revoking, are of the essence. Charles Lever was a master of such games, beginning with whist. Identity games and characters who create counterfeit identities, either playfully, with malicious intent, or out of grim necessity, are prominent in Lever's fiction. In *Charles O'Malley: The Irish Dragoon* (1841), there is Frank Webber, a Trinity student who keeps the college and half of Dublin in an uproar with elaborate, mostly destructive practical jokes. Two of his milder japes entail disguising himself as a faculty tutor who habitually hears his students' recitations while lying abed, and as a spinster aunt from the county "Meeyo," who visits and embarrasses her sophisticated Dublin relatives during one of their elegant evening parties.

Darby the Blast in *Tom Burke of "Ours"* (1844) and Talbot in *The O'Donoghue* (1845), both novels set in the period of the United Irish Rising, are masters of disguise who approach the status of intelligence agents. In *The Knight of Gwynne*, Lever's novel about the Act of Union and its immediate aftermath, Bagenel Daly and his sometime cohort, Freney the Robber, put on their masks and play their tricks largely from disillusionment with the corruption of Irish society and politics. While partly a throwback to the "fire-eating" Anglo-Irish rakes of an even earlier generation, Daly is also a disenchanted idealist-adventurer, who has never really felt at home since he left the Canadian Indian tribe with whom he harbored in his early manhood. Freney, like many highwaymen and gentlemen criminals, claims to live by a code superior to that of regular society. He would never rob a poor man; nor would he dream of walking into Parliament House in Dublin and casting a vote for the Legislative Union in exchange for a title or a cash bribe.

Lever's last novel, *Lord Kilgobbin* (1872), contains his most developed and also his most sociopathic pretender, Joe Atlee, who is another perpetual Trinity student like Frank Webber. Studentship for Atlee, however, is mainly a blind for such other activities as issuing literary forgeries and writing anonymous political articles for the European press from any ideological posture that may be in demand at the moment. One of Atlee's tricks is to publish a left- or right-wing analysis, then hotly reply to it from an opposite viewpoint. This curiously modern man without qualities or convictions of his own holds secret correspondence with Fenian elements while at the same time exploiting contacts supplied by his college roommate to become a confidential aide to the new viceroy for Ireland. There is a revealing scene when Atlee visits the viceroy's Welsh castle. Having arrived ahead of his valise, he must borrow something to wear from the lord-lieutenant's secretary, Cecil Walpole. A gorgeous blue uniform coat, "which formed the appropriate costume of the gentlemen of the viceregal household," catches his eye and he cannot keep his hands off it: "By one of the contrarieties of his strange nature, in which the desire for an assumption of any kind was a passion, he . . . tried on that coat fully a dozen times" (1:241), each time acting before a mirror the strutting part of a Castle aide-de-camp.

What is at the bottom of such a man? Perhaps he is a bottomless fraud. Or he might possess one of those modern selves-in-performance that collects its sense of being real from the reflections and refractions of itself in the eyes of others. More traditionally, we may surmise that Atlee is profoundly self-alienated and search for the roots of his malaise in his personal and social situation. He is penniless, and there are too many unportioned sisters at home for his father, a northern Irish Presbyterian minister, to support. Joe's social and cultural problem of identity begins with his low minority status in a chronically distressed country and conflicted culture. He might solidify his identity or forge it anew by becoming a nationalist rebel; instead, he pursues journalism, a risky trade for one alienated from self and fascinated with literary and other forms of forgery and fraud. Joe's real talent is for public relations. It is as a public-relations counsel and press secretary that he becomes known and necessary to the viceroy, though, strictly speaking, these trades have yet to be invented.

No doubt the tricksters, pretenders, and quick-change artists in Lever's fictions were projections of Lever himself. At least they expressed what he may have feared was the truth about himself when he became depressed and imagined that he had misused his gifts. But of course he was not without firm commitments and standards, beginning with the love of family: of the wife who had brought no marriage portion with her and was ailing with heart disease for many years before her death; of the single son who ran him heavily into debt with extravagant follies and gambling losses, and who broke his heart by dying early of an apoplexy; of the daughters he delighted to go swimming with in the bay at La Spezia, and who consoled his later years, one by making a prosperous marriage to a likeable man, the other by showing a literary gift of her own and becoming the guardian and editor of his literary *oeuvre.*[1]

One can also make out a certain attachment to determinate values in Lever's lifelong admiration for the British uniformed service, for its code of honor, courage, and patriotism. This admiration is most sharply focused in the cult the novelist made of Wellington, hero of the Peninsular War and of Waterloo. Wellington makes several appearances in *Charles O'Malley*, and he is always the same, a man utterly incapable of donning a costume or a disguise:

> A short, slight man, in a gray undress coat, with a white cravat, and a cocked hat, entered. The dead silence that ensued was not necessary to assure me that he was one in authority,—the look of command his bold, stern features presented; the sharp, piercing eye, the compressed lip, the impressive expression of the whole face, told plainly he was one who held equally himself and others in mastery. (1:364)

> . . . I had ample time to scan his features and canvass their every lineament. Never before did I look upon such perfect impassibility; the cold, determined expression was crossed by no show of passion or impatience. All was rigid and motionless, and whatever might have been the workings of the spirit within, certainly no external sign betrayed them. (1:366)

The young officer who takes these impressions just before the Battle of the Douro River, and who is himself of an ebullient, rash, and headlong temper, clearly regards the Iron Duke as his perfect opposite and antitype, utter "English" in emotional constitution to his own utter "Irish," and also as a stern father figure and fixed mark. However, if we contemplate this fixed mark—this monument—in the light of certain historical facts, its outlines begin to flow and vibrate and its colors to shift about. To begin with, Wellington was Irish, specifically Anglo-Irish, not English at all. Before his eldest brother, the second earl of Mornington and Marquess, changed the family name to Wellesley, he sat in the Irish parliament during the 1790s as plain Arthur Wesley of Trim in County Meath. Like so many Anglo-Irishmen of his generation, he made his career by absenting himself from his native place, going first to India, where he made his military reputation and personal fortune in campaigns against rebellious native rulers, then moving on to England, where the military threat posed by Consul, later Emperor, Napoleon Bonaparte gave him his opportunity at supreme British command.

So it appears that Wellington, too, was a consummate identity changer, right after Lever's quick and changeable heart. Even the civilian dress he assumed while leading the troops was a deliberate choice of costume, designed to encourage an army largely made up of civilian volunteers, short-term draftees, and county militia men,[2] while undermining the aplomb of Napoleon's gorgeously caparisoned marshals and the French rank and file of colorfully uniformed *Grande Armée* professionals. It was a clever trick but no more so than the mysterious sleight of hand by which the landowner from Meath, who was married to Kitty Pakenham, a connection of the Edgeworths of County Longford, convinced an Ireland-hater such as Tennyson, and millions of other English patriots, that he was the greatest British captain since Cromwell and Marlborough.

The Military Novels: *The Confessions of Harry Lorrequer* (1839); *Charles O'Malley: The Irish Dragoon* (1841); *Tom Burke of "Ours"* (1844)

As a group these books achieved a sustained popularity and were still being reprinted on both sides of the Atlantic, often in deluxe editions, almost until World War I. The carnage of the Great War, the agony and pity of it, made Lever's representation of war and military life as a picturesque and panoramic deployment of men, horses, and ordnance, as a set of moves on a game board—feints and skirmishes, attacking the enemy's center while rolling up his flanks—instantly obsolete. Lever always presented war and army service as occasions for boyish adventure, ordeals of courage resembling adolescent rites of passage, male bonding, storytelling, singsongs, pranks, and practical joking along the route of campaign. When dramatic tension slackened, he could always be counted on to throw in a duel, a dalliance with a beautiful foreign woman, chance encounters with some high-ranker known to history—Wellington or the duke of York; Napoleon or Marshal Soult—or even a bloody battle, to recapture the reader's attention and save the day.

Of course, Lever did not get it all wrong. War was and remains a young man's game, while not only he but also the important nineteenth- and twentieth-century war novelists, from Stendhal and Tolstoy to Stephen Crane, Ernest Hemingway, and James Jones, showed some version of the love of comrades and young men maturing under fire. Lever simply seems less serious about such things. Cheerfulness and light-heartedness keep breaking in. After August 1914, this tone and mood were perhaps no longer acceptable to adult readers.

It is not to be concluded, however, that Irish Charles O'Malley shows a passionate enthusiasm for entering British military service merely because his creator entertains superficial views of the military and of war.

Such service was, in the era depicted and for several more generations to come, a main way that Irishmen could overcome the colonial disadvantage and transcend the split sense of social and cultural identity that was every Irish person's burdensome heritage. This can be readily illustrated. Early on in *Charles O'Malley*, when Charley meets the supercilious and disdainful Captain Hammersley at his relatives', the Blakes', Galway establishment "Gurt-na-Morrow," he deeply resents him, not only because Charles has become smitten with Miss Dashwood, who apparently prefers the English officer, but also because, in the nature of the case, the Englishman *must* act out his superiority, while the Irishman must act out his bitter resentment over being in an inferior position. Hence ensues the mad attempt of both young men to outdo each other's dangerous riding exploits during the fox hunt, where both end up severely injured.

Later, when he is a dragoon in the Peninsula, Charles meets Hammersley again and discovers that he is friendly, even though their rivalry over the young lady continues. They meet as equals, as brother officers in the service. This service is a freemasonry, if not a democracy. For as long as it continues, the Irish-English difference, and even class differences, scarcely matters. There is, however, a world where troubles continue to accumulate, where there is no suspension of the Irish disadvantage. Uncle Godfrey's letters from the Galway property regularly report setbacks and disasters, from failing crops and tenants failing to pay their rents, to rapidly accumulating mortgage debt. When Charley is invalided out, after long and meritorious service in Portugal and Spain, he arrives home to find that the uncle has just died and that the property he inherits is in a ruinous condition.

Lever can be a careless writer. Nothing much is done about these problems, despite a lapse of years, before Charles is suddenly caught up in the excitement of the Hundred Days. He reenlists, makes a beeline for Brussels, Quatre-bras, and Waterloo where he gets to look on at the final battle, first with Napoleon (Charley has been captured), then with the victor, Wellington (Charley has escaped). At the end of the novel, Major O'Malley brings his bride, the former Miss Dashwood, home to Ireland. At Portumna the faithful tenants, removing the coach horses from the traces, draw the carriage home to the O'Malley house amid general rejoicing, while bonfires are lighted on the hills.

This happy outcome is, of course, cloud-cuckoo-land fantasy. Unless the new bride were rich, and even if he were to apply himself and learn the difficult business of estate management, Charles has almost no chance of rescuing the O'Malley agricultural estate from its intractable problems, which are largely structural, reflecting the unviability of the Irish agrarian system at that period.

Naturally, one does not expect a work like *The Irish Dragoon* to shed much light on the most profound Irish problems. We turn to it for its bright narrative of youthful adventure in foreign parts, supplemented by a veritable moving feast of stories and anecdotes related on shipboard, along the lines of march, and in bivouac by a rich variety of secondary narrators, most of them in uniform; for the droll characterizations of Major Monsoon, the crooked and companionable commissary officer; of Dr. Maurice Quill, the unflappable military surgeon and roisterer from Cork; and of Mickey Free, Charley's bat man, male nurse, and philosophizing sidekick; for the many splendid ballad poems and songs punctuating the narrative at frequent intervals, with titles like "Oh Once We Were Illigint People," "Bad Luck to This Marching," and "The Pickets Were Fast Retreating, Boys"; and for occasional self-contained episodes like "Patrick's Day in the Peninsula" (2: Chap. 21), which convey the joy of life, even in the midst of ghastly suffering and extreme danger.

Charles is a Roman Catholic, but that affiliation is given no force whatsoever in the plotting. The letters that Father Rush, the parish priest, writes to his former Latin scholar contain only local gossip and information about a keg of bootleg poteen he hopes to smuggle out to him. What really counts in this book is that the O'Malleys are not alienated from the British connection. Charley may bridle at what he takes to be English arrogance and putting on airs, yet he is perfectly loyal.

Lever followed up *Charles O'Malley* with *Tom Burke of "Ours,"* which also is about a young Catholic who is a landowner's son coming of age and making a military career in the Napoleonic Era. The crucial difference is that Tom turns against the British connection, first consorting—the tale opens around 1800—with men on the run and under cover who are all that is left of the shattered United Irish movement, then escaping to France, acquiring a military education and a French commission through attendance at St. Cyr, and becoming the most loyal of Emperor Napoleon's adherents, fighting through and witnessing all the major French campaigns up to Waterloo.

Even at the Bourbon Restoration, when *Grande Armée* officers are shown taking advantage of amnesty and the chance to swear a new oath of allegiance, Tom sticks by the lost cause of the now forever exiled Bonaparte. That makes Lever's reading of the moral of his own tale, coming in an epilogue, rather puzzling:

> The moral of my tale is simple—the fatal influence crude and uncertain notions of liberty will exercise over a career, which, under happier direction of its energies, had won honor and distinction, and the impolicy of the effort to substitute an adopted for a natural allegiance. (2:492)

Tom Burke did win honor and distinction—on the French side. Further, it would appear for an Irishman of that day, especially a Roman Catholic, allegiance to either the British or the French cause would be an adoptive rather than a natural one. The "natural" allegiance for those political orphans, the Irish, would be to an Irish sovereignty. This in fact was the "crude and uncertain" notion to which Tom Burke was exposed while still a boy, when he became involved with elements of the expiring rebel cause of the United Irish in the year of the voting of the Act of Union. For our purposes, these early experiences are the most interesting and suggestive. After Tom's escape to France, the book is largely travelogue, military campaigning, and romance.

Tom Burke opens in an atmosphere of gloom and sorrow uncommon in Lever's fiction. The senior Burke, a small landowner from the east side of the Shannon, near Athlone, lies comatose and dying in a rundown house attended only by old Lanty, a witless huntsman who has not been quite himself since his rageful master brained him with a "loaded" whip.[3] A cynical, neglectful physician and a corrupt attorney, who is also agent to the Burke property, sit just outside the sickroom, greedily eating and drinking while discussing the size of the bills they will levy against the estate. Poor Tom, who is about fourteen and the neglected yet loving younger son, sits apart, waiting for his father to ask for him. This never happens. Mr. Burke only calls for the favored older son, who is away at school in England and does not bother to turn up for the funeral.

The social level of this household is that of the late-eighteenth-century "half-sir."[4] It is a little grander than Carleton's "bodagh" or large farmer, but at the lower margin for the landlord class as a whole. Burke has been a bad landlord, physically violent, and swift to rackrent and evict. His harshness has not made him prosperous.

After the funeral, the orphaned boy sits with the servants in the kitchen. "Darby the Blast," a picturesque figure of great size and strength, comes there. This itinerant performer upon the Irish pipes saves Tom from a forced apprenticeship to the crooked attorney by taking him on the road. Before they have gone far, they encounter a witch-like old woman, whose husband and children, she says, were done in by the oppressions of Tom's father. She curses the boy upon learning who he is. Tom Burke, then, sets out on his wanderings as a neglected younger son and an accursed, despised orphan. There is nothing between him and despair but Darby.

It is more than enough, for Darby, showing a constant devotion to Burke, proves truly resourceful. Not only a fine musician, he is also a master spy for the United Irish remnant and for the French. He draws Tom deeply into the underground network of Irish dissidence, while outwitting Barton, a "thief-catcher" and British agent, and putting the boy in touch with Lieutenant de Meudon, a romantic young Frenchman of high lineage and a consumptive tendency. Going underground in Ireland after the survivors of General Humbert's expedition in autumn 1798 were rounded up and sent home by their British captors, de Meudon hopes to build an effective Irish rebel force, even though experience has taught him of the native Irish tendency to fall quarrelling among themselves or turn informers. In these early chapters Tom is kept busy indeed, spending an idyllic time with de Meudon in a remote glen of Wicklow until the lieutenant dies of hemorrhaging lungs, meeting Dublin conspirators in a house on Kevin Street, leading a mob protesting the vote for Union in front of Parliament House, and receiving several wounds and injuries, including a severe concussion during the street demonstration. In various disguises, Darby always turns up to rescue Tom and to nurse him through his injuries. He is a surrogate father yet more than a father. Darby is part of, and represents, the "hidden Ireland" that has remained resistant and essentially unknown to the British presence, forever plotting to bring about a restoration of native Irish sovereignty.

Darby's last service to his protégé in Ireland is to carry him to a French ship lying off Howth. Tom has been grievously wounded and may die. Theirs is a touching farewell, for Darby has completely replaced in Tom's affections the cold, brutal natural father, who oppressed his tenants and spurned the love of his younger son. Luckily, in fact magically, by the time the ship makes landfall along the French coast, Tom's wound is distinctly on the mend. As the ship drops anchor, there is a spectacular description of the French invasion army, drawn up troop by troop on an immense sandy plain beside the sea. Most of the French fleet displays itself nearby. It is a glorious picture. Tom Burke is being reborn from his deathy wounded state to his new French career.

We have seen that getting abroad could be a sort of rebirth for Charles Lever also. For all the loyalist verbiage about "natural allegiance" in the Epilogue, there was something of Tom Burke in Lever himself. If Charles O'Malley was his right hand, Tom was his left. One way of locating this writer culturally and politically is to postulate that one hand does not always know what the other is doing.

Before closing this section, let us return briefly to *Harry Lorrequer*, the immensely successful first-person "confession" with which Lever made his literary debut. Perhaps what caught the public's fancy most was a new voice and intonation. It was the voice of a social adventurer, certainly; also the voice of an outsider determined to become an insider. That is to say, it was an Irish voice trying to sound English—Lorrequer claims to be English while admitting he was educated in Ireland—but missing the mark out of excessive Irish liveliness and nervosity:

> One dark doubt shot for an instant across my brain. Mayhap her ladyship had registered a vow: never to syllable a name unchronicled by Debrett, or

was only mystifying me for mere amusement. A minute's consideration dispelled this fear; for I found myself treated *en seigneur* by the whole family. (1:34)

The circumstance is that a titled English family, the Callonbys, residing for a season on their Clare estate, have taken up Lorrequer socially, even though he is a mere subaltern in a marching regiment. He guesses they mistake him for his well-heeled and socially prominent cousin Guy, but he plays out the role because he has fallen in love with the daughter, Lady Jane. The language in which he appraises this circumstance, we see, is facetious, schoolboyish, rather vulgar, nervously insecure, self-conscious, and a little self-mocking. Behind it is the Anglo-Irish notion—it has previously turned up in the Edgeworths—that the English need a spirited Irish infusion to rescue them from too much Teutonic gravity. At the level of high culture the same point would be made by Matthew Arnold when he gave his Oxford lectures "On the Celtic Element in English Poetry" a generation later.[5] Harry Lorrequer's liveliness wins Lady Jane in the end. Lever's lively writing found its mainly Anglo-Saxon audience on both sides of the Atlantic.

One cannot be lively all the time. Lever soon mastered a tone of seriousness—it was already emerging in *Tom Burke*—and turned to graver concerns than the social and military adventures of young men during the Napoleonic Era. Chief among them was the perplexed condition of his native land, which drew his uneasy attention, no matter how far from Ireland he traveled, and how long he absented himself.

The Matter of Ireland: *St. Patrick's Eve* (1845); *The O'Donoghue* (1845); *The Knight of Gwynne* (1847)

St. Patrick's Eve, a sort of fable, modeled in part on Dickens's Christmas books, was Lever's attempt to explain the condition of Ireland to his offspring—and no doubt to himself—just before the parlousness and divisiveness of that condition drove him abroad again. The main setting is "a little village on the bank of Lough Corrib . . . shut in by lake and mountain . . . apart from all the world" (xxxvii). The action, taking place in three distinct eras, focuses in each era on the village fair preceding St. Patrick's feast day.

The First Era is pre-1800. Young Leslie, the landlord's son, is attacked by a gang arrived at the fair to participate in a faction fight between Connors and Joyces. Owen Connor, who loves Mary, the sister of his chief Joyce opponent, Phil, rescues Leslie but is himself savaged by Joyce adherents. When Owen recovers from his hurts, the older Mr. Leslie gratefully offers the Connors a richer farm holding near the lovely lake. They decline to move from their mountain tenancy but do accept a permanent exemption from paying rent.

We are told that in this era, "while Mr. Leslie lived in ignorance that such people existed on his property, they looked up to him with a degree of reverence almost devotional. There was a feudalism, too, in this sentiment that gave the reverence a feeling of strong allegiance" (329). These feelings of reverent allegiance to an owner of a different religious faith, whose original property title arose in invasion, conquest, and confiscation, are evidently Pavlovian reflexes, for the Connors, hitherto living totally unknown to the landlord, have never received any form of service or patronage from him. First Era peasants seem a different kind from *homo sapiens.* Owen Connor has had his skull shattered in the fight with the Joyces; yet his recovery is rapid and complete. "He soon got better, far sooner perhaps than if all the appliances of luxury had ministered to his recovery; most certainly sooner than if his brain had been ordinarily occupied by thoughts of a higher order than his were"[6] (336).

The Second Era starts shortly after 1800. The formerly resident landlord, Mr. Leslie, takes his family to live in England. Returning for a visit, he is carried off by the *cholera morbus.* Control of the estate passes to a new, rent-driving agent. Owen Connor and Phil Joyce meet up in the village graveyard and are cautiously reconciled.

The Third Era is in effect the 1840s, though this makes characters like Owen and Mary mysteriously exempt from ordinary aging. An undeclared war is raging between the landowners—served by their agents and the armed police—and the hard-pressed tenants, egged on by the terrorist secret societies that so exercised William Carleton. In this era, Owen Connor is ordered to pay off the previous years of rent exemption by the new agents, who operate from a commercial premises in Galway City. Long-standing verbal agreements go unhonored. Owen tries to see the younger Mr. Leslie in London but he is out of town. Returning to the mountain farm, Owen discovers that he has been evicted and an armed ruffian put in his place. In despair, Owen joins a band of White Boys, whose meeting place is a ruined mausoleum in the village graveyard. Through a wicked ruse, he draws the card that designates him as the assassin of an agent named Lucas. Just as he is about to bushwack this gentleman, Mr. Leslie arrives, prevents the assassination attempt, is properly grateful to Owen for having saved him from the cudgels of the Joyces, and restores the Connor tenancy to its old basis of rent exemption.

In a wonderfully sappy epilogue, Mary Joyce is shown, on one last St. Patrick's Eve, being guided up a steep mountain path by Mr. Leslie, who is on horseback, she to be united in matrimony with Owen Connor. Connor is on a beetling rock, with the orphan child Patsy, whom he has informally adopted, standing beside him. In the Phiz illustration, all the space between the bride below and the groom above is filled with capering peasants.

Lever's mystic notion of a feudal bond between landowners and their tenants, which had been mysteriously ruptured and which could be mended or restored whenever the proprietors got around to it, was sheer fantasy. Neither Maria Edgeworth nor Carleton went this far in the direction of wishful thinking. After *St. Patrick's Eve* we find Lever not only retreating to the Continent but also falling back upon the relative security of historical perspectives in his approach to Irish problems. He will make one last effort to address the contemporary Irish scene in *Lord Kilgobbin*, but before that come works such as *The O'Donoghue*, set in the years 1794–96, and *The Knight of Gwynne*, subtitled *A Tale of the Time of the Union.*

Generally, Lever's waywardness with history has a certain entertainment value. In *The O'Donoghue*, he shows Major Luttrell—the notorious "Luttrell the Traitor" who had turned tail with his cavalry troop at Aughrim in 1691, supposedly causing the Irish to lose this crucial battle—on his way to attend a viceregal ball at Dublin Castle in 1796. When the street crowd catch sight of him in his carriage, they hiss and boo. Unless he is an apparition, they really should be cheering him for having established a new Irish longevity record. He would have to be at least a hundred and fifty years old. Of course in Ireland, where the past is ever green, historical figures, especially sinister ones, have a way of outliving their own deaths. It is a theme we shall see Le Fanu, for one, exploring fruitfully.

The O'Donoghue and *The Knight of Gwynne* need not detain us long. In the former, the old "Gaelic" chieftain O'Donoghue, harboring in an ancestral castle that is half-ruin, half-barracks, is played off against the wealthy English gentleman Sir Marmaduke Travers, a retired London banker who comes to live in the district, the rugged and picturesque Vale of Glenflesk on the Cork-Kerry border, not far from Bantry. The young people at the castle—the chief's two sons, Mark and Herbert, and their cousin, Kate O'Donoghue—become involved with the children of Sir Marmaduke, Sybella and Frederick. Frederick is an English Guards officer. But there is no blending of the two lines through romantic attachments leading to love and marriage. Presumably that is because the military plot played out in the novel, the ill-adventured scheme to put Wolfe Tone and several thousand French invasion troops ashore along the great bay, in coordination with a rising of the native Irish throughout the Southwest, sharpens Irish and English differences and loyalties beyond any hope of genial compromise.

The O'Donoghue himself is not an impressive figure. Bone idle and besotted with family pride, he takes a Micawberish line with the family finances. He has let his business agent in Cork City put the remnant of the vast acreage his grandfather once held under heavy mortgage, and he has stooped to forging Mark's signature on property deeds in order to raise ready money. This elder son is, not surprisingly, of a sullen and angry temperament, yet he is devoted to the cause of a native Irish revival and loves his cousin Kate faithfully if jealously.

History records that a devastating storm blew the French ships out of the bay before they could land troops. Lever adds the fictional detail of an explosion of hidden gunpowder and arms at a shebeen house in Glenflesk, which levels the ancient seat of the O'Donoghues. Son Mark manages to survive and catch the last French ship out. Many years later he will revisit the Vale in company with Kate, now his wife. The year is 1825 and Ireland, from Mark's standpoint, is still enslaved. His bearing is military and he has lost an arm, no doubt while fighting under the French flag. This couple, rather like the Lever family, appear foreign, and they speak French together. This does not prevent old Mary M'Kelly, formerly keeper of the subversive shebeen, from recognizing them. Now a roadside beggar, she bitterly accuses them of deserting their country and spurns their proffered alms. Both the Travers and the O'Donoghue estates—the English and the Irish—are deserted ruins. However, there has been one successful accommodation, as between opposed traditions. Mark's younger brother Herbert, whom we saw as a boy acquiring Homeric Greek and good Latin from the parish priest, has turned Protestant, studied for a law degree at Trinity, and gone off on British imperial service to be a judge in India.

The ending conveys bitterness and a sense of impasse. The Irish uprisings of the late 1790s have failed, we are meant to believe, owing to the treachery and cowardice of the mere Irish. The United Irish movement has proved a hotbed of informers and government spies. In the Bantry Bay operation, when the French fleet came sailing in, the local rebel recruits disgraced themselves by failing to show up for the appointed rendezvous with French ships. Lever's final attitude seems to be, A plague on both your houses, Irish and English. This is the mood in which he clears off to Brussels after those several years of residence in the fractious Dublin political and social scene of the early 1840s.

Maria Edgeworth read to the family circle at Edgeworthstown the early chapters of *The O'Donoghue* as these were appearing in monthly numbers. She evidently liked the part about the Englishman coming with his daughter Sybella to live in rural Ireland. She wrote Lever an appreciative letter that quite delighted him (Downey, 1:117). *The Knight of Gwynne* may have pleased her less. This aristocrat, an influential member of the Irish Parliament during the debates on the Act of

Union, is against it yet fails to get to Parliament House to cast his vote at the final reading. Having just learned that his business agent, "Honest Tom" Gleeson, has absconded with a large sum of his money, he is too upset to appear. We recall that R. L. Edgeworth was a member of the last Dublin Parliament who voted against the bill to protest the corrupt means employed to secure its passage. Nothing would have prevented him from turning up on that historic evening to vote according to his conscience.

In writing *The Knight of Gwynne*, Lever tried to portray a great Anglo-Irish landlord who was perfectly honorable and honest. If he could bring it off, then the honor of an entire class, in the very era when a deep stain appeared on its historic record, might be vindicated. However, his failure with Lord Gwynne is nearly complete. The man is pompous and sententious rather than judiciously wise. His spectacular hospitality at Gwynne Abbey near Clew Bay in County Mayo is wasted on parasites and visiting English firemen, while he is never seen performing charitable acts or attending to the needs of his many hard-pressed tenants. The knight enjoys wagering large sums at Daly's Clubhouse in Dublin, and the reader is expected to admire him when he gambles away enormously valuable property—almost the only thing he has left after the malfeasance of his agent, Gleeson—under circumstances that would perfectly entitle him to claim a misdeal of the crucial hand of cards and give him a second chance to win. But he lacks the courage to do this in front of the usual staring crowd of loungers and fellow gamblers.

Lord Gwynne does not even have the excuse of immaturity, for he is elderly, with an English wife of mature years, Lady Eleanor, and grown children. However, there is little point in belaboring him for faults common to so many of his class in 1800.

"Finishing Creditably": *Lord Kilgobblin* (1872)

By the time Lever became British consul at Trieste in 1867, he had been reporting to the Foreign Office for almost two decades. Writing in 1868 to his publisher and close friend, John Blackwood, he claimed to know "more of the Continent and foreign questions than the whole lot of them," and he wondered, only half-jokingly, why they wouldn't make him "Under-Secretary, F. O." (quoted by Stevenson, 281). He knew the answer, of course. It comes out in a letter of that same period to his fellow countryman, the journalist William Howard Russell: "You and I do labour under a distinct disqualification. It is not merely our brogue. . . . It is our Irishry in fifty ways. We offend susceptibilities every hour of our lives by our haste and over-quickness. The 'I know that' tone we have offends the how-and-why Bull, who knows he could buy us all out to the fourth generation; he cannot see why we presume to think faster than he does" (Stevenson, 282).

Disliking Trieste, especially Triestine society; always concerned about his wife's worsening health, and in poor health himself, Lever at this time felt that his literary career was nearly at an end—"I am always hoping that each book will be my last" (Stevenson, 283). In this mood he proposed to Blackwood a "story of modern—that is, recent—Ireland, as opposed to the old Erin, with all its conflicting agencies of Tory and Whig, radical, rebel, and loyalist, dashed with something of that humour that even poverty and famine have not exhausted, without a bit of sermonizing or anything at all 'doctrinaire.' I think I could put many strong truths forcibly forward, and insinuate much worth consideration and reflection. I believe I have *one* more effort in me, and I don't believe I have two; but I'd like to give myself the chance of finishing creditably" (Stevenson, 284).

Lord Kilgobbin: A Tale of Ireland in Our Own Time is the work in which Lever finishes. It came out as a book in the year of his death. In light of its accomplishment, "creditably" is too modest. He began the writing in late 1869 and expected to take a close-up look at Irish conditions during a spring trip in 1870. That was not to be, for his beloved wife died in April of that year and he was plunged into many months of grief and depression. Nevertheless, the writing continued and he was able to pay a visit—it would be his last—to both London and Dublin during April 1871. People made much of him in both places. There were festive dinners at the Garrick Club, and Trinity College, Dublin, awarded him an honorary degree. One senses that the world was cheering a departing guest. More narrowly, it was a world from which Lever had voluntarily removed himself for much of his adult career.

Kilgobbin's is the Ireland of Church Disestablishment, of the Fenian raids and risings and the furious reaction they bred, of a new Whig administration that wants to replace the old Tory politics of coercion, hangings, and transportation with some conciliatory moves toward the Irish tenants and the Irish Catholic clergy. In 1870, Gladstone's first Land Act—the first attempt by government to regulate landlord-tenant relations on principles of fairness and economic common sense—was launched, and there was a faint stirring of a Home Rule movement under Isaac Butt, M.P. All these stirrings of change impinge upon Kilgobbin Castle, where the "Lord," Matthew Kearney, is in residence, along with his daughter Kate, who manages the estate, and occasionally with son Dick, a Trinity student. The title is an old Catholic one. Local nationalists accept its legitimacy for as long as Kearney professes undying nationalist sentiments—at meetings of the "Goat Club," of which

Lord Kilgobbin is president or "Chief Capricorn." When however, Kearney turns Whig in order to support his son's candidacy for parliament, the nationalists are furious and put up their own candidate, Dan Donogan, an itinerant Fenian "head-centre" and escaped convict. Donogan comes in at the top of the poll. As with the Sinn Feiners elected to the Westminster Parliament after 1916, he declines taking his seat. This linking of electoral events fifty years apart is not altogether specious, for the seeds of Irish independence were certainly planted in the time *Lord Kilgobbin* depicts.

Avoiding the romantic west, the seaside, and the mountains, Lever locates the Kilgobbin property in the workaday midlands, near Moate, in King's County, on the edge of the immense and featureless Bog of Allen. This is the right locale for a novel that in places, though not consistently, shows a command of prosaic reality as dense as Trollope's, and that gets along without the sort of nonsense about "feudal" bonds to which Lever had recourse in *St. Patrick's Eve*. The bogland is Ireland demystified and dead level. At the same time, being uncharted and full of unmarked sinkholes brimming with brown water, it is easy to get lost in and be drowned: the dead level can give way under a person's feet like a banana peel or quicksand. Certainly that is the experience of Cecil Walpole, secretary to Lord Danebury, the new Whig-appointed viceroy. He ventures into the neighborhood of Kilgobbin while out hunting, bringing little with him except his English hauteur and the expectation of getting his own way, especially with young women.

By keeping the focus of action at Kilgobbin Castle, the novel demonstrates a structural economy unwonted in Lever's books. Everyone comes there—Walpole and his friend, the Dublin Castle aide-de-camp; a party of rural terrorists demanding arms; the exotic Greek cousin, Nina Kostalergi; Dan Donogan, who appears to be modeled after the famous Fenian leader, James Stephens; the infatuated cousin of the Kearneys, Gorman O'Shea; and son Dick, when Trinity terms are out. Joe Atlee comes there, too, but he also gets to go to North Wales and on a long "fact-finding" trip to Turkey and Greece for Lord Danebury. Joe is the chief centrifugal element of the plot. That is not true at the end when he gets his comeuppance and is almost literally bogged down, as the ever-surprising Nina and the Fenian fugitive rush into marriage and seek an unknown future in America.

For all its centeredness, this is Lever's one novel on Irish themes where he manages to draw freely and imaginatively on his vast knowledge of Europe and experience of diplomacy. His development of Nina Kostalergi as a character—tying together the two ends of Europe where the British exert strong influence, Ireland and the eastern Mediterranean—amounts to a full-blown proto-Jamesian "international theme."

But there is also the quite subtle and rather teasing handling of Lord Danebury, the Foreign Office peer. With a flair for intrigue and intelligence work, he had been a highly successful envoy in Turkish Ottoman territory and was given the Irish lord-lieutenancy as a reward for brilliant service "out there." When he tries a comparable style of intrigue in Ireland, working through Walpole and then Atlee, he is drawn straight on into disaster: he is richly fed on misinformation and encouraged to enter into secret dealings with the Fenians—for proper and patriotic ends of course—until he finds himself involved in a major scandal when his attempts at secret diplomacy are leaked in full to a press quite eager to embarrass the new Whig administration. In the ensuing debacle, Lord Danebury has no choice but to resign a viceregal term of office barely begun and to count himself lucky to be allowed to resume a diplomatic post in his familiar territory, the Levant, where intriguers are not as bottomlessly duplicitous and unappeasable as the Irish have proved to be. Walpole, who had been the hapless go-between and chief conduit for the false information given Lord Danebury, is fed to the wolves, though not exactly. His next post will be Guatemala, where, Danebury acidly remarks, yellow fever or a hungry crocodile may be counted on to finish him off.

What did the English think they were doing, sending to rule in Ireland an expert on the Balkans and a snobbish youngster whose beckoning future is Guatemala? The Irish do not usually ask such forthright questions, especially of their rulers. Nina, however, exercising all sorts of privileges, including that of outsider, certainly does, as when she asks the Fenian hunter, Inspector Curtis, "Do pray, Mr. Curtis, tell me all about it. Why do some people shoot the others who are just as Irish as themselves? Why do hungry people kill the cattle and never eat them? And why don't the English go away and leave a country where nobody likes them?" (323). It is noticeable that these questions strike against self-destructive Irish factionalism as well as against the British colonial presence.

Nina is half-Greek, half-Irish. Once again, the heritage and sense of identity are halved and hyphenated. One might add that she is part waif, part vamp. With so much in the mix there is always the danger of an explosion. It is impossible to be sure until the end whether Nina will turn out to be a villainess or a proper heroine, a demon or an angel. She is splendid in her elopement with Donogan, after having collected passionate avowals and marriage proposals from all the conventional young men. Yet one notices Lever makes sure they leave the country. America may be just big enough for this pair.

How did she get to Ireland in the first place? The book gives a detailed answer. Into it went Lever's ripened knowledge of how the world wags in mid-nineteenth-century Latin and Levantine Europe. Matthew Kearney had a sister Mathilda, who, finding herself still single at thirty, embarked on a continental tour. At Naples she was courted by an unprincipled scoundrel calling himself Prince Kostalergi. She imagined she loved him and he mistook her for an English lady with a fortune, so they were married. On hearing of it, Matthew broke off all communication with his sister. An infant girl, Nina, was born. The Kostalergis went to live at Palermo after a scandal: the prince was found to run the Greek legation at Naples as a gambling den, and he killed one of the heavy losers in a duel, causing him to lose his post. Soon Mathilda died, worn out by the prince's bad treatment and final abandonment of her. He took the child and turned up in Rome, becoming a music and language teacher, appearing in less than the best Roman society, doing a little spying for the English and French on the side. As Nina grew up, she was trained as a singer and in the arts of fascinating men. The prince anticipated selling her to some dissolute rich man for a large sum. Marriage might even be part of the arrangement. But Nina would not be sold. She wrote a letter to Uncle Matthew, who was slumbering through his middle years beside his brown bog, entreating him to save her. He offered her asylum at Kilgobbin Castle and she came running. Her part in this novel begins and ends with a flight toward freedom.

A farfetched story? Lever had surely heard stranger ones in his long years of consular work. After all, Greece and Ireland—or Greeks and Irish—have a certain rapport in an age of Great Powers and client states that are treated virtually as colonies. Dan Donogan, the Fenian, had fought during early years in Greek wars of independence and picked up a speaking acquaintance with modern Greek. This detail, as believable as Lord Byron's meeting his death at Missolonghi, will help make the newlyweds compatible during the inevitable strains accompanying resettlement in the United States. The British do not regard Matthew Kearney's old Irish title as legitimate. In parallel, whoever rules Greece at that time refuses to allow Prince Kostalergi his claim to the principality of Delos. However, Kostalergi's better Irish equivalent is Joe Atlee. They even meet and cut a deal during Joe's special fact-finding mission to Italy, Greece, and Turkey for Lord Danebury. Theirs is a dance together of sham existences—the term originates with the great Polish émigré Joseph Conrad—East and West.

One does not want to make exaggerated claims for *Lord Kilgobbin.* Given his class affiliations, the fantasy games he liked to play with his own uncertain sense of self, and his habits of diplomatic absenteeism—to say nothing of his ills and sorrows while doing the book—Lever was not well situated to write the great novel of mid-nineteenth-century Irish politics and society before the advent of Parnell changed all the rules. Nevertheless, it is an arresting performance and a strong finish in the point-to-point race Lever had been running ever since he took his first look at the world beyond Dublin.

"Anglo-Irish" in a Novel by John Banim (1798–1842)

How does the curious fate of being Anglo-Irish in the nineteenth century appear to writers who are not themselves Anglo-Irish by heritage or, in the singular case of William Carleton, by appropriation? Some light on this question may be shed by our briefly considering the nationalist novelist John Banim's *The Anglo-Irish of the Nineteenth Century* (1828). Banim was an older contemporary of Lever's. The late Robert Lee Wolff referred to this novel as Banim's most significant book, pointing out that while it purports to relate how young Gerald Blount, son of an absentee Ascendancy viscount, comes to terms with his mixed "English-Irish" heritage, it is in fact a powerful satiric attack mounted against the very existence of Anglo-Irish identity as such (Wolff, brochure, 18). By the time Gerald opts for an all- or mere or "real"[7] Irish role, he has been led through a series of encounters and recognitions tending to inculcate the lesson that to be Anglo-Irish is truly to be a nullity, a self-cancelling proposition, a palpable void. Banim gets his confidence from the fact that, though set just before the Peninsular War, his tale was actually being written in the full tide of O'Connellite agitation for Catholic Emancipation, and looks beyond Emancipation to repeal of the Union. Yet he hedged his bet, inasmuch as the book was brought out anonymously.

Challenges to the viability of Anglo-Irish identity occur in many episodes. There is a scene at Dublin's Theatre Royal, where young English officers annoy young women in the audience by staring, making rude remarks, even tripping them up with their spurs. Gerald is furious, understanding that this behavior expresses insolent contempt for the Irish people: the officers would not have behaved this way in their own country. He then reflects that it is the lack of a settled Irish character which elicits these bad English manners. He concludes that the natives and the settler class must sink their differences in the formation of a solid national character. Then there will be no more contempt.

The Anglo-Irish are criticized for behaving in a fawning, servile manner when in England, while acting overbearing and arrogant toward the Irish people at home. We are introduced to obsequious Mr. Gore of Dublin, who borrows £350 from Gerald when they become acquainted in England and of course never repays. In Dublin Mr. Gore is burdened with a spendthrift wife and three high-living adult daughters, who abuse him while running up vast debts at the most expensive shops. He squeezes his country tenantry and borrows from everyone within reach, but this domestic Anglo-Irish Lear must break in the end. On the very night the Gores have given an especially showy and pointless dinner party, the bailiffs take possession. Wife and daughters are packed into a cab, the father joins them in an unwonted mood of philosophic resignation, though not until he has unscrewed and carried away the brass nameplate from the door of the fine townhouse where they had lived, and the family decamps for parts unknown.

But the most far-reaching challenge to Anglo-Irish cultural and social hegemony comes just halfway through the book. On a bright February morning, Gerald takes a lengthy stroll through the heart of Dublin, visiting en route nearly every site of architectural renown and civic distinction in the city. This walk is elaborately yet clearly organized, and the entire passage—running on for some dozen or so closely printed pages—is nothing less than an inventory of urban treasures, as these had been accumulated almost entirely during the great age of the Anglo-Irish, from late in the seventeenth century to 1800.

Gerald begins in the Merrion Square area, where he is impressed by the fine houses and spacious street plan. After passing through a quarter of mean houses and starveling shops, he finds himself at the quays of the Liffey. Here he is taken with two classical buildings—someone tells him they are the "ould Royal Exchange and the Four-Courts, long life to 'em"—and he notices how the paved quays and the arrangement of principal streets at right angles to the Liffey open the river to the city on both sides, whereas in London the Thames is far less accessible and more "chartered." He crosses to the north bank, reaching a point in or near elegant Mountjoy Square, where he can see how the shape of the town plan relates in one direction to the sea, its "suntipt" waters crowded with shipping, and in the other direction to "picturesque sweeps of land, some blue and bare, some showing villages or villa." Impressed in spite of himself, Gerald says, "very beautiful, Dublin; very beautiful, I admit" (2:178).

Further walking brings him back across the river to the front of the Royal Exchange once again, and thence by a broad avenue to College Green. He is very admiring of the Bank and the front of Trinity College, and has a colloquy with a leg-pulling news vendor, whose dialect—"a vile Dublin brogue (the vilest of any in Ireland, for it is slang-brogue)" (2:180)—is as hard to make out, at least in Banim's try at phonetic transcription, as English back-slang.

The last part of Gerald's walk leads to the middle of Carlisle, later O'Connell Bridge. Here he takes the full measure of the central Dublin panorama as it organizes itself along two main axes and in four cardinal directions: north up Sackville Street to the Nelson monument and General Post Office, with the distant Rotunda and a fine church steeple closing the view; south along the same axis to the Bank and University; west, up-river, along the quays and the arching bridges to the Four-Courts, with the Castle and the two cathedrals massing together on the south side; east, down-river, to the Custom House, a forest of masts and rigging, and the Liffey mouth beyond. Transported by his viewing, Gerald reflects how superior are these buildings and thoroughfares, including the river itself, to anything he has known in London. With a sort of rapture he concludes: "I must admit that I now stand in the center of perhaps the most beautiful city-picture in the world" (2:184).

During this promenade Gerald Blount, on the way to becoming an Irish nationalist, resurveys Dublin as a preliminary to reclaiming it as capital (in more than one sense) for a reviving nation. The city becomes the brightest jewel of a pure or mere Irish diadem. The time for lamentation or even derision over the disgraceful flitting of the parliament has passed. In fact, the Act of Union contains this hidden benefit to the Irish majority: by voting it, the Anglo-Irish in effect surrendered their Irishness, ceased to be contenders for a significant role in the Irish future. Now the unrepresented native people, who surrendered nothing because they held nothing, can claim what, after all, they had built with their sweated labor—"the most beautiful city-picture in the world'—and build on toward a nation all their own.

We know, of course, that the Anglo-Irish were not to be so easily dismissed into the dustbins of history. For that matter, young Blount, in spite of becoming an enthusiastic nationalist, remains indismissibly a hybrid—half-English, half-Irish in lineage and upbringing. And why should Banim devote a novel to the conversion of an intelligent, energetic, and scrupulously honorable young Anglo-Irishman to the national cause unless he recognized a certain value for Ireland in the class that had produced him? With the failure of Repeal the problem of a final disposition of the Anglo-Irish "case" could be postponed. Yet it is only a postponement. Their case remains unsolved, not only to the national novelist John Banim, but also even more, as Lever's "mercurial" career of identity games and shifting about perhaps suggests, to themselves.

VI

THE POLITICS OF ANGLO-IRISH GOTHIC: CHARLES ROBERT MATURIN, JOSEPH SHERIDAN LEFANU, AND THE RETURN OF THE REPRESSED

Mystery is the shadow of guilt.
—J. S. LeFanu, *Wylder's Hand*

Gothic authorship seems dominated by
outsiders— Irishmen, Scotsmen, and women.
—Judith Wilt, *Ghosts of the Gothic*

Introductory

THE BATTLE OF CULLODEN in 1746 secured the hegemony of British Protestant power against any likelihood of Stuart and Catholic revival. It may be significant that the English Gothic Revival can be dated from the following year, when Sir Horace Walpole purchased his estate of Strawberry Hill near Twickenham and commenced his Gothic erections in what he took to be an authentic medieval architectural style. Nearly twenty years later, in 1765, Walpole wrote and brought out the first Gothic novel or romance, *The Castle of Otranto*. From that date to about the end of the 1820s, Gothic fiction proved a very popular subgenre of English prose fiction. It opened a literary—sometimes a subliterary—career to many minor, if few really outstanding, imaginative writers, especially women writers, and it significantly influenced the course of the novel on the Continent and in America. At least in Britain, the impulse to produce generic Gothic fiction wanes at about the time the Catholic minority of the population wins emancipation from the legal and civil disabilities Catholics had suffered ever since the Protestant revolutionary settlement of the seventeenth century.

Typically, Gothic fiction, from Walpole to Ann Radcliffe and "Monk" Lewis, was set in a Catholic Mediterranean country—Italy, Spain, or Provençal France—at a medieval, or at least a pre-Enlightenment remove of time.

At worst, Gothic fiction, emerging when Catholic power seemed to have gone down to final defeat, pandered to the insular and sectarian prejudices of the common English reader, especially those marginally educated. There is, however, another and more positive side. The later eighteenth-century efflorescence of the Gothic constitutes in itself a remarkable "return of the repressed" into the general awareness, from whence it had been banished for generations. Feudalism, ecclesiasticism, the Catholic culture of Latin Europe might be presented as haunts of corruption, oppression and *diablerie*, yet their presentation at all, in however distorted and unhistorical a form, stimulated the general imagination, nourishing a taste for the hierarchic and hieratic, along with the marvelous and strange, which Neoclassicism and the rationalism of the Enlightenment could not satisfy.

The capacity of the Gothic to survive, and particularly to interbreed with other imaginative modes so as to engender much more complex and valuable literary phenomena than itself, was extraordinary. In the Enlightenment period proper, Gothic romance was that monster unchained during the sleep of Reason which demonstrated how much of the unconscious and incalculable remained after mere Reason had completed its survey.[1] At the beginning of the nineteenth century, Gothic made a confluence with romanticism, being enriched by and enriching the romantic quest after the numinous and the transcendental. During the development of the Victorian and early modern novel, detective and crime fiction, especially in their "black" varieties, were drawn from Gothic entrails, while the psychological novel, particularly fiction delving into the unconscious or "night" side of the psyche and of human character and motive, owed much to the Gothic matrix. There is reason to believe that Gothic fiction helped to produce modern science fiction, following a line from Mary Shelley's *Frankenstein* to the "scientific romances" of H. G. Wells at the turn of the century. The Brontë sisters adapted the Gothic mode to the exploration of women's oppressions and aspirations in early Victorian society and to the more intense reaches of love between the sexes, while Dickens used Gothic techniques and effects to represent the fantastic distortions of personality, roles, and relationships accompanying the Industrial Revolution and the rise of megalopolis.

Most surprisingly, but just as certainly, the Gothic mode in American literature, engendering with certain Puritan obsessions about "the power of blackness,"[2] about Nature as a realm of potent demonic otherness, and with a harsh Calvinist theology of predestined election and reprobation, produced a central tradition of prose fiction, or prose romance, running from Charles Brockden Brown, through Hawthorne, Poe, and Melville, to the moderns William Faulkner and Flannery O'Connor. It is still alive and somewhat viable in such contemporary

American romancers as Joyce Carol Oates, E. L. Doctorow, and Toni Morrison.

A peculiar distinction of the Gothic literary style and a clue to its staying power, is its ability to convey, through oblique, symbolic, or allegorically encoded language, truths, feelings, and desires that the official culture and "mainstream" writing little notice and sometimes suppress. In that sense, Gothic literature often carries a heavily political or metapolitical charge.[3] The Gothic seems to flourish in disrupted, oppressed, or undeveloped societies, to give a voice to the powerless and unenfranchised, and even, at times, to subvert and contradict the official best intentions of its creators.[4] It is no accident that D. H. Lawrence hit upon his axiom, "Never trust the artist. Trust the tale" (*Studies*, 2), while tracing the richly Gothic designs of classic American literature through Poe, Hawthorne, and Melville. And it was certainly no accident that Jane Austen's narrator in *Northanger Abbey*, when she repudiates Gothic romance as a suitable imaginative instrument for exploring the real character of life in the most settled parts of "middle" England, says she is willing to abandon to the Gothic not only all of Italy, Switzerland, and the south of France, but also "the northern and western extremities" of her own country (165). That meant the "Celtic fringe" of Highland Scotland, Wales and Cornwall, and the whole, presumably, of Ireland.

Politically oppressed, underdeveloped in the far west and southwest, disrupted and distressed by famines, clearances, uprisings, and the depredations of the rural secret societies, devoutly Catholic in its majority population, and full of romantic scenery and prehistoric, not to say feudal, ruins, nineteenth-century Ireland was an impressive candidate for Gothic treatment. The country was in fact sometimes seen as a sort of living Gothic, or agonized Gothic romance that had turned real. That is what Charles Robert Maturin meant when he wrote in the preface to his *Milesian Chief* that Ireland was "the only country on earth, where, from the strange existing opposition of religion, politics, and manners, the extremes of refinement and barbarism are united, and the most wild and incredible situations of romantic story are hourly passing before modern eyes" (1:20).

Les Huguenots: Charles Robert Maturin (1782–1824); Joseph Sheridan LeFanu (1814–1873)

Maturin and LeFanu occur along the time line of nineteenth-century Anglo-Irish letters in an early and middle position, respectively, a little more than a generation apart. Both writers essentially belong to the Dublin-dwelling, rather than the landed, estate-dwelling part of the Ascendancy class; both took degrees at Trinity College, Dublin; and both garnered their incomes from a combination of literary with other vocational pursuits centered in the city. Maturin was a clergyman fated never to rise above the rank of curate, even though he was a popular preacher at the most fashionable of Dublin's Established Churches, St. Peter's. He operated a crammer for Trinity aspirants in his home and also realized some trifling financial return from selling the copyrights of his prose romances and stage melodramas to London publishers and theatrical managers. Maturin had the misfortune to start an artistic career just when Dublin was temporarily abandoned by people of substance as parliamentary power was transferred back from College Green to Westminster. After the passage of the Act of Union, his comparison of Dublin to a corpse, a skeleton, and the bones of Behemoth has already been cited. An early attempt to make a name as a dramatist in London ended disastrously, and he rarely left Dublin in later life. Yet a steady friendship with Sir Walter Scott, maintained entirely through correspondence, helped him to combat feelings of neglect and isolation (Ratchford and McCarthy, eds.).

LeFanu as well had close connections with the Church of Ireland. While his father was rector at Abington in East Limerick at the beginning of the 1830s, the entire family became targets for the intense resentment felt by the local Catholics—outnumbering the Abington Protestants by twenty to one—over tithe collecting. LeFanu became a barrister and went to London in 1838 to follow a career in law. Whatever happened, he returned precipitately to Dublin after only a few weeks in the British capital. Abandoning all plans to practice law, he increased his output of sketches, articles, and stories, which he had been contributing to several Dublin journals and papers since the middle 1830s. His first novels came out in the 1840s. After 1851, he intermitted novel writing for nearly a dozen years. The 1850s were a time of heavy domestic responsibilities and a period when LeFanu was preoccupied with *Dublin University Magazine*, of which he was the owner-editor, and as a spokesperson for Conservative-Unionist political interests. But after the death of his wife in 1858, he resumed fiction writing and rapidly produced the series of stories and novels, notably *The House by the Churchyard* (1863) and *Uncle Silas* (1864), for which he is most celebrated.

Both men shared a Huguenot inheritance. Although the Irish Huguenots were strongly identified with Irish Protestantism as a whole, and had been readily assimilated into the Ascendancy class from their first appearance in Ireland toward the end of the seventeenth century,[5] there were certain differences. If the Anglo-Irish Protestants felt isolated from and threatened by the overwhelming majority of the unfranchised and confiscated Catholic native Irish, "brooding over their discontents in sullen indignation," in the memorable words of John Fitzgibbon, (Lord Clare), then the Huguenots, as actual historic victims of Catholic massacre and expropriation in sixteenth- and seventeenth-century France, should have felt more isolated and threatened still. Yet paradoxically, there was a basis for covert identification between the Huguenot Protestants in Ireland and Irish Catholics. Both traditions showed a similar pattern of persecution, confiscation, and flight abroad in approximately the same era of the seventeenth-century wars of religion.

One must, however, proceed cautiously. For instance, although LeFanu's early stories offer sympathetic portrayals of exiled and attainted upper-class Irish Catholics of the Penal Era, this may less reflect the Huguenot connection than the romantic Irish nationalism Joseph Sheridan absorbed from his mother, a member of the Dublin Anglo-Irish Dobbin and Sheridan families who had made a cult in her girlhood of the aristocratic rebel, Lord Edward Fitzgerald.

Maturin reflected upon his Huguenot inheritance with greater extravagance. His first Gothic tale was the story he told, and may even have believed, about the origin of his own family. During the reign of Louis XIV, a great aristocratic lady stopped her carriage in a Paris street to pick up a swaddled infant abandoned there. She then raised this child as her own. Unfortunately the boy turned Protestant and became a minister. For that he was sent to the Bastille after the revocation of the Edict of Nantes in 1685, languishing there for twenty-six years and losing the use of his limbs. After release from prison the crippled cleric came to Ireland where he was reunited with his wife and two sons. From this persecuted and exiled family the Maturin Irish line was supposedly descended. However, Maturin also believed that his surname derived from a French Catholic religious community, *Les Maturins* (Ratchford and McCarthy, eds., 3).

In his historical romance *The Albigenses*, Maturin tried to trace the origins of the Huguenot sect to one Hugues of the Black Tower,[6] an Albigensian robber baron active in Languedoc in the thirteenth century. That was to connect oneself to a tradition of dissent ancient indeed. There is, however, no basis in history or etymology for interrelating Huguenots and Albigensians. Maturin annoyed his Arminian ecclesiastical superiors by espousing a "high Calvinism" and scandalized them by having stage works put on in London. At the same time he won little admiration from the other persuasion with his sermons on "the errors of Catholicism."[7] Deliberately seeking identification with persecuted ancestors, he moves toward the position of an internal migrant or exile in his Irish life. Of course, his greatest creation, John Melmoth the Traveller, even though he commands utter physical freedom in a work crammed with images and instances of imprisonment, sounds the exilic note in his extraordinary world traversals. In origin not precisely a Huguenot, the Wanderer is the next thing to it, being brother to an English Cromwellian who established himself on the Wicklow Coast in the mid-seventeenth century, founding an Anglo-Irish Protestant line, while brother John was mastering necromancy in Catholic Poland and bartering his soul for the doubtful advantage of a long life and a few spectacular Faustian powers.

Reading Maturin

Like the genre of Gothic prose romance itself, Maturin's writings are a mixture of absurdity and grandeur. He was never very sure of the audience for which he wrote, though that was normal for Anglo-Irish authors. However, some of Maturin's spectacular miscalculations in the conduct of his literary career suggest a downright will to fail.[8] A couple of examples will suffice. For his first published work, *Fatal Revenge; or, The Family of Montorio*, Maturin used the pseudonym Daniel Jasper Murphy. This name, in the opinion of his friends, "quite as much injured his literary reputation as the use of his own name could have damaged his professional standing, by reason of its 'vulgar and merely Irish sound'" (Ratchford and McCarthy, "Preface," 2).

Near the end of his writing life, hoping to revive his literary fortunes with a historical novel in the manner of Scott, Maturin largely wasted sixteen hundred pages in four volumes on *The Albigenses* (1824), a subject he could not possibly command, despite his undeniable learning, owing to his having no direct knowledge of Provence and the Pyrenees, and his having little access to essential documents concerning this remote and complex episode in medieval and papal religious politics. Not even sure how the heretics comported themselves as they were harried about the *Alpes-Pyrenees* by papal crusaders, he gave the Albigensian rank and file the look, the ranting religious rhetoric, and the quarrelsomeness of Scottish Covenanters.

Nevertheless, at other times Maturin well understood the basis of his strength as an imaginative writer:

> If I possess any talent, it is that of deepening the sad; of painting life in extremes, and representing those struggles of passion where the soul trembles on the verge of the unlawful and unhallowed.

Those last phrases presage Oscar Wilde, Maturin's blood kin, who borrowed half a nom-de-plume from Maturin's most famous romance. The passage is excerpted from the "Preface Dedicatory" to *The Milesian Chief* (1812). It is there also where he asserts that the representation of extremes is accomplished through depicting the actual, Ireland being the land where romantic and Gothic developments come to pass "hourly . . . before modern eyes" (1:20).

While this claim may be admitted up to a point, it did not always follow that Maturin's principal works combining Irish actualities with wild romantic story—*The Wild Irish Boy* (1808), and the aforementioned *Milesian Chief,* and *Women*—succeeded as works of art. In fact, Maturin's art accomplishes more with a purer Gothic, in the more encoded and symbolic modes where melodrama serves to elicit unacknowledged truths and buried feelings about Irish cultural dividedness.

Maturin's stage melodrama in blank verse, *Bertram; or, The Castle of St. Aldobrand*, is a case in point. Set in Sicily at an indeterminate period, its protagonist, Bertram, a Luciferian figure of "ruin'd grandeur," is a nobleman who early on sounds an exilic or Wildgoose note: "I have no country— / And for my race, the last dread trump shall wake / The sheeted relics of my ancestry" (2.3.26).

The story of Bertram is crazily simple and most evocative. The Lady Imogine has loved the noble Bertram, but the more powerful territorial usurper, St. Aldobrand, drove Bertram and his followers into exile, while Imogine, in order to save her father from dying of famine, became the usurper's wife. Languishing abroad, Bertram has become the leader of a traveling robber band and arrives back in the territory of St. Aldobrand, through the accident of shipwreck, at a time when St. Aldobrand is absent fighting a crusade. Bertram is recognized by the local prior, then meets up with Imogine, who at first does not recognize him. He begs a tryst of one hour, to which Imogine consents. Though she has been a faithful if melancholy wife, she now succumbs to her old love. While his robber band discreetly withdraws, Bertram lingers in concealment near the castle and slays St. Aldobrand from ambush as he returns from the crusade. Bertram then sequesters himself with his victim's corpse and makes no resistance when the castle knights arrive to arrest him. Imogine, torn between true love and wifely fidelity, goes mad, wandering out into the storm with her baby son (by St. Aldobrand, of course) who quickly dies of exposure. She puts the dead baby in a cave and is found close by in a distracted state by a search party—a procession really—consisting of the prior, monks, knights, sundry servants, and the manacled hero-murderer, who is being led out to execution.

An end-scene follows. Mad Imogine expires slowly in the enchained Bertram's arms. He snatches a weapon from an attendant knight and kills himself with it. The knights have little to say. It is left to the prior and an old nurse named Clothilda to sum up and clean up the shambles.

Must we read this farrago as coherent, intentional allegory? Obviously not. The London audiences, who cheered the play during an exceptionally long run of twenty performances when it was first produced, were apt to have missed its subtext entirely. But if we do allegorize our reading, here is how it may go. Assuming that Sicily, that much invaded island kingdom, equates with Ireland, then Imogine is the familiar dolorous archetype of Ireland as unhappy woman beset or contested, while Bertram is obviously the supplanted native aristocracy, and St. Aldobrand the English supplanter. At the roots of this fantasy exist both dread of a native revival and some longing for it, except that the covert wish is overbalanced by pessimism. For the consequence of attempted return is imagined as a murderous, maddening conflict in which virtually all lose. One notices that the baby son, even though he blends and reconciles the aboriginal and the supplanting strains or traditions, must die. The only nonloser of any stature on the scene at the end is the representative of the Church.

Of course, Maturin did not deliberately squirrel away a political allegory about Ireland in his Gothic melodrama of Sicily. Rather, the Anglo-Irish literary imagination is ineluctably haunted, cloven into duality by the cleavage in Irish society between settlers and natives. Nor is there any conviction, from the Ascendancy perspective, that the conflict can be negotiated to a solution. Not in 1816, not a hundred years and twenty years later. That is why the Old Man's cry at the end of Yeats's *Purgatory*—"O God / Release my mother's soul from its dream"—so perfectly echoes the prayer of the old Prior in *Bertram* as he surveys the wreckage of Imogine's sanity in the last scene and begs, "All-pitying Heaven—release her from this misery." The Anglo-Irish, then and later, as a class and a culture, are locked into their fate and must suffer it out to the very end.

Melmoth the Wanderer: A Tale (1820) is the one work where Maturin lives up to the fullest promise of his literary gift. It is probably the greatest of Gothic romances in English, and it is certainly a major work of Anglo-Irish literature. The romance is a marvelous baroque machine for generating (and detonating) narratives, for transforming, reversing and inverting, undermining and confounding relationships among narrators, characters, and readers, and it operates consistently at the highest level of literary intelligence. The style, sustained throughout the framing narrative and the six framed and nested main tales, the whole shaping an intricate verbal labyrinth that anticipates such works of structural exorbitancy as *Ulysses* and *At Swim-Two-Birds*, is sumptuous yet always controlled and functional, richly colored when the tale is of Immalee—Isadora on her fragrant and flowery Indian spice island; of burning eloquence in "The Tale of the Spaniard"; more spare and realistic in the tale of Guzman's starving family, the Walbergs, and in the opening chapters, set at old Melmoth's rundown lodge on the Wicklow coast in 1816.

This opening shows Maturin for once accomplishing his project of combining Irish actualities with the "wild and incredible" so effectively that the reader is swiftly drawn in and captivated. The key to that effect is, of course, the Wanderer himself, but how to understand that far- and swift-traveling Anglo-Irish man-demon, who is well over two hundred years old as the book opens and who is missing, presumed dead, only a few weeks later, at its close?

One cannot deal thoroughly with that question here. What can be done, however, is to suggest to what a large extent Melmoth's aggressions upon others, his sufferings, and his damnation are, from the beginning, entangled with, and emerge from, the background of Irish Ascendancy history in its darker aspects. Consider only the beginning of the work, as it is well-analyzed and summarized by its American editor, William F. Axton:

> Wherever the reader turns in *Melmoth*, he is confronted by . . . religious perversity, economic injustice, or political and social despotism. An omniscient third-person narrator's account of young John Melmoth's return to the deathbed of his miserly uncle gives way quickly to Biddy Brannigan's account of the Melmoth family's complicity in Cromwell's pitiless reduction of Ireland . . . and in the ruthless expropriation of Irish Catholics' lands by ambitious Roundheads. She also tells him the strange tale of an immortally young ancestor, the Wanderer. Thus from the beginning Melmoth is closely linked to the interrelated evils of sect and faction, and their exploitation by greedy and ambitious men. (xv)

On the final day and night of the Wanderer's presence on earth, the Anglo-Irish Protestant, John Melmoth, and the Spanish Catholic, Alonzo di Monçada, keep vigil outside the Wanderer's locked door in the nearly ruinous Wicklow Big House of the Melmoth clan. A point is made of telling the reader that the title character consumes his final hours in the very room where he was born. Thus is closed a circle that was drawn very far and wide in experience between the mid-seventeenth and early nineteenth centuries. In their much briefer lives the youthful John and Alonzo have abundantly experienced the consequences of sect and faction and the tyrannies these breed, the former vicariously as principal audience for the entire narrative's immense burden of pain and horror, the latter as the main victim in his own superbly narrated story, "The Tale of the Spaniard"; and as decoder and copyist at Madrid, in the old Jewish scholar Adonijah's underground refuge, of "The Tale of the Indians." Together they hear frightful sounds coming from the room during the night and in the morning find it empty. They then make out a trail from the house to the top of a tall rock overlooking the sea, where, presumably, the Wanderer jumped or was flung by devils to his death. At this conclusion John and Alonzo "exchanged looks of silent and unutterable horror, and returned slowly home" (412).

The moment is curiously ecumenical for that time and place. Inheriting Irish Protestant and disinherited Spanish Catholic wend their way toward a temporary shelter, which in its terminal dilapidation provides no safe harbor. They are bonded together by their youth, by one's having rescued the other from drowning, and by a shared knowledge of the "unutterable." Is one to think that John and Alonzo have learned sufficiently from what they have been through and from what has been related to avoid repeating the errors and excesses of their respective traditions? The subsequent history of Ireland, of Spain, and of the world suggests otherwise. The doggedly optimistic must contend with a sound of hideous laughter, which seems to bubble up from the depths of the Irish sea.

Mere generalization and structural diagrams convey little sense of the book's richness of style, its compelling narrative rhythms, its peculiarly satisfying imaginative eccentricity, and its emotional power. The following sketch of a commentary and occasional paraphrase, covering some aspects of the first half of the book, through the "Tale of the Spaniard" and Alonzo's election to the role of transcriber of the "Tale of the Indians," simply reports on a reading in progress, without any pretense of being a definitive interpretation, even of a part. It may, however, suggest why the work deserves to be much more widely known and appreciated.

"In the autumn of 1816," John Melmoth, a Dublin University student surviving on a very reduced allowance from his penurious uncle, hurries to the family seat on the Wicklow coast, where this uncle has become fatally ill. As it comes into view, the Melmoth estate is seen to be in appalling decline, with the gate lodge in ruins, the broken main gate hanging by a single hinge, all fences down, and the former great lawn changed to a wilderness of "pebble-stones, thistles, and hard mould. . . . The house itself stood strongly defined even amid the darkness of the evening sky; for there were neither wings, or offices, or shrubbery, or tree, to shade or support it, and soften its strong harsh outline" (7). It shows grass-grown main steps, boarded windows, and a knockerless front door. John fumbles his way to the kitchen entrance, where he discovers the old cook-housekeeper, in company with her neighborhood gossips, awaiting the master's end. There has been no medical attendance on the dying proprietor apart from a witchlike old woman, who has a local reputation as a practitioner of what may charitably be called "folk medicine." The foundational third-person narrator explains how this mostly means practicing on the ignorance and superstition of her clients:

> No one, in short, knew better how to torment or terrify her victims into a belief of that power which may and has reduced the strongest minds to

> the level of the weakest; and under the influence of which the cultivated skeptic, Lord Lyttleton, yelled and gnashed and writhed in his last hours, like the poor girl who, in the belief of the horrible visitation of the vampire, shrieked aloud, that her grandfather was sucking her vital blood while she slept, and expired under the influence of an imaginary horror. Such was the being to whom old Melmoth had committed his life, half from credulity, and (*Hibernice* speaking) *more than half* from avarice. (8)

The longer sentence above becomes more astounding as it prolongs itself. It exhibits in miniature Maturin's general narrative procedure of allowing new fictions to proliferate in the midst of a story already under way. It is not so much a method of digression as one of superfetation. The second sentence shows Maturin paying his respects to Maria Edgeworth's "documentary" realism, while also playing self-consciously to his presumed English readership by deliberately perpetrating an "Irish" (*Anglice*) bull. Soon the narrator will remark that the housekeeper's friends have names, "which we shall spare the English reader the torture of reciting, (as a proof of our lenity [giving] the last only, Cotchleen O'Mulligan)" (10). This Anglo-Irish *mauvaise honte* disappears even before the primary narration is broken into and transformed by the long series of actor narrators, both major and minor.

Just off the miser's bedroom is a closet anteroom containing an ancestral portrait inscribed "Jno Melmoth, anno 1646." Before sinking into death, old Uncle Melmoth tells his nephew that the original of the picture is still alive. He looked middle-aged in 1646. In 1816 he ought to look indescribably ancient. As the miser dies, the door of the death chamber opens twice; each time the nephew sees peering in a man closely resembling the portrait. The second time he is "beckoning and nodding to him with a familiarity somewhat terrifying" (15). Every distinguished family has a skeleton, but here is one still clothed in flesh and still vigorously living. If only he would talk, his reminiscences would beat even the conscientious indiscretions of *The Black Book of Edgeworthstown* into a cocked hat. It is the Wanderer himself who looks in. He will talk, but not before the book is nearly done, when he speaks at length in the surprisingly class-conscious "Tale of the Mortimers." Be that as it may, a will is found designating John the nephew as sole heir to the dead man's considerable if neglected estate. A note found with the will adjures the heir to destroy the closet portrait and to discover a manuscript tied with black tape, which he may read or omit reading before burning it. This manuscript proves to contain "The Tale of Stanton," and, of course, he reads it.

But first, Maturin's reader must attend to the old housekeeper's story of the tall figure seen in the courtyard at the very moment the uncle had his fatal stroke, and the "odd story" told by Biddy Brannigan, the practitioner in folk medicine, of how the Melmoth family established itself in Ireland, how the portrait of the brother was painted in 1646, how this brother, coming to be known as the Traveller or Wanderer, lived on and on, only appearing at the Wicklow demesne to augur the death of family members of evil character, and how the unfortunate Englishman Stanton came searching for the Traveller in the Restoration Era of the seventeenth century, leaving behind the manuscript describing his transactions with Melmoth when that man or demon himself failed to appear.

The reader by now may begin to wonder who does *not* have a tale to tell or write. Or is Maturin conducting a clinic on storytelling per se? Both these accounts are structured as *oratio obliqua*—indirect discourse—the servant's subsumed within the general narrative, the practitioner's internal to young Melmoth's reflection, during sleepless hours spent alone in the gloomy house, upon what she has revealed to him. He now goes to find the secreted manuscript and begins to read it to himself by bad light—the candles are burning blue[9]—just after midnight in the autumn of the year.

Stanton's story is recapitulated by the foundational narrator of *Melmoth* as a whole. While traveling across a darkling Spanish plain near the ruins of a Roman amphitheater and a Moorish fortress, he met some peasants carrying the corpses of a pair of lovers killed by lightning. An Englishman with a maniacal laugh suddenly arrives on the scene. Here the manuscript becomes illegible. When it becomes legible again, Stanton is just entering a house in Valencia, the mistress of which has a particular horror of Englishmen. She starts a story of the house, only to have the Stanton manuscript become illegible again, though only for a few lines. Her tale-within-Stanton's-within the general narrative is about the splendid Cardoza family nuptials, held in this very house in a festive chamber hung with tapestries depicting the "beautiful" torturing of "a few Moors who refused to renounce their accursed religion" (24). An Englishman had been a silent member of this happy party. Father Olavida, a distinguished casuist, attempted to engage the foreigner in theological debate. However, it proved no contest when the Englishman, exercising supernatural powers, simply willed the sudden death of both the priest and the bride, escaping in the horror-struck confusion that ensued.

Just once in this reported account do the actual words employed by the Valencian lady appear: "He [the bridegroom] never recovered his reason; the family deserted the mansion rendered terrible by so many misfortunes. One apartment is still tenanted by the unhappy maniac; his were the cries you heard as you traversed the deserted rooms." (27). After that comes a new outbreak of hiatuses and illegible passages. The reader begins to suspect that these narrative breaks are arranged so as to cover up various revelations about the Wanderer's activities, which he does not want exposed. In short, *he* has been at Stanton's manuscript, perhaps not writing anything in but editing out and erasing—what? Perhaps anything that might put a future reader on guard against his baleful influence. Maturin's reader will make this surmise, while Stanton's reader, young John Melmoth, will not. These discrepant responses are a part of Maturin's compositional strategy.

The scene of Stanton's story now shifts to London, around the year 1677. The general narrator provides a brilliant guided tour of the Restoration theaters in a style that owes a good deal to Evelyn and Pepys. In one of the theaters poor Stanton encounters the sinister stranger from the plain in Spain. He wishes to question him, but the stranger says it must be another time, adding that they will be sure to meet again: "*I never desert my friends in misfortune.* When they are plunged in the lowest abyss of calamity, *they are sure to be visited by me*" (34). That promise is fulfilled when they next meet in the cell of the lunatic asylum where Stanton's scheming younger relative has put him in order to secure for himself the family inheritance. While awaiting processing by the keepers, and in fact before even realizing where he has been brought, Stanton discovers a manuscript volume—"the album of a madhouse"—in which inmates have recorded from time to time their deranged fantasies and demented conceptions of the world and of themselves. This frequent conversion of agents and patients into writers and readers is one of the most arresting features of *Melmoth.*

Stanton's chief torment in this place is to know that he is sane, whereas the other inmates merely suppose that they are.[10] The stranger, who is, of course, the demon Melmoth, cruelly predicts, "You will wish to become one of them, to escape the agony of consciousness" (45). The sane inmate is particularly disturbed by the yelling and screaming that goes on: for instance, from the religious bigot whose moral denunciations in daylight, through the law of the return of the repressed, change at night into hideous and obscene blaspheming of God, the Cross, and the Christian faith; the howlings of someone suffering from alcoholic dementia; the pitiful crying of the mad mother who has lost all her little ones and her husband in the Great London Fire: "It was remarkable that when this sufferer began to rave, all the others became silent. The cry of nature hushed every other cry,—she was the only patient in the house who was not mad from politics, religion, ebriety [*sic*], or some other perverted passion;[11] and terrifying as the outbreak of her frenzy always was, Stanton used to await it as a kind of relief from the . . . ravings of the others" (40). Here emerging for the first time, this emphasis on natural feeling and the moral authority of nature will become the leading positive theme of *Melmoth*, underlying all its investigation of corruption in high civilization, in organized religion, in familial and other personal relationships, in human passion.

The "Tale of Stanton" is drastically foreshortened when the last fifteen manuscript pages prove illegible. Again one suspects it is a trick of the Wanderer, in his other guise as roving editor. Stanton escaped the lunatic asylum somehow, came searching for Melmoth in Ireland, "of which I find he is a native," and his last bit of decipherable writing says, "Perhaps our final meeting will be in——" (45). The blank is not as easy to fill in as one might imagine. It will not be Hell, because Stanton never did barter his soul's salvation as Melmoth tempted him to do; and it will not be Paradise, because Melmoth, despite Immalee's dying hope to see him there, will not be allowed in. Nor is it easy to surmise why Stanton should come after this sinister and threatening being in the first place. For he has already withstood the demon's temptation to exchange his salvation for his freedom, and it's unlikely he tried to follow him to his Irish abode merely to gird at him. Stanton knows the fate of Father Olavida, who merely tried to debate the "Englishman." The same questions come up in connection with the next major story, the "Tale of the Spaniard," since it will be narrated by someone who had been another of Melmoth's targets for temptation, and who came all the way from Madrid to Wicklow, presumably because he was tracking the Wanderer to his ultimate lair.

Before turning to this splendid narrative, an entire Gothic romance in itself, we must come back briefly to the framing narrative, which commenced with the book's first sentence. Following his uncle's wishes, young John Melmoth destroys the portrait. A night of severe storm ensues and a ship begins to wreck off the coastal shoals and cliffs. John hastens to the shore, where he glimpses the vessel in distress, then notices his own living ancestor, the Traveller, standing on a tall rock, laughing his demoniac laugh and crying, "Let them perish" (50). While clambering up the rocks to reach Melmoth and to protest his outrageous behavior, John faints and falls into the water. From there he is rescued by a sole survivor off the wreck, the young Spaniard, Alonzo di Monçada, who is swimming ashore and carries John with him to safety. After a period of delirium and general illness, John is visited by a "grave and decent" local priest, Father Fay, who alerts him to the fact that he, the young Irish Protestant, owes his very life to Alonzo, the young Spaniard of Catholic background. The least John can do is thank him and inquire whether he has a tale to tell. Alonzo has one indeed.

The tale told to John Melmoth over many nights is a triumph of style as well as an account of long-continued resistance to tyranny in many forms, from improperly exercised parental authority, to the thought-control exercised by a decadent monastic rule, to the spectacular oppressions of a revived Spanish Inquisition. Its language is elaborate and polished, marked by extraordinary analytical power, and a daunting intellectual poise and authority. It is a fantasticated style, whether we speculate—fruitlessly—as to how a neglected, callow, tormented, and continuously imprisoned Spanish stripling came into its possession, or revert to its ultimate sources in the literary gifts of a shabby and neurotic Dublin clergyman, scribbling in solitude through the night, sustained by copious draughts of brandy.

Even as a child Alonzo was a monastery inmate, owing to his illegitimacy and the intention of his noble parents, egged on by their priestly director, to force him to take monkish vows at the earliest possible time. He did, however, enjoy one visit home, during which he briefly met his grandfather, his younger brother, and his now properly married parents, a glamorous pair whose youthful good looks, wealth, and prominence in Madrid society apparently cannot erase their guilt for having conceived their child out of wedlock. Alonzo has only a glimpse of this grandfather and here, in part, is how he records his impression: "I was hurried through several apartments, whose splendour made my eyes ache, amid an army of bowing domestics, to a cabinet where sat an old nobleman, whom, from the tranquil majesty of his posture, and the silent magnificence that surrounded him, I felt disposed to fall down and worship as we do those saints, whom, after traversing the aisles of an immense church, we find niched in some remote and solitary shrine" (55).

The impression is dreamlike, for the boy is still young enough to confuse fantasy and reality, while his worshipful reaction to the old man's presence is "Catholic" and "idolatrous."[12] Alonzo is still a considerable time away from his discovery, after being forced, or rather, emotionally blackmailed,[13] into a novitiate at the Convent of the Ex-Jesuits, that he has instinctively "Protestant" leanings. These will appear in his attachment to the Bible as God's full revelation of Himself, by his habit of appealing to reason and conscience, instead of to ecclesiastical authority and tradition in determining moral cruxes, and in his spontaneous revulsion against such mortifications as self-flagellation and fasting. The very form, however, of the beautiful sentence quoted above tells us at least as much as its content. It is splendidly baroque, especially in the processional swing of its successive dependent clauses, its highly organized balance of phrases, its orotundity and majestic pointing. Alonzo handles his bewildering and demeaning experience, and it *is* demeaning to be rushed without explanation through strange rooms to encounter an imposing stranger, in the language, not of a victim, but of a grandee.

The effect is for the language to set at defiance the misery and lack of personal autonomy about which the language is reporting. This effect can be made out again and again in the "Tale of the Spaniard." For example, during his forced novitiate, Alonzo attends an old monk on his deathbed in the convent infirmary and hears from him that a lifetime of religious devotion and self-suppression has revealed only that monasteries are identical to secular prisons. Quite convinced, for that has been his own impression, the despairing novice rushes away to the convent garden:

> The garden, with its calm moonlight beauty, its innocence of heaven, its theology of the stars, was at once a reproach and a consolation to me. I tried to reflect, to feel,—both efforts failed; and perhaps it is in this silence of the soul, this suspension of all the clamorous voices of the passions, that we are most ready to hear the voice of God. My imagination suddenly represented to me the august and ample vault above me as a church,—the images of the saints grew dim in my eyes as I gazed on the stars, and even the altar, over which the crucifixion of the Saviour of the world was represented, turned pale to the eye of the soul, as I gazed on the moon "walking in her brightness." I fell on my knees. (90)

If the monastery-prison is labyrinthine in its capacity to thwart all escape attempts—except into death—we here see Alonzo temporarily flying free on winged words. Perhaps in this instance they are words smuggled to him out of Maturin's reading in the major English romantics. However, as the novice's situation becomes more desperate we shall need different images: language as a tunneling device, as rations for mere survival, and finally, as light shining at the end of a tunnel, making real the dream of escape.

The climax of Alonzo's desperate career in the monastery is reached when he undertakes to escape, in company with the brutish parricidal monk, through the underground vaults and passages, only to enter a narrow *couloir* ending at a blank wall. Their candles gutter out in the noisome air. It is impossible to find the way back. Evidently both are doomed to die there in the dark. Part of Alonzo's torment entails his intuition of a certain kinship to his criminal companion, who originally claims sanctuary in the convent after murdering his own father during a drinking bout. For Monçada, in keeping up his determined refusal to take final vows, has opposed himself to both parents and to such compelling authority figures as the director, the monastery superior, and even to the Catholic Church as a whole. At his worst moments the novice worries that his resistance may be a damnable defiance of God's will (*Melmoth*, 150). Not long before they entered the cul-de-sac, the parricide had declared that they must escape together or not at all, and that they must remain permanently together, whether and if they ever got out. Even escape appears as the equivalent of another life sentence. But what does it matter, thinks Alonzo, since their situation at the wall is patently without hope?

Immediately ensues a brilliant disquisition on hopelessness—"this fiery thirst of the soul for communication where all communication was unutterable. Perhaps the condemned spirits will feel thus at their final sentence, when they know all that is to be suffered, and dare not disclose to each other that horrible truth which is no longer a secret, but which the profound silence of their despair would seem to make one. The secret of silence is the only secret. Words are a blasphemy against that taciturn and invisible God, whose presence enshrouds us in our last extremity" (151). This says quite the opposite of what it seems to say. Silence is the language of despair. Words "blaspheme" against a "taciturn" God, but that deity is the giant Despair. In hopelessness, words are the only hope. It seems less the insight of a distressed religious in love with religion than of a distressed writer in love with writing. In any event, these eloquent words help Alonzo to survive at the dark wall until hope flares up again and a way out is found.

Eventually Alonzo will escape his oppressors, and it is appropriate that the way out should be through writing, writing as the physical act of putting marks on paper and as literary production. This happens as he arrives at the underground cell of the old Jewish savant Adonijah, after having escaped the monastery, escaped the dungeons of the Inquisition during a fire most likely started by the Wanderer himself, escaped that gentleman, who, during Monçada's stay with the Inquisition, had been up to his old trick of offering a prisoner immediate freedom in exchange for his hope of salvation, and even escaped the pressing attentions of the parricide when that bloody man was torn to pieces by an aroused street mob. Quite by accident Alonzo has sought refuge in the house of a Jew named Solomon, who passes for Catholic. When agents of the Holy Office rap on the door, Solomon shows him a trap door and Alonzo drops down it like a hunted rabbit, finding himself once again in a tunnel: "Amid this temporary magnanimity of despair, this state of mind which unites the extremes of courage and pusillanimity, I saw a faint light" (201). This shining comes from the strangely furnished room of Adonijah, at the end of the tunnel. The Sephardi is extremely old—and, by a remarkable coincidence, has been slowly compiling that part of the Wanderer's history comprised by the "Tale of the Indians." He needs a copyist, someone who can read a Spanish written out in the Greek alphabet, and that Alonzo can do. The Spanish youth's sudden arrival at his hideout and study—it is also a paleontological museum filled with a variety of articulated skeletons—must seem to Adonijah like the work of heaven.

The episode is one of the oddest, yet most charming, versions in literature of someone's being pursued and overtaken by the literary vocation. Adonijah's skeletons include several of his own deceased relations and those of personages in the "history" he has been setting down. Even the remains of Immalee-Isidora, the pathetic heroine of "The Indians' Tale," may have their niche there. When Alonzo is reluctant to begin his task, fearing that Melmoth will be furious with him for writing down some of his secret life, Adonijah admonishes him that he must write precisely because his own encounters with the Wanderer link him in sympathy to persons in the story he is to copy. "Snatching a skeleton from its receptacle, he placed it before me, saying to the skeleton, 'Tell him the story thyself, peradventure he will believe thee, and record it'" (208). The Jew then points a hand at the manuscript as bony and bleached "as that of the dead." A lovely brief paragraph follows, serving as prologue to the "The Indians' Tale," the story of Immalee's doomed love for the Wanderer:

> It was a night of storms in the world above us; and far below the surface of the earth as we were, the murmur of the winds, sighing through the passages, came on my ear like the voices of the departed,—like the pleadings of the dead. Involuntarily I fixed my eye on the manuscript I was to copy and never withdrew it until I had finished its extraordinary contents. (208)

The passage suggests a compelling reason for going to the trouble of reading and writing—to heed the pleadings of the dead to be remembered.[14] Alonzo now seems caught up in the complete literary act as he winds up his story about himself that he has been *telling* John Melmoth in Wicklow and goes on to *relate* how he *read* and then *inscribed* afresh, in a partial act of *translation*, *transliterating* from one alphabet to another the final major story in the narrative chain comprising *Melmoth the Wanderer*. It is an edifying moment, perhaps intentionally designed to distract the reader from realizing that Alonzo di Monçada has not, after all, found his way to freedom. He has only exchanged cell for cell, the tedium, viciousness, and risk of the monastic and inquisitorial confinements for the drudgery—and the risk—of literary occupation. He will, nonetheless, escape in good time, arriving in Wicklow with several good stories to pass on.

The Sephardi's rather capacious cell also contains the articulated skeleton of a giant elk. Such a prehistoric trophy has been on display at Trinity College, Dublin, during several centuries. Was this a way for Maturin to signal the reader that he, not Adonijah, or Alonzo either, was the underground writer to whom everything narrated in *Melmoth* should ultimately be credited? If so, the reminder was unnecessary. We never escape Charles Robert Maturin, of Huguenot descent, at least on his father's side, whose work, as with so many of the great romantics, shows a strong autobiographical impulse. Four principal themes of the "Tale of the Spaniard" are illegitimacy, persecution for "Protestant" convictions, imprisonment, and an escape abroad that exchanges one Catholic country and society for another. These same themes were central to what I called Maturin's first Gothic tale, his account of the tribulations of his Huguenot ancestors and how the family came to be established in Ireland. Like the *Aeneid*, this part of *Melmoth* is or contains a myth of founding. More narrowly, Maturin's alienation from Irish Catholic culture and society, along with his difficulties vis-à-vis ecclesiastical superiors in his own Established Church are mirrored in the woes and frustrations of young Alonzo. To recognize this is to take nothing away from the great achievement of Anglo-Irish Gothic's greatest prose romance.

Reading LeFanu

In Maturin's time the social pattern of Ireland shows a fairly straightforward contrast between Ascendancy haves and native have-nots. The chief event was the debacle of the Union, that discreditable episode by which all the Irish lost. Living later in the century and living longer, LeFanu was involved in more complex and changing social and political conditions—from Catholic Emancipation and the Tithe War, through the great famine and the abortive Rising of 1848, to the era of "Fenian Fever," Church Disestablishment, and the first stirrings of Home Rule in the final years of his life. By 1873 Anglo-Ireland had entered its phase of final contraction, though it was not evident at the time and there was still a way to go before nightfall. Not surprisingly, the sensitive antennae of the artist picked up signals of an end to come:

> One of the most recurrent of the weird dreams that haunted LeFanu . . . was of a vast and mysterious crumbling old mansion—of the type which he had often recounted in his tales—threatening imminently to fall upon and crush him. (Varma, ed., ii)

It would be too obvious to comment that this is the house of Anglo-Irish tradition itself, which has been crumbling ever since *Castle Rackrent* and even earlier. Two other points to make about LeFanu's fiction—certainly organizing principles of "metapolitical" character—are perhaps less obvious.

In LeFanu's writing there is a significant interplay, sometimes a willed confusion, between the idea of possession, by apparent demons or ghosts, and the idea of dispossession, as in the loss of property, power, status. Put another way, there is a convergence in LeFanu's imagination between demonic and supernatural "possession" and the age-old Irish tragedy—never to be eluded by Anglo-Irish persons of tender conscience—of appropriation and dispossession. Second, LeFanu's fiction is full of hauntings: his special gift and effect, however, is often to make it appear that the living are being haunted by the living, by material creatures commanding fell physical force and an intense mental desire to exact revenge and do mischief far beyond the powers of the insubstantial dead.

Perhaps that is a common effect in nineteenth-century Irish life because of the two communities: one apparently in control yet outnumbered; the other in servitude yet much larger and longer in the land; both occupying the same small territory side by side and sometimes closer than that, but not reconciled, the majority constantly watching the privileged minority, coming to haunt its dreams, which are of crumbling mansions under ghostly siege, or at the point of falling. One does not even have to go to ghost stories for literary illustration. Major Yeates in Somerville and Ross's "Great Uncle McCarthy," the opening story of *Some Experiences of an Irish R. M.* (1899), suspected his house was haunted by famished spirits, owing to night noises and the fearful rate at which his kitchen provisions and liquor were disappearing. Only it turned out that there was a numerous family of native McCarthys squatting in a remote, unvisited attic, coming and going by unknown passages, and living high off his food and drink. There is a chapter called "Spinsters' Ball" in George Moore's *A Drama in Muslin* (1886). At the height of the Land War, the daughters of the estate owners in a western district organize a dance party at a vacant school and become uncomfortably aware—those who are more sensitive—of the hungry and ragged country people outside in the dark, crowding at the windows, gazing in like specters upon the far-from-brilliant scene.

With LeFanu, the matter typically goes beyond merely gazing and spying, as the specter or demon presses upon and assaults its victim like a living enemy. A story called "The Familiar," in another version called "The Watcher," provides the essential paradigm.[15] In 1794, Naval Captain Barton, retired to Dublin after British service during the American Revolution, is stalked by a "familiar," who begins by dogging and echoing his footsteps on a deserted street late at night, then sends him hate letters signed "A Watcher," then is manifest as a rageful little man in a fur cap and red vest, perhaps like a radical republican or rank-and-file United Irishman of the period, and believed by Barton to resemble closely a former crewman in the vessel he had commanded. After the captain has been fired upon from ambush along the same lonely road, he consults a learned Trinity College preacher, Dr. Macklin, and describes experiences that sound like a sublimation of Ascendancy political *angst* in the context of late-eighteenth-century tension between the two communities:

> I have been mercifully allowed intervals of repose though none of security; but from the consciousness that a malignant spirit is following and watching me wherever I go, I have never, for a single instant, a temporary respite. I am pursued with blasphemies, cries of despair, and appalling hatred. I

> hear those dreadful sounds called after me as I turn the corners of the streets; they come in the night-time, while I sit in my chamber alone; they haunt me everywhere, charging me with hideous crimes, and—great God!—threaten me with coming vengeance and eternal misery. (*Best Ghost Stories*, 226)

Dr. Macklin surmises that Barton's essential problem is one of conscience, but another friend, tough-minded General Montague, thinks the captain is being harassed by an agitator:

> a certain little man in a cap and greatcoat with a red vest and a bad face, who follows you about, and pops upon you at corners of lanes. . . . Now my dear fellow, I'll make it my business to *catch* this mischievous little mountebank, and either beat him to a jelly with my own hands, or have him whipped through the town at the cart's tail, before a month passes. (229)

The malignant little man—the familiar—will not be denied, even though Barton sequesters himself behind the stout walls of a fortified house at Clontarf.[16] The demon will invade the captain's living space and the captain in the end must surrender his tormented existence with the acknowledgment that there is a certain rough justice in his fate:

> "A grudge, indeed, he owes me—you say rightly," said Barton with a certain shudder; "a grudge you call it. Oh, my God: when the justice of Heaven permits the Evil One to carry out a scheme of vengeance—when its execution is committed to the lost and terrible victim of sin, who owes his own ruin to the man, the very man, whom he is commissioned to pursue, then, indeed, the torments and terrors of hell are anticipated on earth." (237)

Six years earlier, at Plymouth, Captain Barton had ruined and harassed to his death a man in his command who had bitterly protested Barton's seduction of his young daughter. The familiar is the demonic specter of that outraged father.

A similar pattern is evident in LeFanu's many stories centering on the Faustian pact, including "The Haunted Baronet," a novella of 1861, which is one of his most brilliantly styled works. In both "Sir Dominick's Bargain" (1861) and the much earlier "The Fortunes of Sir Robert Ardagh" (1839), the unfortunate aristocrats are called to pay with their lives and their souls in identical words of "leveling tendency": "If he'll not come down to me, I'll go up to him." Also, the demon figure in the former story changes over its course from spruce young recruiting officer offering gold, to sooty smith, to a squat, powerful stranger who appears to be spoiling not only for poor Sir Dominick's soul but also to tear the social fabric to tatters.

With respect to the motif of possession and dispossession, the most haunting, because most literal, use comes in the tale called "Ultor de Lacey: A Legend of Cappercullen," dating from 1862. It is set in Ireland during the years following Culloden. The noble de Laceys, twice attainted owing to the father's Jacobite political sympathies, retreat to the ruins of the family's former vast estates at Cappercullen, and the lovely daughters pass themselves off as fairy folk in order to stop the children of the local peasantry from spying on the family's illegal repossession of the demesne. All goes well and the story has a weird charm until it ends horrifically when a resident demon at home in the ruins, a "real" ghost this time, captures the affections, and the life, of one of the daughters.

LeFanu in his fiction sometimes used Swedenborgian definitions of evil and evil spirits. A few of these notions are conveniently brought together in the third chapter of LeFanu's famous story "Green Tea," when Dr. Heselius, practitioner in "metaphysical medicine," having gone to see his tormented patient, the Reverend Mr. Jennings, takes note, while waiting in the library, of certain underlinings Jennings has made in the eight-volume Latin text of Emmanuel Swedenborg's *Arcana Caelestia* (1749–56). These underlinings make four main points: 1) Man has a faculty of interior sight; it is ordinarily sealed up yet may open, even from an accidental cause such as drinking too much green tea. When this "unsealing" occurs, the subject becomes aware of a world of spirits interpenetrating, or co-inhabiting with man, the visible and material world. 2) With every person are two evil spirits, one harsh and reproving, the other creeping and thought-invading. Until someone's interior sight is unsealed, these spirits remain as ignorant of that person's existence, as the person was ignorant of them. 3) When evil spirits perceive their association with a person they feel an intense hatred and use a thousand means to torment and destroy the person. 4) Through a principle of correspondence, an evil spirit, as it becomes known to its human host, may take a bestial form ("fera") representing the spirit's particular "lust and life" (*Best Ghost*, 187). Thus we get the monkey in "Green Tea," the panther in LeFanu's great vampire story, "Carmilla," the owl that goes crashing out through the skylight just as Captain Barton's friends discover him dead in "The Familiar," and the macaw, jay, kite, and ape in "The Haunted Baronet."

A couple of these points are worth taking up. There may seem something a little childish and wishful in the idea that what cannot be apprehended in the realm of the spirit cannot harm. Against this forlorn hope must be weighed the sad fact that in Swedenborg's scheme of things the human subject, as he or she falls under the influence of evil, is usually singled out and overmatched. At the very least it will be two against one. Of course, the victim in "Green Tea" is attacked by a single demon—though Mr. Jenning's monkey disappears from time to time, presumably to consult with others of its kind, and there is something besides the monkey creeping into his thoughts and driving him toward suicide. On the other hand, Sir Bale Mardyke in "The Haunted Baronet" comes under attack by at least four or five spirits: the three represented by the birds—these also showing a human form from time to time—; the water demon whose shadow is seen just under the surface of the lake during some fateful crossings; and whatever has gotten into Philip Feltram after his drowning, resurrected him, and is somehow controlling his body until Sir Bale has been safely ensnared. Carmilla, Countess Karnstein, that most ingratiating and lively of vampires, goes pretty much one on one as she settles to her work, yet the older woman who poses as her mother, the servants manning her crested coach-and-four, and even the black horses that go wild at the sight of the old stone cross in the Styrian forest must be demons too. It seems after all that Carmilla owes her success to something like a backup crew, if not an entire corporate organization.

Victims of evil in LeFanu divide up into sinners—mainly the Faustian Bargainers—and those more or less innocent like the de Laceys and Mr. Jennings. Then there are the sheer innocents such as Maud Ruthyn in *Uncle Silas*, whose only crime has been to come into the property desperately coveted by her homicidal uncle and his brutish son, Dudley Ruthyn. Though permeated by Swedenborgian atmosphere, this best-known of LeFanu's novels does not use his doctrines as a key to the novel's mystery plot and moral themes. It may even offer a critique of Swedenborg and his followers' understanding of how wickedness actually operates in the world.

To begin with, in *Uncle Silas*, as in Henry James's "The Turn of the Screw," to which it bears strong resemblance, evil, even without settling the question of its origin and nature, whether natural or supernatural, flourishes where a parent abdicates the duty to care for and protect his vulnerable, isolated, dependent child, the seventeen-year-old Maud Ruthyn. The irony is that while Austin Ruthyn is mooning about at his Swedenborgian exercises and devotions, the sadistic French governess, Madam de la Rougepierre, is handed her chance to exercise malign influence at Knowl. Ruthyn is even more at fault for his decision, embodied in his will and carried out after his death, to put Maud and her vast inheritance under the guardianship of his reprobate brother Silas, until she is twenty-one.

This decision flies in the face of known facts—about Silas's earlier career of vicious folly and depravity, his persisting opium addiction and distressed fortunes, his bad public reputation as a murder suspect who was never charged by a grand jury only because the victim's body was never located. Austin thought he would clear the family escutcheon of a large stain by giving brother Silas the chance to show the world how well he can look after his niece. But when the girl, following the reading of her father's will, moves from Knowl to Silas's estate at Bartram-Haugh, she is moving into a death trap. The first cause of her deadly peril is her own father's insensate pride of family, his willful indifference to obvious truths, and a type of moral isolationism, or moral experimentalism, his esoteric studies may well have fostered.

Perhaps all we are saying is that Austin was somewhat unbalanced in his mind and feelings, for whatever reason. Let us turn then to the dry and sensible Swedenborgian physician and family adviser, Dr. Bryerly. He certainly cares about Maud's well-being and is very concerned for her safety after she moves to the walled demesne of Bartram-Haugh. It's hard, however, to approve the advice he gives her as he senses her loneliness and exposure following her father's death:

> "Remember, then, that when you fancy yourself alone and wrapt in darkness, you stand, in fact, in the centre of a theatre, as wide as the starry floor of heaven, with an audience, whom no man can number, beholding you under a flood of light. Therefore, though your body be in solitude and your mortal sense in darkness, remember to walk as being in the light, surrounded with a cloud of witnesses." (125–26)

Where is the comfort or use in this counsel? To stand blind amid a myriad of sighted witnesses who look on but never help, or to attempt to walk about under such conditions may be worse than learning to stand and move in desert darkness. Maud actually survives Uncle Silas's and Cousin Dudley's murder plot against her by finally making friends with the dark, standing perfectly still in the shadows while Dudley butchers the snoring governess by mistake, stealing out of the death house along unlighted corridors and stairways, and making her way to safety at Lady Monica Knolly's through dense woods under the night's protective cover. This development is not new in LeFanu's fiction. His first novel, *The Cock and Anchor* (1845), a book quite free of Swedenborgian coloration, shows his heroine, Mary Ashbrooke, saving her virtue and probably her life as well by escaping in the dark from a house near the Phoenix Park, where she was being held close prisoner.

As long as one remembers that the chief evildoers in *Uncle Silas* are human malefactors, not demons, one is free to enjoy and admire the many demonic touches in their presentation. Operating as a technique of "defamiliarization," the demonic imagery strengthens, and sometimes subtilizes, the representation of evil. Maud herself is the narrator. As she was brought up sharing a sequestered life with a father deeply absorbed since the death of his wife in spiritualist studies, it's no surprise she sees things as she does. Thus, of Madame de la Rougepierre at Knowl she says, "she had designs of domination and subversion regarding the entire household, I now think, worthy of the evil spirit I sometimes fancied her" (23). Glimpsed eavesdropping outside Austin's study door, she looks to Maud like "a great avid reptile." When Maud and Madame go walking in the woods the latter talks of knowing a monkey ghost and appears "as if she expected to see something unearthly, and, indeed, looked very like it herself" (27). Mrs. Rusk, the commonplace and routinely xenophobic Knowl housekeeper, can endorse this impression in her own way. For her, Madame is not only "this inauspicious foreigner" (30), but also "a nice limb [of Satan]" "an old cat," "a devil," "not right" . . . "a witch or a ghost—I should not wonder" (31).

Also, Madame plays at being an evil or unclean spirit, or warlock, or animated corpse on her own initiative. There is her favorite song, said to be a Breton ballad, about a lady with the head of a swine:

> This lady was neither pig nor maid,
> And so she was not of human mould;
> Not of the living nor the dead.
> Her left hand and foot were warm to touch;
> Her right as cold as a corpse's flesh! . . .
> A mongrel body and demon soul.
>
> (32)

The governess drags Maud to the graveyard at Church Scarsdale and cackles, "See 'ow many grave-stones—one, *two* hundred. Don't you love the dead, cheaile? I will teach you to love them. You shall see me die here, today, for half an hour, and be among them. That is what I love . . . I am Madam la Morgue—Mrs. Deadhouse! I will present you my friends, Monsieur Cadavre and Monsieur Squelette" (34). Her motive in this display is to break Maud down by frightening and horrifying her. For the governess is already in touch with Uncle Silas's establishment through Cousin Dudley and is part of the developing conspiracy to get the youthful heiress under Silas's total control. Madame de la Rougepierre is truly morbid, sadistic, perhaps necrophilic, and more than a little mad, but these qualities define her nature, not her supernature.

While the governess is lavishly awful, the touches of the horrible in the portrayal of the reclusive Uncle Silas, who pretends to be a visionary like his older brother—probably as a cover for his frequent opium trances—are more subtle. When Maud finally comes face to face with him she registers "a face like marble, with a fearful monumental look" (192). He is an "apparition, drawn as it seemed in black and white, venerable, bloodless, fiery-eyed" (192). The startling contrast the eyes make looks back to Melmoth the Wanderer. He, too, exhibited the contrast between a dead white countenance and eyes lighted with a hellfire glow. Silas's eyes are "wild . . . hollow, fiery, awful! It sometimes seemed as if the curtain opened, and I had seen a ghost" (197). The more she sees of her uncle, the more he seems to her neither living nor dead. Instead, his is "a dubious, marsh-fire existence, horrible to look on" (261). Even commonsensical Lady Monica compares Silas to Michael Scott, "a dead wizard, with ever so much silvery hair, lying in his grave for ever so many years" (264).

How does an innocent recognize, confront, and escape from the bad intentions of a marsh-fire existence? It cannot be easy to avoid going all passive and unresisting, like a hypnotized bird. Maud, however, will manage to remember something else Monica said about Silas—"his utter seclusion from society removes the only check, except personal fear—and he never had much of that—upon a very bad man" (248). And she will fight him on that very issue of his having sentenced her to a solitary confinement which can only end, unless she fights, in the utter seclusion of death. Evading the murder gang, getting out of the locked mansion and beyond the patrolled estate walls, and joining her friends at Elverton, she can then look back at the Bartram-Haugh nightmare and see that her danger came from bad and violent men, not from a conspiracy of demons. Becoming a wife, a mother, and the mistress of her own large fortune she will be too taken up with living life to waste her energies on the sort of solitary studies of a mystical kind, which caused her own father to neglect his responsibilities as a parent, and further corrupted the already vicious nature of her uncle.

We come now to a troubling point. Works like "The Haunted Baronet" and *Uncle Silas* are not set in Ireland at all but in a fully described and particularized rural region of northern or "Northumbrian" England. Why should they have any claim on our attention as Anglo-*Irish* literary works? First, it can be shown that LeFanu in midcareer began giving his stories English instead of Irish settings owing to a direct demand from his London publishers, Bentley and Company, that he should do so (McCormack, 238). This did not mean, however, that the essential and symbolic content of the fiction turned English as well.[17] Elizabeth Bowen, who must be listened to in this matter, called *Uncle Silas* "an Irish story transposed to an English setting." She then went on to say:

> The hermetic solitude and the autocracy of the great country house, the demonic power of the family myth, fatalism, feudalism and the 'Ascendancy' outlook are accepted facts of life for the race of hybrids from which LeFanu sprang. For the psychological background of *Uncle Silas* it was necessary for him to *invent* nothing. Rather he was at once expressing in art and exploring for its more terrible implications what would have been the

> norm of his own heredity. Having . . . pitched on England as the setting for *Uncle Silas*, he wisely chose the North, the wildness of Derbyshire. Up there, in the vast estates of the old landed stock, there appeared, in the years when LeFanu wrote (and still more in the years of which he wrote: the early 1840s) a time lag—just such a time lag as, in a more marked form, separates Ireland from England more effectually than any sea. (*Collected Impressions*, 4)

Uncle Silas's implied politics have little direct bearing on the cleavage between native and Ascendant communities though that is always in the background. Rather, it is the intricate, involuted "psycho-politics" of country-dwelling Anglo-Irish families, suffering a fearful and historic isolation and loneliness, in pride and obstinacy offering their children as sacrifice to that isolation and loneliness, with which the book is taken up. We have noticed how Maud Ruthyn finds her way out of the tomblike house in the nick of time. For once, the lively expectations of the young are not devoured by the guilts and errors of their elders.

VII

HISTORY AGAIN: THE ERA OF PARNELL—MYTHS AND REALITIES

At the door Dante turned around violently and shouted down the room, her cheeks flushed and quivering with rage:

—Devil out of hell! We won! We crushed him to death! Fiend!

The door slammed behind her.

Mr Casey, freeing his arms from his holders, suddenly bowed his head on his hands with a sob of pain.

—Poor Parnell! he cried loudly. My dead king!

He sobbed loudly and bitterly.

Stephen, raising his terror-stricken face, saw that his father's eyes were full of tears.

—Joyce, *A Portrait*

THE TWO GREATEST Anglo-Irish public men of the nineteenth century are the first Duke of Wellington (1769–1852) and Charles Stewart Parnell (1846–91). Not only are both prodigious, but they are also prestidigitators of their own identities. The first, beginning as plain Arthur Wesley of Trim, County Meath, a country gentleman and younger son with a seat in the late-eighteenth-century Dublin Parliament, magically changes into the Iron Duke, Napoleon's conqueror, greatest English captain since Marlborough, later serving as British prime minister in the very year, 1829, that saw passage of the Catholic Emancipation Bill.[1] His state funeral was very grand and he is buried in St. Paul's Cathedral. Tennyson's equally grand and paradelike "Ode on the Death of the Duke of Wellington" breathes not a syllable about this "foremost captain of his time's" Irish origins:

> Lead out the pageant: sad and slow,
> As fits an universal woe,
> Let the long, long procession go,
> And let the sorrowing crowd about it grow
> And let the mournful martial music blow,
> The last great Englishman is low.

The second, Parnell, seems to work his transformations of identity the other way around, beginning as an Anglo-Irish landlord in Wicklow, with an interest in quarrying and a hobbyist's enthusiasm for assaying minerals, coming to place his political hopes and goals with those of the Irish majority, and becoming—until his precipitous fall from popularity owing to the Katharine O'Shea divorce scandal—native Ireland's "uncrowned king."

The reality of Parnell's identity and career is rather more complex. Consider even his long clandestine involvement with Mrs. O'Shea, with whom he had at least two children and lived an intense and faithful, if secretive, connubial experience from 1880 until their marriage in 1891, just a few months before his death. Despite her Irish-sounding married name, Captain O'Shea's estranged wife was wholly English, born Katharine Wood, daughter of an English rector. The long relationship with Parnell was conducted almost entirely at the homes Mrs. O'Shea occupied with her children, the first house at Eltham, a district of South London, and the next two in Brighton on the south coast. Though they occasionally encountered discreetly on the Continent, they were never together in Ireland. In fact, Katharine Wood O'Shea was never in Ireland. Nor were any of Parnell's Irish confederates and lieutenants admitted to their chief's domestic circle in England. What they knew or surmised of the affair they were expected to keep to themselves. But all such agreements would be tacit, for Parnell was notoriously reserved and aloof, a disposition that grew stronger in the later 1880s as his difficulties with the resentful and extortionate Captain O'Shea, Katharine's husband, mounted.

Many public men have led rigorously separated private lives, yet surely it is not usual to lead one's private life a nation away from one's public life, and a hostile nation at that. Something in Parnell may have positively enjoyed this situation, as he tied knots in the tail of the British lion through his effective tactics of parliamentary obstruction, while holding in that lion's very lair a shocking secret ripe for disclosure. Certainly Charles Stewart Parnell was an enigma, perhaps even to himself. The following brief sketch of his career accepts that as its premise. The late F.S.L. Lyons's distinguished biography of 1977 opens with testimony by three contemporaries as to Parnell's essential nature. According to Michael Davitt, he was "an Englishman of the strongest type"; to an editorialist of the *Drohgeda Argus* writing in 1875, "Mr. Parnell was an Irishman, Irish bred, Irish born, 'racy of the soil'"; and to T. P. O'Connor, a long and close associate from parliamentary days, "both in appearance and to a large extent in character Parnell was much more American than either English or Irish" (*Parnell*, 3).[2]

His mother was, of course, an Alabaman. She held outspoken anti-British views, which were perhaps typical of her generation of Americans, and these were not much modified during a long residence in Ireland. Parnell's sister Fanny contributed verses in the mid-1860s to the Fenian publication *The People*. During the suppression of the Fenians in 1867, the Parnells' Dublin residence was visited and searched by the police. Charles was away at Cambridge University at the time. He later told Justin McCarthy, the Irish novelist and MP, that it was this incident which made him conscious of Irish political problems. There is also this: "Parnell's eyes lit up with fire as he told me that if he had been there he would have shot the first man who endeavoured to force his way into Mrs. Parnell's room" (McCarthy, 2:109).

We probably should not make too much of the maternal and American influence—not unless we wish to follow a Freudian route, making the son's unconscious Oedipal fixation on his "foreign" mother the key to his later overwhelming attraction to the English mother, Mrs. O'Shea. On the male side the Parnells were a distinguished Anglo-Irish clan, long established in Ireland, showing an important early-eighteenth-century poet, Thomas Parnell (1679–1718), in the family tree, and noted in Wicklow for a tradition of public service in such posts as justice of the peace and high sheriff of the county.

In Parnell's part of the nineteenth century, the tradition of Irish nationalism showed two faces, that of physical force and that of constitutionalism. The former, in combination with conspiracy, was manifest in the various bands of agrarian agitators, in the Fenians, in the Irish-American branch of the Fenians called Clan-na-Gael, and in the Irish Republican Brotherhood (IRB), a secret organization founded as early as 1858, which survived to provide leadership, tactics, and most of the republican ideology during Ireland's final break with England in the period 1916 to 1922.

Constitutional nationalism was mainly represented by the Irish group of M.P.s at Westminster. Those who were not Ulster Unionists tended to work together in favor of such things as Tenant Right and Catholic Defense. This group's long-range goal was a type of Home Rule which essentially would restore the old Dublin Parliament, this body to have control of Irish internal affairs, while questions of imperial defense and foreign policy were to be left to the British Parliament. To achieve its goals, the Irish party, beginning in the 1850s, conceived a policy of independent parliamentary opposition aimed at winning concessions from whichever major party happened to be in power at the time. Discipline and cohesiveness in the Irish caucus left much to be desired, however. The English government found it relatively easy to co-opt Irish members, as when Keough and Sadleir, in 1852, accepted office in Lord Aberdeen's ministry. By the time Parnell won his first parliamentary election in 1875, there had been progress in shaping the Irish bloc of M.P.s, yet much remained to be done. On election, he moved swiftly into a leadership position, becoming president of the Home Rule Confederation of Great Britain and chief of the Irish parliamentary caucus by 1877.

When Parnell entered parliament for Meath, his platform called for denominational education under clerical control, release of political prisoners, security of tenure and fair rents for the tenants, and Home Rule, all this delivered with a warning that England should remember what had happened in America a century earlier. Lyons calls this last point "Home Rule with a Fenian edge" (52). Thus, at the very start of his "constitutional" political career, one sees Parnell maintaining an opening toward the other more rebellious type of nationalism. That would remain his keynote. He was to walk a line between, and sometimes attempt a braiding together of, the two ways. Never quite becoming an enemy of the British state—no matter how often the London press, especially *The Times*, relegated him to that category—he yet will maintain close relations with agrarian radicals and Fenian ticket-of-leave men, sometimes using funds from Irish-American conspiratorial groups to push on parliamentary goals, but only once, and that very deliberately, overstepping the bounds of strict legality and going to prison for it.

That came in 1881, at the height of the near-revolutionary Land War, which had been joined between Irish landlords and their tenants since 1879. In that year, poor harvests, falling prices, and mounting evictions had fostered predictably an increase of rural agitation and crime. But this time a broad-based defense organization, the Irish National Land League, was founded, largely through the organizing efforts of Michael Davitt, with Parnell as its first president. By the next year we find Parnell, in a famous speech delivered at Ennis in Clare, advocating a tactic of social ostracism, whereby any farmer who tries to lease land falling vacant through the eviction of the previous tenant shall be utterly shunned by all. For advocating this policy, Parnell and other Land League leaders were prosecuted on November 2, 1880, only to have the jury fail to agree. Then in 1881, Gladstone, the Liberal Party prime minister, promulgated a new Land Law Act for Ireland. It proposed substantial reforms, such as provision for fair rent,[3] fixity of tenure, and free sale by the tenant of his improvements upon termination of tenure, plus the setting up of a Land Commission to adjudicate disputes. However, at the convention of the Land League that same September, Parnell urged the membership to "test the Act." By that he meant that tenants should immediately demand wholesale rent reductions, release from eviction proceedings-in-progress, and also demand immediate hearings before the Land Commission.

The government regarded this response as seditious, an attempt at radical undermining of the law before it could take hold. Moving on the basis of a coercion act passed the previous March, it ordered the arrest of the entire Land League executive. From prison on October 18, 1881, Parnell issued a "no rent" manifesto. Two days later the Land League was suppressed by government decree. However, the historians' consensus is that Parnell saw advantages in his term of imprisonment in Kilmainham Jail. It enabled him to consolidate his popular support in Ireland,[4] consult with his lieutenants, all of whom were jailed with him, and treat at leisure with the government on key points. On May 2, 1882, after agreeing to let the Land Law Act proceed without further disruptions—the so-called Kilmainham Treaty—Parnell and the others came out of jail. The shocking bloody murders of Under-Secretary Burke and the new Chief Secretary, Lord Frederick Cavendish, in the Phoenix Park, Dublin, a few days later tarnished, but did not destroy, Parnell's new standing with the English Liberal leadership. After Kilmainham, we find him setting the land question a little to one side while he concentrates on further shaping the Irish M.P.s into a fully disciplined minority party, which can act as a fulcrum of power between the major British parties, Conservative and Liberal.

It all came together in the election of 1885, when the Liberals took 335 seats, the Conservatives 249 (of which 25 were dependent on the Irish-in-Britain vote), and the Parnell bloc 86. This meant the Irish could either double the Liberal majority or turn the other way and cause a stalemate of 335 to 335 on any legislative vote. Gladstone was swift to appreciate these elementary facts. Within a month he announced his conviction that some sort of devolved government for Ireland was only right and proper. In January 1886, the Liberals, partnered by the Irish M.P.s, drove the Conservatives from office. By April, Gladstone was ready with his first Home Rule for Ireland Bill. Though it failed to pass on the second reading by 40 votes, it sealed the alliance between the Liberal leadership and Parnell until his fall. The year 1886 also saw revival of organized, widespread Irish land agitation. Called the "Plan of Campaign," its new feature was rent withholding, or, rather, payment of rent into a special escrow fund. Money was then dispensed from this fund to pay the tenants' legal costs in court actions and to relieve the distress of the evicted. Perhaps as a *quid pro quo* to Gladstone for his support of Irish Home Rule, Parnell's expressed attitude toward the Plan of Campaign was unenthusiastic and distant.

The alliance with Gladstone and the Liberals represents the high point of Parnell's public career. Now forces of fate began accumulating to bring him down. The threat came from two directions. In 1887, *The Times* published a series of articles on "Parnellism and Crime," which charged him with treasonable acts and associations during the Land War and purported to include extracts from his correspondence implicating him in atrocities such as the Phoenix Park murders. However, a special commission of high-court judges, sitting during 1888 and into 1889, exposed the extracts as forgeries carried out by an unstable former nationalist, Richard Pigott. Pigott committed suicide and Parnell was cleared of the various charges and aspersions. For a brief time he was even popular with the large British public as it deplored *The Times*'s shoddy and politically tendentious journalism.

The other threat was Captain O'Shea. As an M.P., O'Shea had always refused to take the voting loyalty oath of the Irish bloc, hewing instead to an independent, opportunistic line. In 1886, Parnell forced the Galway constituency to accept O'Shea as its candidate, much to the disgust of his lieutenants and the constituency itself. Four months later, O'Shea refused his vote to the Irish Nationalists on the Home Rule Bill's second reading. He then resigned his seat. It was obvious he no longer had any use for Parnell's patronage. The scandal of a divorce action was in the offing. Katharine's fortune, however, depended on her inheriting from her ninety-three-year-old Aunt Pen. The gallant captain was waiting for the aunt to die. Then he would institute a double action, a suit for divorce and a probate action claiming most of Katharine's inheritance for himself and for those children born to Katharine before 1880.

We scarcely need reminding that we are in Victorian times. The aunt died, the Captain filed for divorce at the end of 1889, the hearing came on eleven months later, and the verdict against Mrs. O'Shea, naming Parnell as culpable corespondent, bred a widespread reaction. The first blows were aimed at Parnell's continuing leadership of the Irish parliamentary party. The Irish Catholic bishops, proceeding cautiously at first, hinted they might be satisfied with his resigning leadership temporarily. Prime Minister Gladstone, coming under pressure from the nonconformist sector of the Liberal electorate, including some wealthy party contributors who were Baptists, asked Parnell to resign in order to save the Liberal-Irish voting coalition and future prospects for passing Home Rule. When Parnell refused, Gladstone published the text of a letter to John Morley, which repeated these points. A few days later, on November 29, 1890, Parnell issued a manifesto to the Irish people appealing for their support and understanding. On December 1 began the notorious debates in Committee Room Fifteen of the House of Commons on a resolution to change the Irish bloc leadership.

Gladstone wrote of these debates to the English Roman Catholic primate, Cardinal Manning, while they were still in progress. His rather hectic language may remind us of what Maturin said of Irish Gothic—it is not something merely imagined but actually occurs: "The proceedings of this week have opened to our view a new chapter of human character and the experience of life. It is like a demoniacal possession when the evil spirit will not depart without rending the body in which it has resided" (letter, Gladstone to Manning, Dec. 4, 1890; quoted in Lyons, 540). Parnell, of course, was the evil spirit and the Irish M.P.s the torn body. Just down the road was the tearing to pieces of Parnell's Irish constituency as a whole. In the end the vote was 45 to 29 in favor of Parnell's dismissal as parliamentary leader of the bloc. When he refused to bow to this majority decision, those opposing him stood up and walked out, thus insuring a split in the Irish party ranks that would endure for over a decade.

Now Parnell went over to Ireland to play out the hand that fate and his passion for the Englishwoman had dealt him, appealing directly to the Irish people in a series of wearing public appearances and hard-fought by-election campaigns. The story is universally known as it is reprised in the Christmas Dinner scene of Joyce's *A Portrait of the Artist as a Young Man*, and that version corresponds quite well to reality. The pious people, sermonized by their priests, did turn away from the great charismatic leader, even though there were many pious people, and even some priests, who stood by him. It is also true that he wore himself out, hastening his death, in the attempt to turn the political tide by winning at least one of the by-elections. Though the margins of defeat varied, along with the qualities of the local Parnellite candidates, from North Kilkenny, to North Sligo, to Carlow, he lost them all.

Those who stayed with Parnell to the end tended to be the Fenian survivors and "hillside" men of the diehard physical-force tradition. Sensing this, Parnell in his final public appearances sounded more radical and more disaffected from constitutionalism than ever before. These late developments guaranteed Parnell a prominent place in the official pantheon of primary nationalist heroes, which began to be added to under IRB auspices when effective Irish political struggle against British control revived in the early years of the present century. This is quite ironic if we consider that Parnell's greatest accomplishments were parliamentary and constitutional; whereas the Supreme Council of the IRB, as far back as 1877, had resolved to leave the parliamentary movement unsupported.

Another irony emerges as the man is changed into legend. For Yeats, Parnell epitomized "Anglo-Irish solitude," a high-tragic quality showing up in a few great Anglo-Irish personalities and reflecting the historic isolation, difference, and minority status of this class as a whole. But Parnell's habits of reserve and solitariness were not in fact profound character traits or even a matter of class tradition. They were mainly devices to keep friend and foe alike sufficiently at arm's length so that his secret life with Kitty might go on unnoticed and undisturbed. He loved his mistress to distraction and his letters to her—some written in disappearing ink—are boyish, eager, and sentimental. At home with Mrs. O'Shea, who at the very end became Mrs. Parnell, there was nothing solitary or lofty about him.

Still, Yeats was right in another sense. The pathos of the Anglo-Irish hero of Parnell's type lies in his difference at bottom, and therefore his isolation, from the people he aspires to represent and serve. In Yeats's peculiar dramatistic and visionary terminology, he is a Player perpetually doomed to play Anti-Self to the Native Irish Self.[5] Unfortunately, when a serious flaw in the hero becomes evident, this same people can say, "He is not one of us," and spit him out of its collective mouth. Of course the larger tragedy was that of a subject people, poorly positioned at the time to generate its own native leadership, making do with the fascinating hybrid, Charles Stewart Parnell, until certain embarrassing facts of a personal nature happened to come out.

VIII

SPINSTERS BALL: GEORGE MOORE AND THE LAND AGITATION

There ensued a somewhat lengthy pause . . . Mr. Bloom, so far as he was personally concerned, was just pondering in pensive mood. He vividly recollected when the occurrence alluded to took place as well as yesterday, some score of years previously, in the days of the land troubles when it took the civilised world by storm, figuratively speaking, early in the eighties, eightyone to be correct, when he was just turned fifteen.
—Joyce, "Eumaeus," *Ulysses*

Introductory

HERBERT HOWARTH properly describes George Moore (1852–1932) as "the annalist of the death of the landlords," citing in support some plangent phrases which may have been written as late as 1911: "We are a disappearing class, our lands are being confiscated, and our houses are decaying or being pulled down to build cottages for the folk. All that was has gone or is going" (*Vale*, 245). However, these lines are anachronistic in that they refer to a decline which had already been going on for a very long time, and which certainly had become irreversible by the 1880s. Well before 1911, economic and legal machinery had been created for defeudalizing landlord-tenant relations and for replacing the landlord system as such with a native proprietorship made up of family farmers.

Moore's sentences may need some correction along with some interpretation. He hands the reader a warrant for such impudence when he writes in *Ave*, the first volume of *Hail and Farewell*, that "in Ireland we don't mean all we say" (*Ave*, 77). Yet sometimes "we" may mean more or other than what overtly appears. Thus "our lands are being confiscated" is probably meant to recall the wicked phrase about the Protestant Colony used by the earl of Clare, chief whipper-on of the Union—"their common title is confiscation"—and to suggest that a reconfiscation by the natives is in progress. But that, of course, was not the case.

Instead, the Wyndham Land Act of 1903 legally entitled the Anglo-Irish proprietors to a buy-out of their land when and if they chose to sell, on highly favorable terms secured for the indefinite future by a government bond issue.[1] In 1912, George Moore, as absentee owner of the large though unproductive Moore estate in Mayo and Roscommon, chose to be bought out for the then substantial sum of £30,000, while keeping back for his personal use and for his heirs Moore Hall and five hundred acres of woods, hunting fields, and lakefront property. Though the house burned in 1923, the fire may have started accidentally. In any event, it was not rummaged for materials with which to build cottages for the folk. Moore's phrases in *Vale* include a perfect bull: "All that was has gone or is going." Such a mystifying verbal construction from so calculating a stylist as Moore signals that the language of dying fall, coming at the very end of *Hail and Farewell*, a work Moore had originally thought of calling *Ruin and Weed*, is deployed for pathetic effect and not with any strict regard for socioeconomic facts and historical chronology.

Moore had done his best work as annalist a quarter century earlier, when he described the land agitation and the collapse of the power and prestige of the landlords in his third novel, *A Drama in Muslin: A Realistic Novel* (1886), and in its nonfictional supplement, *Parnell and His Island* (1887). The novel is several things at once: a fictional exposure of the moral funk, incapacity for leadership, and low morale of the rural proprietors at the time of Parnell's jailing in Kilmainham and of the Phoenix Park murders, which followed his release; an effective satire of Dublin Castle society—that is, viceregal society—and the vulgar and cruel rituals of its winter season; and it is also a penetrating and largely sympathetic study of a set of provincial Irish and Anglo-Irish young women during the year or two after they leave convent school and attempt to maneuver in the marriage market so as to avoid the "muslin martyrdom" of becoming old maids. *A Drama in Muslin* also has a distinct heroine, drawn from the group of school leavers, whose inner growth of conscience and intellect leads her to cast off the trammels of family, class, religion, and, to a degree, nationality. Alice Barton marries a district doctor in the face of parental disapproval and moves with him to Kensington, where he has bought a practice. Their marriage is sedate yet liberated as Alice takes up writing as a trade and helps support her growing family by producing popular novels and enlightened articles on contemporary issues for London magazines. On this level *A Drama in Muslin*, despite its portrayal of Alice's flying by a number of Irish and Anglo-Irish nets, is something less than an anticipation of Joyce's *A Portrait*; yet it does adumbrate some trends of English protofeminist New Woman fiction and drama soon to emerge.[2]

Parnell and His Island developed from articles in French, which Moore published in *Le Figaro* during the summer of 1886. These made up to a book which appeared in March 1887 as *Terre d'Irelande.* Though *Parnell* carries a publication date one year later than the novel, it draws on the same notebook jottings recording observations of Ireland in crisis. A slighter work than *A Drama in Muslin*, it can be conveniently disposed of before we turn to the novel. However, before examining either of these texts I want to establish three things: the particular, even peculiar, Moore family tradition out of which the novelist emerged; certain circumstances at the beginning of the 1880s that forced him to turn his attention back to Irish affairs after a long absence from the country itself; and finally, those traits of character and temperament in George Moore which made him, even though himself a landlord and eldest son, an unabashed critic as well as a close observer of the Irish landlord system in its crisis and accelerating decline.

In 1785, the first George Moore, of an Old Catholic settler family claiming descent from Thomas More, who had garnered a large fortune in the Spanish wine trade at Alicante, founded the Moore estate in County Mayo, the westernmost, poorest, and most rugged of the Connaught counties. Its full extent was about 12,000 acres supporting four to five thousand souls when times were good. The Hall, an exceptionally grand and imposing big house fronting on Lake Carra, was built in 1795, and the Moore family also held property to the northeast, in Roscommon, in the townland of Ballintubber.

Coming to Mayo at a time when the penal strictures against Catholics had been relaxed through a series of Relief Bills passed by the Dublin Parliament, the Moores experienced little if any social disadvantage in remaining Catholic and soon numbered among their connections the Brownes of Westport, who held title to the earldom of Sligo. Even without the tolerant climate of the 1780s and early 1790s, this was the way of the far west, where Protestant gentry were widely scattered and so few in number that living on good terms with educated papists of large property made compelling sense. At the same time, the Moore family's politics were not always class-typical. During the rising of 1798, the writer Moore's great-uncle John joined the rebel cause and was proclaimed president of "The Republic of Connaught," a distinction for which he was quickly arrested and held for execution by hanging. This fate he only avoided by dying of a prison fever in Westport Jail before the sentence could be carried out.

George Moore's father, George Henry Moore, M.P., was a Nationalist in the desolate parliamentary period between the great famine of 1845–48 and the rise of Parnell. Noted for his liberal views on tenant right and his fiery speeches against English rule in Ireland, he yet received his death blow owing to discontent among his tenants. In 1870, he found it necessary to travel the long distance home from London to Moore Hall in foul weather in order to cope with an agitation for rent reduction. Arriving exhausted from the journey, he almost immediately succumbed to a fatal stroke. Eighteen-year-old George, the inheriting son and future writer, was away from home at the time. Hurrying to his father's bedside, he found the dead face already "changed," settled in the unyielding expression inflicted by rigor mortis: "And it is this changed face that lives unchanged in my memory" (*Hail and Farewell*, 3:31) . There are a number of compulsive references to faces changed in death scattered through Moore's writings. It is also true that he has described his father as "the one pure image of [my] mind, the one true affection" (*Confessions*, 63). Perhaps whenever one encounters hostile or repellent descriptions of Irish poor tenants and their way of life in Moore's writings, and there are many such, even perhaps when one learns that "the two dominant notes in my character [are] an original hatred of my native country, and a brutal loathing of the religion I was brought up in" (*Confessions*, 84), one should bear in mind this anguished experience of an oldest son.

There are other things to bear in mind. On his mother's side the writer was a Blake of Ballinafad. Blakes were of squireen or, in Carleton's native Irish term, "bodagh" social standing, altogether too close to the despised peasant for comfort.[3] Moore certainly disparaged his mother's family, though he did not hesitate to employ his own uncle, Joe Blake, as his estate agent during the years he spent in Paris, from 1873 to 1880, learning the French language, studying French literature, and trying to become a painter. He was also cultivating friendships with Manet and Degas, Turgenev and Zola, writing unsuccessful stage pieces and quasi-decadent verse, in general concealing a certain industriousness behind the pose of a dilettante and a stroller of the new Baron Haussmann boulevards. But this is going too fast. Moore's boyhood needs putting into the picture.

Certainly it was suitably adventurous and even wild on the huge Mayo demesne. George Moore, the M.P., kept a large racing stable and entered horses, including some famous winners, in all of the top steeplechase and flat races in the British isles. Young George hung about the stables, becoming an expert rider and excellent shot before he reached his teens. His primary education was with the village priest, who taught him some Latin along with the three Rs. Later he was sent to Oscott College, an English public school for Catholics, where he carried on as the class dunce until removed from school by his parents at age fifteen. Then followed a full year at home given over to "hunting, shooting, and attendance at race meetings" (Hone, 31). Such a year would have great value in bringing the eventual writer into close touch with the countryside and its people, their pace and style of life, this despite his later professed loathing of the peasants. By comparison, young Yeats's forays during summer holidays, notebook in hand, into the cabins and boreens outside Sligo town appear a little wan and bespectacled.

Encountering his oldest son in the miry stable yard during that year of rustication, the M.P. and Gold Cup winner, George Henry, may well have wondered whether he was raising up a half-sir with a loaded whip if not an outright firbolg or bog man. Though this sort of reversion or leveling downward was common enough in Irish rural life—it is actually discussed in both *A Drama in Muslin* and *Parnell and His Island* and is a major concern of the great realist writers of the succeeding generation, Edith Somerville and Martin Ross—that was not the direction in life which George Moore was destined to take.

The land agitation did not occur in a vacuum, but grew from agricultural distress all over Ireland in the late 1870s. Moore, attitudinizing in Paris, just as *La Belle Epoque* was getting under way, heard from Joe Blake in 1880 of a pressing claim for £3000 against the estate. Along with the indebtedness there was a problem of disorganized accounts. Moore decided to change agents and adopt a plan of frugality. It entailed selling off timber—a precious commodity in bare, windswept Mayo—giving up Paris altogether, and moving to London, where he began to make money from his first attempts at novel writing and from a busy production of articles and reviews on contemporary literature and contemporary French and English painting.[4] He also began paying long annual visits to Moore Hall and to Dublin, staying at the Shelbourne Hotel, storming the guest lists of the lord-lieutenant and his aides-de-camp at Dublin Castle, and discovering the shortcomings of the Dublin social establishment that he would highlight in *A Drama in Muslin*:[5]

> But it was his dress in particular that created astonishment. He wore a little top hat on the side of his head, high-heeled boots, and wide trousers, looking like a caricature of a Frenchman in an English paper; he kept to this costume even when he went out shooting, but he recovered respect by shooting as well as anyone else. So anxious was he to be regarded a stranger in his own country that he at first pretended that he had forgotten how to speak English. . . . In spite of his seven years' sojourn in France, an Irishman could still recognize him as a fellow countryman as his spoken English had Irish traits. (Hone, 86–87)

However, and despite the undeclared war raging between tenants and proprietors, Land Leaguers and the police and military sent to protect the large landowners, Moore's tenants, recalling that the father had never evicted except for cause, looked benignly on the young Frenchified master as he went everywhere unarmed. As for what Moore really thought about these newly militant and organized toilers, one answer lies in our knowing how to sort out the negatives and judge the tone in this outburst from *Confessions of a Young Man*, first issued in 1888, when the land agitation, which had been in remission for several years, flared up again in the scheme of rent withholding called the Plan of Campaign: "That some wretched farmers and miners should refuse to starve, that I may not be deprived of my *demitasse* at *Tortoni's*; that I may not be forced to leave this beautiful retreat, my cat and my python—monstrous" (*Confessions*, 104).

Finally, there are the traits in Moore's character, at least in his character as a writer, which made him effective in exploring the Irish scene during the land troubles. For one thing, he liked to find out things for himself, was a passionate self-educator behind all the languid posing with python and cat. Much on the spot investigation nourishes the realism of *A Drama in Muslin* while *Parnell*, though it is tricked out with fictional and semifictional devices and portraiture, is essentially a piece of investigative reporting. Second, though perhaps not quarrelsome by nature, Moore never ducked a quarrel when one was threatening. In writing these books he did not hold back or soften things out of concern that he would raise up enemies, particularly enemies from his own Anglo-Irish and landlord group.

But perhaps his most important and useful trait was a certain shamelessness. Deep in the Irish character lies the conviction that one must not carry false tales, but even deeper lies the taboo against giving scandal by letting shameful truths emerge. However foul the secrets one holds about oneself, one's neighbors, or one's kind, one does not foul the nest by uttering them. Moore did not subscribe to this profound taboo. Whatever fairies gathered at his cradle when he was born, their number did not include the sprite bearing the tribal gift for discretion.

Parnell and His Island

> The conversation then turned on . . . the Irish difficulty,
> which it was agreed could only be solved by sinking
> the island in the sea for twenty-four hours.
> —Moore, *A Modern Lover*

Moore's book-length pamphlet, despite its considerable range of useful observation, is quite unbalanced and at times lurid. If the writer is to be believed, Dublin is a cesspool, its social rounds a sordid farce; Moore's own class and generation of landlord, a spineless and idle lot, are doomed; the poor Irish tenant, with few exceptions, is a disgusting animal, scarcely differentiated from the bogland harboring him and far behind the rest of the European "races" in his evolution. The "regime" of Parnell, established through the Land League, has made murder an Irish fine art (*Parnell*, 235). Soon a doddering Gladstone will grant the island a free parliament. Then the Irish-Americans, a sinister cabal wearing wide-brimmed hats and flourishing dynamite sticks, will pour in. "And looking still further into the future, I see the inevitable war with Russia beginning on the Afghan frontier, and following on England's first defeat . . . the Irish-Americans, who will then be governing in Dublin, will declare the independence of their island" (*Parnell*, 253–54).

Holding such views and revealing such limited powers of political forecasting, Moore blessedly did not follow his father into a parliamentary career. Yet his lack of balance was scarcely unique at this time. In the 1880s the Irish climate of violence bred violent responses. Even Tennyson, not content with having made reference to "the blind hysterics of the Celt" in *In Memoriam*, confided to his friend William Allingham, the Anglo-Irish minor poet and diarist, that the solution to the Irish problem would be to blow the island to pieces with high explosives.[6] Moore's French and English readers were ready to believe almost anything he wanted to tell them, just so long as it was blood-curdling and Irish.

The survey in *Parnell* is organized in terms of a trio of oppositions: Dublin and the countryside; the privileged and the deprived; man's life as opposed to woman's life in the strifeful Ireland of the land crisis. Moore alternates distant with closer observation. The pattern is established early as the narrator describes the Dublin suburbs of Dalkey Village and Killiney Hill in their seaside setting as one of the most alluring and "voluptuous" prospects in Europe, then moves in to notice "a front door where the paint is peeling, and a ruined garden" (5). These discoveries elicit an economic analysis that is accurate for the most part. Though "no town in the world has more beautiful surroundings than Dublin . . . in such ruin life languishes here" (5–6). That is because all Irish wealth comes directly from the land and the peasant. The agrarian disturbances, by cutting off the flow, are immediate causes of dilapidation in the capital:

> In Ireland every chicken eaten, every glass of champagne drunk, every silk dress trailed in the street, every rose worn at a ball, comes straight out of the peasant's cabin. (7–8)

From Dalkey, along roughly the same route as young Dedalus would follow in the "Proteus" episode of *Ulysses*, the reader is led straight into town. Despite Dublin's "absence of any characteristic touch" (12), it is said to resemble an old clothes shop. There, society visibly consists of a multitude of "illbred young girls" (15) making eyes at a few petty officials, briefless barristers, and their clerks, for "Dublin is a town of officials" (17), where yet the women much outnumber the men. Every man, or nearly, is in the pay of the Castle. This structure, Britain's administrative center of rule in Ireland is "an immense police barrack . . . devoid of all architecture. It rises like an upas tree[7] amid ruins and death" (20). For all that, and though its menacing inscrutability outdoes Kafka well before Kafka, the Castle remains the focus of all Irish social striving.

As Moore describes the Castle balls of the Dublin season, he becomes less harsh in tone and betrays some sympathy for the young women, many unchaperoned, many from the provinces and staying for the winter at the Shelbourne Hotel or at boarding houses, who flood into these parties in a female-to-male ratio of three to one and torment themselves and each other in a virtually hopeless search for eligible suitors: "It is pitiable to see these poor muslin martyrs standing at the door, their eyes liquid with invitation, striving to inveigle, to stay the steps of the men as they pass by" (25). Every season the absence of men becomes more noticeable. Where, for instance, are the sons of the landed gentry? They, it seems, are a species of nonstarter in the matrimonial steeplechase. Those in town remain sequestered in the Kildare Street Club:

> This club is a sort of oyster-bed into which all the eldest sons of the landed gentry fall as a matter of course. There they remain, spending their days drinking sherry and cursing Gladstone in a sort of dialect, a dead language which the larva-like stupidity of the club has preserved. The green banners of the League are passing, the cries of a new Ireland awaken the dormant air, the oysters rush to the window—they stand there open-mouthed, real pantomime oysters, and from the corner of Frederick Street a group of young girls watch them in silent admiration. (31–32)

The emphasis in the sections of *Parnell* dealing with agrarian Ireland is on the breaking apart of the traditional social compact between those who own and those who work the land. The crisis is conveyed through scenic vignettes and a series of imaginary portraits. Some of Moore's section titles—"An Irish Country House," "A Castle of Yesterday," "The House of an Irish Poet"—evoke a long tradition of travel writing about Ireland in which English or continental observers, entranced by the quaint and picturesque, totally miss the distressful underlying realities; yet the country house of Moore's description turns out to require round-the-clock police protection, the castle ruins, despite their melancholy charm, warn of the impending fate of this generation of estate owners, and the Irish poet, a plain surrogate of Moore himself, is only at home because the land troubles have cut off his allowance for living abroad. A reader who expects to meet with the appalling in a section called "An Eviction" will not be disappointed, but things are scarcely brighter in "The Patriot" and "A Hunting Breakfast."

This patriot is an imagined Catholic Nationalist M.P. called "James Daly." Beginning as a rural terrorist, he advanced to the rank of Land League organizer by acts of arson, cattle maiming, and murder. Taking advantage of the broadened electoral franchise after 1867, he has now found his way to Westminster. Here he divides his time between spreeing on whisky and turning out to vote as his leader, C. S. Parnell, dictates. Historical research does not tend to support Moore's characterization of a typical Irish nationalist M.P. of the 1880s. Were it accurate, one would need to be all the more impressed with Parnell for having shaped so disciplined a voting bloc from such very unpromising material.

In "A Hunting Breakfast," the scheduled meet—one of the few rural pursuits that traditionally all classes and conditions of Irish country dweller can enjoy together—is broken off when Land League agitators, appearing in the field on foot, frighten the horses and stone the hounds away from the scent. As the old huntsman turns home, trailed by his limping and bloodied pack, he says, "No, no, I have had enough of it; I have seen Irishmen stone my hounds. . . . I believe in the country no more" (230). For him it is the end of the world. For the frustrated and rattled gentry, who can still look forward to a luncheon party at "Mrs. Jack's," it is an occasion for exclaiming, "Those brutes of Land Leaguers! Gladstone and Parnell ought to be hanged!" (235)

Moore portrays one landlord, a woman, who is so hard and unscrupulous that she makes a good thing out of the Land War insofar as it offers opportunities for clearing off distressed tenants and devoting the cleared land to the vastly more profitable activity of fattening cattle. Miss Barrett, of County Mayo, is the antithesis of the kindly, self-denying Miss Martin of Ballinahinch, who beggared herself in trying to relieve the sufferings of her tenants during the great famine of 1845–48. The former's "one desire is to evict her tenants; to harass them with summons is her sole amusement" (190). Just how are these forced evictions carried out? Moore gives full details:

> At last the door gives way and Pratt and the police force their way into the black den. There is the father, the wife, and her six half-naked children. The father, covered only with a pair of trousers, his heavy shoulders showing through the ragged shirt, rushes out like a wild beast to strangle Pratt, but he is seized by the policemen; and the clearing of the house of furniture is

> commenced—an iron pot, a few plates, three logs of wood that are used as seats, a chair, a cradle, and some straw and rags on which the whole family slept. . . . Miss Barrett looks on with evident satisfaction. (197–98)

The dreadful scene continues. The wife is kicked in the stomach, suffering internal injuries, and a crowd of onlookers make low remarks about Miss Barrett's presumed sexual proclivities and ugliness. One becomes uneasy over Moore's unrestrained inventiveness here. Given nineteenth-century British libel laws, it's clear that Miss Barrett was not taken directly from life, while it seems unlikely that Moore, who never evicted his own tenants, was a casual bystander at some other landlord's heartless proceedings.[8] The action of Pratt and the others is based on hearsay then, or it is worked up from accounts published in the press. Authenticity suffers, no matter how *saisissant* the scene might have been to Moore's original French readers.

Parts of *Parnell and His Island* do render authentically Irish life in that troubled time. In "An Irish Country House" one meets "Tom," the oldest son, a superannuated London swell whose "remnant of fashion—scarfs from the Burlington Arcade, scent from Bond Street, cracked patent leather shoes, and mended silk stockings" (40–41), far from rendering him derisory to the local young women, make him a beau ideal. Here is Tom in the idle round of his rural occupations:

> Then he is seen slouching through the laurels on his way to the stables; and, whistling to their dogs, his sisters rush after him, their hands thrust into the pockets of their cotton dresses, the mud of the yard oozing through their broken boots. Behind the stables there is a small field lately converted into an exercise-ground, and there the three stand for hours, watching a couple of goat-like colts, mounted by country-lads, still in corduroy and hobnails, walking round and round. (42)

This *tranche*—or it is a trance?—*de vie* tastes as real, and for some may lie as heavily on the stomach, as Irish soda bread. Karl Marx would have found it typical of what he called the "idiocy" of country life, by which he meant qualities of privacy, isolation, and remoteness which the ever-busy, urbanized, and distracted twentieth century has come to value more highly than the last. The little scene has possibilities—dramatic ones—especially when we focus upon the girls. Unlike the brother, they seem eager and fresh, not having lost their edge during several years of a wastrel existence in London. They are ready for—if not quite anything—then certainly for more than they are being offered. To realize this dramatic potential, here represented in the arresting and arrested figures of two unidentified sisters, George Moore wrote *A Drama in Muslin*, the work with which the rest of this chapter is concerned.

A Drama in Muslin

I confess I only love woman or book, when it
is a voice of conscience.
—Moore, *Confessions*

W. B. Yeats, whose judgments on prose fiction are always his own, placed *A Drama in Muslin* among five great novels Moore would write, adding the qualification that all five "gain nothing from their style" (*Autobiography*, 293). The late Peter Ure, an English critic whose views on Anglo-Irish literature are always to be attended to, wrote of Moore's third novel in an essay called "George Moore as Historian of Consciences" that it "came straight out of the drawing room and demesne at Moore Hall. It is one of the prime documents of the last phases of Anglo-Irishry, belonging to the group of which *The Real Charlotte* . . . and some of Yeats's tragic poems are worthy members" (Hughes, ed., 95–96). According to Ure, the novel in its original form shows the education of Alice, the older of the two Barton sisters, to reject the "communal conscience" and its typical institutions, such as the middle-class marriage mart. The individual conscience simply develops from what one learns by looking and attending: "Alice's conscience does not simply strive against the communal one—it is educated by it to reject it. In the same way, in the year of *Esther Waters*, Shaw was to make Vivie's role in *Mrs. Warren's Profession* one of both repudiating and being educated into awareness by her wicked mother, who is the emblem of the communal conscience as it decays" (Hughes, ed., 98).

The comparison is apt, though I think Ure misses an evolutionary dialectic in English society, as depicted by Shaw in *Mrs. Warren's Profession*, that is certainly not there in Moore's depiction of the Irish society. That is to say, just as Vivie went morally in advance of her mother, so had Mrs. Warren gone in advance of those poor working girls, including her own sister, who let themselves be done to death in pestilent sweatshops and factories, owing to what the communal conscience dictated then. In Shaw, that good socialist fallen among Fabians, as Lenin so wittily put it, progress through the social dialectic determines the validity of conscientious action in the individual. In Moore, as we shall see, conscience in origin and operationally is rather more mysterious, granted that there are one or two passages where the narrator does try to base the development of the faculty in Alice on an evolutionary process.

Ure is also helpful on the relation of the 1886 *A Drama in Muslin* to the revised *Muslin* of 1915. Stylistic revision was not very extensive, mostly amounting to correction of obvious mistakes and the elimination of some "inelegancies." By no means was the book recast or "translated" into Moore's later manner of continuous, uninflected narrative *oratio obliqua*. In revising, the writer cut back a little the part of Alice, much reduced the descriptions of social and political conditions in Dublin and the Galway countryside, and, according to Ure, "excised some of the element of hysteria and melodrama and baleful political anger" (Hughes, ed., 107). That element is perhaps most evident in the long description of the invited families proceeding in their carriages to the viceregal audience and Castle ball as the Dublin poor, pressing forward out of the teeming slums nearby, look on under lurid and gloomy skies, where a display of thunder and lightning is in progress (*A Drama in Muslin*, 170–72).

Such a perfervid atmosphere made the original version of the novel a product of its time, or of the time just past, 1881–84, within which all of the events of the story are framed. We must notice Moore's careful and precise emplacement of his imaginary tale and characters in a definite chronology of public events and developments. The Barton sisters and their set leave school in early summer of 1881. Coming home to Galway, they find the tenantry so aroused, following the government's Irish Coercion Act of the previous March, that armed police are required to keep guard around the clock at many estates, including the Barton property, Brookfield.

In order to amuse themselves during this bad time and to get the anxious and lugubrious postgraduate business of husband hunting under way, the young women of the district organize their ball for "spinsters." It is held at a remote, unused schoolhouse and hall, and few eligible bachelors show up. One who does is the diminutive Mr. Burke. Before the evening ends, he becomes that much more eligible when news is brought that his older brother, the marquis of Kilcarney, has been shot dead from ambush by an unknown terrorist.

The Barton daughters, with Mrs. Barton as duenna, arrive in town to make their social debuts in January 1882. The time is not propitious, for the land agitation has reached its darkest point. Parnell and the rest of the Land League executive have been confined to Kilmainham Jail since the previous October. Every Dublin dinner table is buzzing with speculation as to who is winning this climactic battle of wills between the English government and the Irish leader, whose popularity with the common people has increased for every day spent in jail. Though her egregious social blunders are her own, it is a poor time for Mrs. Barton to attempt to ensnare the little marquis, formerly Mr. Burke, or anyone else of high social standing, for her beautiful but quite lack-witted daughter, Olive. Convinced that everything is coming down and eager to snatch a little happiness for himself, Kilcarney slips out of Mrs. Barton's carefully cast nets, gasps out a declaration of love and proposal to the girl who genuinely attracts him, the epicene Violet Scully, then wanders in the dark through central Dublin, imagining doom for people like himself. Passing the O'Connell statue in Upper Sackville Street he thinks:

> This was the man who had begun the work; it was he who had withdrawn the keystone of the edifice, soon to fall and crush all beneath its ruins. Then he found himself walking beneath the colonnades of the Bank of Ireland. Here was the silent power that protected him; but soon the buyers and sellers would be scourged out of the temple, and a new power established . . . that would turn him a beggar upon the world. And sometimes he was seen examining the long line of Trinity College. All this would go too. This ancient seat of wisdom and leaning would perish before the triumphant and avenging peasant. For him the country and for him the town. And for the old race of the Kilcarneys poverty and banishment. (218)

Poverty and banishment are an old Irish story, only now it's the turn of the proprietors to be sent whistling down the wind. So the love-struck yet woebegone marquis imagines. Nor does the darkling ebb and flow of the nearby Liffey afford any relief or contrast. Just as the city has been given over to incendiarism, conspiracy, and political murder, so has the river turned accomplice as it carries assassination victims toward the concealing sea, and hides the knives of assassins in its polluted bottom mud (219).

These knives foreshadow the Phoenix Park murders of Burke and Cavendish, which will take place within a few weeks, on May 6, 1882. By that time the Barton women will have returned home to Brookfield, where Mrs. Barton's dinner party is thrown into panic and confusion when the shocking news is brought. A day or two earlier there had been a picnic excursion—under police escort—to Kinvara Castle in South Galway, where the pedantic but liberal-minded estate owner, Mr. Adair, had put forward the optimistic view that Parnell's release did not involve the secret deal between him and the government which the newspapers want to call "the Kilmainham treaty." With this new evidence of savagery from conspirators everyone agrees must be connected with the Land League, Mr. Adair finally curbs his social optimism , while Olive quaintly exclaims, "I think they ought to hang Mr. Parnell; I believe it was he who drove the car" (240).

Though it may seem surprising, henceforth in the narrative there is little further reference to politics and to social crisis. That is because the Gladstone Reform Act of 1881, now at last taking hold in the Irish countryside, in conjunction with those agreements quietly worked out between Parnell and the Government which won his release from jail in April 1882, have defused the main issues of contention between the landowners and the tenants and brought the Land War to a close for at least the next few years. And this despite the Phoenix Park incident, an atrocity that was intended to derail the new agreements:

> Peasants and landlords rubbed their eyes, stared aghast, and then, laughing like people awakening from a nightmare, they resumed their ordinary occupations. The change was as marvelous as any transformation-scene. People thought differently, spoke differently, acted differently; stock was bought and sold without restrictions of any kind; carriages filled with pink-dressed young ladies travelled the country, and the training of horses occupied every manly and many a female mind. The stoning of the hounds, the poisoning of the covers were only remembered as a bad dream; in a trice the gentry disbanded their black-coated bodyguards and resumed their own red coats. (265)

A Drama in Muslin several times shifts scenes between the capital and the countryside. In this design the two most important sites are Dublin Castle and Brookfield, the Galway property of the Catholic Bartons. Until the English left Ireland the Castle served as a prison, a police barracks, a hive for spies and undercover agents, a killing ground for political prisoners charged with high treason, *and* as a viceregal court. Moore is well able to suggest the potential for humiliation to Ireland generally in those scenes where nervous and frightened young girls are pushed into the throne room of this unsavory place and kissed on both cheeks by the viceroy, before being moved along by bored chamberlains to the state ballroom, where they must hunt, usually in vain, for invitations to the dance.

At Brookfield the father, Arthur Barton, who is at least half-mad, and an epitome of a class in terminal decline, paints historical pictures when he is not warbling romantic Italian songs to his own guitar accompaniment. One picture, a huge, frequently repainted study called "Julius Caesar Overturning the Altars of the Druids" appears to be an allegory of Gaelic Ireland's conquest by the English. Before the Kilmainham settlement, Barton's tenants presumably have wished to kill him; hence the four armed police mounting guard at his hall door around the clock. However, he is incapable of an intense response to this situation or to any other. We are told he was so upset at receiving an anonymous death threat that he was unable to tune his guitar for a week. It seems just right for a man who has secretly matched the painted heads of his own wife and daughter Olive with the bodies of voluptuous nudes provocatively posed, and who has overlooked his wife's sexual affair with a dithering Protestant neighbor, Lord Dungory—her "twenty years of elegant harlotry" (204)—during the entire period of their daughters' growing up.

At Brookfield the Barton daughters, plain, intelligent Alice, and pretty, feather-brained, maybe father-brained, Olive struggle to find a future for themselves after the privileged seclusion of the convent school. Olive quickly falls in love with a visiting young officer, Captain Hibbert, and is made desperately unhappy when Mrs. Barton refuses to let him court her after grilling him on his income and future prospects. This drawing-room scene of negotiation is synchronized with a scene outside the house in which Arthur Barton and his estate manager negotiate with the tenants over rent reduction. Here Moore's debt to a famous scene in Flaubert's *Madame Bovary* is obvious. Many of the girls from St. Leonard's will come to grief as Olive does and some will come to something worse. May Gould, the liveliest and warmest in temperament, by the end of the novel has born an illegitimate child which quickly dies, and become an easy sexual target for the dirty old men in the local hunt club. Lord Dungory's lame daughter Cecilia, after developing a passionate crush on Alice that is more than halfway to a lesbian declaration of love, has turned hysterical man-hater, converted to Catholicism, and joined an order of nuns. Then there are the somewhat older, postdebutante Brennan sisters, famous for dressing exactly alike, who travel up to Dublin year after year for the Season, and have never attracted the slightest notice from any man.

Though Alice has the misfortune of being intensely disliked by her own mother, her superior talents are established early on when the story opens with a theatrical performance of her little play about King Cophetua and the Beggar Maid by the girls of St. Leonard's. The point of its fable is the King's discovery of a poor, despised maiden's merits and his making her his wife. Without dramatic foreshortening, Alice's journey to the wedded state takes time, thought, and strong moral effort. She reads George Eliot (an author Moore sometimes pretended he could never bring himself to read), discovers her religious faith is withering away, sets herself in conscientious opposition to her mother's schemes of exploiting Olive's good looks by hawking her about in the marriage mart, gains some independence from her successes at magazine writing, and finally escapes both parents' influence and control by marrying Doctor Reed, a stout older man without social position whom she respects without loving.

After a quick vestry wedding that is boycotted by both Barton parents, but obligingly witnessed by the kindly Brennan sisters, the couple set off in heavy rain for London. On the way to the train they pass an eviction-in-progress. Alice stops the eviction by persuading her husband to pay the rent arrears. It is a matter of indifference to the police and the bailiffs; they simply march off to the next farm on their long eviction list. On that unyielding note of Irish agrarian misery, Alice's career in her native country comes to an end.

Moore has put a lot of himself into Alice's characterization. Like him she is an oldest child underrated by her parents and is physically unprepossessing. Beginning to write, she finds she has a flair for autobiography and produces the "Diary of a Plain Girl." Though she finds male mentors such as the English novelist Harding—he is carried over from Moore's previous novels, *A Modern Lover* (1883) and *A Mummer's Wife* (1885)—she is also doggedly self-reliant in holding out against parental disfavor and in realizing a sufficient return from her pen so that her decision to accept Dr. Reed is free of the constraint imposed by dependency. Finding no common ground with her parents, she does feel a covert rapport with a grandfather who had written and left in manuscript a whole series of historical works. This detail was taken over without change from Moore's own family circumstances.

How does someone with such awful parents develop a superior character? Mrs. Barton is a person "who had worked her way through life by means of numberless by-paths, all lying a little to the left of the main road along which the torrents of men and women poured, and who had been known to them only at intervals as she passed furtively down the end of a vista or hurriedly crossed an unexpected glade. The bent shoulders hinted at a capacity for stooping under awkward branches and passing through difficult places. There was about Mrs. Barton's whole person an air of falseness, as indescribable as it was bewitching" (23). Alice avoids this fate of furtive falseness in part through ceasing to be Catholic. Moore's conviction of this period was that Roman Catholicism stunted the development of moral conscience by leaving its management too much in the keeping of priests, both in their role of confessors and as interpreters of Scripture and the moral law. Also, as earlier pointed out, Moore believes that conscience develops through directly confronting real conditions, while Mrs. Barton's whole life has been based on skulking and evasion.

When Alice begins examining the situation in which she finds herself after leaving school, she poses the following questions:

> "How then," she asked passionately, "can we be really noble and pure, while we are still decked out in innocence, virtue, and belief as ephemeral as the muslin we wear? Until we are free to think, until we are sisters in thought, we cannot become the companion, the friends, the supports of men." (101)

Here Alice's dissociation of "the really noble and pure" from the trappings of conventional maiden innocence is quite bold and puts late Victorian cant in its place, though without abandoning the period's typically idealizing moral idiom. From here on she determines she will only outwardly conform to "social laws," as she has already been doing for some time with "religious laws." Still, it can't be easy, in an age when the codes of both organized religion and society retain so much of their traditional authority, to shape an individual morality so sweeping in its repudiations without grounding it somewhere. In a late scene with her friend Cecilia, who is about to become an ex-friend, Alice tries to ground the moral in the natural:

> "I cannot but think that the best and the most feasible mode of life is to try to live up to the ordinary and simple laws of nature of which we are but a part." Here Alice paused, and she sought vainly to define her ideas. She was conscious of the truth that conscience is no more than the indirect laws—the essence of the laws transmitted by heredity; and had she been able to formulate her thought she would have said "and the ideal life should, it seems to me, lie in the reconciliation—no, reconciliation is not the word I want; I scarcely know how to express myself—well, in making the two ends meet—in making the ends of nature the ends also of what we call our conscience." (228)

When Alice Barton uses her own words, the thought is pretty muddled. But when the narrator tries to take over, putting words of his own in her mouth, the muddle gets much worse. Perhaps Moore should have attended to George Eliot after all. But it may not matter. The most significant test of Alice's nonconforming moral conscience may lie in the quality of the life she lives after cutting loose from creed, class, family, and country. On this ground the heroine appears headed for a modest triumph as the book ends.

George Moore called *A Drama in Muslin* his "best subject" but unfortunately his "worst written." He thought that in 1902[9] when there were still many books to come in the course of three more decades in an exceptionally dedicated writing life. Certainly there is overwriting and lusciousness in the descriptions of young women's "embonpoint," "haunches," and ball gowns. At the same time there is evidence of care in construction, as in the parallels suggested between the Spinsters Ball of Book 1 and the first Castle Ball in Book 2. There is also some arresting scenic description. Here is a specimen with which we can end our investigation of Moore in the 1880s. Replete with Zolaesque touches and painterly effects evoking Sickert, if not Degas, the passage shows some ambivalence on the narrator's part toward the conflict of haves and have nots it brings into view. The anxious well-to-do are driving to the Castle in front of the gazing poor:

> Notwithstanding the terrible weather the streets were lined with vagrants, patriots, waifs, idlers of all sorts and kinds. Plenty of girls of sixteen and eighteen come out to see the "finery." Poor little things in battered

bonnets and draggled skirts, who would dream upon ten shillings a week; a drunken mother striving to hush a child that dies beneath a dripping shawl; a harlot embittered by feelings of commercial resentment; troops of labourers battered and bruised with toil: you see their hang-dog faces, their thin coats, their shirts torn and revealing the beast-like hair on their chests; you see also the Irish-Americans, and their sinister faces, and broad-brimmed hats, standing scowling beneath the pale flickering gas-lamps, and, when the block brought the carriages to a standstill, sometimes no more than a foot of space separated their occupants from the crowd on the pavement's edge. Never were poverty and wealth brought into plainer proximity. In the broad glare of the carriage lights the shape of every feature, even the colour of the eyes, every glance, every detail of dress, every stain of misery were revealed to the silken exquisites who, a little frightened, strove to hide themselves within the scented shadows of their broughams; and in like manner, the bloom on every aristocratic cheek, the glitter of every diamond, the richness of every plume were visible to the avid eyes of those who stood without in the wet and cold.

"I wish they would not stare so," said Mrs. Barton; "one would think they were a lot of hungry children looking into a sweetmeat shop. The police ought really to prevent it."

"And how wicked those men in the big hats look," said Olive. "I'm sure they would rob us if they only dared."

Alice thought of the Galway hall, with the terrible faces looking in at the window. (171)

Outside the Galway hall it had been the poor as well, gazing in at the dancers like spectres. Almost as if looks could kill: as unlucky Captain Barton was gazed to death by the dreadful single watcher in LeFanu's tale. Only now, in an age of near-revolutionary strain and violence, it is a multitude, and the class basis of the conflict is plain for all but the most willfully blind to see.

IX

"THE STRAIN OF THE DOUBLE LOYALTY": EDITH SOMERVILLE AND MARTIN ROSS

"This is the last dance I shall give," went on her ladyship unappeased; "the men in this country consist of children and cads."

I admitted that we were a poor lot, "but," I said . . .

—Somerville and Ross, *Some Experiences of an Irish R. M.*

Indian Summer

IN IRISH HISTORY, conditions of an appalling and intransigent kind sometimes have a way of dissipating quickly, like mountain mist. An example of this is the great change in a few years from the poisonous and wrenching socioeconomic conflicts of the 1880s to the relative tranquillity of the Anglo-Irish 1890s. If this easing depended upon a piece of luck—the sudden fall and death of Parnell—and on the Anglo-Irish recovering a sense of security in their lives that would swiftly evaporate only a generation later, it was, nevertheless, the atmosphere in which Anglo-Irish culture produced its characteristic expression at that time. At the same time, part of the poise and temper of Anglo-Irish culture in the 1890s may well entail an awareness deep down that the entire historic enterprise of the Anglo-Irishry, so largely based on landownership and country pursuits, is actually close to an ending. It is possible to find that awareness in the work of Edith Somerville and Martin Ross, both in a major tragicomic work like *The Real Charlotte* (1894) and in the wryly narrated, sometimes anarchic comedy of the Irish R. M. stories and their sequels (1899–1915).[1] But before coming to the work of these marvelous writers who were cousins, single women by choice, life partners, and such close collaborators in writing that they went on composing books together for years after one of them died, it will be useful to turn once again to Elizabeth Bowen's rich family history, *Bowen's Court*, for her picture of the Anglo-Irish *fin-de-siècle*.

Bowen emphasizes an Indian Summer glow and mentions some of the conditions creating it. In politics, Liberal Unionism, sponsored by the Conservative Party, which hoped to kill Home Rule aspirations with kindness, aimed at a final settlement of the land problem through redistribution of land, as much as possible to those actually working it. However, as noted earlier, tenants had to buy from their landlords, property which some felt was already theirs by ancestral right.[2] In that 1890s era it was hoped that aggressive nationalism was discredited owing to the Parnell scandals and the consequent split of the Irish parliamentary group into factions. The new Gaelic League, founded by the Roscommon Protestant landowner Douglas Hyde in 1893, which aimed at restoring to the Irish people a sense of their native heritage through Irish language study and rediscovery of a distinguished literary tradition composed in Old and Middle Irish, did not touch the Bowens or their kind, and did not seem to contain the rebellious political potential it later revealed: "The Parnell scandal, and the succeeding tragedy, had been far from the *bois dormants* of Mount Temple and Bowen's Court. These, like woods in the sunset, glowed in the golden close of the British nineteenth century. No unkind wind blew. The 'nineties, for Anglo-Ireland, were a decade of fine consciences and a humour that was uncombative, mellow and disengaged. Protestantism became less bigotted" (*Bowen's Court* 1964, 398).

There were, though, indications of the impending breakup of a system. Elizabeth tells us that her parents were the first generation of Bowens since the building of the house in 1776—a house "which was, in essence, a family home . . . a symbolic hearth . . . the focus of generations of intense living" (ibid., 403)—to live away from Bowen's Court for years at a time. We are in the era when the great house and the surrounding farms begin to disengage from each other as the demesne is broken up through purchase and as expropriletors begin to live off capital and income realized through these sales. If it is not the breaking of an organic bond, it is certainly the weakening, and sometimes the elimination, of an association that had been going on for centuries. This account of what happened is somewhat oversimplified. As estate land came on the market under provisions of the Wyndham Act, some of it was bought up by members of an expanding provincial middle class comprised of former estate managers, country solicitors and physicians, and a smattering of large shop owners and small manufacturers. These are the people whom the peasants too poor to bid successfully for their own leaseholds often called "grabbers." Edith Somerville and Martin Ross in their earlier fiction were among the first writers to investigate, sometimes disdainfully, this new class.

First Meeting, Final Separation

Edith Oenone Somerville (1858–1949) and Violet Martin (1862–1915), whose pen name became Martin Ross, first met in 1886, laying the ground for their literary collaboration. It was the year of Moore's *A Drama in Muslin*, a book purportedly demonstrating that there was no room in Ireland for single women of talent and spirit. Edith and Violet were of the landed elite, that class about which W. B. Yeats was to develop so much curious literary fantasy somewhat later on. They were also blood relatives, claiming descent through their mothers from a common great-grandfather, Charles Kendal Bushe, called "the incorruptible." Bushe had been Irish solicitor-general and a member of the Dublin Parliament during the debates over the Union. He could not be persuaded to cast a yea vote by either money bribes or the offer of a peerage. In 1932 Edith would publish a book about him and his wife, Nancy Crampton.[3]

When the cousins first saw each other, Edith Somerville, the oldest of seven, was at home at Drishane House, Castletownshend, West Cork. Her family were part of a large "tribe" of interrelated Somervilles, Townshends, and Coghills who had been in Munster since the sixteenth century as landlords and as part of the loyal Anglo-Irish Protestant garrison. When landlording entered its historic decline in the wake of the land agitation, many of her brothers and male cousins opted for military service in the British armed forces and for civil service abroad in the Empire. These escape routes were not open to Edith. After a casual and limited "lady's" education at home, she had spent several years of her early to middle twenties applying herself in painting and drawing classes at studios in Düsseldorf and Paris. She must have started as an art student about the same time as Moore was giving up his efforts to become a painter. Her autobiographical novel *French Leave* (1928) reveals that she won the right to pursue such studies over the bitter protests of her mid-Victorian father, a retired general and at one time high sheriff of County Cork, while her mother quietly connived at furthering her daughter's artistic ambitions.

Conventionally, Edith was expected to marry and settle to the raising of a large family. But she had resolutely set herself against marrying. A favorite cousin, Ethel Coghill, deserted to matrimony in 1880, and it took Edith years to get over the loss of her intimate friend. On February 6, 1886, Edith wrote in her diary: "Heard from Ethel, who is suffering from five babies and five nurses—and is down on her luck. And no wonder."[4] This entry was written when she was becoming acquainted with Violet Martin, who had recently come to Castletownshend with her mother and her sister Selina for an extended visit. They arrived on January 16 and stayed at a village house called Tally-Ho. The visit would continue for nearly a year.

Violet Florence Martin was the eighth and youngest child of the Martins of Ross Castle, a Galway demesne near Lough Corrib on the way west into Connemara. This originally Norman family had been in West Galway immemorially and was related to the Martins of Ballinahinch. Violet's family had been Catholic until the middle of the eighteenth century, a rather late date for a Norman gentry family to swear the Oath of Conformity. Her grandfather Robert had even married a Catholic, yet all offspring in the next two generations were baptized and raised as Protestants. There was, however, a tradition in the family of double baptism, the Catholic ceremony being carried out surreptitiously, at the instigation of family retainers fearful for the immortal souls of their beloved charges, yet also with the tacit acceptance of the family. As a small child Violet Martin was in and out of the cabins of the Irish-speaking tenants and house servants, looking on at weddings, wakes, and funerals. She used to attend chapel with her nurse and later recalled sermons spoken by priests in Irish and English. These details become significant, as her writing, to the extent it can be distinguished from her collaborator's, reflects a more intimate and earthy knowledge of the native Irish condition.

But by 1886 Violet and her family had been living in Dublin for more than a decade and might have appeared citified to Edith, as her memories of working in the women's art classes of the Studio Julien in Paris began to recede. She was, though, to return to Paris for further studio work that very spring. In Dublin the Martins were on visiting terms with all the leading Ascendancy families. Violet had studied Greek, French, and the fine arts with private masters. She had read a paper before a Dublin law society and at eighteen had been a guest at the Dublin wedding of Augusta Persse to Sir William Gregory.

The Martins' long absence from Ross Castle, which ended in 1888, when Violet returned there with her mother to help refurbish the house and restore the gardens, orchards, and lawns, directly reflected the vicissitudes of landowning during the Land War. Her idea of the estate up to about midcentury was feudal if not edenic: "My father came and went among his people in an intimacy as native as the soft air they breathed. All were known to the Master and he was understood by them" (*Irish Memories*, 4). When Robert, the oldest son, was born in 1846, "the workmen in the yard kissed the baby's hands, the old women came from the mountains to prophesy and to bless, and to perform the dreadful rite of spitting upon the child for luck" (*Irish Memories*, 15).[5] But even this fantasy version of a social history is penetrated at one point by Violet's "dreadful" gift for ironic deflation: "Life at Ross was of the traditional kind, with many retainers at low wages, which works out as a costly establishment with nothing to show for it" (*Irish Memories*, 24).

Martin believed that the Ross estate survived the troubles of the Fenian 60s as though it "had borne a charmed life" (*Irish Memories*, 25–26). Apparently the charm stopped working in 1872. In that year the estate tenants, many newly enfranchised by the Reform Act of 1867, followed the instructions of their priest by electing to parliament a Home Ruler. This was a blow from which Violet's father James never recovered, for he died in that same year at only forty-six. A few months later, Robert Martin the heir turned his back on the estate, moving off to London to try for a career in journalism and light literature.[6] About the same time the widow Martin closed Ross and moved with her six other surviving children to Dublin.

Violet and Edith's friendship, which was to ripen into a lifelong mutual love very like a marriage, and to entail a famous literary partnership, the products of which were something like children,[7] was begun casually enough. At first the two young women's diary entries seem to show that there was more eagerness on Edith's side. The dark-eyed Miss Martin, with her flower petal complexion, silken-soft hair, daintiness of person, and slender hands and feet—these are Edith's descriptions from much later on (*Irish Memories*, 103)—was the magnet drawing the steel of strong, soldierly Edith's attention:

V. Sat Jan 16 1886: Left Dublin. . . . Came on to Castle-townshend in the Somervilles' carriage, and established ourselves at Tally-Ho. *Very* cold.

E. [same date]: Violet and Selina Martin arrived at Tally-Ho.

Over the next several days Violet was sick in bed, though she did manage to come to St. Barrahane's Church, where Edith was the organist, that first Sunday:

E. Sun Jan 17: Violet Martin came to church and sat in the choir. Thank goodness as we were fairly badly off.

E. Mon Jan 18: Had tea with Violet who is seedy in bed.

In Violet's diary entry for that day Edith is not singled out among those who visited. For the moment Edith is the more eager to make a new friend.

E. Feb 3: Saw her for a moment. Violet M. Came up to tear paper for a paper chase.

E. Feb 14: Sunday. Very cold. Showery. Church. Aunt Fanny better. After 2d service Violet had tea up here + then Violet and I went for a walk.

Violet's diary entry for that Sunday in its entirety is: "Went to Church twice. Tea at Drishane—very fine."

Violet Martin's first separate and distinct reference to Edith in her diary does not appear until February 27: "Drishane in the morning. *Sat* to Edith." Edith's diary entry of that day begins, "Lovely day. Began to sketch small panel. Violet M." The sketching went on and became Edith's oil portrait of Violet at age twenty-four. A reproduction of this picture appears in Maurice Collis's double biography of the cousins (48). One guesses that this picture, inscribed "To V.F.M. from E. Somerville," sealed the intimacy developing between them.

As 1886 went on, eager interest in the other becomes evident. During early spring and into May, Edith was busy in Paris with her art and Violet missed her. By now she was used to Miss Somerville's addressing her as Martin in order to distinguish her from another relative or acquaintance named Violet. No doubt this was the origin of the rather princely pen name Martin [of] Ross. In September, Edith paid a week's visit to Waterford. On the fourteenth, Martin's diary records, "Wrote to Edith." On the eighteenth it is "Did nothing in particular, being too excited by the return of Edith. At 6.30 walked up to the Skibbereen Road in torrents of rain and met Edith." In October they carried out their first publishing collaboration, an article on palmistry for the *Graphic*, which Martin wrote and Edith illustrated.

Though they did not always live under the same roof during the next few years, they were never again to live essentially separated lives.[8] For neither was there ever anyone else. It would take Martin's death to sunder them, and when that death came, diary entries and portraiture again played a leading role. Martin's last jotting in her own diary came on Monday, September 6, 1915. Ever since a bad hunting accident in the fall of 1898, which had confined her for months with a "bruised spine" among other injuries, Martin had suffered bouts of ill health and invalidism. Now she was experiencing constant head pain and spent the next few weeks having many of her teeth pulled and consulting one or more physicians, who hypothesized that the basic problem was with her eyes. On November 27, a Saturday, Edith wrote, "Martin and I went to Cork by 12 train." She was bringing her to be admitted as a bed patient to Cork Hospital. There on December 7, Martin lapsed into a coma. At last it was generally recognized that she was suffering from a well-advanced, inoperable brain tumor.

At this point Edith begins to make her day-to-day entries in a special notebook with silver gilt paper pasted over the regular covers.[9] On the front cover in black capitals is lettered "DECEMBER 1915." This death book contains Edith's daily observations of Violet Martin's last days.

Pasted inside the front cover is Edith's drawing of Martin on her death-bed, and attached to the inside back cover is an enlarged signed photograph of Martin. The drawing shows only her face against the pillow. Gaunt and lined, the mouth dropping open, it is the face of someone who looks all of her fifty-three years, who is *in extremis.* The photograph, a formal one, is of a much younger woman. Martin is seated on a white and gold couch, wearing a cream-colored ball gown decorated with pearls. She is in left profile to the camera and very upright. Her hair is up, revealing shapely ears and a slender neck encircled with a black ribbon. The large eyes and strong chin of the old oil portrait are still in evidence, but the upper lip, an Irish one, is longer.

The writing in this notebook does not show Edith going to pieces. That was not her wont. By the same token, the drawing shows an unyielding *faithful* realism. Nevertheless, the book was a gift of love to Martin, the last thing on earth she could do for her: "The Church of Ireland minister came on Tuesday, December 7, He was anxious that Martin should in some degree realise the service. I knelt by her holding her hand, and told her what was proposed—she gave my hand a little pressure. Madden read some of the prayers and then read the communion service. She could not swallow, but I whispered to her, and her lips were touched with the Bread and Wine. She again gave my hand a faint pressure."

As the coma deepened, Martin was moved to a nursing home. Edith came every day, staying on into evening. Sometimes her sister Hildegarde and Ethel Coghill, a younger namesake of the friend who had married, came with her. For Tuesday, December 14, she wrote: "Sat there till dinner time. Went up there again after dinner. I sat there till after the night nurse, Miss Sweeney, had been installed. . . . The streets noisy and blazing. Recruiting meeting raging in Patrick Street." On December 18 she mentions the drawing: "It was hard to get the point of view, harder still to get the single artistic effect." Then the final entry: "At 5 a.m. on Tuesday, Dec 21—they say the breathing changed, and began to fail, and at a quarter to eight this morning it ceased."

The notebook entries end with an inscription centered on a separate page: "December 21. Tues. EOES. 1915." It seems as if she were recording her own death. For a part of her that was undoubtedly so. On the twenty-third she got up early and wove a big E out of violets; she took it to the church where Martin was laid out and placed the E above her heart. And she wrote to her brother Cameron in England—"No one but she and I can know what we were to each other" (quoted in Collis, 172). She went to attend the burial in St. Barrahane churchyard but found she could not stay: "Hildegarde and I went away to the cromlech field, where Martin and I have so often sat . . . stayed there while the incredible, impossible happened." Edith Somerville would outlive Violet Martin by thirty-four years. She once called meeting her "the hinge of my life" (*Irish Memories*, 122). Now that hinge was broken.

Ross without Somerville

The small body of imaginative writing done by Martin alone is extraordinarily interesting, some of it distinguished, and as a whole it tends to support the view of their contemporaries that she was the poet of the two. For one thing, she is apt to use riveting figurative language, as when she says of a woman who went mad from her sufferings during the great famine, "reason had stopped in that whelming hour, like the watch of a drowned man" (*Irish Memories*, 16). Afraid of, yet drawn to, burial places while a small girl, she wrote most powerfully on scenes of suffering: sickness, death, and funerals. This morbid streak or metaphysical shudder in her imagination is relieved by great comic gifts and the ability to modulate rapidly between dark and bright tonalities. Both cousins worked frequently in the vein of tragicomedy. To the extent they can be distinguished, Martin's tragic effects seem to tend more toward the Gothic and spectacular while her comedy is wilder, less jocular than Edith's.

I said earlier that Martin Ross knew the native condition more intimately. One might add that her approach to it is much more tension-ridden and more ambivalent than Edith Somerville's. The latter's casual references to the native Irish are replete with comparisons to bush negroes, wild Indians, and primitives. At the level of anecdotage she knew all there was to know about the country people, especially Cork people, but she knew first and last that they were of a different, inferior species to herself, her family, and her class. Whether the result of double baptism or not, Martin knew no such thing. She could speak ill indeed of the "other Irish," but she could not keep away—could not distance herself emotionally, in memory and imagination, and sometimes in fact—from the people she had been raised among.

One of the mysteries that drew her attention more than once was the enigma of peasant marriages, unions entered into for apparently casual or harshly materialistic motives, but nevertheless enduring and often loving "after the fact." She also writes of the peasant girls' readiness to marry into conditions of squalor and female victimization without a backward glance, owing to the fact that continuing single by choice was inconceivable in rural society. This, of course, ignores the large number of young women who chose to enter religious orders in preference to marrying and those who emigrated while still single. One guesses that her own choice of "another way" than matrimony in her intimacy with Edith gets caught up in these reflections (*Irish Memories*, 125).[10]

Her deepest fascination and partial identification with the native Irish, however, come in the area of English language usage. Despising the British invention of the loose-lipped stage Irishman, she reports the speech of West Galway people, even those who are primarily Irish speakers, as unfailingly eloquent, dramatic, rich in image and anecdote, yet always pure in idiom, spare and reticent, in all respects the opposite of the common English misconception of Irish loquacity, barbarisms, and illogic.[11] Here she echoes, more or less unconsciously, the Edgeworths' idealization and partisanship of native Irish verbal talents, with the added complication, one feels, that some part of her own identity and aspiration as a literary artist is taken up with achieving a "mere" Irish eloquence and power of "deep speaking." We can begin to bring this out by quoting from her memoir of the Martins of Ross as given in the first chapter of *Irish Memories*: "Many years ago a mission priest delivered a sermon in Irish in the bare white chapel that stands high on a hill above Ross Lake. I remember one sentence, translated for me by one of the congregation. 'Oh, black seas of Eternity, without height or depth, bay, brink, or shore! How can anyone look into your depths and neglect the salvation of his soul!'" (40). She was so struck with this, especially, one imagines, with the shuddery metaphysics of the apostrophe, that she introduced it word for word into the brilliant sketch "At the River's Edge," to be later discussed.[12]

The lines are quoted at the end of her account of the Phoenix Park murders and other atrocities of the Land War period. Martin relates how she attended the trial of the so-called "Invincibles," the group charged with the killings, and paid particular attention to a seventeen-year-old defendant, Timothy Kelly, and his unhappy mother, who took the witness chair to provide her son with an alibi. Her evidence was not believed: "The trapped creature in the dock, with the men who were his confederates, went down into the oblivion into which they had thrust their prey" (40). Martin clearly approves of the death sentence. As for the sentence about black seas of eternity—"it expresses all that need now be remembered of the Phoenix Park murders" (40). In this sequence the flip-flop of sympathy from native to Anglo, from murder conspiracies among the colonized to lofty punitive judgments issuing from the colonial masters, is so swift that a reader may suffer a sort of vertigo. Vertiginous also is the effect of her garbing the official judgment on this native murder gang in the language of Catholic religious rhetoric. It is brought home to a reader how complex, conflicted, and paradoxical could be Martin Ross's relation to the fissured world of her Irish experience.

Martin's strong reaction to the Phoenix Park murders of May 1882, and to the ensuing trial of suspects, probably normal for someone of her class and loyalties living in Dublin at the time, led to one of her earliest pieces of fiction, the short story "Two Sunday Afternoons." It is well done—of its sensationalistic kind—and bears a certain resemblance to Joyce's "Two Gallants," which was not to come for another fifteen years. According to Edith Somerville, the subject "was suggested to her by what she had heard and seen in Dublin, when little more than a child during the dark time of conspiracy of 'the Invincibles'; and . . . it seemed too sordid and too tragic, and she put it away." This is from Edith's foreword to a collection of their fugitive pieces called *Stray-Aways* (1920), where the story finally appeared.

Kate Byrne, maid of all work for the McKenzies, who keep a respectable lodging house on Mount Street, is seduced and victimized by Joe Devine, an Invincible who pretends to love her. His real object is to get into the house and murder Mr. McKenzie, a former custom official who intercepted some illegal dynamite shipments. Devine's confederates include the Irish-American Mrs. Nolan, whose apparently friendly visit to Kate on the second Sunday is a ruse to get the several assassins across the McKenzie threshold. During the ensuing ruckus Kate is fatally stabbed by her own lover, while McKenzie escapes with minor wounds. The gang is captured when police are alerted by the girl's screams. Feverish and on her deathbed, she refuses to identify Joe as her slayer, but she may in delirium have said enough to hang him anyway.

The opening is interesting for its hostile representation of Dublin commoners and for its anticipation of the much better known opening of *The Real Charlotte*—"An August Sunday afternoon in the north side of Dublin . . ." —only here it is in May and the scene is on the south side:

> It was Sunday afternoon, and the swards of St. Stephen's Green, Dublin, were blotted and littered with hot humanity. Peter Street, Patrick's Close, and the dingy labyrinth that lies between the two cathedrals, had sent forth contingents from their teeming population, leaving still an ample residue to fill the windows with lolling forms and jeering faces, as the churchgoers passed below. The soft grass of May was bruised by supine and graceless figures, unshaven cheeks were laid on it, and tobacco and whisky were breathed by sleeping lips into its mystery of youth and greenness. Above them the hawthorn trees trailed branches embroidered to the tip with cream and pink, children played shrilly about the fountains, with curses, laughter, tears and guile, happy beyond all comprehension, unhampered in their games by sense of honour, truth or cleanliness. (*Stray-Aways*, 255)

For the early 1880s Martin is certainly taking the *aroused* view typical of her class toward the currently unruly Irish plebs. The two cathedrals are the Protestant ones, St. Patrick's and Christ's, while the "dingy labyrinth" in between is comprised of the Yeatsian "little streets"[13] where unplanned parenthood, Catholicism, and sedition supposedly flourish. At the park, the people manage to offend and besmirch springtime nature by their sprawl, and the narrator is swift to cut off hope of improvement in the rising generation, for the children's games already act out mere Irish profanity, falseness, and dirtiness. Also, the references to whisky breath and unshaven cheeks convey the suggestion—a most unlikely one—that the Catholic Irish do not use Sunday, as decent Protestants do, for attending church.

When Kate is introduced she is at one with the vulgar crowd of the Irish. However, some sympathy struggles with distaste in the narrator's initial description: "Her dress proclaimed her the maid-of-all-work out for Sunday; the coarse colour that covered cheek and high cheek-bone spoke of youth and strength; her mouth was good-humoured, Irish, and vague. The blue eyes were well and darkly set, the slant of the eyebrows downwards to the snub nose might have been sinister, or might have been merely vulgar; the rest of the face gave the casting vote in the latter direction" (256). More compassion is displayed when the girl is shown at lovemaking, for she is, after all, an innocent whose seduction will end in the most tortured discovery that she has been used, even as it ends in mortal wounding: "His arm came closer around her, and the present moment rushed in upon her, shutting out past and future. To the passerby she was merely a clumsy girl with a large head, sprawling on the shoulder of a dingy artisan, yet love and its dreadfulness are there expressed, a fire struck from the heart of life, to burn itself out in slow despairs or mild regrets, or in some sudden agony or extinction of death" (258).

"Love and its dreadfulness." The next time he puts his arms around her his hand will hold a "sharp and slender" knife, which he will plunge into her body. Without belaboring the issue it seems obvious that lowborn Kate in this early story acts as surrogate to wellborn Martin Ross's own dread of grownup sexuality, her nervousness about what may happen when a girl abandons herself to passion or comes to depend upon a male lover. Sexual fears are not the point of "Two Sunday Afternoons," but they are certainly a ground note under the manifest plot.

Beginning in 1889, the year after her return with her mother to Ross Castle, Martin composed a series of prose sketches focusing on native life in West Galway and Connemara. One of these, "Children of the Captivity," has already been cited. Her better pieces deserve comparison with Turgenev's classic *Notes of a Hunter*. The best of them all, "At the River's Edge," is one of the masterpieces of Anglo-Irish prose, a work that is exquisite, lucid, and yet boundlessly mysterious and suggestive.

In these sketches, which travel a line between fiction and actual lived experience, Martin draws freely on memory, sometimes going back to early childhood. Frequently she will come to focus on a female figure from the native community in terms of whom or against whom she can play off her conflicted sense of her Irishness, the battle in her spirit of two cultures, two loyalties, even two somewhat distinct senses of reality. It seems true that she was never to get beyond this conflict. In the last pages of *Irish Memories* appear several of her letters to Captain Gwynn, M.P., to whom she was writing in November 1912. In one letter she says, "I told him that my foster-mother took me secretly, as a baby, to the priest and had me baptised. It was done for us all, and my father and mother knew it quite well, and never took any notice. I was also baptised by Lord Plunket in the drawing-room at Ross, so the two Churches can fight it out for me!" (322).

In the sketches of 1889, "A Delegate of the National League," and "Cheops in Connemara," the female figures are, respectively, the delegate's grown daughter and a national school mistress at a lonely primary school out on the moorland of the far west. The delegate is presumed to have alienated himself from the big house and its family, but when he dies, a root compulsion draws the narrator down from the castle to the house of mourning. There his daughter leads her into the bedroom where the delegate is laid out, and she says: "There he is for you. What do you think of him now?" (*Stray-Aways*, 17).[14] It is a strange question, echoing and reechoing in the mind. Later, when the burial procession is passing the estate gates, the cart carrying the coffin and mourners is stopped, and the keeners cry out "a moment or two." The delegate's daughter, with unbound red hair, raises her arms in a wide-flung gesture and keeps them raised as the cart begins to move again. The gesture would be seen again, in *The Real Charlotte*, setting off the final catastrohe.

She is saying something to the big house and the family there, claiming some ancient right or connection, but what is it? The narrator tries to spell it out, but unfortunately ends up sounding like Gabriel Conroy at his genteel Christmas speech-making in Joyce's "The Dead": "Her arms seem as if lifted in bearing testimony of some kind, and it is, perhaps, a prejudiced fancy that further endows the gesture with an acknowledgement of the affection that bound gentleman and peasant in the days held in small estimation by the National League" (23). In later sketches Martin will know better, know what to leave unsaid. This one is about hidden connections—the phrase actually appears earlier—which really do lie too deep for verbal excavation.

In "Cheops in Connemara," the narrator, designated as a "he," feels little rapport with the native school mistress in her one-room building standing on uncharted bog—"the Steppes of Central Asia"—as she rote-trains her little scholars in standard English texts and bad Victorian recitation pieces, such as Horace Smith's "Address to a Mummy." The school is without furniture, and the children, coming from poor peasant families barely surviving on the furthest verge of Western Europe, apparently make little sense of the instruction. The visitor, although patronizing while the children are put through their paces, gets quite agitated when he/she is told that no history is taught in the school or in any Irish national school (*Stray-Aways*, 30). Of course that situation would be remedied and overremedied along certain patriotic lines when the natives assumed control over their own history after 1921. Does the visitor know—does Martin Ross know—that the class she belongs to has robbed the people of a history worth teaching to native Irish children in 1889? It is not easy to tell.

A more elaborate sketch, "In Sickness and Health," written some time before 1906, shows Martin using the instrument of memory to explore all those features of peasant marriage that draw her somewhat baffled attention and curiosity. It begins with a small girl's eager impressions of a rural wedding at "Shraft" (Shrovetide), which she attended with her nursemaid. It ends some twenty-five years later with anecdotage designed to show how the peasant possesses a nature "that keenly perceives sentiment and contentedly ignores it" (*Some Irish Yesterdays*, 162). In these anecdotes a woman or man may marry to acquire land, or for a money payment, or, very occasionally, to improve social standing; yet these constrained arrangements, or so she claims, often develop into tender, warm, true marriages.

The paradox of simultaneously perceiving yet ignoring sentiment does not seem exactly what is going on in these marriages. One feels that Martin Ross in this piece may come to the end of her subject before she quite gets to the bottom of it. Conjecturally, that is because she cannot see that human dispositions are shaped by historical conditions and are continuously, if slowly, altering. Particular historical pressures, some of them appalling, led to the odd mixture of the calculated and the sentimental in the postfamine rural Irish attitude toward love, marriage, and family life. Yet for Martin to see this clearly she would have to accept that her own class values and status are equally subject to the shaping of history. She may know this half-consciously yet cannot afford to know it altogether—at least not when she was writing the sketch. She puts herself into a cleft stick, however, with that word "contentedly." Why should it content anyone to be able to appreciate sentiment keenly but have to discount sentiment in the harsh conditions under which he or she is forced to live from day to day? The answer is it doesn't. Fortunately, Martin Ross the artist cannot give a false report. There is very little contentment or even resignation on display in this sketch, apart from what is put on for the "quality," or displayed out of mannerliness on ceremonial occasions.

The little girl has a good time, tasting the holy water when it is showered on the newlyweds, chasing after the cavalcade of lumbering plow horses by which the bride is ritually "dragged home," feasting on an egg and half a glass of port wine in a bedroom apart, while "less honoured guests" "harangue" one another in the kitchen of the bride's mother. This "first distinct glimpse into matrimony" (142) represents the state of innocence from which the narrator must depart as time moves on and experience builds up.

In adolescence, she is much taken with the wisdom of Tom Cashen, the yard man and pig keeper, her "trusted friend and counsellor." Tom thinks men must marry or go mad, owing to the ghastly unremittingness and sheer difficulty of domestic toil in a "swarming" cabin, toil that women are fated and perhaps adapted to perform. As for Mrs. Tom's view—"I think I realised that she was not likely to have one" (144).

Having lost sons to America and the silent—or silenced—toiling spouse to death, Tom comes eventually to his own end. Martin's description of his interment is not only a shuddery one but also tells us more about the real life of the western peasant than she may have intended:

> Within sight of the Chapel . . . stands a ruin, with the ground inside and outside of it choked with graves; mound and crooked headstone and battered slab, with the briar wreathing them, and the limestone rock thrusting its strong shoulder up between. In the last light of an October afternoon I found myself there, in a crowd that huddled and swayed round one intense point of interest—a shallow grave dug with difficulty, where was laid in its deal coffin the quiet body left behind by the restless spirit of Tom Cashen.

It seems an unsuitable and unwholesome plot for further buryings. Why do the quaint natives go on using it? The unquaint answer would take us into the economics of landownership and the power, still substantial, of large landlords in West Galway. The peasantry are to make do with this crowded-out "ruin" because property laws prohibit their digging graves "among a rich man's flowering lawns, / Amid the rustle of his planted hills," where "life o'erflows without ambitious pains." These fine phases are from "Ancestral Houses," the first section of W. B. Yeats's "Meditations in Time of Civil War." It is ironic that Martin Ross, daughter of such a house, should provide witness to the grimness of a peasant's burial place, but that is just the sort of irony she delivers in some of her most characteristic writing.

With the dispersal of the burial crowd the narrator is greeted by the woman whose "Shraft" wedding she attended twenty-five years earlier. As they exchange polite compliments, Martin notes to herself that the other is perhaps forty-five but looks sixty, suffers from chronic head pains and other health problems, and has a habitual drunkard for a husband. She thinks of what her life was, starting out, and what it has become:

> Instead of the broad-backed horse, galloping on roads that were white in the sun and haze of the strong March day, with the large frieze-clad waist to meet her arms about, and the laughter and shouting of the pursuers coming to her ear, there would be a long and miry tramping in the darkness behind her spouse, with talk of guano and geese and pigs' food, and a perfect foreknowledge of how he would complete, at the always convenient shebeen, the glorious fabric of intoxication, of which the foundation had been well and truly laid at the funeral. (148)

However, not to worry. "The possessor of these materials for discontent was quite unaware of them" (148).

There is more to come in the sketch: The story of the young tenant wife who had girl triplets, the story of the Big House cook whose brother would permit her to marry the driver of the butcher's cart but not a man whose family were broom makers. In these and other stories there is evidence of much female hardship, suffering, and humiliation, but no female, if one is permitted a bull, seems to mind. These women must be made unaware of their pain. Otherwise, Martin Ross who, on the one hand, had truly loved her peasant foster mother and her early nurses at Ross Castle, and who, on the other hand, remained a loyal daughter of her class, and of the house of the Martins, would be riven with guilt. Nevertheless, there are moments she comes close to recognizing the contradiction she is caught in, one common to masters, and even more to mistresses, raised among kindly servants in colonial societies.

Martin's last and finest West Galway sketch, "At the River's Edge" (1914), is about not marrying, among other things. Compared with earlier work, the story lacks certain evasions—the claim that an immutable peasant nature exists, and the allied assumption that Irish peasant life lies outside history. Here for the first time a broad distinction is drawn between what the people were like "long ago" when they could still call their souls their own, and what they are like at present, in the era of what Martin elsewhere names the people's "captivity." This is vague enough as an instance of historical periodizing, but it does the job. By 1914, Martin has lived through the full cycle of her own femininity. At fifty-two she has probably reached menopause. That fact may partly explain the detached elegizing mood in which her colloquy with her companion in the sketch is carried on.

In this lovely piece of writing the narrator enjoys what Major Yeates of the R. M. stories, with only a trace of irony, called "the incommunicable gift of being talked to" by the native Irish person (*Further Experi-*

ences, 289). The scene is a house situated on a tributary stream of the Galway River. Here someone unnamed is very ill, so that the narrator and a companion, a "cowlike" illiterate countrywoman named Anastasia, are obliged to sit up together all night long.

Anastasia does most of the talking, the narrator being struck by the utter contrast between the beautiful phrasing, rhythm, and imaginative power of her speaking and the passionless matter-of-factness with which she treats the topics of love and marriage. Her imagination easily encompasses in memorable anecdote startling episodes of a supernatural kind, but makes little or nothing of "romance." And at one point it is suggested that the incongruity stems from inexplicable, because forgotten, circumstances in history: "'The Irish were deep-spoken people long ago,' continued Anastasia, yawning lamentably; 'it was all love-songs they had. The people used to be in love then. Sure, there's no talk of love now'" (*Stray-Aways*, 10).

The sun comes up and shines upon a whitewashed convent wall visible across the river, and a servant girl goes down from the house to wash out milk pans in the clear cold water. On the opposing bank a young man appears, wearing cream-colored flannel boneen and riding bareback a yellow Connemara pony. With utter offhandedness he proposes marriage to the girl washing out the pans: "Mary Ellen, I'm going to be married this Shraft, and I'll give you the preference." With utter offhandedness she refuses him: "Thank ye, Johnny, I'd sooner stay as I am" (12). A little later the narrator hears Mary Ellen talking and laughing in the kitchen with Anastasia. Between the convent and the house of single women the young man intent on a Shrovetide wedding doesn't stand a chance.

From here the sketch moves to its exquisite close in a paragraph that transposes native into Anglo-Irish deep-spokenness:

> In the grass between the window and the river the young spikes of the daffodils were grouped like companies of spearmen, resolute in the cold opposition of January. A thorn-tree leaned stiffly over the hastening water, and the robin that had been drinking near its roots shot up as if tossed from the ground, accomplished a lofty curve, and sank again in exquisite transitory yielding to the earth-force that would someday defeat it forever. The low wind gathered purpose, and a mist began to thicken the sky. It went and came, as though it must return to press the house to its bosom, and tell those within of its love and despondency. (13)

The daffodil spearmen evoke the native Irish partisans of James, who gathered with their pikes at the Boyne River in 1690. They would be routed by the more modern weaponry and superior fire power of the Williamite Protestants, thus reviving the long subjection of Ireland to

English power. The robin that shoots up and sinks back again performs the trajectory of Martin's female life. It also puts us in mind of her actual death, impending within a single year. The low wind that wants to press the house to its bosom, while telling of its despondent love, is mourning Irish separatedness, the sadness of two peoples who can only meet and mingle and speak together on special occasions, at a wedding or a funeral, or at the house of someone desperately ill.

Writing Together

Since I have turned to allegory—that spectre!—at the end of the previous section, and also in the chapter on Irish Gothic and its social and political encodings, I want to cite here a critic who makes strong claims for the role of allegory in Anglo-Irish letters. In *Ascendancy and Tradition in Anglo-Irish Literary History from 1789 to 1939* (1985), William J. MacCormack says: "Resisting the orthodox pleas to assimilate content and form, we may find in *Castle Rackrent* the origins of an allegorical mode of writing and interpretation which will take us through to the late work of Yeats and Joyce as a characteristic of Anglo-Irish art" (104). He then proceeds to make an interesting argument for interpreting *The Absentee* as an allegory of reconciliation between Anglo-Irish and native traditions, one going well beyond the kindly anticipations created by the overtly happy ending. He also claims, much less convincingly, that *Uncle Silas* "is the only Irish novel between *Castle Rackrent* and *Ulysses* which approximates to a total apprehension of social reality," basing this claim—pretty thinly—on allegorical reading that treats the wicked Silas, and his brother, the reclusive Austin Ruthyn, as jointly representing an Ascendant class's guilt over mismanagement and the shirking of its responsibilities and powers (182, 187).

A trend toward allegorical or equivocal writing may indeed develop from several factors in the Anglo-Irish artist's situation. We can agree that one of these might be a sense of social guilt, which a writer cannot openly acknowledge without appearing as a traitor to her class, and which therefore must be smuggled, as it were, into expression. We saw this form of indirection in Irish Gothic, particularly in LeFanu's ghost stories and mysteries. LeFanu also supplied the formula of its operation: "Mystery"—for mystery read allegory— "is the shadow of guilt." Something else reinforcing the Anglo-Irish writer's turn toward equivocal or veiled writing may be her or his despair, after Union, of remaining in or joining the mainstream of English writing. To put it brutally, it was no longer socially rewarding to go to London and make sounds (and gestures) like an Englishman. To stay at home and do that was not rewarding either. Hence the incentive to discover another way of writing, perhaps one that drew from very old traditions indeed of Irish indirectness, reticence, and implicitness in speaking, in manners, and in mien. The formula for this might be, "To say what one means one says what one does not mean."

Finally, there is the allegorizing tendency that proceeds from an individual writer's conflicted or double sense of identity, which we tried to analyze for Martin Ross/Violet Martin in the last section. This chapter is subtitled "The Strain of the Double Loyalty." In simplest terms, for both Somerville and Ross the implied strain is between an Irish and an English side. But what are we talking about here? Is it a writer's "real" character or her literary persona? Other dualities crowd in. Both people were conflicted about being women, yet not in identical ways. Martin Ross, as we have seen, felt herself to be both Protestant and Catholic. The phrase about the double loyalty comes from Violet Powell's study of Somerville and Ross, *The Irish Cousins* (198). Lady Violet does not always make clear whether she is talking about national, class, or religious loyalties. The "strain" may be different for each. For Edith, whose father had been a high-ranking British army officer and Crimean War hero, national issues may have been paramount. For Martin the religious strain might have mattered more. Incidentally, three dictionary definitions of "strain" are applicable here: "burden or ordeal"; "lineage or heritage"; and "the manner, style, or mood of a book" (*Webster's New World Dictionary*).

Perhaps we are now in a position to look at a fascinating passage in *Irish Memories* where Edith relates how her collaboration with Martin, which was already launched, took on serious purpose. It is sometimes quoted with no indication that it may offer problems in interpretation or be saying more than it appears to be saying. Edith's context is the writing together of their first novel, *An Irish Cousin*, published in 1889. At Drishane in October 1887, they had begun writing fiction, working in a sort of family storeroom, where old broken furniture was kept, aiming low, hoping to finish a piece of salable melodramatic claptrap or shilling shocker. As the result of their paying a long day visit, thirteen miles on horseback, to the sequestered seaside house of a remote kinswoman of Edith's, "a pathetic little old spinster lady," they received their first "genuine literary impulse" (*Irish Memories*, 129). However it came about, they found themselves motivated to aim higher and to try and write as truthful and sincere a work of fiction as they knew how. The experience of the visit also provided them with a central subject or theme, which found its way into *An Irish Cousin* and which was to appear again and again both in their collaborative efforts and in some of the fiction Edith went on to write after Martin's death.

What was the revelation forthcoming on that day? Writing of the experience many years later, Edith is anything but forthcoming. She mentions that the relative was old-fashioned but kind, and kept them to tea after furnishing them with a substantial lamb dinner earlier in the day. After this lady's death, the house would be stripped of its furnishings and old portraits, passing into the hands of "farmer people." But it was dying, Edith remarks, even then. She and Martin left for Drishane around sunset. As they turned for a last look, moreover, "some thrill of genuineness was breathed" (130) into their book when they both noticed at a window over the hall-door a white face looking out, which glimmered for a moment before vanishing. Here is what she says happened next:

> As we rode home along the side of the hills, and watched the fires of the sunset sink into the sea, and met the crescent moon coming with faint light to lead us home, we could talk and think only of that presence at the window. We had been warned of certain subjects not to be approached, and knew enough of the history of that house to realise what we had seen. An old stock, isolated from the world at large, wearing itself out in those excesses that are a protest against unnatural conditions, dies at last with its victims around its death-bed. Half-acknowledged, half-witted, wholly horrifying; living ghosts, haunting the house that gave them but half their share of life, yet withheld from them, with half-hearted guardianship, the boon of death.
>
> The shock of it was what we had needed, and with it "the Shocker" started into life. . . . Little as we may have achieved it, an ideal of Art rose then for us, far and faint as the half-moon, and often, like her, hidden in clouds, yet never quite lost or forgotten. (130–31)

As the "half"s and their hyphens pile up we may begin to think we are being teased when in fact a key, of sorts, is being slipped into our hands. The missing "subjects not to be approached" because they are taboo are pretty well comprised by phrases such as "half-bred" and half-breed. The subject the cousins have discovered for literary treatment is the secretive and scandalous mixing, at remote estates, under conditions of extreme social isolation, of gentry blood and genes with those of the common people through love affairs, often illicit, which produce offspring. One of these half-acknowledged, possibly half-witted products—living hyphens and not ghosts, we may be sure—appeared at the window over the hall-door, startling Edith and Martin into recognition of an Anglo-Irish home truth and a literary subject they might make their own. Incidentally, the reason why these offspring of mixed blood are sometimes so deficient, which flies in the face of widely accepted Darwinian principles with respect to "hybrid vigor," points to another dimension of the scandal. Over time and with continued isolation these illicit relations will more and more entail incestuous combinations. Eventually, the only decent fate for the degraded and contaminated ancient stock and what it bred is to finish, "to die at last with its victims round its death-bed."

In Anglo-Ireland nothing happens only once. Twenty-five years later, Martin on her own paid a visit in West Galway that bore a close resemblance to the West Cork visit in 1887. She described her experience to Edith in a letter dated March 18, 1912. If it seems odd that Martin in her letter makes no reference to the earlier visit, it is equally odd that Edith, when she was putting together *Irish Memories* in 1917, and writing of the visit that breathed genuineness into their literary labors for the first time, failed to mention Martin's West Galway visit. It is not as if she had forgotten it, for it was to provide the basis in actuality for Edith's most ambitious and successful work of fiction undertaken on her own long after Martin's death. This was *The Big House of Inver* (1925). The dedication of that book—"To Our Intention, 1912–1925"—and the inclusion in it of the following extract from Martin's letter of March 1912, assigns to the dead writing partner an essential role in the novel's conception and gestation:

> Yesterday I drove to see X—— House. A great cut stone house of three stories. . . .
>
> Perfectly empty. . . . It is on a long promontory by the sea, and there rioted three or four generations of X——s, living with country women, occasionally marrying them, all illegitimate four times over. . . . About one hundred and fifty years ago a very grand lady—married the head of the family and lived there, and was so corroded with pride that she would not allow her two daughters to associate with the neighbors of their own class. She lived to see them marry two of the men in the yard. . . .
>
> Yesterday, as we left, an old Miss X, daughter of the last owner, was at the door in a little donkey-trap. She lives near in an old castle, and since her people died she will not go into X—— House, or into the enormous yard, or the beautiful old garden.
>
> She was a strange mixture of distinction and commonness, like her breeding, and it was very sad to see her at the door of that great house.
>
> If we dared to write up that subject——! (*Inver*, 313)

Here Martin's spelling out in some detail things which Edith's account of the earlier visit merely hinted at makes her letter invaluable. The ending is puzzling, if we read it as still acceding after twenty-five years to the taboo—or *omerta*—conception of "certain subjects not to be approached." But she means something else. The cousins had been approaching the subject of the quality getting under bedsheets with the peasantry ever since their first novel, *An Irish Cousin*. "If we dared . . ." must be about that particular house, already disguised in Martin's letter as X, the house about which Edith was to write, much later on, an ambitious novel under the fictional name of *Inver*.

An Irish Cousin is a fairly close, possibly unwitting, rewriting and "Irishizing" of LeFanu's dark masterpiece, *Uncle Silas*. When the Canadian-born heroine and narrator, Theo Sarsfield, comes for a long visit to Uncle Dominick's gloomy big house in Cork, she finds her uncle pallid and enigmatic, suffering from severe alcohol addiction and frequent fits of hostile depression. He is determined to thrust his son Willy upon her as a prospective husband. Willy's bearish manners reflect a provincial upbringing in neglect that has led to his solacing himself with the village girl, Anstey Brian. Willy, of course, falls in love with Theo. But she, while touched by his devotion, much prefers gentlemanly Nugent O'Neill. The list of main characters is completed by Moll Hourihane, Anstey's peasant mother, who appears quite mad even while she mysteriously enjoys the freedom of Durrus House. Moll shows up one night in a disheveled state at Theo's bedside, thus recalling not only the maniac from the attic in *Jane Eyre* but the homicidal Dutch wife from LaFanu's "A Chapter in the History of a Tyrone Family" as well.

Theo's late father, Owen Sarsfield, the older brother of Dominick, had been found drowned in a bog hole when he visited the estate from Canada back in the 1860s. That is how the younger brother came to inherit the property from old Dick Sarsfield, the reprobate grandfather of Theo and Willy. In a series of late developments, Willy gives up trying to win Theo and impulsively weds Catholic Anstey at the priest's house; Dominick dies raving, but not before confessing how he and Moll together murdered Owen for the inheritance; furthermore, a pattern of illicit relationships comes to light that suggests the possibility of incest or near-incest in the marriage of Will and Anstey. It seems that Moll Hourihane was Old Dick's mistress, and she may have been Dominick's as well. So Anstey could be the daughter of one Sarfield or the other. Willy, having lowered himself by marrying Catholic, may also be playing Russian roulette with the genetic code in cohabiting with a half-sister. Theo cuts away from this sordidness by accepting Nugent's marriage proposal.

The cousins' early fiction, though open to charges of inept plotting and derivative melodrama, contains direct and fresh observation of local life. In *An Irish Cousin* we learn that country women in that part of Munster continue to use their own surnames after marrying, and we are onlookers at Willy's twenty-fifth birthday party, where elderly tenants ceremoniously kiss his hands while their wives actually kiss him "on the mout'." Their next novel, *Naboth's Vineyard* (1891), is even more impressive for its grasp of local detail and the "unwritten law" that may actually control a community. It is set in Land League days, about 1883, in and around a southwestern fishing village called Rossbrin. For an instance, one Donovan, the area "gombeen man"[15] and Land League executive, has a dispute over whose cattle are to be fattened at a temporarily vacant farm, Drimahoon. His argument is with a widow Leonard. Now, while it is clear that a man named James Mahony lost the farm through the rackrent, so all should boycott the widow for offering to take it over, there are complicating factors. Mrs. Leonard is a paid-up founding member of the Rossbrin Land League chapter. She can prove that the Mahonys, years before, had "grabbed" the tenancy of Drimahoon from her own uncle. Furthermore, she has noticed that an anti–Land Leaguer "landlord's man" is after the property, a scheme that must be headed off at whatever cost. When Donovan persists in threatening her with the boycott, she further points out that he once drove the old mother of her laborer Dan Hurley into the workhouse, just so that he could fatten cattle on grazing land that for generations had been leased by the Hurley family. Such attested facts render judgment of individual property rights almost impossible to determine.

The apprentice work of these two books served Edith and Martin well. *The Real Charlotte* (1894), their next novel,[16] is a serious contender for title of the best Irish novel before Joyce. One contemporary Dublin critic goes even farther: "In *The Real Charlotte* they wrote the only great Irish novel that is really and truly a novel and employs all the novelist's devices shamelessly but with finesse" (Cronin, 85).

It is always a little dangerous to legislate what is and is not a novel. The history of the form is strewn with borderline cases. Certainly for its date, the year of Hardy's *Tess of the D'Urbervilles*, *The Real Charlotte* appears a very advanced sort of prose narrative, perhaps more French than English in its scintillating verbal surfaces, its darting (rather than cosmic and massive) sense of irony, the finesse of its intricate yet ample plotting, its amused contempt over middle-class striving and the more pharisaical sorts of middle-class moralizing, its cool anatomizing of a devastating personality such as Charlotte Mullen.

The book is also extraordinary in Anglo-Irish literary tradition for its serious attempt to display a more or less complete society. There are two sides to this. One is the very thorough delineation of the hierarchies, class tensions, and power relations of the local society—Lismoyle and the nearby large landed estate of Bruff, in occupation by the titled Dysart family. The other is the linking of this relatively isolated milieu, through various means and devices, to a larger world beyond. For example, when the young Dubliner, Francie Fitzpatrick, is introduced in the first chapter, the reader is also made acquainted with a lower-middle-class Protestant environment of North Dublin. Though Francie's destiny is bound up with Lismoyle, where she has blood ties, these scenes and later important scenes at Kingstown and Bray[17] bring the Irish capital and its environs into the picture. Christopher Dysart, the gentle and diffident heir to the Bruff estate, has been a civil servant in the West Indies before the story opens and may be expected to return to such a career after he has digested the shattering events of the novel's closing pages. Who then will carry out the landlord's duties is anybody's guess. Finally, there are the English army officers—Captain Cursiter, and young Hawkins, whose heedless pursuit of Francie, both before and after her rash marriage, has such terrible consequences. From a regiment long quartered in the district, the officers are made welcome at Bruff and at certain town households. For all the courtesies exchanged, they remind us that Ireland remains a sort of colony and that the quartering of large numbers of British troops in Ireland is at the convenience of a foreign master.

The lakeside town of Lismoyle bears some resemblance to the pleasant town of Oughterard, on the west bank of Lake Corrib in County Galway, and the distance between it and Bruff may be compared to Oughterard's actual distance from still surviving Ross Castle. At the estate we are shown the leaders of local society and observe evidences of disarray that will carry through into lower ranks and classes. The essential problem at Bruff is the letting go of reins of authority and, concomitantly, a loss of connection with the tenants. On the day Christopher, the inheriting son, turned twenty-one, his chagrined and jealous father, Sir Benjamin Dysart, succumbed to mania and partial paralysis. Now, when he is not being pushed around in a bath chair by an attendant, the baronet is apt to be discovered wheeling his chair after young maidservants, or else pouring verbal abuse on relatives and visitors, none of whom he appears to recognize.

Christopher makes a feint at taking his father's place, but mainly he moons about with a camera—he is too unsure of himself to try drawing and painting—while his agent, Rodney Lambert, encouraged by his employer's lack of push, has begun winkling funds from the estate accounts to carry out property speculations of his own. Christopher will let everything slip through his hands, including the chance of loving beautiful young Francie. He becomes a living instance of the psychological law—out of Freud by Darwin—which says that a man who is unable to show aggression will not be able to love. It may be he thinks that exercising authority will make him dotty and violent like Sir Benjamin. The sister Pamela, as gentle and passive as Christopher, will not give even a faintly welcoming sign when Captain Cursiter, whom she loves, pays a final call. He is hoping to be encouraged to propose, but no signal is forthcoming.

Pamela is destined to remain single and lonesome. The English-born mother, Lady Dysart, must think her grown children are bewitched. This gentlewoman is in command at the tea table, but when she gardens, she manages to transplant row after row of weeds under the impression they are native flowers.

The town of Lismoyle and its immediate surroundings are the precincts of the middle rankers. At one point the narrative refers, indulgently, to the "sloughs" of the middle class out of which several characters are attempting to climb (67). Chief among the climbers are Lambert and Charlotte Mullen, the ugly, intelligent, and ruthless daughter of a former manager of the Bruff estate. Roddy Lambert, upon whom Charlotte has doted ever since he was a juvenile clerk in her father's office, has succeeded to the agency management. By tradition, "brevet rank of gentleman" (22) goes with the job. He and Charlotte remain close even after he marries a sickly local woman for her fortune. They are both speculators in land, what the peasants call "grabbers" after any property whose leaseholder or owner falls behind in rent or mortgage payments, and are prepared to rackrent and evict ruthlessly. Frequently a silent partner in Lambert's business deals, Charlotte shows the greater cunning and toughness. Their association will be strained and then terminated when she realizes that the agent's great passion is for her own cousin-once-removed, Francie Fitzpatrick, whom he has seen on her visits to Lismoyle and during his many trips to Dublin, beginning when Francie was a young adolescent.

Charlotte's house, which she inherited from an ancient aunt, is called "Tally Ho." She is supposed to share the inheritance with Francie but will cheat her out of it, practically as a matter of course. The house name, from the place Violet Martin stayed during her first visit to Castletownshend, is perfect for conveying the note of false heartiness and cheer that Charlotte often sounds in company, especially among her equals and betters. When she is dealing with the poor laundry women of the lake shore, from whom she draws excessive rents for ramshackle accommodation, or with anyone to whom she has loaned money, or with servants, her tone is much more savage. On one side Charlotte is descended from a fox-hunting squire named Butler and claims that her people in their day were the social equals of the Dysarts (72). No doubt that is true though it does not prevent her from making up to the Dysarts, whenever she finds herself in their company.

To this point all the society appearing has been Protestant. With the character of Julia Duffy of Gurthnamuckla, an elderly recluse, we enter a region of anomaly created by religious and class mingling that the cousins had become fascinated with after their visit to Edith's reclusive kinswoman in fall of 1887. It may be appropriate to mention here that

The Real Charlotte is set in 1887–88, during the "Plan of Campaign." Political developments, however, are not emphasized. The main story runs from June of one year through May of the next, with Francie meeting her final fate on June 1, 1888.

Julia is the only child of a substantial Protestant farmer who took to drink and married his own lowly dairy woman, a Catholic. Julia grew up in social isolation and for a time followed the religion of her father. However, after his death she shunned both communions, thus entering the "moral isolation" (34) of those in Ireland who refuse to declare for one creed or the other. Alone and in poor health as the story opens, Julia is barely surviving at Gurthnamuckla, a fine house which has fallen into a ruinous state, where she is attended by a lackwitted old beggar, Billy Grainy. She holds her land on a long lease, renting out the unworked fields for grazing, and is in arrears on her own rent payments. Lambert and/or Charlotte would snap up the property in a trice, thus forcing Julia into the workhouse, were it not that Sir Benjamin Dysart, in the baronet's saner days, had promised her father that she should have security of tenure at Gurthnamuckla until she died.

Though she appears in only a few scenes, the character of Julia is brilliantly "worked" in the plotting and thematics of the novel. No one espouses her cause, yet it becomes entangled in the struggles and projects of all the leading characters. In the end, the widespread failure to treat Julia with justice, to look after her and secure her rights, has the most devastating consequences for these same leading characters. We will spell out some of the details, but not before filling in the bottom layer of the Lismoyle class structure, the poor Catholics in their huddle of cabins along the lake, who support themselves as boatmen, as launderers, as service people at houses in town or at Bruff, or as petty tradespeople such as clothes-menders and small shopkeepers. Norry the Boat, a tall battered single woman with grimy vulturine features, who cooks for Charlotte Mullen, is part of this lakeside proletariat. She is also a kinswoman of Julia's on the humble Catholic side. In time this connection will have "whelming" consequences.

Finally, as a sort of second society, there are the animals: at Tally Ho, the tomcat named Susan in its bitter warfare with the cockatoo, along with the more conventionally named mother cat Louisa and her litters, and all the geese, chickens, and turkeys of the yard: myriad dogs and horses at various locations; the herons, mallards, coots, and "such-like water people" of the lake and its tributary streams. "People" here should be taken more than half seriously. In *The Real Charlotte*, and also in many sketches, stories, and novels to come, animals are often vividly characterized in their own right, quite a few to a point of striking individuality if not outright eccentricity.

In order to establish a social hierarchy, one must discriminate and rank. In *The Real Charlotte*, especially in early chapters, as characters are first introduced, the basis of discrimination and ranking is most often the speaking voice, its tone and accent. On that basis the authors' Anglo-Irish gentry bias is very clear. Though Christopher stammers and Pamela's shyness sometimes makes her nearly inaudible, the Dysarts still speak best. Miss Hope-Drummond, the Dysarts' husband-hunting English houseguest, has a voice that is typically, unsatisfactorily "Saxon." Francie Fitzpatrick speaks in a "pert Dublin accent, that, rightly or wrongly, gives the idea of familiarity" (46). Charlotte speaks passably when she is not using low-comic speech for storytelling and yet has a bad habit of "ponderous persiflage" (28), while Lambert, whenever he is excited or angry, lowers his accent from the would-be genteel to the "raw Limerick brogue" of his social origins (159).

The aspersion of vulgarity in speech is never directed at characters of the lowest rank and no doubt is made too frequently with respect to the middle rankers. Christopher Dysart is not very appealing to a reader of egalitarian views as he reflects on Francie, to whom he is attracted after rescuing her from drowning, "that she must be a nice girl somehow not to have been more vulgar than she was, and she really must have a soul to be saved" (112). The authors betray themselves into a rather "vulgar" rating game, played mainly on behalf of their sometimes listless hero, with—"He wondered how she came to be such a friend of his; Lambert was a first-rate man of business and all that, but there was nothing else first-rate about him that he could see. It showed the social poverty of the land that she should speak to him with confidence and even admiration" (112).

This absentee landlord-in-the-making, for all his modesty and real refinement, is on dangerous moral ground when he tries to disengage Ireland's social poverty from the more basic poverty that he and other landowners have visited on the land for centuries. The cousins could not subject Christopher to the searching critique directed at the likes of Charlotte and Lambert, in part because it would have meant a critical view of their own class. If there is a serious flaw in *The Real Charlotte*, it is the writers' tendency, only occasionally manifest, to confuse young Dysart's social rank with a type of ineffable superiority that can never be explained, but which is only known as it works its magic on one of his "inferiors": "Christopher's character is easer to feel than to describe; so conscious of its own weakness as to be almost incapable of confident effort, and with a soul so humble and straightforward that it did not know its own strength and simplicity. Some dim understanding of him must have reached Francie, with her ignorant sentimentalities and her Dublin brogue; and as a sea-weed stretches vague arms up towards the light through the conflict of the tides, her pliant soul rose through its inherited vulgarities, and gained some vision of higher things" (180).

Let us retreat from this bog of platitudes to the drier, harder ground of Julia Duffy's case. We see that some rather "superior" people contribute to her suffering. As earlier noted, both Lambert and Charlotte were angling after her leasehold. From him she received a legal writ ordering her to pay at least half her rent arrears or quit Gurthnamuckla altogether. This would mean the workhouse. When she tried to raise money owed her from her grazing tenant, he reported that he had been forced into bankruptcy. She walked the many long Irish miles into Lismoyle to consult with Charlotte, who had posed as her friend, visiting her when she was bedridden. Charlotte was not at home but Julia's own cousin Norry was in her kitchen and had been listening at doors. From her, Julia learned that Charlotte had been plotting with Lambert to get Gurthnamuckla for herself. She would then let Tally Ho go to Francie, as her share of the inheritance from the aunt, but only if she, Charlotte, can bring off a match between Francie and the heir of Bruff.

As Chapter 31 opens, Julia is walking further long miles to Bruff to remind the Dysarts of the old promise made to her father securing her for life against eviction. At the estate she has a nightmarish encounter with the maniac in the bath chair (167), who orders her to be thrashed, along with his son Christopher. Julia next walks back to Tally Ho Lodge where she confronts Christopher, who is there visiting Francie. She speaks to him about the promise, mumbling with illness and exhaustion. He thinks she is drunk. In any event, she must make her complaint in writing. She sets out empty-handed on the long road home, only to collapse on route as "brain fever," probably a stroke, overwhelms her.

Julia is out of sight during the next period of the story when Francie rejects Christopher's vague proposal, is jilted by Hawkins, impetuously marries Lambert, who has become a widower through Charlotte's malevolent agency, and revives her dangerous infatuation with Hawkins. Julia is actually coming to the end of her life in pain and neglect at the workhouse infirmary. Now the Catholic side of her mixed heritage takes over. She apparently dies a Catholic and certainly receives a regular Catholic funeral, presided over by her kinswoman, Norry the Boat. This funeral precipitates Francie's catastrophic accident. On the point of running off with Hawkins, the distracted girl, an inexperienced rider, tries to force her nervous mount past the scant funeral procession and the cart holding the coffin and mourners. As a Protestant and a city person she is ignorant of the rural protocol that gives funeral processions priority over all other road traffic. When Norry, a bizarre figure at the best of times, raises the keen, flapping the wings of her cloak like some great bird out of Celtic folklore, the startled horse begins to buck and Francie is thrown onto her head, dying instantly. That, too, evokes Irish legend, the story of beautiful Deirdre, who dashed out her brains on the road stones rather than submit to the Ulster king after he had treacherously slain her lover, Naoise, and his brothers. The important difference is that while the ancient heroine defiantly imposes her will, even though it costs her life, the modern one is merely a victim, buckling under pressure from all sides, a lamb led to slaughter.

The interrelating of Julia's case with the projects of the central characters is one of the cousins' finest achievements in fiction. In terms of the large theme of a divided Irish community, it counts the cost—the strain—of that division with force and subtlety. Though not a perfect book, *The Real Charlotte* may claim a moral maturity working hand in hand with technical mastery, which marks Anglo-Irish fiction's coming of age. That this should happen not much more than thirty years before Ascendancy culture was effectively put in receivership as the Irish majority succeeded in retrieving Irish sovereignty for much of the island is simply one more paradox in a tradition that was a living paradox from the first.

Edith and Martin went deep into themselves for certain things in *The Real Charlotte*. For each author the intimate link is to a particular character. Edith's is to Charlotte Mullen. In this character she was confronting the "mannish," managing, overpowering woman she may have sometimes feared she was or might turn into in years to come. As Charlotte ran a business while running her competition into the ground, and rehearsed the choir and still found time to take the *English Times* and the *Saturday Review*, and read literary classics and "startlingly advanced works of fiction . . . many of them in French" (20), so Edith played senior partner in the literary firm of Somerville and Ross[18] while playing the organ and rehearsing the choir at St. Barrahane's. And she would go on to become the first woman master of a hunt in Ireland and successfully manage Drishane estate through some of its most difficult years. Charlotte is given Edith's passion for reading and identical reading tastes. Of course, we can assume Edith would not stand and watch a helpless woman die, as Charlotte did with the first Mrs. Lambert when she might have saved her by bringing her her heart medicine.[19] There is still plenty of distance between the writer and the created character, including the difference of social position and personal refinement, although Charlotte, if she could snatch a page from the fiction of Flann O'Brien and speak for herself, might want to argue this last point.

For Martin the link is, of course, to Francie Fitzpatrick, from broad resemblances such as the girlhood years spent in Dublin and the tendency for the hair of both "to come down out riding" (*Irish Memories*, 121; *The Real Charlotte*, 39), to their common proneness to accident.

In *Irish Memories* Edith says, "I don't suppose that any little girl had more accidents than Martin" (100), and in *The Real Charlotte* Francie's accidents pretty much spell out her line of fate. We first meet her clinging to a runaway milk float in the opening chapter. Later on she barely escapes drowning when Lambert's sailboat capsizes in the lake. At the end, approximately fulfilling Lambert's prediction—"Some day you'll be breaking your neck, and then you'll be sorry" (38)—she is thrown and killed. There is something eerie in considering that a bad riding accident suffered by Martin a few years after publication of this book undermined her health and may have led to the brain tumor from which she died. Perhaps what Francie and Martin have most in common are their intensely feminine natures. As early as "Two Sunday Afternoons" Martin had shown that to be womanly, a woman, was to be pressured and at risk. Francie's poignantly brief, pressured career is a larger, more compelling demonstration of the same point.

How conscious were Edith and Martin of having written themselves so far into their greatest novel? Certainly they were conscious of having given Charlotte and Francie the exact kind and degree of kinship—common descent from the same great-grandfather—as held between them. Beyond that, nothing is certain.

In *The Real Charlotte* the reader is shown that the class most admired for its social grace—its fine manners and speech and mellow way of life—is also the most deficient in meeting moral responsibilities. Moral paralysis at Bruff begins with the paralyzed and crazed Sir Benjamin and continues in the "deadlocked" invertebrate temperament of Christopher. His diffidence makes him miss his chance with Francie, the lovely and spontaneous girl with the bad Dublin brogue and makeshift rearing. The consequences for the girl are far worse. Although Mr. Woodhouse serenely remarked in Jane Austen's *Emma* that "Young ladies are sure to be cared for," no one takes care of Francie after she leaves Dublin for Lismoyle, and no one was looking after her at the time of her death. In a hierarchical social order one must expect such caring to begin in the higher, more privileged ranks. If fine manners are not for that—if the *noblesse* no longer *oblige*—then what are fine manners for?

We should not, of course, ignore the active force of evil in Charlotte Mullen and, to a lesser degree, in Rodney Lambert. But Charlotte is after all a nemesis raised by the moral absenteeism of people like the Dysarts. She operates precisely in that area of opportunity which opens as the proprietors withdraw from their responsibilities to dependents and former dependents even more precipitately than they give up oversight and control of their vast holdings in land. In a small gossipy community like Lismoyle the Dysarts will be sure to know how vilely Charlotte treats her tenants by the lake and of her activities as a usurer. Yet

Lady Dysart goes on inviting her to Bruff because Charlotte is sufficiently deferential and can tell a good story. She is probably also a little afraid of her. At Bruff the Dysarts maintain a beautiful household, and Christopher is indeed a true gentleman, yet when the family is put to the test, Bruff turns out to lie in the same neighborhood as Castle Rackrent, Christopher bears more than a passing resemblance to Sir Condy, and Charlotte turns out to be Jason masquerading as a cruel, scheming, particularly intelligent and, let it be admitted, passionate and love-struck woman.

What *is* proper conduct for an old ruling class in an age of transition spelling the end to that class's authority and power? *The Real Charlotte* provides at least the beginning of an answer: self-withholding or refined shrinking from contact with the other sorts of one's fellow-Irish are bad; better to embrace the vital Francie with her hoyden ways than to be left alone like Christopher. The decline of the gentle sister Pamela into single lonesomeness is equally regrettable. Otherwise, in some of Edith and Martin's more relaxed and genial literary performances of the later 1890s and just after, the answer might appear to be hunting and riding, the Anglo-Irish recreations centering upon the fetish of the fox, the horse, and the hound.

The sport of fox hunting in its origins was, one imagines, a sort of allegorical activity spelling out in code a feudal lord's dominance and control of his vassals and serfs in a manner that was simultaneously overbearing and protective, and which came in time to be strictly controlled by the rules of an organized game. Without these rules, idle men-at-arms were apt to wreak havoc on cultivated fields and domestic animals under the pretext of ridding the farms and gardens of "vermin." William Somervile's long neo-Miltonic eighteenth-century poem, *The Chace*, which Edith, his descendant, excerpted in her collection of hunting verse, *Notes of the Horn*, calls fox hunting "the Image of War, without its Guilt" (18). The form of warfare is that of cavalry sorties in open country. No doubt it was excellent as an exercise, but a farmer, finding his crops and poultry trampled under and his livestock stampeded after the hunt rushed through, might not agree about the absence of guilt.

Be that as it may, we have seen that in the early 1880s hunting had to be abandoned in some Irish districts when the tenants poisoned the covers, stoned the hounds away from the scent, and sometimes attacked hunting parties with pitchforks. In the 1890s, just at a time when their traditional authority was breaking up, owing to changes in the land laws brought about by the conflicts a decade earlier, the landlords resumed hunting with an enthusiasm that was perhaps obsessive, because it masked a nostalgia for dominance that would never again be satisfied in reality. Similarly for the Anglo-Irish cult of the horse and the hound: the horse, perpetually and everywhere symbolizing lordship, but nowhere more than in Ireland, becomes an end in itself when there are no more genuine lords. The hound, typifying fidelity, replaces the human "villein" in a fossilized survival of an old feudal bond requiring a servility that was always more wished for than real, and which dogs can be trained to supply on demand.

Some Experiences of an Irish R. M. (1899) and its two continuations, *Further Experiences of an Irish R. M.* (1908) and *In Mr. Knox's Country* (1915), are often remembered as very funny hunting stories, even though hunting is the main subject in only eight of the thirty-five episodes. I would suggest that these masterful stories are, in an important sense, about the de-anglicizing of the title character and narrator, Major Sinclair Yeates, and together make a sequel to *The Real Charlotte*, with a new direction indicated for the Anglo-Irish upper classes as they wrestle with the problem of their future in an Ireland that is rediscovering, along many lines of activity, linguistic, literary, and historical, its long disparaged "Celtic" heritage and, at the same time, beginning to move toward the painful confrontation with Britain, in armed struggle, which will bring about independence. De-anglicization was a main concern of the cultural nationalists of the 1890s and the following decade, given wide currency through Douglas Hyde's much-discussed lecture "On the Necessity for De-Anglicizing Ireland," which was published in 1894, and through the clever chauvinist journalism of D. P. Moran, who preached the "philosophy of an Irish Ireland" in his weekly paper, the *Leader*. He coined the term "West Briton" as a term of derision for Irish men and women whose manner and cultural orientation seemed derivative of English models.[20]

With his Oxford education and stint at the Sandhurst riding-school, his British army service in an English regiment, his monocle and self-deprecating manner, Irish Major Yeates is the very model of a West Briton.[21] Yet Somerville and Ross apply themselves to his de-anglicizing with more than a touch of mockery aimed at the chauvinists, for the Major's hibernicizing is an affair of the heart and entails no greening at all of his demeanor, his speech, his taste in poetry, or his loyalist politics. Nevertheless, his experience, once he has leased from Flurry McCarthy Knox the ramshackle big house of Shreelane in West Cork, is one long, bemused, and delighted sinking into intimate relations with the native condition and with the varieties of native temperament discoverable in that highly flavored and distinctive part of Munster.

Story after story, but always in fresh and unforeseeable ways, show "mere" Ireland's power to beguile or ensnare the stranger or outsider into a relation of complicity with itself. In *Poisson D'Avril*, a story where Yeates tries to bring a gift of Irish salmon to an English country house and ends up delivering instead a broken bottle of whisky wrapped up in the "grass-green" costume of a folk-festival step-dance contestant after committing a minor crime, this aspect of Irish life is called "the personal element." To it is due "the magnificent superiority of the Irish mind to the trammels of officialdom" (*Further Experiences*, 57). Since Yeates is an official, this view and the enthusiastic way he expresses it put him wonderfully at odds with himself. More self-contradiction emerges when we consider that while he is a district judge and occasional public prosecutor, he might himself be charged with a variety of infractions, usually committed in company with his landlord, Flurry Knox, that range in seriousness from horse theft ("Trinket's Colt") to poaching ("The Shooting of Shinroe"), illegal consumption of bootleg spirits at an unlicensed tavern ("The Last Day of Shraft"), dognapping ("A Conspiracy of Silence"), and being accessory after the fact to the killing of a white cockatoo ("The House of Fahy"). It appears that Yeates's career as resident magistrate at "Skebawn" (Skibbereen), West Cork, shows that same pattern of happy degeneration which led the English king in medieval times to complain that the knights he sent to subdue and rule the wild Irish all too soon suffered a sea change, becoming "more Irish than the Irish themselves."

Sinclair Yeates is more complicated as a literary construct than those reading the stories for sheer entertainment might realize. He represents a feat of male impersonation on the part of two women that is comparable to Maria Edgeworth's management of Thady Quirk in *Castle Rackrent*. It may have been Martin Ross's fascination with the law and the courts that led to their making him a stipendiary magistrate. One recalls her early attendance at the murder trial of the Invincibles and her involvement with a Dublin law society. While living at Drishane, she would read reports of the local assizes in the Skibbereen paper and make extracts of humorous testimony (Collis, 125). The Irish country people's penchant for false swearing and equivocal and evasive testimony, forming the basis of this humor, reflected the people's long experience with a system of imposed rule in which the native person had less than total confidence.

Over the course of the stories, Yeates's skills in horsemanship and hunting develop substantially until he can occasionally challenge Flurry himself. He reflects the development of Edith's skills as she took over and revived the nearly defunct West Carbery Hunt around the turn of the century. Duties included looking after the hounds. She also supplemented her income from writing and offset losses from the agricultural estate by horse coping; that is, by buying, training, and selling horses.

The major is a constructive development from Christopher Dysart. He has the latter's diffidence and equivalent service in the Empire, but not his paralyzed will, finickiness over vulgarity, and *nolo me tangere* attitude toward the tenant class. In the first story, "Great-Uncle McCarthy," when Yeates learns that Flurry's poor relations have been squatting in his lofts and attics, poaching and selling his live foxes, living on his provisions and doing this with the connivance of his cook and gamekeeper, he is dismayed but not inclined to punish. The McCarthy Gannons remove themselves while loudly proclaiming a prior right to Shreelane through the ancient Catholic line of the McCarthys. Major Yeates has met this attitude, though never so baldly expressed, in his daily work on the magistrates' bench. There he is beginning to sense when to stand his ground on an issue of right or of serious wrongdoing and when to throw up his hands and acknowledge the custom of the country.

This kind of knowledge takes time to acquire. All through these stories we see the major changing, keeping up with changing times. As the second volume opens he is Deputy M.F.H., substituting for Flurry, who has gone to South Africa with the Irish Yeomanry to fight in the Boer War. As soon as the option is available, the major becomes a motoring enthusiast. When a newly rich family of Dublin Catholics, the McRorys, buy property in the district, Yeates, unlike many of the local Protestants, makes friendly overtures toward them. He dislikes the boys' penchant for uproarious practical jokes, but he is taken with a daughter, Larky, for her good looks, flirtatious ways, and unfailing high spirits. This clan, except for the gloomy and distracted father, gets to cross what Yeates call the "bounder-y" line by being good at tennis, golf, riding, and dancing (*Further Experiences*, 232). On the other hand, Yeates remains quite snobbish about a family of prosperous farmers, the Flynns, whose house is ugly and overfurnished, where a picture of the Pope is displayed, and the overdressed daughters prattle on about their trips to London and Paris in affected accents (*Further Experiences*, 103–37).

That Yeates's wife Phillipa is English further helps to make him appear as occupying the classic Anglo-Irish middle ground between English and mere Irish extremes. It also helps that she belongs to the slight minority of English people who love the Irish on sight. The natives, who like to be liked, will love her back, especially if they are not too closely acquainted with the grounds of her affection: "These are the sort of people I love," says Phillipa. "Real Primitives" (*In Mr. Knox's Country*, 109).

The Anglo-Irish indigenes, as distinct from the major, are represented by the extraordinary Knox clan. They are "Black Protestants, all of them" claiming descent from a seventeenth-century Cromwellian venturer, but have shed the severe Calvinism connoted by their name. Knoxes fill all the ranks of local society, "from Sir Valentine Knox of

Castle Knox down to the auctioneer Knox, who bore the attractive title of Larry the Liar" (*Some Experiences*, 7). That does not bring us any way near the bottom, for in rural Ireland, auctioneers— who are usually substantial real-estate brokers in addition to conducting sales of household effects and farm equipment— belong to the prosperous middle class. A character only slightly less important in the R. M. stories than the major himself is young Florence McCarthy Knox—Flurry—who "occupied a shifting position about midway in the tribe," and "looked like a stable-boy among gentlemen and a gentleman among stable boys" (7). Just as Flurry is essential to the rural community in his role of leading huntsman and horse coper, so is he essential to the comic processes of these stories in his role of chief instigator, intriguer, and trickster. He also shows some unique features when we look at him from the perspective of "tribal"—Irish tribal, Knox tribal—concerns.

For instance, he is one of a kind among Knoxes in being of mixed heritage. Although we are told nothing directly about his parents, it is clear that his mother was a Catholic McCarthy with sufficient influence in the marriage to assure that the name Florence, a Munster first name for males that is matched with McCarthy as it is with no other Irish surname, became his. Before the English conquest, McCarthys were "the chief family of the Eoghanacht and one of the leading septs of Munster" (MacLysaght, 39). Flurry's two surnames are a piece of conflictful Irish history. However, he is just as black a Protestant as any other Knox and so loyal that he volunteers service in the Boer War with a British unit. Another volunteer group, the Irish Brigade, fought in South Africa on the Boer side. Flurry could have found himself riding out against Major John MacBride, Maud Gonne's future husband, and against Arthur Griffith, later head of Sinn Fein and of the first Irish Free State government. The native strain in Flurry, or rather the writers' idea of it, is seen in his slyness, his ability to think two jumps ahead of any rival or victim, especially when mischief is afoot.

In yet another aspect, that of his love for his cousin Sally, Flurry is shown as jealous and unsure, largely because he knows that the high-toned Lady Knox is determined to prevent her only child from throwing herself away on a half-bred half-sir, whether he is a loyal member of the Anglo-Irish tribe or not. He is, however, rescued from this difficulty by still another Knox, with whom he has a strong if indefinable rapport. That is old Mrs. Knox of Aussolas Castle, his own grandmother. It is she who provides cover for the successful elopement of Sally and Flurry on the night of the Aussolas Castle servants' ball and chimney fire ("Oh Love! Oh Fire!" *Some Experiences*, 281–309). She also dissolves her daughter-in-law's wrath and wins her assent to the match by willing Aussolas to Flurry and her valuable diamonds to Sally.

For certain thematic purposes old Mrs. Knox is the most important and interesting of all the clan. In her untidy castle staffed by eccentric servants, where every meal is an adventure, she dresses so as to appear like a bundle of rags stitched together with diamonds. That is Lady Knox's catty description. Her memory extends far back. One of the reasons she likes Major Yeates is because she had danced with his grandfather at Dublin Castle. Her memory is also unimpaired, a fact demonstrated by the pleasure she takes in capping English and Latin verse quotations with the Major. In "The Finger of Mrs. Knox," a relatively late story from *In Mr. Knox's Country*, the grandmother is characterized as a "successful ruler" and talented autocrat. Part of that talent is the "power of divining in her underlings their special gifts, and of wrestling them to the sphere in which they shone" (25). Thus, the hen-woman is enlisted to make up the fire and the gamekeeper is called to sweep the chimney. This is being done while "the cook panted in with the teatray," since "the butler, it appeared, had gone out to shoot a rabbit for dinner" (25). In the long history of Irish makeshifts, Mrs. Knox may be the first to treat making shifts as an art and as a principle of order.

In the remainder of the story, which is chock full of "modernizing" references to motor cars, women riding astride, and the cinema, Mrs. Knox interviews a former farm tenant who has fallen into the hands of Goggins the Gombeen and is facing foreclosure and eviction. With a certain grim satisfaction she reminds him that she no longer has power to forgive or postpone payment of his obligations, and that his landlord now, under the buy-out provisions of the Wyndham Act, is the government. But she also agrees to intercede with Goggins at his public house and actually succeeds in stopping the foreclosure on the basis of personal authority alone.

The story is even more political than appears on the surface. Within a generation, men like Goggins are going to sit in Dail Eireann, the Free State Parliament, and begin to legislate for Ireland. In their confrontation Mrs. Knox tells the publican that for a quick profit he has destroyed in an ugly way and in a few short weeks a forest planted by her father, which took eighty years to grow. There is some *parti pris* here of course. Goggins could retort, but does not, being content to bide his time, that it was not his class and "race" which denuded Ireland of her forests. In the native version of history deforestation went chronologically in phase with the English invasions and conquest, and the ensuing exploitation of Ireland's natural resources by the invader.

The metapolitics of the story consist in this. In a manner analogous to W. B. Yeats, though certainly not as consciously and self-consciously as Yeats, the cousins are trying to locate some essential quality, power, or value associated with Anglo-Irish tradition at its best, which might survive or outlast what is left of the rapidly liquidating Anglo-Irish economic, social, and political base. What Yeats called aristocracy and tried to backdate to the eighteenth century of Burke and the rest, Edith and Martin call "autocracy" and attempt to fix in the ancient, eccentric, yet still robust, alert, and authoritative figure of Flurry's grandmother.

The *Irish R. M.* stories were immensely successful and brought the cousins an international audience mainly composed, let it be said, of well-off country-dwelling people in Britain and the Dominion countries and in the eastern and southern United States. The native Irish read Somerville and Ross with particular understanding and amusement, while sometimes pretending they did not read them at all. There were the usual rewards and pressures arising from popularity. During the war in South Africa an English officer wrote to say that reading the stories had saved him from suicide. During World War I, *Irish R. M.* stories were included in the printed sheets that the *Times* sent out to the front-line troops.

The nature of their collaboration was disarmingly straightforward. Each took turns writing chapter by chapter, and each corrected and revised what the other wrote. Before starting to write *Some Experiences* they had "talked and argued into existence" several of its unforgettable characters.[22] And the idiom they consciously aimed to write in was what they actually called "Anglo-Irish." It was a tone or half-tone, a way of speech and writing reflecting a peculiar way of life: "In the speech of the upperclass man or woman what is crudely called the Irish brogue is rarely present in its strength; yet their talk is full of the vivid quality that is theirs, partly by heritage, partly by intimacy with the people who were till almost yesterday their tenants" (*Stray-Aways*, 188–89).[23] This style, which is "Irish enough," and whose subtle music the English ear may mistake for mere Irish "brogue," takes all the trophies.

It is the very spirit of late-nineteenth-century Anglo-Irish culture, autumnal Anglo-Ireland's essential myth of itself that the style conveys. There is a snobbish side to it, of course, but more significant is that this idea of the culture owes so very little by now to the English side of the double loyalty. The Anglo component in the Anglo-Irish oxymoron has nearly melted away, or rather, has become absorbed. Anglo-Irish talk is, once again, "full of the vivid quality that is theirs, partly by heritage, partly by intimacy with the people." The heritage has been Irish for a long time. Edith Somerville and Martin Ross in their bright collaboration are jewels in a diadem of Irish writers.

X

W. B. YEATS AND THE END OF ANGLO-IRISH LITERATURE

Friendship is all the house I have
—Yeats, *Autobiography*

Introductory

AFTER 1921, when the sovereignty of the Twenty-six Counties was established through a formal Truce and Treaty of Peace between the British government and the Irish Parliament of Sinn Fein rebels, the Anglo-Irish remnant coped with the change as best it could. With the partitioning off of the northeastern Six Counties, Free State Protestants became a tiny minority, less than eight percent in 1925 (Terence Brown, 84), in a society overwhelmingly Catholic and mere. The natives had no reason to love this remnant, most of whom had stood aside during the final struggle for independence, clinging at the last to loyalist and unionist political hopes. There were, however, no vengeful retaliations or public humiliations, and no reconfiscations of wealth and land that in past centuries had been seized by colonists in acts of conquest or attainder and then handed on to Anglo-Irish descendants. The setting fire to big houses—some three hundred were destroyed in the Troubles (1918–21) and the Civil War (1922–23)—was a dreadful thing, but during the Troubles much of the arson came from English Black and Tans in retaliatory raids and reprisals, and during the Civil War most destruction of country houses was carried out by I.R.A. raiders in defiance of the Free State and its protective laws. During the shaky first decade of the Free State's existence, the Cosgrave government guaranteed the property rights of all, including extensive holdings by British nationals, and the large properties of the various religious communions. In Dublin the two cathedrals, St. Patrick's and Christ's, had been held by the Protestants since the Reformation. Even though the city lacked a Roman Catholic cathedral church, these grand ecclesiastical establishments would remain with the Protestant Episcopal Church of Ireland. No one in government or in the Catholic hierarchy was prepared to revert to the barbarity of a Reformation-style seizure.

Perhaps the most enlightened act of the new government toward the Anglo-Irish and Unionist group was the careful shaping of the Irish parliamentary upper house, the Senate, so as to include significant representation from this minority. It was decided that a third of the senators would be appointed to the body by the prime minister or Taoseach, after consultation with his ministers, while the remaining two-thirds would be elected by members of the lower house, called the Dail. In this way the poet Yeats, along with such people of note as Lord Dunsany and Colonel Maurice Moore, the brother of George Moore the novelist, were brought into government. Yeats spent two three-year terms, from 1922 to 1928, giving service on various fine-arts committees, including one charged with approving designs for the new Irish coinage, and speaking out against a Censorship Bill and in favor of legislation permitting divorce. During debate over the Divorce Bill the poet recited the historic accomplishments of the Protestant Ascendancy and maintained that certain civilized values that he found central to Anglo-Irish tradition should be protected and celebrated in the new Irish society as it searched out a cultural identity of its own. These included courtesy, disinterestedness in public service, disdain for material gain, and a tradition of high intellect going back to Bishop Berkeley and Jonathan Swift.

Minister Kevin O'Higgins, speaking in Dail debate in 1922, when the bill to establish a Senate was being discussed, had chosen his words carefully in favoring participation by the Anglo-Irish minority:

> These people are part and parcel of the nation, and we being the majority and strength of the country . . . it comes well from us to make a generous adjustment to show that these people are regarded, not as planters, but that we regard them as part and parcel of this nation, and that we wish them to take their share of its responsibilities. (O'Sullivan, 75)

"These people" and "part and parcel" may seem a little cold, yet one should remember that O'Higgins is speaking to men and women who had only recently laid down arms after years of fighting against the English troops, some of whom had known neighbors and relatives savaged in reprisals, and some of whom had been recently released from prison terms for actions that no Irish nationalist would deem criminal.

Many in the Dail at that time would have thought the Anglo-Irish had always taken more than their share of everything *except* responsibility. And a few, because the nationalist memory is so tenacious, would have had no difficulty bringing to mind words about the Anglo-Irish spoken in 1848 by the agrarian radical James Fintan Lalor as he viewed the shambles in the rural districts wreaked by the great famine of 1848, and laid the blame at the landlords' doors:

> They form no class of the Irish people or any other people. Strangers they are in the land they call theirs, strangers here and strangers everywhere, owning no country and owned by none; rejecting Ireland and rejected by England; tyrants to this island and slaves to another; here they stand . . . alone in the world and alone in its history, a class by themselves. (Letter, *Irish Felon*, June 1848; quoted in Hall, 5)

Lalor's "alone . . . alone . . . a class by themselves" may oddly make us think of Yeats's lapidary phrase, "Anglo-Irish solitude," by which he means an admirable quality of heroic subjectivity and self-independence discernible in certain remarkable individuals produced by the Anglo-Irish as a beleaguered and isolated class: in his own time, such individuals as Synge the playwright, Parnell, and Lady Augusta Gregory. In Yeats's Nietzschean imaginative strategy, a term indicating a lack or disadvantage is transvaluated, becoming a term of praise.[1] But this is to anticipate.

By the middle of the 1930s, the Protestant proportion in the Free State population had further fallen to below six percent. Of these, few could be described as culture producers. Under Eamon de Valera, Irish society was slated to become increasingly pietistic and parochial, more or less democratic in constitution but conservative in style, an agrarian society of small and middle-sized family farms, somewhat isolated from the rest of Europe physically, and turned in on itself spiritually.[2] Yeats, along with Somerville and Ross and the main figures of the Irish Language and Literary Revival, belonged essentially to the final generation of the Anglo-Irish minority. After them the Ascendancy strain would persist in memory and commemoration but not as a culture that lived on. There was no longer a sufficient "critical mass" or demographic base to produce it.

Yeats seems to have understood this fact long before he appeared in the Irish Senate to remind his fellow citizens that the Anglo-Irish had done the state some service. His main involvement as a writer with Anglo-Irish themes, and his various attempts to sum up and celebrate the Anglo-Irish as a class, as a type of aristocracy, and a peculiar strain of Irish "intellect" are an effort to preserve what is dying out as a precious legacy of cultural memory. Clearly, his project resembles the activities of the language revivalists, who had been uncovering treasures of Gaelic cultural memory that were lost sight of when knowledge and educated use of the native language went into steep decline somewhere in the eighteenth century. In his services to Anglo-Irish writers he was trying to circumvent that form of tragic forgetting. They, too, he would insist, were Irish ancestral voices that must continue to sound if independent Ireland hoped to achieve a civilization worth much.

Before turning to consider the service Yeats rendered to a minority culture as the actual Anglo-Irish remnant was fading from the scene, it will be helpful to glance at how others of the Yeats generation came to terms with the new post-Treaty Ireland. Again we are primarily concerned with culture producers, the writers and scholars.

Some simply packed up and left. George Moore, who had moved from Ely Place, Dublin, to Ebury Street, London, in 1911, continued to visit Ireland until, in 1923, Moore Hall in Mayo was ravaged by fire. From then until he died in 1932, he was never able to bring himself to revisit his native country. Moore's friend, the fine literary critic and former National Librarian W. K. Magee—"John Eglinton"—was another who went to England. Though Magee was of Ulster Presbyterian stock, his critical perspectives were cosmopolitan and European; he much preferred reading Flaubert and mastering the philosophy of Nietzsche to working up a knowledge of the Irish saga heroes and heroines out of Standish O'Grady's and Lady Gregory's unscholarly compilations. He also lacked the energy and the nationalist convictions to put up with the sheer discomfort and hazard of life in the Free State during the Civil War. Moore, hoping that Magee would become his biographer, beckoned him to London. Settling at Bournemouth instead, he let others like Charles Morgan vie for the title of Moore's first biographer.

It may seem surprising that Standish J. O'Grady, the author of *History of Ireland: The Heroic Period* (1878), of *Finn and His Companions* (1892), and many other works that give a stirring and ennobling idea of ancient Ireland and her myths, and whom Yeats considered the true begetter of the Irish Literary Renaissance, should have moved to Britain in 1918, spending the last decade of his life on the Isle of Wight. By 1918, however, O'Grady was seventy-two and in poor health. During that year and the next two, the worst years of what has come to be called the Anglo-Irish War, Ireland was particularly strifeful and dangerous. Even Yeats had then considered it might become necessary to emigrate. Besides, O'Grady for all his unbridled attacks on the Anglo-Irish landlords as a failing class—in 1901 he described them as "rotting from the land in the most dismal farce tragedy of all time"[3]—was no Irish nationalist but an unwavering supporter of the Union, an Empire loyalist who saw no contradiction between this posture and his glorifications of such legendary heroes as Finn, Cuchulain, and Queen Maeve.

Other Anglo-Irish and Protestant figures in the Literary Revival appear to have used the movement as a sort of Jacob's ladder or rainbow bridge by which they escaped class and minority isolation and exposure and passed into the Irish mainstream. Preeminent here is Douglas Hyde (1863–1947), the landlord's son from Roscommon who cofounded the Gaelic League, delivered his influential lecture on de-anglicizing Ireland, translated and edited ancient texts and memorable collections of Old and Middle Irish poetry like *The Love Songs of Connacht* (1893), and wrote the first Irish language plays for Yeats's and Lady Gregory's Irish Literary Theater. In 1938, when Hyde became the first president of Ireland under the de Valera Constitution, a largely honorary and ceremonial position to be sure, his identification as a great living Irishman would have been accepted by nearly all parties. Sometimes he was called a "Catholic Protestant" by those unsure of the depth of his commitment to Irish political sovereignty, but if the test is survival and integration in an ongoing society, then this "golf-playing, grouse-shooting Anglo-Irishman" (Kiberd, 11) wins first-class honors.

Among major literary figures one can see J. M. Synge's tragically curtailed career as a steady journey away from the narrow and rather sour milieu of Dublin Protestant evangelicals of his birth toward reconciliation and then intimacy with the other Ireland. The stages of the journey are easy to mark: first his sojourns in the Aran Islands, beginning in 1898, and his tours of West Kerry and the Blaskets for the Congested Districts Board; his acquisition of spoken and written Irish and his considerable study in the Old and Middle Irish written record; the writing and staging of his peasant comedies, culminating in *The Playboy of the Western World* (1907), where what is "curious ironical" in his dramatic writing—the phrase is Yeats's ("Samhain 1904," *Explorations*, 157)—becomes dissolved in an imaginative treatment that is fully energized, joyous, and wild; and, finally, just before fatal illness overtook him, his romance and marriage engagement with the young Catholic actress Molly Allgood.

After Synge's death in 1909, Yeats wrote the finest imaginable sentence of eulogy about him: "Synge was the rushing up of the buried fire, an explosion of all that had been denied or refused, a furious impartiality, an indifferent turbulent sorrow" (*Autobiography*, 352). The words are not analytic ones about the general nature of an artist, but rather an attempt to suggest how a particular great artist came to express the inner life of a people at such a depth that the expression produced pain, an immense excitement, and even, from the people concerned, especially on first hearing, a vehement denial. A historically oppressed people is never really seen by or known to its oppressors, and over time, over centuries, comes to be unknown even to itself. Synge, who derived from the oppressor group, came to undo some of the damage, providing in his plays a shock therapy for historic misery and for the shame that settles into a habit of self-mistrust and self-repression. Yeats's is an extraordinary compliment, but Synge's was a deserving achievement.

Lady Gregory traveled her own sometimes arduous route to accommodation with the new Ireland at an age when most people would be content to sit by the fire. To those who know her principally as Yeats's epitome of Anglo-Irish aristocracy and as one of the triumvirate of directors, along with Synge and Yeats, of the Abbey Theater, it may come as a surprise to learn that her political views and values were going through dynamic change throughout the revolutionary epoch that opened with the 1916 Easter Rising. Her first and biggest change was the abandonment of a lifelong Unionist outlook. To avoid conflict with her son Robert, a fervent Imperialist, she kept her conversion to Irish nationalism to herself until 1918, when Robert was killed while flying combat missions for the British over Italy. At the split during the treaty negotiations between the Griffith-Collins group and the diehard republicans, she quietly sided with the latter, mainly because she admired de Valera, the republican leader who was refusing to accept the nominal oath of loyalty and Lloyd George's offer of Commonwealth status instead of full independence.[4] During the Civil War she took her turn night after night, managing the theater hands-on at a time when the republicans were trying to close down Free State institutions, in the case of the Abbey, which received a small government subsidy, by frightening away audiences and performers alike. Here she could not go along with a de Valera tactic and did all she could to keep the theater open.

One night the play was Yeats's *Cathleen ni Houlihan*, and the actress in the key part of the Poor Old Woman, symbolizing Ireland herself, failed to appear. Lady Gregory, knowing every word and gesture of this famous work, dating from 1902, went on and played the part. She had never appeared on a professional stage before, nor would she ever again. The role had originally been written for Maud Gonne. These two most important women in Yeats's adult life seldom met, although Yeats, who was fascinated with linkages of the incompatible and antithetical, would sometimes introduce them as characters in the same poem. He does this in "Beautiful Lofty Things," a late poem, which ends, "All the Olympians; a thing never known again" (*Poems*, 303). Perhaps there is something Olympian, certainly not to be known again, in Augusta Gregory's acting Maud Gonne MacBride's part in order to keep the theater open against the will of the republicans so many years after Madame MacBride's bitter, intransigent, and radical republicanism had estranged her from the poet and led her to abandon an acting career as well.[5]

Yeats: Myths and Facts

Yeats's final undertaking for Anglo-Ireland was to bear witness to the end of its tradition as a distinguishable strand in the fabric of Irish life, to pipe a former ruling class to its grave. He worked at it with the aid of several falsifications of actuality which proved serviceable as poetic myths or fictions. Let us grant that "actuality" and "facts" are fictions too. Even so, distinctions must be made.

One myth was that of the natural nobility and spiritual dignity of the Irish peasantry, the "Gaelic race." Its complement was the myth of a true Anglo-Irish aristocracy of gentle "blood," high character, and superior intellect. Both fictions were given a pseudohistorical grounding running somewhat as follows: before the English conquest, the culture of the Gaelic folk was a dignified unity. Admirable qualities of this culture included natural refinement of manners, an instinct of deference to leaders and masters, powers of spiritual intuition, unbridled imagination, and expressive speaking. During the long occupation by the English, these qualities were driven underground to varying degrees, yet managed to survive, surfacing at the end of the nineteenth century under the encouraging stimulus of the Irish Language and Literary Revival and a renascent cultural nationalism. This revival could not, of course, bring back lost leaders—a Lord Edward Fitzgerald, a Parnell, and, more distantly, the native aristocrats who had taken their swan- and gooselike flights at the end of O'Neill's Rebellion, during the era of Cromwell, and at the end of the Jacobite war. Nor did it extend to improving the peasants' economic position, or to providing them with a modern education and a chance for their children to climb into the middle class. But that was just as well, since middle-class values and modern intellect were largely corrupted by materialism. Better to go unlettered and in rags than to be trained for a "huxter's"[6] career of fumbling in greasy tills.

In parallel, the culture of the Anglo-Irish gentry class before the Union was transvaluated through Yeats's myth of a late-seventeenth- to late-eighteenth-century intellectual ascendancy whose luminaries were Berkeley and Burke, Swift and Goldsmith, and the College Green parliamentary orators. These figures demonstrated a late-arriving Renaissance in Ireland that compared favorably to the European Renaissance, especially to the urbane aristocrats and humanists of the fifteenth- and sixteenth-century Italian city states of Urbino, Florence, and Ferrara. About the extent to which this high culture had endured and been transmitted during the nineteenth century the poet remained of two minds. He saw certain families and houses—the Gregories of Coole

Park, the Gore-Booths of Lissadell in Sligo, the Persses and Shawe-Taylors of Roxborough House, Galway, where Lady Gregory spent her girlhood—as legitimate heirs of a golden age. But other families and houses, including the Moores of Moore Hall, were not recipients and transmitters of golden-age culture to the same extent, if at all. It appeared that Anglo-Irish tradition at its finest was continuous and discontinuous at the same time. Such contradictions, which would be quite disturbing in the realm of the factual, are acceptable when one is dealing in myths.

Another fiction was that of "kindly" relations between peasantry and aristocracy. This amity had somehow magically returned after the merely incidental disruptions caused by the great famine of the 1840s and the struggle over landownership during the 1870s and 1880s. Over long reaches of time amity was the norm, though close examination of any particular phase of Irish history from the twelfth-century invasion onward might be hard put to demonstrate its presence.

Many Yeats critics have accepted his mythmaking for the truth. In the opening chapter of his standard work, *The Lonely Tower: Studies on the Poetry of W. B. Yeats*, T. R. Henn lays out as history nearly everything I have just called fiction. He begins by quoting stanza one from "Meditations in Time of Civil War," written during 1921–22:

> Surely among a rich man's flowering lawns
> Amid the rustle of his planted hills,
> Life overflows without ambitious pains;
> And rains down life until the basin spills,
> And mounts more dizzy high the more it rains
> As though to choose whatever shape it wills
> And never stoop to a mechanical
> Or servile shape, at others' beck and call.
>
> (*Poems*, 200)

Instead of treating as somewhat idealized the poem's image of rich life endlessly expending and renewing itself—a perpetual-motion machine of privilege— Henn takes it for a description of how life was actually led on Irish "great estates" before the Rebellion. He sketches the following genre picture:

> To this society, in the main Protestant, Unionist, and of the 'Ascendancy' in character, the peasantry was linked. The great demesnes had their tenantry, proud, idle, careless, kindly, with a richness of speech and folklore. . . . The days of *Castle Rackrent* and the absentee landlord were, in the main, over; the relationship between landlord and tenant varied, but was on the whole a kindly one, and carried a good deal of respect on either side.

> The bitterness of famine, the evictions and burnings . . . belonged to an earlier period. The members of the family would be known either by the titles of their professions: the Counsellor, the Bishop, the Commander, and so on; or by the Christian names of their boyhood. They mixed with the peasantry more freely and with a greater intimacy (especially in childhood) than would have been possible in England. . . . Sport of every kind was a constant bond: the ability to shoot, or fish, or ride a horse was of central importance. At its best there was something not unlike a survival of the Renaissance qualities: . . . "Soldier, scholar, horseman, he". (Henn, 5–6)

Here is someone swallowing whole Yeats's mythifying of big houses and adding a few touches of his own. "The Counsellor, the Bishop, the Commander" are like titles in a glamorized version of antebellum American plantation culture, where every proprietor is an honorary colonel and the slaves, wearing powdered wigs and satin knee breeches, are called Pompey and Cincinnatus. Henn refers to the bond created by sport and horsemanship. For that we might recall the violent attacks on hunting parties carried out during the Land War. George Moore remembered a day of hunting when he was caught in a violent thunderstorm and had to stable his nervous mount in a tenant's cabin, the family being forced outside until the weather cleared. So much for renaissance qualities and bonding through sport.

More soberly, the problem is to determine at what period before the Rebellion of 1916–21, Henn's dividing point, these kindly relations on the estates were enjoyed. Moving backward, it could not have been at the time of the Wyndham Act, for that was a response to long-standing angry differences between leasehold farmers and owners over rent, security of tenure, and landownership. Obviously it was not during the Land War or in the period of the great famine. If relations were less than kindly during the "hungry forties," they certainly could not have been better in the Tithe War of the early 1830s, when tax collectors—"tithe proctors"—were sometimes buried alive, flayed with furze bushes, or mutilated by tenant mobs. During the 1820s there is the intense struggle over Catholic Emancipation disturbing tenant-landlord relations, and before that the atrocities and conspiracies of the peasant secret societies about which Carleton wrote. We have arrived at 1798, year of the major rising famous for its having set Protestants against Catholics, peasants against landowners, and for the ferocity of acts committed on both sides. Before that there is the era depicted in *Castle Rackrent*, a work presenting a model of landlord-tenant relations, which Henn has already characterized as bad.

When then? Most likely never. Kindly relations *as a norm* are really not in the case. They are what someone infers as a child from the gentleness of servants and then in adulthood nostalgically projects back in time. Henn was himself Anglo-Irish and grew up on an estate in County Clare. He says, "The relations between Protestants and Catholics might be bitter, and memories of the Penal Laws were long; but in the years before the First World War I remember little trouble in the West" (7). Why should he have remembered trouble at all? In those years T. R. Henn was a tiny boy.

This mistaking of myth for actuality has had wide currency in later Yeats criticism, especially among American critics. Donald Torchiana's *W. B. Yeats and Georgian Ireland* (1966), the standard work on its subject, essentially takes Henn's chapter on the Anglo-Irish background as its starting point in "reality." Finding this approach unsatisfactory, the English Yeatsian Peter Ure said in a review of Torchiana that "both patriot and the mythopoeic poet are entitled to their simplicities, [but] the scholar is not." According to Ure, Yeats chose to live by myth "first (to put it with a crudity), by going 'Gaelic' and then by going 'Anglo-Irish'. It is most important for our general sanity that he should be very clearly seen to have lived by myths" (Ure, xi). Though Torchiana's work is indispensable, it does tend to foster the illusion that Yeats's Anglo-Irish golden age, a highly imaginative construct, is actually what happened.

During the 1970s, Daniel Harris in *Yeats: Coole Park and Ballylee* (1974) could present rich readings of Yeats's "Jonsonian" country house poems of the 1920s and early 1930s without worrying the question whether the Anglo-Ireland the poems constructed corresponded to underlying realities. More recently, however, a group of critics has emerged for whom the issue is paramount. Irish-born, they include Seamus Deane, W. J. MacCormack, and Declan Kiberd, all of whom came to maturity in the civil-rights decade of the 1960s and saw the old sectarian and political conflict between Protestant majority and Catholic minority in partitioned Ulster reignite after 1968. As strife has continued, writers from this group have tended to be impatient and ironic when dealing with such topics as the autonomy and privilege of the poetic imagination, Yeats's cult of violence—his "Saito's sword" complex—and the notion of a high-minded, disinterested Protestant aristocracy and golden age.

In Deane's *Short History of Anglo-Irish Literature* (1986), "Protestant Ascendancy," a term he discovers was first used by a cabal of Dublin politicians and businessmen in 1792, is simply "a system of privilege based on the interests of one group, which defined itself in politically sectarian terms" (54). Here Ascendancy is hard to distinguish from Orangeism, a movement whose origins can be traced to 1795 in which religious passion and sectarian bigotry were manipulated for economic advantage. Whatever Yeats had in mind as he praised Anglo-Irish Ascendancy, it certainly was not that. Deane has also written, in "Literary Myths of the Revival," that "the most seductive of all Yeats's historical fictions is his gift of dignity and coherence to the Irish Protestant Ascendancy tradition. . . . We tend perhaps to forget how much retrospective glamour the Ascendancy has gained from the Yeatsian version of its achievement in literature. The literary tradition has absorbed this version as a truth. As a consequence we fail to see that the heroic impulse which rather ambiguously transforms the physical force tradition in politics (as in "Easter 1916" or "The Statues") also produces the intellectual chauvinism of that Yeatsian recitation of the great eighteenth century names" (*Celtic Revivals*, 28).

Deane somewhat overstates the glamour shed backward by the Yeatsian version, at least among the Irish themselves. As recently as 1956, Constantia Maxwell could remark in the new preface to her brilliant social history of *Dublin under the Georges* (1936, 1957) that "for long the Protestant Ascendancy . . . has been in bad odour in Ireland," adding that "its cultural heritage is now at last being valued, and will, one sincerely hopes, soon become completely absorbed in the national tradition" (Maxwell, 16). So was it Yeats's hope as he trafficked in historical fictions, as poets will, and proceeded, in Ure's words, to "go Anglo-Irish" at a certain stage of his complicated career.

Going Anglo-Irish

> And we asked ourselves why our Willie Yeats
> should feel himself called upon to denounce his own
> class; millers and shipowners on one side, and on the other
> a portrait painter of distinction; and we laughed. . . . All
> the romantic poets have sought illustrious ancestry.
> —Moore, *Hail and Farewell*

On his mother's side Yeats derived from middle-class Protestant stock. The territory was Sligo on the Irish west coast, and the important family names were Pollexfen, Armstrong, and Middleton. These were the sort of people who had comprised the loyalist yeomanry in the 1798 United Irish Rising. Through his mother, Susan Pollexfen, Yeats was connected to millers, merchants, and a sea captain, his grandfather, who carried cargoes and passengers in his own small shipping line between Irish western ports and Liverpool. The gentry families of the county, the poet tells us in an early autobiography, performed public duties and attended church with families like his, but did not exchange visits with them.[7]

Not until he was a young man domiciled elsewhere, with a growing reputation as a poet and man of letters, did Yeats receive an invitation to visit Lissadell, seat of the Gore-Booths and birthplace of those two strong-minded daughters—"one a gazelle"—Eva and Constance.

On his father's side Yeats derived from northern and western church ministers, and from Dublin people who included an eighteenth-century Castle official and a linen merchant. More remotely and uncertainly, there was a link through the Butler name with the family holding the dukedom of Ormond, centered in Kilkenny in modern times. The poet's father, John Butler Yeats, was a Trinity-educated barrister who abandoned the law for portrait painting and lived mainly in London before emigrating as an elderly widower to New York. During several generations the Yeats family had collected rent from a small landholding at Thomastown, County Kildare. This source of income disappeared as a direct result of the Land War. The last of the Kildare land was sold to the tenants, as directed by the Ashbourne Land Distribution Act, in 1888. The Yeatses then, to the extent they could be considered landlords, were petty, hard-pressed, absentee, and failing.[8] When William was a boy, his mother "reminded the children constantly of the financial difficulties in the family. They were told they could not have things they wanted badly till Mrs. Flanagan, a delinquent Thomastown tenant, paid the rent. So they named a rag doll Mrs. Flanagan, and, when the rent did not come on time, ill treated the doll" (Murphy, 86).

These facts are not so riveting in themselves as in their indicating that Yeats's discovery of an ennobled and intellectually distinguished Anglo-Irish tradition proceeded, not from what he was born to or experienced in early life, but from what he lacked and wished for. That is as it should be, according to his own notion of self and antiself, or self and opposing mask, the theory of creativity first laid out in *Per Amica Silentia Lunae* (1917) and later much elaborated in the two versions of *A Vision* (1925, 1937). In this compensatory scheme of the creative imagination, the artist shapes himself and his given circumstances or "body of fate" anew in an image, myth, or assumed personality ("persona") that is only connected to himself as origin by being an opposite. Thus in Yeats's poem "*Ego Dominus Tuus*," comprising the second part of *Per Amica Silentia Lunae* (*Mythologies*, 321–24), Keats is said to make "luxuriant song" from a life experience of debility and deprivation, while Dante makes high religious art from a life experience in which lechery has played a large part.

Ideas of aesthetic self-reinvention in Yeats owe something to Oscar Wilde, who was a kindly influence when Yeats began to make his literary way in London in the late 1880s (*Autobiography*, 88–93). Wilde's aesthetic of posing, dandyism, and the brilliant surface makes much of a personality deliberately constructed and of "the truth of masks" (Wilde, 408–32). Another source was Nietzsche, whom Yeats began to read and reread as early as 1902, especially the Nietzschean doctrine of "self-overcoming." To be ordinarily Anglo-Irish was to experience a divided and conflicted social identity. It was not, however, until Yeats became friends with Lady Gregory that he saw how to reinvent himself as Anglo-Irish in a grand style.

They met in summer of 1896. She drove over from Coole Park to Tullyra Castle, where the poet was visiting Moore's cousin Edward Martyn in company with the poet and critic Arthur Symons. On that day she invited Yeats to come stay with her. He accepted the invitation to be her houseguest and with surprising ease formed a lifelong friendship with this widowed upper-class lady of forty-five, and with her family. The connection was useful in giving him somewhere to spend his summers for the next two decades, until he bought and refurbished his own country home, the Norman tower at Ballylee about a mile from Coole, a site linked to one of the Coole lakes by a rapid mill stream and underground channel ("Coole and Ballylee, 1931," (*Poems*, 243–45). But it was more than useful. Yeats's father well understood his son's poetic genius; writing to him in one of his last letters, from New York, in June 1921, John Butler Yeats says: "When is your poetry at its best? I challenge all the critics if it is not when the wild spirit of your imagination is wedded to concrete fact. Had you stayed with me and not left me for Lady Gregory, and her friends and associations, you would have loved and adored concrete life for which as I know you have a real affection" (J. B. Yeats, 280–81).

We may set aside the old bohemian painter's quite mistaken assumption that he ever provided any of his offspring the security of a place to stay with him, but not his conviction that his oldest son's relation to Lady Gregory and her world was crucial for his entire career in maturity. Nor would the poet himself have disagreed. Some twelve years after their first meeting, on February 4, 1909, Yeats wrote of Lady Gregory, who was dangerously ill at the time: "She has been to me a mother, friend, sister and brother. I cannot realize the world without her—she brought to my wavering thoughts steadfast nobility. All day the thought of losing her is like a conflagration in the rafters. Friendship is all the house I have" ("Journal," *Memoirs*, 160–61). His admitting to an essential homelessness apart from homing on this Anglo-Irish Penelope, Augusta Gregory—rings true. The burning-rafters figure is arresting, prophetic even, when one considers that the history of the big houses was soon to become the history of their fiery destruction. When the rafters went, all was over—with Roxboro House, where Lady Gregory was born, fated to go down in flames along with Moore Hall and so many others. But most important is Yeats's revelation in an intimate journal of his great, dependent love for his patron and collaborator, of the cult he has made of her and her unwavering nobility.

When the friendship began, Yeats was not exactly unknown and unconnected. In his London-based activity he was already the leading younger poet of his day, the most talented survivor of the early 1890s Rhymers group, and about to publish his most important poetry collection thus far, *The Wind among the Reeds* (1899). And he was not thinking about abandoning his English base, for Woburn Buildings, Bloomsbury, would remain his permanent winter residence during the next twenty years, until he married.

In his Irish undertakings at this time, Yeats was equally a figure to be reckoned with. Returning to Dublin from prison and exile in 1886, the old Fenian, John O'Leary, had recruited him to the cause of Irish nationalism, instructing him in the political traditions of Thomas Davis and the Young Ireland movement of the 1840s, and designating him heir apparent of the poets of Young Ireland, such as they were. Ever since, Yeats had been active and leading in every project and controversy of Irish cultural nationalism that arose, whether it was a scheme for circulating books reflecting the native culture and national aspirations throughout rural Ireland, the founding of Irish literary and debating societies among young émigrés in Britain, or propagandizing through reviews and articles on behalf of Douglas Hyde's new translations of poetry from the Irish. Though never active in it, Yeats, on whom a file was kept by the Castle intelligence apparatus, was briefly a member of the Irish Republican Brotherhood (IRB), the secret revolutionary organization that sprang, Phoenixlike, from the smoking ruins of the Fenian uprising of 1867. Also through O'Leary, in 1889, Yeats had met tall, beautiful Maud Gonne, with a complexion like apple blossoms, who, he writes in the *Memoirs*, "had received the political traditions of Davis with an added touch of hardness and heroism from the hand of O'Leary" (41).

Maud Gonne, with whom Yeats fell forever in love, brought into his life, whether he saw her in Dublin, London, or abroad in Normandy or Paris, the "overwhelming tumult" of her fierce and active Irish republicanism. Eventually a certain distance grew between them, after she married Catholic John MacBride, an IRB rebel whom Yeats loathed—he is the "old bellows full of angry wind" of "Easter 1916." Their estrangement also grew from her close involvement in political agitation among elements of the Dublin lower middle class and working class whom Yeats had come to despise for their moralistic and philistine approach to the fine arts and for what he thought was their conformism and bigotry as Catholics. But in 1897 he and Maud were still working together on political projects, one of which was in preparation for the centennial of the Rebellion of 1798.

Yeats was nominal head of an agitprop group calling itself the Wolfe Tone Memorial Association. On the evening of June 22, 1897, he found himself in the midst of a street demonstration organized by Maud and directed against the participation of loyalist Dubliners in public celebrations of Victoria's sixty-year jubilee of reign. We have available the poet's own impression of the Jubilee Riot that ensued: "That evening there was a meeting of our council in the City Hall, and when we came out after it the crowds were waiting for us all around the Hall. We were going to the National Club in Rutland Square, and they came too. Outside the National Club, a magic lantern was to show on a white screen statistics of evictions, deaths from starvation, etc., during Victoria's reign. Somewhere in front of us was a mock funeral Maud Gonne devised, a coffin with 'the British Empire' printed upon it, and black flags with the names of all those who had been hanged for treason during Victoria's reign. Presently they began breaking windows where there were decorations." These were loyalist decorations, including the union jack and pictures of Victoria. At this point he notes that "Maud Gonne was walking with a joyous face." He next describes how police proceeded to baton the demonstrators, treating a group of old women watching the magic-lantern show with particular brutality. "My memory is that two hundred people were taken to hospital and that one old woman was killed"(*Memoirs*, 112–13).

Maud Gonne was not Irish. Her father was a British general, "Tommy" Gonne, and her mother was a connection of the English Cook family, which pioneered the travel business. Growing up in Ireland and France after her mother's early death, she became anti-English and antiimperialist as only a renegade can be. Even before she found the blackjack of Irish nationalism with which to strike at John Bull, she had conspired with French Boulangists to clip the claws and flea the rump of the British imperial lion. Lady Gregory was at that time a loyalist, as might be expected of the widow of Sir William Gregory, baronet, South Galway's premier landowner, former governor-general of Ceylon, and a descendant of an eighteenth-century director of the East India company to whom, Yeats claimed, the great Edmund Burke committed the care of the people of India, "now that he himself had grown old" (*Autobiography*, 261). Her house and its mode of life were the very epitome of Anglo-Irish planter culture as it had evolved for centuries under the protection of British power, where "every generation had left its memorial" (*Autobiography*, 260). Yeats's ability in that period of his life to turn from one woman to the other, from nationalist to unionist, may still seem surprising and in need of further discussion.

"I must have spent the summer of 1897 at Coole" (*Autobiography*, 267). If so, he went there straight from the Jubilee Riot. The usual explanation, based largely upon his late autobiographical work *Dramatis Personae*, is that the poet, overworked and driven close to a breakdown by Maud's resolute rejection of his love, was glad enough for the invitation from a perhaps lonely yet highly intelligent and cultivated gentlewoman, who shared his interests in the folk beliefs and superstitions of the country people and in spiritualism, and who, in the generally more tolerant political climate of the late 1890s, would have been neither terrified nor shocked by his nationalist fervor. In Sligo, Yeats had collected folklore from the cottagers, from the well-stocked memory of his own mother, Susan Pollexfen Yeats, and especially from Mary Battle, his Uncle George Pollexfen's mediumistic housekeeper; this material had enriched his early poetry and his collection of Irish country tales and legends, *The Celtic Twilight* (1893). Similarly now, on the Coole Park estate and in the villages nearby, he would go from cabin to cabin with Augusta Gregory, collecting folkloric protocols while slowly recovering from his nervous crisis: "and every night she wrote out what we had heard in the dialect of the cottages. . . . She wrote, if memory serves, two hundred thousand words, discovering the vivid English she was the first to use upon the stage" (*Autobiography*, 267).

Later on, Yeats would testify that he was drawn to Lady Gregory, her house, and the elevated traditions of life both she and it embodied out of a peculiar instinct to give service. He uses the term in a sense that dignifies and sweetens it, placing it at a feudal and bardic remove from servility. Thus, early in *Reveries over Childhood and Youth* (1914), after talk of various seventeenth-century ancestors, including several adherents of William and one Jacobite who followed Patrick Sarsfield and the native Irish cause, Yeats says: "I am delighted with all that joins my life to those who had power in Ireland or with those anywhere that were good servants and poor bargainers" (*Autobiography*, 12). Again, in the *Autobiography—First Draft*, begun in 1915, describing that first visit to Coole, he says: "But here many generations, and no uncultivated generation, had left the images of their service in furniture, in statues, in pictures, and in the outline of wood and field. I think I was not meant for a master but for a servant, and that it has been my unhappiness to see the analytic faculty dissolve all those things that invite our service, and so it is that all images of service are dear to me" (*Memoirs*, 102).

To some extent, the kind of service he is talking about, and despite his disclaimer of being meant for a master, is that of a governing or aristocratic class. It is well rendered by the French expression *noblesse oblige*. One recalls that one of the Pope's titles is "servant of the servants of God." During Holy Week he stoops to wash the feet of a poor prisoner, but not during the rest of the year. Comparable aristocratic humility is expressed when the sister of a belted earl stands to be introduced, whether the arriving guests are women or men. Surely one source of Yeats's imaginative play with "service" and "servant" is his pride of ancestry surrounding his middle name. The dukes of Ormond were first gentlemen of the Norman king's household, hence "butlers." By that route Butler becomes a proud cognomen suggesting anything but a servile role.[9]

Finally, in some of his last poems, where an aged Yeats commemorates an Anglo-Ireland no longer above ground, that only exists insofar as it has been alembicated into poetic images, he assumes, with an effect mingling pathos and haughtiness, the persona of a confidential servant left behind by, or surviving, a beloved and admired mistress or master. That is the role he takes in remembering Coole in the fifth stanza of "The Municipal Gallery Revisited":

> My mediaeval knees lack health until they bend,
> But in that woman, in that household where
> Honour had lived so long, all lacking found.
>
> (*Poems*, 320)

And the same role is played out to the end in "The Curse of Cromwell," where the speaker appears as an ancient survivor, part bard, part tattered seneschal, endearingly like poor Thady Quirk, except that he belongs to a wider sweep of historical time. The great house in the poem is the entire habitation of Anglo-Irish culture, from first to last. But it is also seventeenth-century "Old Catholic" and Cavalier in its particular represented qualities. That sets it in flat opposition to "Cromwell's house and Cromwell's murderous crew," which represent the iron-sided puritan obsession with material accumulation, with whiggery, hucksterism, "making it,"—all those qualities which J. B. Yeats taught his son to despise long before he fell in with Lady Gregory "and her friends and associations":

> You ask what I have found, and far and wide I go,
> Nothing but Cromwell's house and Cromwell's murderous crew,
> The lovers and the dancers are beaten into the clay,
> And the tall men and the swordsmen and the horsemen where are they?
> And there is an old beggar wandering in his pride—
> His father served their fathers before Christ was crucified.
> *O what of that, O what of that*
> *What is there left to say?*
>
> . . .
>
> But there's another knowledge that my heart destroys
> As the fox in the old fable destroyed the Spartan boy's

Because it proves that things both can and cannot be;
That the swordsmen and the ladies can still keep company;
Can pay the poet for a verse and hear the fiddle sound,
That I am still their servant though all are underground.
O what of that, O what of that
What is there left to say?

I came on a great house in the middle of the night
Its open lighted doorway and its windows all alight,
And all my friends were there and made me welcome too;
But I woke in an old ruin that the winds howled through;
And when I pay attention I must out and walk
Among the dogs and horses that understand my talk.
O what of that, O what of that
What is there left to say?

(*Poems*, 304–5)

It appears then that to be the servant and the bardic mourner of a ruined noble cause is the highest form of service left. Some of the natives had thought this for a very long time. Now it was the turn of the Anglo-Irish to think it.

The Final Service

In 1927, Lady Gregory sold the Coole estate to the Irish Free State Ministry of Lands and Agriculture, leasing back the house and a scrap of ground for a small annual rent until her death in 1932. Then the house was taken down and the ground on which it had stood was planted over with evergreens as a forest preserve. Reflecting on these changes, we may well wonder what service Yeats might have thought he could perform, not just for her, but by extension for the class and culture she and Coole were emblems of, when these had so little time left. The answer may be evident from the way the question is put. Yeats's service would be to praise what was worthy about Anglo-Ireland and the culture created by an agrarian, largely Protestant gentry during three centuries or more of their presence in Ireland; to champion or defend what was defensible in the values of Anglo-Ireland against the attacks that would be, that were, leveled against it as a new order took over and a new nation came to be; and finally, to commemorate it, to make the best of what had to die seem vivid and ever living through the myth-making powers of his art.

Three services then, to each of which can be assigned an approximate span of time and a characteristic factor of risk. *Praising*: From about 1902 to 1918, from the first poem set at Coole, "In the Seven Woods"

(*Poems*, 77), to the great elegy "In Memory of Major Robert Gregory" (132–35), where courtly compliment ("Soldier, scholar, horseman, he, / As 'twere all life's epitome") is checked by the need to acknowledge a loss so grievous that it cannot be uttered: "but a thought / Of that late death took all my heart for speech." The risk run is fulsomeness, the courtier's false note, the mincing Osric tone, praise meant to be overheard by a patron, with a suitable payoff to follow.

Championing: From about 1919 to 1927, from "On a Political Prisoner" (*Poems*, 183–84), where the values of Anglo-Irish tradition are challenged from inside, through the example of the well-born prisoner's having rejected them as she took up the career of bitter nationalist agitation and armed insurgency that led to her imprisonment, to "Blood and the Moon" (237–39), written in August 1927, where "Goldsmith and the Dean, Berkeley and Burke" are recruited as luminaries of an elevated conception of Anglo-Irish art and intellect reaching back to a presumed golden age. Here the risk is that the championing or defense will be not only of values central to civilization, but also, in a reactionary spirit, of class arrogance, intolerable pride, and mere privilege.

Commemoration: It was already in progress by the time Augusta Gregory disposed of her estate, and runs straight on to Yeats's death in January 1939. A poem such as "The Tower" (*Poems*, 194–200), written in October 1925, seems to be on the cusps between defense and memorializing. This is seen particularly in Section 3, where the speaker, representing himself as the veritable embodiment of Anglo-Irish pride of accomplishment, wills that quality to "upstanding men" who will follow after:

I declare
They shall inherit my pride,
The pride of people that were
Bound neither to Cause nor to State,
Neither to slaves that were spat on,
Nor to the tyrants that spat,
The people of Burke and of Grattan
That gave, though free to refuse—

This works splendidly at the level of myth, somewhat less well when confronted with certain facts. Grattan's people, if they are anybody, include the late-eighteenth-century Irish Parliament, which could have voted for full Catholic Emancipation but did not, and against the Union but did not. In important respects, the last line quoted makes a truer history when changed to "That refused, though free to give." The risk in commemoration, then, was of being drawn to indulge in a type of historical nostalgia that could turn into amnesia or be used as a stalking horse for certain illiberal ideas and pseudo-ideas with which the poet toyed during the 1930s. This was the period of his brief dalliance with the program for Ireland of General Eoin O'Duffy and his fascist Blue Shirts.[10]

The later Yeats has been called reactionary and fascist before.[11] I would not go that far. Agreeing with Auden that "he was silly like us" is far enough. But perhaps no one has cast the aspersion of "courtier" before. Was Yeats in fact ever a lackey of the Ascendancy in the period 1902–1918? The question legitimately comes up in connection with his widely known and quoted poem "Upon a House shaken by the Land Agitation" (*Poems*, 95–96), and there is now in print some fascinating material to help settle it. Yeats wrote the poem during August 1909, while summering at Coole. George Moore, egged on by his friend AE, pretended to believe that the house in the poem was the British House of Lords:

> How should the world be luckier if this house,
> Where passion and precision have been one
> Time out of mind, became too ruinous
> To breed the lidless eye that loves the sun?
> And the sweet laughing eagle thoughts that grow
> Where wings have memory of wings, and all
> That comes of the best knit to the best? Although
> Mean roof-trees were the sturdier for its fall,
> How should their luck run high enough to reach
> The gifts that govern men, and after these
> To gradual Time's last gift, a written speech
> Wrought of high laughter, loveliness and ease?

The three quatrains shape toward a sonnet of Shakespearian type, except that there is no concluding, clinching couplet. That is a pity, since it might have interrogated the very questions which structure the rhetorical argument. Instead, the claims of privilege are luxuriantly displayed while "mean roof-trees" really do not get to speak. The poem keeps its hand over the mouth of the commonalty. This is deference with a vengeance. Now for the documentation.

Although the actual events directly inspiring "Upon a House" did not come into full view until summer 1909, Yeats's private journal, which he had begun to keep in 1908, shows that by March 1909 he was already brooding on questions of class superiority and the role of wealth in the making of "high" civilization: "In spite of myself my mind dwells more and more on ideas of class. Ireland has grown sterile, because power has passed to men who lack the training which requires a certain amount of wealth to ensure continuity from generation to generation, and to free the mind in part from other tasks" (*Memoirs*, 178). Then on August 7, 1909, he enters in the journal "Subject for a poem: 'A Shaken House,'" followed by a prose version of the poem he was to write. This procedure of preparaphrasing a poem still to come is not uncommon in Yeats. In this he was following one of his acknowledged masters in poetic craft, Ben Jonson:

> How should the world gain if this house failed, even though a hundred little houses were the better for it; for here power [has] gone forth or lingered, giving energy, precision; it gave to a far people beneficent rule; and still under its roof living intellect is sweetened by old memories of its descent from far off? How should the world be better if the wren's nest flourish and the eagle's house is scattered? (*Memoirs*, 225)

The next entry, on the same day, is a first metrical draft of the poem, followed by—"I wrote this on hearing the results of reductions of rent made by the court" (226). A reader may be taken aback to realize for the first time that the "land agitation" did not entail rioting or attacks on life and limb but only an action at law. What are the facts? Denis Donoghue, the *Memoirs* editor, supplies them in a note: "Fifteen tenants of the Gregory estate at Coole Park applied to the Land Court to have their rents reduced. The Land Commissioner, the Honourable Gerald Fitzgerald, granted their application, reducing the rent by approximately twenty percent. . . . At the same time, the Land Purchase Act of 1909 and certain provisions of the Finance Bill of 1909 imposed new burdens of taxation on Irish landowners . . . the Encrement Value Duty and the Reversion Duty. Much of this new revenue was earmarked for the payment of old age pensions" (226). It's easier to be against mean rooftrees, even against wrens' nests, than against pensions for the aged.

One last journal entry. It comes immediately after the reference to rent reductions: "One feels always that where all must make their living they will live not for life's sake, but the work's, and all will be poorer. My work is very near to life itself, and my father's very near to life itself, but I am always feeling a lack of life's own values behind my thought. They should have been there before the strain began, before it became necessary to let the work create its values. This house has enriched my soul out of measure, because here life moves~~-creates~~ [*sic*] without restraint through spacious forms. Here there has been no compelled labour, no poverty-thwarted impulse" (226). The strain here mentioned is pretty clearly that entailed in making a living.

Certain reflections may come up, now that we are able to see the poem more fully in relation to the circumstances occasioning it. For one thing, the poet does array himself against the claims of economic and social justice as determined by a court that was in no way ill-disposed toward the landlord interest—if anything, quite the contrary. Second, there is Yeats's confession in a personal journal never intended for publication of his self-involvement in the situation when he says that his own artistic work, and his father's, would have been better if they had been born to riches and leisure, and did not have to work so hard at other things than poetry and painting. To be fair, Yeats's fundamental idea of great art as something created out of an abundance of life, out of the horn of plenty, embraces more than the Anglo-Irish landed rich, or for that matter, the high Renaissance nobility of Urbino and Ferrara—though it may sometimes take these fabled places' rumored way of life as a Platonic image or analogy for such art at its best.

Finally, one must recognize an element of anachronism in the poet's carry-on about the Shaken House. Strictly speaking, there was no severe land agitation in 1909. The land question, which convulsed agrarian Ireland in the 1870s and 1880s, had been settled, mainly through the program for redistribution of land set out in the Wyndham Act of 1903, reform legislation developed as the result of a conference on agrarian problems organized by Lady Gregory's own nephew, John Shawe-Taylor, the heir of Roxboro House.[12] If Yeats had appeared before a crowd of tenant farmers in an Irish village in the early 1880s, and delivered the prose burden of his poem as a speech, he might have been beaten up or even buried alive in a dung pile. If he had done it in 1909, his listeners would have turned their backs on him and gone off to complain to the land commissioner. More anachronism appears in the fact, as Yeats would have been well aware, that in writing his poem of unbridled praise to the Gregories and their lineage while living under their roof, he is acting much like those household bards retained by the Gaelic and then the Hiberno-Norman aristocracy, whose poems glorifying the pedigree, exaggerating the exploits, and defending the privileges of their masters constituted payment for value received in the way of shelter, sustenance, and protection from harm.

Did the Gregories like the poem? Not entirely, for that following summer, when Yeats was again at Coole, a coolness grew between him and them, largely based on his suspecting that they found him calculating and materialistic. Lady Gregory had written to Edmund Gosse, asking him to use his influence in securing the poet a Civil List pension, and had received back what she considered a distinctly uncivil reply. She and her son Robert decided it was appropriate for Yeats to fire off an indignant letter of his own to Gosse, and all that August he drafted version after version of a letter but sent none. The Gregories could not understand his delay. Yeats, realizing this, confided his discomfort to his journal: "This has been a painful thing. It has been the one serious quarrel I have ever had with Lady Gregory, because the first that has arisen from irreconcilable differences towards life" (*Memoirs*, 257). He was discovering that service to the rich had another side—dependency. Just a year after writing "Upon a House," on August 8, 1910, he wrote: "All the time I spoke of the thing with Lady Gregory or Robert, I knew that they thought that I hesitated not because I wished to do right, but because I thought Gosse might be useful to me. If I had kept silent I would have escaped that." He so longed to be taciturn and aloof like Parnell, but found himself gregarious,[13] voluble, and now, he imagined, under the suspicion of being conniving and low: "Why do I write all this? I suppose that I may learn at last to keep to my own in every situation in life; to discover and create in myself as I grow old that thing which is to life what style is to letters: moral radiance" (257–58).

Moral radiance sounds like something out of Matthew Arnold or Bishop Colenso. It sounds distinctly middle-class. "How am I fallen from myself," as the Confucian motto at the beginning of Yeats's volume *Responsibilities* puts it. Yeats did get his pension and the misunderstanding with the Gregories cleared up. But not before he had glimpsed the steel talons concealed by the velvet gloves of his friends with the lidless eyes.

Ending

Yeats married Georgie Hyde-Lees in 1917, when he was fifty-two, and the couple had their first child, Anne Butler, in the troubled year of 1919. During the Troubles, they mostly kept out of Ireland, spending much of 1920 and 1921 at Oxford, and giving consideration to emigrating permanently. The poet decided against this step, even while recognizing that he might be condemning his offspring to a heritage of bitterness. It was after all *their* heritage. Returning to Ireland, he bought his Dublin house at 82 Merrion Square and intensified the championing and defense of Anglo-Irish values earlier referred to. The battle was mainly fought in two places or houses: in the Free State Senate, and at the refurbished Norman tower called Thor Ballylee, a kind of blockhouse, itself threatened by IRA raiders during the Civil War and ringed round by the burned-out or threatened big houses of his friends. At both sites he mounted the same campaign, though the means—parliamentary debate and journalism in Dublin, meditation and poetry at the tower—were different.

The aim was to espouse the Anglo-Irish heritage, to convince every Irish person in or out of power to whom his influence might reach, that this "people" belonged in Ireland, and to insist that a viable culture for the newly independent country should draw from Anglo-Irish as well as native Irish traditions, to the extent that these could be distinguished. As he wrote in an article, "Ireland is not more theirs than ours. . . . We must glory in our difference, be as proud of it as they are of theirs" (quoted in Torchiana, 119). And in "Pages from a Diary in 1930," sounding a less-polarized note, and rather beautifully, he wrote, "Preserve that which is living, help the two Irelands, Gaelic Ireland and Anglo-Ireland, so to unite that neither shall shed its pride" (*Explorations*, 337).

One of Yeats's great discoveries of the middle 1920s was the early-eighteenth-century philosopher George Berkeley: not merely because this Anglo-Irishman "proved that the world was a vision" (*Senate Speeches*, 172), which could not help but delight a visionary poet; nor just because he could be fitted, with some forcing, into an anti-Whig line that included Swift, Goldsmith, and Burke; but even more because "this fierce young man," a fellow of Trinity College, Dublin, had written in his Commonplace Book, repudiating Locke, Newton, and other British empiricists, "We Irish do not think so" (Berkeley, 124; quoted in *Senate Speeches*, 180). In short, the finest intellect the Anglo-Irish ever produced had defined itself, without self-conscious patriotism, as an Irish, not an English, phenomenon. Yeats returned to this declaration in the diary of 1930, where he makes even wider—and wilder—claims:

> Between Berkeley's account of his exploration of certain Kilkenny laws which speak of the 'natives' came that intellectual crisis which led up to the sentence in the *Commonplace Book*: 'We Irish do not hold with this'. That was the birth of the national intellect and it caused the defeat in Berkeley's philosophical secret society of English materialism, the Irish Salamis. (*Explorations*, 333–34)

Reflecting on education, Yeats rather thought that in the new Ireland the children could thrive on a mix of "Gaelic literature," which holds "something English-speaking countries have never possessed—a great folk literature," and of Berkeley and Burke, "a philosophy on which it is possible to base the whole life of a nation" (*Senate Speeches*, 172). This was poet's talk, yet it was consistent with his more senatorial reflections at that time in urging a kind of cultural pluralism—it seems anything but fascistic, as the key to a creative and peaceable Irish future: "The basis of Irish Nationalism has now shifted, and much that once helped is now injurious, for we can no longer do anything by fighting. We must persuade, and to persuade we must become a modern, tolerant, liberal nation. I want everything discussed, I want to get rid of the old exaggerated tact and caution" (*Senate Speeches*, 160).

This last is from "An Undelivered Speech on Divorce," which somehow was excluded from the June 1925 Senate debate on a divorce bill.

In the debate itself Yeats stood out, invoking Milton, explaining lucidly why the well-being of a nation in which most people are of one opinion may depend on the effective right of a small minority to a contrary opinion, and delivering in his peroration stirring remarks that carried the listeners' minds to the great days of the Dublin Parliament : "We against whom you have done this thing are no petty people. We are one of the great stocks of Europe. We are the people of Burke; we are the people of Grattan; we are the people of Swift, the people of Emmet, the people of Parnell. We have created the most of literature in this country. We have created the best of its political intelligence. Yet I do not regret altogether what has happened. I shall be able to find out, if not I my children. . . . whether we have lost our stamina or not" (*Senate Speeches*, 99).

Colonel Maurice Moore, the novelist's devoutly Roman Catholic younger brother, presiding over the Senate when Yeats spoke, wanted to know about the Milton reference. He could not believe that so religious a poet as Milton had ever expressed an opinion, much less a favorable one, on divorce. Before the Senate even debated the divorce bill it had been overwhelmingly defeated in the lower chamber. The Senate could debate but not reverse Dail decisions.

At the blockhouse, the square Norman tower of Ballylee, the defense was no different, except that the language and force of language were that of poetry. From "Meditations in Time of Civil War" to "The Tower" to "A Dialogue of Self and Soul" and "Blood and the Moon," from 1921 to 1927, Yeats's big poems—they are *ensembles* of poems, elaborated in from two to seven sections, each section with its own stanzaic design—sum up a heritage and tragically meditate on violence that is immediate and close by: "a drunken soldiery / Can leave the mother, murdered at her door, / To crawl in her own blood, and go scot-free" (*Poems*, 207). It is also part of that universal history of gyres and phases that Yeats was concurrently diagramming in the successive drafts of *A Vision*, though no amount of overviewing and long viewing can remove the Irish flavor. First the mother is murdered and then she crawls in her own blood. It is a bull for the collection of the Edgeworths and a perfectly calculated one at that.

The year 1927 may just be the year in which Anglo-Irish culture came face to face with its own ending. It was not so much a forced eviction as a notice to quit at the party's earliest convenience. In March, Lady Gregory sold Coole to the Government. In July, the Free State minister of justice, Kevin O'Higgins, a brilliant and severe young statesman who back in 1992, we recall, had moved in the Dail the acceptance of the Anglo-Irish minority as "part and parcel" of the nation, was murdered by IRA gunmen while returning from mass to his home in Booterstown, Dublin. Yeats had been one of O'Higgins's fervent admirers, including him as the only Roman Catholic on a short list of all-time great Irishmen around whom a Free State style of civility and probity might be shaped. To make Yeats's cup of bitterness overflow, there was a rumor in Dublin that one of the young assassins was Sean MacBride, Maud Gonne and John MacBride's only offspring (Blythe, 7).

In August, Yeats retreated to Thor Ballylee where, he confessed in a letter to Olivia Shakespeare, he was doing a new suite of Tower poems, "partly driven to it by this murder" (*Letters*, 727). These would see light as "A Dialogue of Self and Soul." At the end of that summer, the republican leader de Valera came in from the mild Irish cold, taking his seat in the Dail after somehow evading the required oath of loyalty to H.M. the King, and beginning the successful drive for power which would mean that in the short run at least the new Ireland would take more of its tone and coloration from the hybrid vigor, canniness, conservative instincts, and Catholic piety of a Clare peasant boy with a Cuban-American father than from the Protestant Sligo child who, in his father's beautiful compliment, "gave a tongue to the sea cliffs" and grew up to be not only Anglo-Ireland's but Ireland's greatest poet ever.

After that, it was all commemoration, of "all the Olympians," a thing never to be known again, and

> You that would judge me do not judge alone
> This book or that, come to this hallowed place
> Where my friends' portraits hang and look thereon;
> Ireland's history in their lineaments trace;
> Think where man's glory most begins and ends
> And say my glory was I had such friends.
>
> (*Poems*, 321)

until Yeats, who faulted himself for gregariousness and speaking out of turn, and who deliberately designed his art to celebrate and even to resemble the "lonely and proud" things he most admired, at last, in his epitaph and then in death, became one with Anglo-Irish solitude.[14]

> Cast a cold eye
> On life, on death.
> Horseman, pass by!
>
> (328)

XI

AFTER THE END: THE ANGLO-IRISH POSTMORTEM

Nothing in Ireland is ever over.
—Elizabeth Bowen, *Collected Impressions*

These P.M.s are gruesome, but I often find them—(*Krapp switches off, broods, switches on*)—a help before embarking on a new . . . (*hesitates*) . . . retrospect.
—Beckett, *Krapp's Last Tape*

He's dead, if he had the wit to stiffen.
—Humorous invective of an Ulster woman born in 1890

Introductory

A POSTMORTEM is an evaluation or discussion occurring after the end or after the fact (*Random House Dictionary*). Other meanings are the examination of a dead body, and the analysis of a game—a hand of bridge, say—which has already been played through. Here we shall look at several writings coming at the end of the line of Anglo-Irish tradition that carry out a sort of postmortem on the tradition. There is Yeats's ghost play *Purgatory* (1939), a brief, violent, and problematic work that has been widely admired, particularly for its dramatic line and its starkly effective stagecraft, even while there has been no real consensus on what the play is saying. Next, we shall consider the case of Elizabeth Bowen, whose life in one aspect was a virtual allegory of Anglo-Irish uprooting and ruination, while several of her finest works of fiction superbly enacted the same themes in imaginative terms. Not surprisingly, one discovers both Yeats and Bowen exploiting certain resources of Gothic literary style in their writings about the death—or is it the struggle to die?—of Anglo-Irish tradition. The great Gothic works, including those looked at in an earlier chapter, show that there is no disabling contradiction between imaginative vitality and morbidity, between artistic coping and a dying culture. It may take imagination to die, "wit to stiffen," as the Tyrone woman put it.

One needs that assurance in turning, finally, to investigate Samuel Beckett's *Watt* (1953), a work of terminal morbidity, which is offered here, with a certain arbitrariness, as a terminus ad quem both of the tradition itself and my study of it. One may say of *Watt*, emphasizing the central episode of the title character's adventures in the big house of Mr. Knott, that it subjects Anglo-Irish writing to a parody so devastating and cold that it has the effect of canceling its own subject. Looking for analogies to the reduction process carried out in *Watt*, one imagines something that might be called the Doctor Crippen procedure—the virtual destruction of a body in an acid bath. One says "virtual" because there is always a telltale remainder. *Watt*'s notorious "Addenda," which only "fatigue and disgust" prevented "Sam"'s incorporating in the book's main body (*Watt*, 247), correspond to the traces of bone, tooth amalgam, garter, glass eye or whatever, remaining after the Doctor finished his devoted steeping.[1]

Purgatory

Sooner or later we must limit the families of
the unintelligent classes
—Yeats, *Explorations*

"Scoundrel! Why did you engender me"
—Hamm to Nagg, in Beckett's *Endgame*

One of the oddest features of the play is that the main character, of two—or of three if one counts the mute apparitional mother silhouetted against the lighted window—is both the play's principal malefactor and its raisonneur, the character who interprets its brief, terrible, and perhaps "tragic" action. That is the Old Man, and he is a very bad old man indeed. He has been the murderer of his own father and will now murder his only child, the Boy, in full view of the audience. Of these crimes the latter would seem by far the worse. His father, who does not appear in the play, had been drunken and brutal, and the Old Man killed him when this brute was burning down the house that had come into his possession through his marriage to the Old Man's well-born mother, and which he had already brought to ruin through his low drunken carouses. The father killer can dramatize himself as a judge and executioner combined, both declaring and carrying out meet punishment of his father for a major crime:

> . . . he killed the house; to kill a house
> Where great men grew up, married, died,
> I here declare a capital offence.
>
> (Yeats, *Collected Plays*, 432)

It isn't much of an excuse for murder, but perhaps we can sympathize up to a point, especially in light of the horrible Anglo-Irish exposure to the deliberate destruction of their estate houses between 1919 and the middle 1920s.

For the killing of the son there is not even the ghost of an excuse, and the act itself, death by repeated stabbing "on the same jack-knife" as killed "my father," though it may show a commendable rage for order and symmetry, is bloody, cruel, and sneaky. It is the latter because the Boy had covered his eyes with his hands just before the Old Man struck at him.

For all that, it is in no sense an *acte gratuite*. The father kills his son for a grand purpose, in order to rescue his mother's soul from purgatory, this feat being symbolized by the bathing of the solitary tree in white light: "Study that tree. / It stands there like a purified soul" (435). We are not, of course, dealing here with a Christian conception of purgation. Rather, it is a Buddhistic one, reflecting Yeats's studies in and adaptations from the Buddhist Noh theater of Japan.[2] Probably also there is an infusion from Swedenborgian thought about the afterlife.[3] In both conceptions the spirit returns as an apparition to the scene of a major transgression it committed in life, and must reenact the sinful deed for an indefinite period. In the play, release and purgation will come when the ghost knows and understands its transgression and when the consequences of sinning are put to an end. But there is a complication. Consequences may operate upon others or upon the sinner, or even upon both together; if upon others only, then they may intervene to bring consequence to an end, thus relieving the soul of the transgressor of its tormenting repetitive dream. If, however, the consequence is mainly or also upon the transgressor herself, then action by another will lack efficacy. In such a case, "there is no help but in themselves / And in the mercy of God" (431).

The Old Man killed his son on the assumption that he was the only still vital consequence of the mother's sin, and for a time the tree, in lighting up, appeared to support that idea. But when the hoofbeats sounded again in the avenue, the Old Man had to realize that there was another consequence, upon herself, which has not ended. The window will light up again and the brute's bride, the Old Man's mother, will eagerly prepare herself for the drunken, lustful couplings that in life engendered him who is "twice a murderer and all for nothing" (436). On this shattering irony the little play ends, leaving the killer-raisonneur with nowhere to turn except to prayer. There is added irony, in that the God who is supplicated sounds at last quite broadly and familiarly Christian.

> O God,
> Release my mother's soul from its dream!

> Mankind can do no more. Appease
> The misery of the living and the remorse of the dead.
>
> (436)

But what was the mother's transgression, which set off so much dreadful and seemingly interminable "consequence"? Her sole "sin" was to marry and "engender" out of her own class, when, as a young girl, she met and fell in love with "a groom in a training stable" at the Curragh. The Old Man is quite clear about this. He says—this half-bred man—"she should have known he was not her kind" (434). "Kind" here means the big-house Anglo-Irish seen as a sort of extended family or clan, bound together by a common religion, shared social values and style of life, and claiming common descent from predominantly English settler stock. This notion of "kind" appears quite frequently in Yeats's later writings, for example in "Pages from a Diary in 1930," an essay devoted to defining and praising the high tradition of "Protestant Ireland" anchored upon Swift and Henry Grattan. There the poet remarks that "tradition is kindred" (*Explorations*, 312). That would mean that tradition can be ravaged by marrying out of one's own "kind."

The Old Man, however, goes beyond merely chiding his ghostly mother for her having married down and out. He actually says to her, after stabbing his son, her grandson, to death—

> you are in the light because
> I finished all that consequence.
> He would have struck a woman's fancy,
> Begot, and passed pollution on.
>
> (435)

"Pollution" here sounds like a venereal disease. In *Purgatory*, however, it merely designates what racial bigots call "race-mixing." In an Irish setting it is the mixing together of the two Irish strains or "kinds," the natives and Anglo-Irish, people of the "half-door" and those of the "hall door," through the engendering act, which the apparitional mother is doomed to repeat indefinitely and may even enjoy, that determines pollution.[4] In case there is any doubt, we can return to a canceled line in an early version of the text. In context it reads:

> I killed that lad because he had youth
> And soon would take some woman's fancy
> ~~And he pass the blood pollution on~~
> And so pass the pollution on.
>
> (*Purgatory*, 9)[5]

The story then in *Purgatory* of a woman who married down is much like the story from real life which, so they claimed, set Edith Somerville and Martin Ross on the path of serious authorship and which Edith came back to by herself in her last novel, *The Big House of Inver.* I mean the account of the cousins' visit on horseback to Edith's elderly kinswoman whose remote house was by the sea. This was the experience that showed them there was a likely literary subject in the scandal of Irish mixing of kinds, either in illicit relations or in marriages that both communities professed to deplore. An equivalent anecdote appears in Yeats's *Autobiography* (34). He tells of the "brawling squireen, married to one of my Middleton cousins," whom he once visited with his cousin George at Castle Dargan. This is Yeats's only acknowledged link to the half-world of low-bred half-sirs, and he is careful to show that the connection is by marriage, not blood. The Castle Dargan story is sometimes brought up as an autobiographical source for *Purgatory* (Henn, 316).

There is perhaps nothing trivial in the theme of the Irish mixing of kinds, considering that the end result of a small minority interbreeding with a large majority population virtually guarantees absorption of the former by the latter. Still, Somerville and Ross, for all their pride of ancestry and convictions of social superiority, appear to have looked at the possibility of such an outcome with a certain amount of equanimity or resignation. With Martin in fact, who was conscious of mixed ancestry, a deep attachment to people of the cabins is in tension with her "Protestant" sense of a different, though still Irish, identity. Yeats, on the other hand, and on the evidence of *Purgatory* and its apparently racist doctrine of "blood-pollution," is in bitter recoil from the prospect of Irish population merging.

But in fact Yeats's ideas of race and racial exclusivity were not very coherent or consistent. For example, in 1919, at a time of severe Irish disunity, he was all for synthesis, confessing in "If I Were Four-and-Twenty" that he dreamed of writing poems about the Irish holy places Croagh Patrick and Lough Derg, where in future would be carried out rituals uniting both sorts of Irish Christian with pagan cults in revival (*Explorations*, 278). On the other hand, in "On the Boiler" (1939), the ranting political pamphlet to which *Purgatory* was attached on its first appearance in print, he likens the typical native Irish legislator in the Dail to "a youthful chimpanzee, hot and vague," and proposes to solve the problem of quality in the Free State population, in the face of Anglo-Irish numerical decline, through a quasi-scientific method of population control called eugenics: "Sooner or later we must limit the families of the unintelligent classes" (*Explorations*, 426).

These views, which are intentionally provocative and controversial, should not blind us to the fact that Yeats could also be quite sane and sound on the question of an Irish racial stock or stocks. His most considered statement in this area appears as a footnote in his preface to *The*

Words Upon the Window-pane (1931). In the main text he has just remarked how the Battle of the Boyne "established a Protestant aristocracy, some of whom neither called themselves English nor looked with contempt or dread upon conquered Ireland." The note adds: "Nor were they English: the newest arrivals soon intermarried with an older stock, and that older stock had intermarried again and again with Gaelic Ireland. . . . Ireland, divided in religion and politics, is as much one race as any modern country" (*Explorations*, 347).

But let the play *Purgatory* have the last word. It is a miracle of compression, carrying in its brief compass not only a complete action but a play within a play as well—what goes on within the frame of the alternately dark and lighted window. There is also room in it to present and refute the case for eugenics, defined as a selective breeding of the best by any means necessary. Setting aside the problem of how a mere mortal can know what is best in the human race and for it, it can be said that the Old Man as eugenic scientist follows a method which Nazi population science by 1939 was already beginning to employ. That method is murder, and the Old Man's aim, like the Nazis' is "purification." His failure also is like theirs—total—quite discrediting the method and that bastard product of late-nineteenth-century Social Darwinism, eugenics itself.[6]

Purgatory uses a Gothic panoply—ghosts, bloody crime, and a "secret" family scandal to enforce a tendentious meaning: the house of Anglo-Irish culture is down and native brutishness, in combination with "low" female sexual tastes, are to blame. Yeats was capable of thinking differently at other times, yet this is the thought to which *Purgatory* gives expression. There may be critics who choose to see the Old Man as one of Yeats's "lonely antithetical heroes"—the phrase is Denis Donoghue's[7]—but that is no reason not to grasp what this hero is actually up to as he attempts to finish up the wicked business of a lifetime.

Elizabeth Bowen (1899–1973)

We are dead, and all our fathers and mothers
[from the ritual for burying the coffer]
—Bowen, *The Little Girls*

Life works to dispossess the dead, to dislodge and
oust them. Their places fill themselves up; later people
come in; all the room is wanted
—Bowen, *A World of Love*

As time passes since her death in 1973, we are beginning to see Elizabeth Bowen as one of very few great writers of prose fiction at work in Ireland and England between the end of the First World War and the end of the 1960s. Her best novels and stories—*The Last September*, *The House in Paris*, *The Death of the Heart*, "Summer Night," and "Ivy Gripped the Steps" among them—are already classic, while her elegant formulation of what fiction is about—it is "the non-poetic statement of a poetic truth" (*Impressions*, 250)—seems perfectly to suggest the synthesis in her work of imaginative inwardness, a scrupulous attachment to the highest modernist ideals of organic form and answerable style, and an acute, sometimes devouring awareness of her own time and place.

It makes her art more, not less, interesting to remark another element in it, a dark vein of troubled feeling; a touching, shy anxiety; moments when deep grief comes welling up, turning her beautiful life-celebrating forms into shapes of mourning. More often than not this pain of heart and mind centers on the troubles of children. Bowen's children are among the most vivid and memorable in English writing since those of Dickens and Henry James, and many of them have been made unhappy by the death, actual or feared, or simply the disappearance, of a parent. Thus, in the early story "Coming Home," Rosalind, a girl who loves her rather cool and self-possessed mother almost to distraction, is tormented by fears that her mother will die and tries to hurt her as a way of getting closer to her, of penetrating the mother's surface blandness. Rosalind thinks, "Life's nothing but waiting for awfulness to happen and trying to think about something else. . . . A person might be part of you, almost part of your body, and yet once you went away from them they might utterly cease to be. . . . There was no security. Safety and happiness were a game that grown-up people played with children to keep them from understanding, possibly to keep themselves from thinking. . . . Anything might happen, there was no security" (Bowen, *Collected Stories*, 98).

A similar anxiety motivates the compulsive weeping of the fatherless boy in "Tears, Idle Tears," a story of the 1930s, set in the Regent's Park. Frederick cannot stop bawling, even when his plucky mum, who thinks tears at seven are unmanly, walks off in disgust. An unemployed servant girl on a nearby bench bucks Frederick up by telling him about another little boy of her acquaintance, George, who cries all the time. Her unspoken reflection, at the same time, might unman any one of us: "The eyes of George and Frederick seemed to her to be wounds, in the world's surface, through which its inner, terrible, unassuageable, necessary sorrow constantly bled away" (*Stories*, 486). She may seem surprisingly sensitive for a servant, but in Bowen's milieu women servants are often the only characters who do notice and offer solace to the misery of the young. This is especially true when there has been some break or impediment in the regular bond between parent and child, a divorce or separation, a death.

Youthful grief must reach some sort of climax in a central scene of Bowen's 1936 novel *The House in Paris*. We are in the drawing room of the Maison Fisher, itself a sinister parody of a parental home, and Leopold, a nine-year-old whose father was a suicide, and who has been brought there to rejoin the mother he has not seen since early infancy, has just learned that she cannot and will not come to take him. He stands rigidly against the mantel until Henrietta, another temporarily accommodated child who is eleven and motherless, and no sort of relation of Leopold's, goes to stand with him:

> Leopold's solitary despair made Henrietta no more than the walls or table. This was not contempt for her presence: no one was there. Being not there disembodied her, so she fearlessly crossed the parquet to stand beside him. She watched his head, the back of his thin neck, the square blue collar shaken between his shoulders, wondering without diffidence where to put her hand. Finally, she leant her body against his, pressing her ribs into his elbow so that his sobs began to go through her too. Leopold rolled his face further away from her, so that one cheek and temple now pressed the marble, but did not withdraw his body from her touch. After a minute like this, his elbow undoubled itself against her and his left arm went round her with unfeeling tightness, as though he were gripping the bole of a tree. Held close like this to the mantlepiece he leant on, Henrietta let her forehead rest on the marble too: her face bent forward, so that the tears she began shedding fell on the front of her dress. An angel stood up inside her with its hands to its lips, and Henrietta did not attempt to speak. (219–20)

Elizabeth was the only child of Henry Bowen, himself the eldest of nine. She calls him Henry VI in her great family history, *Bowen's Court*, because he was the sixth Henry in descent from the founder of the estate in northwest Cork, the Welsh Colonel Henry Bowen, who received thousands of acres of rich farmland near Spenser's Kilcolman for his services to Cromwell in the Irish wars of the Great Rebellion. Her father was also the first Bowen landlord who did not stay at home and tend to the ancestral patrimony. Instead he became a Dublin barrister, being called to the bar in 1887, the year of the revived land agitation centering on the scheme of systematic rent withholding called the Plan of Campaign. She tells us in *Seven Winters . . . and Afterthoughts* (1962) that she was meant to be a boy, Robert, and that Robert continued to be expected until her parents realized that no more children would be coming. *Seven Winters* recalls her signally happy earliest childhood spent at Herbert Place, Dublin, with summers at Bowen's Court. Houses are always very important points of references for this writer and for many of her fictional characters.

This secure early period ended when her father fell prey to psychiatric illness. Diagnosis was uncertain, but his physicians advised, indeed ordered, strict separation from his wife and daughter, a sort of medical divorce or annulment. Elizabeth and her mother Florence left Ireland when the child was seven, leading for the next five years or so a fairly unsettled existence at English south-coast resort towns such as Folkstone and Hythe. They put up in hotels, spent time in boarding houses and furnished flats, and visited for varying periods in the homes of some English-based aunts and cousins. The girl's attachment to her mother was intense and surely became colored with anxiety after her parents' separation. In *Seven Winters* she remembered plotting to get Florence off to herself, without the interposition of her governess, but she then came to see that a certain remoteness was part of her mother's temperament: "She often moved some way away from things and people she loved, as though to convince herself that they did exist." Even so, Elizabeth thought, perhaps rather wishfully, "When she was not with me she thought of me constantly, and planned ways in which we could meet and be alone" (29).

Under the circumstances, the worst thing that could happen was for Florence Bowen to die, as she did when her daughter was twelve. Elizabeth was away on visit, pretending to herself, as children will, that her mother's illness was not very serious, when Florence succumbed to cancer. The motherless girl, like Henrietta in *The House in Paris*, was looked after by aunts during the next two years; her father appears to have played little part in her life at this time. She then entered school at Downe House, Kent, from which she passed at age eighteen, going straight to London to launch a career. Elizabeth claimed to have been not unhappy at school in Darwin's former home—"A tough thickish child, I did not in fact suffer in any way" (*Impressions*, 192). Some holidays were spent at Bowen's Court even though her school years coincided with the First World War, when travel to Ireland could be difficult.

Henry Bowen sufficiently recovered from his obscure mental demons to marry again. He survived until 1930, and there is nothing to indicate that his relations with his daughter were anything but cordial, or that he thought he owed her particular explanation or excuse for her early uprooting. Elizabeth did not so much bury her pain as secrete it in her stories and novels. The only outward sign of what growing up had cost her was a chronic lifelong stammer, which indeed added charm to her voluble, witty, and often brilliant conversation.

When Elizabeth inherited Bowen's Court in 1930, her family-centered traumas and the harsh experience of being set adrift in the world could begin to connect with the historic experience of her Anglo-Irish class and clan. This was an experience of economic decline, loss of authority in the Irish community, and cultural disintegration. Before asking how her imaginative writings incorporate and give an individual form to these broad developments, I want simply to describe how she sustained a tie with her ancestral home through most of her adult life and also how Bowen's Court ended up.

During the 1930s, when she was a leading younger writer living outside Oxford and then in London, admired and fully accredited by what was left of Bloomsbury and by her generational peers—Waugh, Greene, O'Faolain, Connolly, and the rest—she was also the absentee holder of an Irish estate, which a review of hers in that period describes as "something between a *raison d'être* and a predicament." In the same review—it is of Joseph Hone's biography of George Moore—she mentions how absentees are plagued by "fateful letters in dogged handwriting, sure to begin inside, 'Sir, I am sorry to tell you. . . ,' letters that make the absentee's heart sink at sight of an Irish stamp" (*Impressions*, 161, 163).

Clearly, one thing that had not changed between Moore's 1880s and a half-century later was the hard-luck small farmer or farm laborer in hot pursuit of a proprietor who was apt to be short of cash himself. Still, there might have been an advantage in being of "hybrid kind" after 1939, when de Valera's Ireland chose to be neutral in the Second World War. Elizabeth Bowen, however, refused that advantage. She stayed on in London with her British husband, Alan Cameron, throughout the war, surviving—but just!—the blitzes of 1940 and 1941, and the later assaults by V-1 and V-2 rockets.[8] According to Angus Wilson, editor of her collected stories, who was himself in London throughout the war, Bowen became the greatest of literary witnesses to London and Londoners under siege.[9] Looking back, she said of the experience: "During the war I lived, both as a civilian and as a writer, with every pore open" (*Impressions*, 47). For her, it was a profound, nearly mystical experience of solidarity with a community in primary terms: "It seems to me that during the war in England the overcharged subconsciousness of everybody overflowed and merged." This class- and ego-obliterating experience was at its most intense during nights of blackout and bombing. She said that the only writing relevant to it was Lawrence's "The Blind Man," his story about "blood-consciousness," of touching in the dark and being touched to the quick (*Impressions*, 8).

A London of houses on fire from incendiary bombs and streets torn apart by high explosives was also a reliving of her late teens and early twenties, when country houses and whole towns in Ireland were raided and burned out, either by the Black and Tans or the outlawed IRA. It was then she first learned about "the violent destruction of solid things," witnessed "the explosion of the illusion that prestige, power, and permanence attached to bulk and weight." In 1940 she may have been somewhat ahead of her English contemporaries in appreciating that what deeply matters in a time of catastrophe is a person's felt connections to others. Londoners, however, were catching up fast. "Walls went down, and we felt, if not knew each other" (*Impressions*, 48). This was written in 1945, but it is part of what Lois, the young heroine of *The Last September*, Bowen's 1929 novel of the Irish Troubles, may have finally grasped, though only when it was too late.

As the war intensified between 1940 and 1942, Elizabeth's principal literary project was the writing of *Bowen's Court*, her magisterial history of a beloved rural seat in "neutral" Ireland over the course of centuries. At intervals she visited Ireland for the British government, reporting back to the Coalition Cabinet her impressions of Irish morale under the British-sponsored and -enforced blockade of commercial shipping to Irish ports, and attempting to assess the delicate question of which side the Irish and their famously deceptive, even sibylline leader Eamon de Valera were anticipating to win. These visits gave her the fine short story "Sunday Afternoon." It may get its title from the old wisecrack to the effect that in Anglo-Ireland the time is always midafternoon after a heavy Sunday meal.

After V-E Day, Alan Cameron, a gas victim in the First World War whose difficult duty in the Second World War was as chief civil servant in charge of the physical security of BBC London, came to Bowen's Court for a time to recover from total exhaustion. Until 1952, when Cameron retired, the couple spent summer holidays at Elizabeth's Irish home, while continuing to winter in London. In 1952, looking forward to "full and continuous habitation, such as it had been built for" (*Bowen's Court*, 2d ed., 458), Elizabeth brought back furniture that had been long absent from the house, first in Dublin, then in England. But within months Cameron died. For the next seven years she tried to maintain the house alone, meeting its expenses from her writing income and from occasional lecturing in the United States and Canada. But the task proved impossible. Bowen's Court and its remaining acreage were sold to a local farmer, who, Elizabeth hoped, would raise his family in the house. Unfortunately, that was not practicable for him. After considering taking off the roof, which would have avoided certain taxes, he had to demolish the house entirely. Elizabeth's comment: "It was a clean end. Bowen's Court never lived to be a ruin" (*Bowen's Court*, 2d ed., 459). As a child she had been fascinated by the rural ruins from all eras with which Ireland is strewn, could never pass one without running to look at it close up. Such a fascination is easily developed in Ireland.

Elizabeth Bowen's greatest Irish story is "Summer Night," from her 1941 collection *Look at All Those Roses*. In it a small girl named Vivie, taking advantage of her mother's overnight absence and the inattention of her father, the Major, and his fretful Aunt Fran, runs a little wild on a sultry summer night at her family's "obscure country house," where life, only apparently, proceeds in safe monotony while the great air, sea, and land battles of the early Second World War rage elsewhere. After her little sister falls asleep, Vivie slips off her nightdress, races naked through the upper house, and then tries to get out the front door for a gambol in the apple orchard, only to find that the door has been bolted and barred. Next she decorates her body with snakes and stars drawn in colored chalks and spends some time before the long mirror in her mother's bedroom, admiring the effect and looking at parts of herself she usually cannot see. The narrator comments, apparently without shock or censure over such prepubescent erotic display and Vivie's compulsion to escape the house as if it were a cage, "One arbitrary line only divided this child from the animal: all her senses stood up, wanting to run the night" (*Collected Stories*, 598).

Shock and concern do appear when Aunt Fran detects Vivie at her hell-raising. This high-toned old Christian woman wants to be sure the girl has said her prayers. In response to Vivie's challenging "In my skin?" she tries to gather, cover, and restrain her:

> She drew the eiderdown from the foot of the bed and made a half-blind sweep at Vivie with it, saying: "Wrap up, wrap up." "Oh, they'll come off—my snakes!" said Vivie, backing away. But Aunt Fran, as though the child were on fire, put into motion an extraordinary strength—She rolled, pressed and pounded Vivie up in the eiderdown until only the prisoner's dark eyes, so like her mother's, were left free to move wildly outside the great sausage, of padded taffeta, pink.
>
> Aunt Fran, embracing the sausage firmly, repeated: "Now say to Our Lord." (598)

The aunt's move to constrain and imprison this "wild child" goes pretty far. Vivie's confinement suggests straitjacketing, and the cause is not hard to find, since Aunt Fran thinks so many things are going wrong in the world, the terrible war suggesting a sort of blood poisoning of the entire globe. She has a conviction that there is no zone of safety, so that even in this "apart" household "the enemy is within it, creeping about" (599). No wonder she wraps up Vivie and no wonder that her thoughts shift to Vivie's mother—Emma—who has left home that very evening after vague explanations about paying an overnight visit to a woman friend. To Fran, "Emma flying away, and not saying why, or where," is more evidence of global blood poisoning, the world fever. Unfortunately, "to wrap the burning child up did not put out the fire" (599).

Vivie's instinct "to run the night" is only what her mother is in fact doing. The story opened with this small woman in a big touring car driving south toward an adulterous tryst, while a fiery, molten sunset gives way to warm dusk and a starry, tropical night of a sort the Irish summer occasionally provides. Initially she seems an instance of that "disorientated romanticism" which Bowen in her introduction to the *Faber Book of Modern Short Stories* claimed the modern story was particularly well equipped to render (*Impressions*, 38). Her lover is one Robinson, a factory manager living separated from his wife in a village some sixty miles from her home. An obvious novice at sexual intrigue, Emma leaves a readily detectable trail on route, stopping at an AA hotel to call home and ring up her lover, and then dawdling in public places until the time of her tryst.

Beginning with his occupation and his name and going on to his "abstract and perfectly automatic" (588) style of womanizing and his coldness and fairness of mind, Robinson is a compendium of those "whiggish" traits that Yeats so loathed in the modern world and so regularly denounced in poems like "The Curse of Cromwell" and "Fragments I." His house is of compact stucco, and he has the only motor-driven grass mower in the village, even though much of his land is graveled over for the convenience of his wide-tired automobile. In the winter Robinson's polished windows, glassed-in porch, and empty conservatory send out "uncaring" flashes on sunny days. Like his home, the manager is well regulated and well groomed, especially "about his ears, jaws, collar, and close clipped nails" (589).

As disoriented provincial romantic, this Anglo-Irish Emma clearly derives from Flaubert's great forerunner, but she is also, as a denizen of the country-house world, related to Jane Austen's charming, errant, yet always well looked after and protected Emma Woodhouse. In Jane Austen's settled world, a woman running away, or even out alone after dark, is a social disaster, but in this coming-apart Anglo-Irish milieu, a certain case for flight can be made. It depends upon what one is running from as well as toward.

At home Emma has left a husband, described as deep in a mood of preoccupied doubt, whose frowning is frequent and intense. When the younger daughter Di asks Vivie, "What makes him so disappointed, do you know?" Vivie answers, "I know he thinks about the war" (596). The Major, whose military service was surely in the First World War, is humiliated—"disappointed"—that his country chooses to stay out of the current conflict. That is because he belongs to a class whose very identity over the centuries was bound up with commitments of loyalty and service to Britain, especially in periods of crisis. Irish neutrality heightens a sense of alienation and isolation in the failing and fading Anglo-Irish minority to which the Major belongs, though this is never spelled out in so many words.

As he goes about the house that evening, closing and barring heavy shutters as well as the main door, he ignores the warm weather and acts as if the house were actually under siege by lurking invisible enemies. Aunt Fran falls in with this feeling as she sits in the drawing room, "rigid, face turned to the door, plucking round and round the rings on her left hand." Other worrisome, or even forboding, details pile up: "in one corner stood a harp with two broken strings. . . . The silence for miles around this obscure country house seemed to gather inside the folds of the curtain and to dilute the inside air like a mist. This room Emma liked too little to touch already felt the touch of decay; it threw lifeless reflections into the two mirrors" (594). The house is haunted by lonesomeness and exudes a sort of deathliness. We begin to see the impetus behind the little girl's instinctive and her mother's more considered yet still rash desire to get out and run. It appears to be a run for dear life.

That is a frequent motif in Bowen's fiction, heroines or children fleeing from closed-up houses that have in some way gone to the bad. One recalls Portia's flight in despair from the Regent's Park house in *The Death of the Heart*, the wonderful, unlooked-for release of Leopold and Henrietta from the house in Paris. This motif returns us to Ireland by way of Elizabeth Bowen's study of J. S. LeFanu and her striking, persuasive analysis of *Uncle Silas* as the great exemplum of the Anglo-Irish "family romance."

Between the time when LeFanu's Maud Ruthyn made her successful bolt for dear life and when Bowen's Emma attempts hers—in the guise of a "discreet" affair—the proportions and implications of a class's power and status have changed. Once Maud escapes from Silas's house of murder and death she is free to come into her own as a great lady. On the contrary, with Robinson, Emma is experimenting at putting the entire sad business of a social standing behind her. He would not recognize her social standing, in all likelihood, if it hit him on the head; by the 1940s there was little Anglo-Irish status and authority left to recognize.

Two other important characters in "Summer Night' are the brother and sister, Justin and Queenie Cavey, who pay an unscheduled call on the factory manager that same evening, thus complicating and delaying his scheduled appointment with Emma. Queenie is pretty in middle age, stone deaf, and shows, perhaps in compensation for her handicap, a quality of extreme imaginative inwardness that Bowen usually reserves for her child and adolescent characters. The brother Justin, unmarried like his sister, is a tediously cultivated gentleman who ordinarily lives abroad and is concerned with the arts and literature. Forced back from the Continent to his home village for the duration of the war, he thinks

Robinson is the only interesting man in town and has taken him up in a manner that irritatingly combines superior airs with abjectness. When Justin and Queenie call on Robinson, it becomes evident that Justin has been drinking. That is perhaps why he vaticinates, somewhat unsteadily, about the crisis of the times: "I say, this war's an awful illumination; it's destroyed our dark; we have to see where we are. Immobilized, God help us. . . . We've got to break through to the new form—it needs genius. . . . We're precipitated this moment, between genius and death" (590).

The culture babble is vintage D. H. Lawrence, with a trace of Dostoevsky. It is that dated. Even more parochially, and probably unintentionally, it also parodies the apocalyptic style of the Anglo-Irish novelist Francis Stuart, Iseult Gonne's husband and Yeats's literary protégé, whose search for the "new form" by 1941 had carried him all the way to Nazi Germany. But Justin breaks off angrily when he realizes that Robinson, too polite to admit it, has one eye on the clock in anticipation of another visitor. He is quite hateful in taking needless offense. After leading Queenie home, he spends the rest of the night writing a cleverly aggrieved letter to Robinson. In it he heaps abuse on himself for presuming to take up the manager's time and purely ironic compliments on his host. The letter is a brilliant invention; yet, one wants to know what Bowen means by this character and his absurdities. Probably that Justin and the Major are in parallel. If the latter represents the bankruptcy of the power and social authority of the old Anglo-Irish strain in modern Ireland, then Justin represents the bankruptcy of Anglo-Irish cultural claims and intellect. It was the fear of such bankruptcy that drove Yeats in his later essays, poems, and plays to struggle to preserve what was living of the high traditions of the Protestant Ascendancy, in the hope that this heritage might retain influence in the Post-Treaty society. But it has not worked out. By 1941 the unraveling of Ascendancy in the cultural sphere produces a Justin Cavey, a peevish village culture snob whose pretense to *saeva indignatio* is merely an excuse for bad manners and bad faith.

While Justin scribbles in impotent rage, the technocrat Robinson, a genuinely new type in Ireland, strolls the night with Emma in his rather limited garden, pointing out to her the old abandoned demesne along the far side of his road, where local lovers can harbor under ancient trees and along the shores of a considerable lake. There is even an abandoned and fire-marked big house or castle. Except that it is so far south, it might be Coole Park, or the lakeside estate where George Moore grew up. Robinson, however, is only killing time and giving Emma, who lacks experience of infidelity, a chance to relax. Soon enough he reenters the house, where he equably and courteously awaits her coming in so that he may begin the efficient and abstract lovemaking with which he likes to fill his few leisure hours.

Blessedly, the story ends, not on this whiggish note of efficient love-making, but with poetic truth, with Queenie, whose gift of imaginative fantasy, perhaps Bowen is saying, is the only power that could save modern Ireland from itself by binding the present to the past in a spirit of loving kindness. Simply, even queerly unaware of divisiveness, Queenie has nothing to forgive or thrust bitterly from memory, because she does not even know that she has been injured or is deprived. For her, the evening has been a romantic one. Going to bed,

> she unhooked her muslin dress at the wrists and waist, stepped from the dress and began to take down her hair. Still in the dark, with a dreaming sureness of habit, she dropped hairpins into the heart-shaped tray. This was the night she would find again. . . . On just such a summer night, once only, she had walked with a lover in the demesne. His hand, like Robinson's, had been on her elbow, but she had guided him . . . because she had better eyes in the dark. They had gone down walks already deadened with moss, under the weight of July trees: they had felt the then fresh ruin totter above them; there was a moonless sky. Beside the lake they sat down, and while her hand brushed the ferns in the cracks of the stone seat emanations of kindness passed from him to her. The subtle deaf girl had made the transposition of this nothing . . . into an everything—the delicate deaf girl that the man could not speak to and was afraid to touch. She who, then so deeply contented, kept in her senses each frond and breath of the night, never saw him again and had soon forgotten his face. That had been twenty years ago, till tonight when it was now. Tonight it was Robinson who, guided by Queenie down leaf tunnels, took the place on the stone seat by the lake.
>
> The rusted gates of the castle were at one end of the square. Queenie, in her bed facing the window, lay with her face turned sideways, smiling, one hand lightly against her cheek. (*Collected Stories*, 607–8)

Queenie's "then fresh ruin" could almost be Danielstown, the big house in the Cork countryside, overlooked by mountains, that is set afire by Sinn Fein rebels at the end of *The Last September* (1929). Placed in 1920, in the time of the Troubles, it is the one novel of hers set deliberately in the past. Her preface to the 1952 edition speaks of being caught, as if in an undertow, and carried unresistingly back (*Impressions*, 199). She knew as she wrote it that the book must end with a burning, and in that holocaust all her fears for Bowen's Court were rehearsed if not dispelled. Unlike Lois Farquahar, who is only the niece of Sir Richard and

Lady Naylor, the proprietors in the novel, "I *was* the child of the house from which Danielstown derives. Bowen's Court survived—nevertheless, so often in my mind's eye did I see it burning that the terrible last event in *The Last September* is more real than anything I have lived through." Yet she also confesses, "This, of all my books, is nearest my heart" (*Impressions*, 204).

Why did so many cherished houses of the landed Anglo-Irish have to burn? The immediate answer, especially for the period 1919–1921 and especially in Cork, one of the hotbeds of the Rebellion, was that if the proprietors showed sympathy for the rebels, they would be burned out by the Black and Tans, and if they were friendly to the British forces and supported the efforts of the Royal Irish Constabulary to enforce what was still the law of the land, they had an excellent chance of being burned out by the rebels. It was Catch-22 in an earlier version.

All that summer and into September the Naylors have performed a balancing act. They invite the young English officers to their tennis parties and teas, while Lois actually attends a dance at the married officers' quarters near Cork city. But they also fail to report to the authorities their suspicions that rebel arms are being buried in remote corners of the estate and their certain knowledge that a son of one of the hill tenants, a fugitive with a price on his head, is hiding out at his family's farm. Given the nature of the situation, the balancing act cannot work. The Naylors should realize this as the calm of their dinner table is disturbed by sounds of armored cars grinding past the estate walls as the Auxiliaries go out on increasingly savage punitive forays, making illegal arms searches in which sick people are ousted from their beds and terrorized farmers are beaten up or tortured. Lois spots a man in a trench coat prowling through the grounds at night, following his own route from the nearby mountains where guerrillas are dug in; and when she, Hugo Montmorency, and the fascinating Marda Norton follow a local watercourse to the ruins of an old industrial mill, they find an exhausted fugitive sleeping there, who threatens them with a revolver when he wakes up. Lord and Lady Naylor are in a war zone but pretend not to know it. Yeats's emblematic peacocks and swans have been replaced by the ostrich, which hides its head in the sand. If the Sinn Fein had not arrived first with their petrol tins at Danielstown, the English, led by a sick and violent Ireland-hater such as Daventry, would have done the job themselves.

Another way of answering the question is suggested by something Bowen wrote in 1942, in her essay "The Big House."

> And in this struggle for life, a struggle that goes on everywhere, that may be said, in fact, to *be* life itself, and should not therefore have anything terrible about it, the big house people were handicapped, shadowed and to

an extent queered—by their pride, by their indignation at their decline and by their divorce from the countryside in whose heart their struggle carried on. (*Impressions*, 197)

Of these factors, the last is surely the most important, and it is the one most memorably rendered in *The Last September*. The deepest failure of the big house was its failure to provide a vital center for a community. This must be stressed, for certain critics continue to assume that the Irish estates, at least emblematically, were centers of community. They were not, though they perhaps should have been. Richard Gill, in "The Country House in a Time of Trouble"[10] flourishes this *idée recue* about human community even after he has quoted Bowen's admission that her family "got their position and drew their power from an inherent wrong." Irish and English country houses were not the same—the Irish big house is about as convincing a symbol of community as the House of Usher.

The failure of Anglo-Irish culture at its point of disintegration fell hardest on the young. It is terrible that Lois is so displaced and at a loss in her life that she cannot return the love of Gerald, the English subaltern, even though he is lovable, faithful until death, and fights hard to conquer her diffidence and bewilderment about who she is and what she wants. Marda Norton is scarcely better off as she tires of shifting about and prepares to throw herself away in an English society marriage. As one mounts the scale of age a certain habituation to makeshifts sets in. The Montmorency couple are a case in point. Funking the challenge of Canada, they have gotten quite good at living hand to valise as something close to professional house guests. Hugo will always fall in love with whatever woman appears, while continuing to provide ostentatious nursing care to his wife. Mrs. Montmorency will do her part by steadily becoming more of an invalid, wearing her decrepitude somewhat nakedly so as to provide dramatic contrast to Hugo's air of jaded youthfulness.

As for Sir Richard and Lady Naylor, these tough Anglo-Irish birds will flourish in the long run. After the shock of losing the house has worn off, they will qualify for compensation money and perhaps end their days at Rushbrook, the community of mini-estates overlooking Queenstown Harbor (now called Cobh), to which many of the Munster proprietors retreated after their ancestral houses were destroyed. Bowen wrote of this place in *The House in Paris*: "Rushbrook is full of Protestant gentry, living down misfortunes they once had. None of them, as a matter of fact, had done too badly, or they would not be here, for most of the big villas are miniature 'places' that need some keeping up. The nineteenth-century calm hanging over the colony makes the rest of Ireland a frantic or lonely dream" (74–75). Typically, the walls of these new villas bear photographs of the old estate house, before and after it was burned: "ghastly black staring photographs of the ruins . . . hung outside the bathroom door."

After seeing the man in the trench coat cross her path in the dark, Lois admitted to herself that she "could not conceive of the country emotionally" (37). Yet there are some extraordinary panoramic passages where Bowen, looking through Lois's eyes but with her own power of vision, accomplishes just that. At one point the girl is coming back from a visit to a neighboring estate, Mount Isabel, and from a high place views Danielstown down below:

> Looking down, it seemed to Lois they lived in a forest; space of lawns blotted out in the dusk and pressure of trees. She wondered why they were not smothered; then wondered still more they were not afraid. Far from here, too, their isolation became apparent. The house seemed to be pressing down low in apprehension, hiding its face, as though it had her vision of where it was. It seemed to huddle its trees close in fright and amazement at the wide light lovely unloving country, the unwilling bosom whereon it was set. (78)

The deliberate anthropomorphism brings out the pathos of the beleaguered, beautiful, lonesome tradition that the natives are struggling to be rid of. She sees the estate as a jewel; others, spying from the mountains and attacking from under the protective dusk of dense trees, see instead the chains by which jewels like Danielstown hung upon the "unwilling bosom" of the country. The rest of the description is heart-stoppingly beautiful, a paean to the countryside of Spenser and the Bowen ancestors, country that the Irish of the little white cabins and "the pink and yellow farms" are taking back. This process will not complete itself until the English soldiers pack up and go. Meantime the "hidden Ireland"—the phrase is from the nationalist critic and regional Cork story writer Daniel Corkery[11]—will watch, biding its time, spying out the best opportunities for an ambush or a seizure.

A sense of being spied on, secretly watched, is as constant and nearly as paranoid in *The Last September* as it was in the Gothic tales of LeFanu. At a summer party at Mount Isabel, the Naylors' son Laurence, an Oxford undergraduate who claims to support Sinn Fein, is abashed by "the sense of a watcher, reserve of energy and intention." A feeling "of exposure, of being offered without resistance to some ironic incuriosity, made Laurence look up at the mountain." When Lois attends the dance at the officers' compound, she and her chum are nervous about being seen and recognized from some vantage point in the nearby hills: "They walked rather silently up past the barracks and picked their way over the mud between the huts. A chill of darkness was coming down on the air.

The wind came, knifelike, down . . . over a gulf of land where the farms were dark—apprehensive, the young girls patted the whorls of their hair" (182). Lois wonders if attending the dance at all was too rash: "Would this annoy the Irish?" She is, of course, Irish herself, but of the other "kind." Beyond the wall, its top heavily barbwired, and beyond the sentry inhumanly pacing, "the country bore in its strong menace" (183).

To go with this heavy menace of mountains and woods, there might well be a Gothic castle or dungeon. These are lacking, but there is a strongly Gothic work-up of the ruined mill already mentioned. Lois, Marda, and Hugo Montmorency come upon this nineteenth-century industrial ruin around a bend of the valley stream. It "startled them all, staring light-eyed, ghoulishly" (151). In the best tradition of terror literature, the young heroine's instant fear has its voluptuous side—"It was fear she didn't want to get over, a kind of deliciousness." The narrator remarks, "These dead mills—the country was full of them, never quite stripped and whitened to a skeleton's decency: like corpses at their most horrible" (152). To this the character Hugo appends, "Another of our national grievances. English law strangled the—." But both young women, avid to encounter a *worst* which the custom, ceremony, and privilege of Anglo-Irish life have conspired to cover up, hurry on ahead, leaving to be delivered to empty air the rest of his lecture on how English tariffs, custom levies, and shipping laws strangled Irish industrial development in the very century when England's own industry dominated the world. And it is a worst:

> The river darkened and thundered towards the millrace, light came full on the high facade of decay. Incredible its loneliness, roofless, floorless, beams criss-crossing dank interior daylight, the whole place tottered, fit to crash at a breath. Hinges rustily bled where a door had been wrenched away; up six stories panes still tattered the daylight. Mounting the tree-crowded, steep slope some roofless cottages nestled under the flank of the mill with sinister pathos. . . . Banal enough in life to have closed the valley to the imagination, the dead mill now entered the democracy of ghostliness, equalled broken palaces in futility and sadness; was transfigured by some response of the spirit, showing not the decline of its meanness, simply decline; took on all of the past to which it had given nothing. (152)

The last part of this remarkable description is not very easy to construe. One grasps the romance inherent in ruination, but it is more difficult to grasp how the mill had "given nothing." People must have made an honest, perhaps agonizing effort in those six stories, coming home after toil to cottages "now roofless," before "conditions" made going on impossible. One may recoil from the spectacle of the ruins of the nongiving mill to a thought that if the dominant and empowered class in Ireland during the nineteenth century, that is, the class to which Lois, Marda, and Hugo all belong, had given more—had given *something*—to the country, then perhaps that Gothic strangler, English law, might not quite have been able to do its worst. Some such thought may be struggling for expression in the reference to the "democracy of ghostliness." As a broken mill may equal broken palaces, so may a vast famine producing millions of deaths among humble people rival the passing of kings and the tribulations of mighty heroes.

However that may be, Lois, recognizing that these "brittle, staring ruins" are her "nightmare," and that the mill really is "like the House of Usher," presses on with Marda to a confrontation with the sleeping gunman. Suddenly waking, he is more frightened than threatening. He does, however, wave his revolver at them as he backs away, and it accidentally discharges. The bullet grazes Marda's hand, which she, quite spontaneously, puts to her mouth. Hugo hurrying in, discovers this woman, with whom he is beginning to fancy himself in love, with blood on her lips. The ruined mill as graveyard of economic hope now acquires its final touch of the macabre—the vampire touch, the nightmare vision of the "undead," the dead still putting on an act at living.

Watt (1953)

> Each house seems to live under its own spell . . . that falls on the visitor from the moment he passes in at the gates.
> —Bowen, "The Big House," in *Impressions*

Like Maturin and LeFanu, Samuel Beckett was of Dublin Protestant and Huguenot stock. One grandfather, a late-nineteenth-century building contractor of substantial means, may be compared to Charles Lever's father, the English-born architect-builder in Dublin, whose projects included remodeling the College Green parliament building into a commercial bank. Beckett and Lever also have in common that quite early in their literary careers both relocated to the Continent, neither having found London a congenial alternative after deciding to leave Ireland. Following in his own father's career path, Samuel Beckett's father, William, was a quantity surveyor, though he gave his occupation as architect on Samuel's birth certificate. Critics occasionally speculate that William's choice of occupation, at which he proved highly successful, influenced the son's bizarre passion for quantification and numerical permutation. One example among many would be the several pages in

Watt given over to a list of all the attempts of all the members of the Trinity College research grants committee to catch one another's eye.

Beckett's biographer, Deirdre Bair,[12] describes his family as Anglo-Irish of the second rank, basing this on their not being landed, on William's being in business, and on his not having attended Trinity in Dublin or Oxford or Cambridge in Britain. Such social placements this late in the twentieth century, made about a disintegrating minority, in a country that underwent a largely successful nationalist revolt during Samuel Beckett's adolescent years, are bound to be somewhat tentative. But it is probably safe to say that the family house which William Beckett built around 1909 in the pleasant South Dublin suburb of Foxrock was meant to reproduce or at least recall something of the amenity of the traditional Anglo-Irish country house situated on its own demesne. Cooldrinagh, a three-story structure in Tudor style, faced the Dublin Mountains, and stood in several acres of grounds, including gardens, an orchard, a tennis court and a wooded tract, with outbuildings that included stables, a garage, and a donkey shed.

Cooldrinagh also resembles the house of Mr. Knott in *Watt*, where the greater part of the novel's events take place. Both dwellings are within walking distance of a local railway line and employ staffs of three, including a full-time gardener. Both houses are claustral in atmosphere, somewhat opaque and mysterious to the outside world. No one would dispute this characterization of the house where Watt goes to serve. As for Cooldrinagh, the mother, May Beckett, kept the blinds down all day, refused to entertain, and discouraged her two sons, Frank and Samuel, from bringing home school friends. She was also apt, like Mr. Knott, to prowl the upper stories at night, in her case because of chronic insomnia.

Above all, the two houses are alike in being places where misleading signs are given out and where all meanings are far from clear. For Cooldrinagh, the focus of the problem are in the parents as they appear to the older son Frank and to Samuel during their growing up years. May Beckett was outwardly devout yet not really religious. A very strict disciplinarian, she was given to outbursts of uncontrollable rage, episodes of manic hilarity, and long brooding sulks, these moods following or interrupting one another unpredictably. In addition, she was physically violent, sometimes inflicting severe disciplinary beatings on the boys when it was not always clear what rule had been broken. May's sensual bond with William seems to have been severed or at least attenuated soon after Samuel's birth in spring of 1906. From that time she slept apart from her spouse in a room that neither he nor the children were encouraged to visit.

The husband, by contrast, was hearty in temperament, a sportsman, and physically robust. His entire social life, however, including entertainment of friends and business associates, was led outside the home. He saw people at one or another of the Dublin clubs, overwhelmingly Protestant in membership, to which he belonged, and on the golf course. William Beckett seems to have carried his parental duties rather lightly. Usually he would phone home in early evening, just before his sons were sent to bed, to ask how the day had gone. On weekends he was more available; that is when he was not hiking—alone—in the Dublin Mountains or on the links with business associates. Seamus Deane has remarked that Ireland was the perfect site for Beckett's enigmatic metaphysics of absence (*Celtic Revivals*, 130). I would only add that both the enigma and the absence began at home, in the persons of May and William Beckett, the author's parents.

Watt as well as many other Beckett works may indeed issue from the neurosis induced by growing up in such a family, but here is not the place to pursue the speculation. Nor have I any intention of spending much space on what the book may ultimately mean. Beckett himself seems to think his writing is a doomed attempt to express the inexpressible. In Gottfried Büttner's "gnosiological" study of *Watt*, the author is reported as saying "*Jedes Wort ist eine Luge*"—"Every word is a lie" (Büttner, 27). Büttner, speculating on Beckett's meaning in this Anglo-Irish version of the Cretan paradox, remarks that in the depths of the soul words no longer exist. The dilemma of Beckett's writing consists in his trying to use words to express soul-experience,[13] where there are no words (Büttner, 27–38).

For *Watt* I would put the matter a little differently, so as to avoid terms of faith like "the soul," about which there is so little agreement in our time. The central relation of the book, that of Watt and Mr. Knott, may be put in question-and-answer (catechistical) form. The question is "What is it?" and the answer, invariably and relentlessly, is "It is not that." To grant something like the soul its claims, one may assume that the catechizing goes on intrasubjectively, even intracranially or "speleologically." One surmises that the names of both the servant and the master end in double "t" because they are both, in some sense contained in "Beckett." But enough of this effort to reduce intriguing fiction to mere philosophy—*Dichtung* to *Wahrheit.*

How does *Watt* connect with Anglo-Irish literary tradition so as to provide it with a terminus ad quem? Frank Kermode has said of Beckett's writing that it is full of canceled humanistic designs, that its way of acknowledging a humanism is through this very act of canceling.[14] In a similar way, *Watt* acknowledges Anglo-Irish tradition by a series of parodic reductions amounting to cancellation. Perhaps we should say by embalming or freeze-drying, except that we have played with this type of comparison sufficiently at the beginning of this chapter.

Beckett's servant-protagonist Watt is a final dilapidation or ruination of the entire line of big-house serving men that originates in Thady Quirk. As Thady told the story of the Rackrent decline in his own words, the "editor" transcribing these words and adding a preface, notes, and a glossary, so has Watt told the story of his service in the house of Mr. Knott to "Sam," who has retold the story mostly in his own words, while adding a few editorial notes and the glossarylike "Addenda." In the middle of *Watt* Part II, which tells of Watt's experience on the ground floor of the house, Sam says, "For all that I know . . . on the subject of Watt, and of all that touched Watt, came from Watt, and from Watt alone" (*Watt*, 125). This information came to Sam when they were both in the asylum of many "pavilions" described in Part 3, and at no other place and time. Confirmation of this point is provided in a letter Beckett wrote Büttner on April 12, 1978: "Only one part is in the asylum, *though all told there*, the other three in Knott's house" (Büttner, 159, emphasis added).

In Part 3, Sam provides numerous direct examples of Watt's speech as it began to "invert." These passages, taken down from dictation as it were, carry us back to Maria Edgeworth's powerful fantasy, as she began writing *Castle Rackrent*, that the former Edgeworth family steward John Langan stood at her elbow dictating. She submitted, faithfully rendering his authentic Irish idiom on the page. At the same time, she asserted authorial control and proprietary rights through her pretense of being the memoir's only authorized editor. On the very first page of *Rackrent* appears the extended note on Thady's great-coat, which he wears winter and summer and which the note links to the Irish cloak of "high" Celtic antiquity. Watt, too, wears a long overcoat in all seasons and weathers that is a further *reductio* of the antique mantel. Its weight is unknown, but it is still "green" here and there. It reaches to the feet, helping Watt's baggy trousers to conceal the bad shape of his legs. The coat is of "a very respectable age" as such coats go, purchased secondhand by Watt's father "some seventy years before." It has never been washed or cleaned, except by accidental immersion in rain, snow, sleet, and bog water. Nevertheless, it retains some formerly elegant features: patches of velvet on the collar, remnants of a purplish-red chrysanthemum in the flower hole. One recalls that Thady's overcoat was worn cloak-fashion and was fastened by a single button, which corresponded to the bronze or gold Celtic brooch fastening Irish cloaks in antiquity. Watt's coat has no fewer than nine stout buttons. What appears to correspond to the brooch is the rakish bit of reddish flower in the flower hole.

Thady was perfectly faithful to the "family" and to the succession of Rackrent masters he served. We have seen how Yeats glorified this "feudal" virtue of fidelity in some of his poems and in constructing for himself a role to play as a bard "of serving kind," never happier than when he could bend his "medieval knees" in homage to the Gregories and their aristocratic Anglo-Irish circle. Watt, too, is faithful. He never takes a day off or asks for a raise. It is not even clear that he gets paid for what he does. His devotion, however, is unglorified and matter-of-fact, apart from his intense concern to make out the nature of the mysterious individual he serves, and when it is time to go, he goes.

As the servant figure and the ideal of service are reduced, so correspondingly are the master figure and the ideal of mastery. I am not, of course, saying anything about Mr. Knott in his transcendental aspect—if he has one. We may observe this reduction in two of the examples Sam gives of Watt's inverted manner of speech. In both these excerpts Watt is speaking of Mr. Knott:

> *Say he'd, No, waistcoat the, vest the, trousers the, socks the, shoes the, shirt the, drawers the, coat the, dress to ready things got had when. Say he'd, Dress. Say he'd, No, water the, towel the, sponge the, soap the, salts the, glove the, brush the, basin the, wash to ready things got had when. Say he'd, Wash. Say he'd, No, water the, towel the, sponge the, soap the, razor the, powder the, brush the, bowl the, shave to ready things got had when. Say, he'd, Shave.* (*Watt*, 167)
>
> *Dis yb dis, nem owt. Yad la, tin fo trap. Skin, skin, skin. Od su did ned taw? On. Taw ot klat tonk? On. Tonk ot klat taw? On. Tonk ta kool taw? On. Taw ta kool tonk? Nilb, mun, mud. Tin fo trap, yad la. Nem owt, dis yb dis.* (*Watt*, 168)
>
> [Side by side, two men. All day, part of night. Dumb, numb, blind. Knott look at Watt? No. Watt look at Knott? No. Knott talk to Watt? No. What then did us do? Niks, niks, niks. Part of night, all day. Two men, side by side.]

In the first of these passages mastery is pretty much reduced to the power of capricious countermanding of previously issued orders. In the second, a type of numbness takes over. As Watt prepares to leave the house he has found that the master-servant relation, in his experience of it, was no relation at all: "Niks, niks, niks."

Mr. Knott changes shape, size, and complexion, one cannot say at will—because he does not say—and promptly at noon and at seven p.m. is served a species of universal food, a mess concocted from all possible materials, animal, vegetable and mineral. Going to bed, he puts on his nightclothes over his day clothes. Watt once saw him in the garden with his head inclined, apparently in benign contemplation of a flower and an earthworm. On closer inspection it was revealed that the master had his eyes closed in slumber. Mr. Knott sometimes climbs a tree in the garden and temporarily disappears. We can multiply these mysteries and oddities about him without our ever coming any closer to understanding him than Watt does.

But the notion of mystery points in another direction too—toward the Gothic element in Anglo-Irish literary tradition which, as seen earlier, is usually focussed on and around the large, claustral, unvisited and isolated house in the Irish countryside. Despite the occasional frivolities and levities arising in the speeches of the serving men Arsene and Arthur, and appearing in Sam's account of what the title character got up to with Mrs. Gorman the fish-woman every Thursday, and even despite the sheer ontological frivolity of Mr. Knott's changes of size, shape, and complexion, there are certainly sufficient elements of the eerie and strange to win for the Knott mansion, which on Watt's first view of it, is utterly dark, its chimneys etched by moonlight (33), its own place in the line of spooky Anglo-Irish estate houses and ruins going back to Maturin, if not to Edgeworth herself.

Let us try to follow the track of mystery as Watt, who has been battered about at the train station, and has been hearing voices "singing, crying, stating, murmuring things unintelligible" (33–34), and has spent a period of time lying face down in a gravelike ditch, comes to the house by moonlight, progresses there from ground-floor servant to servant of the "upper regions" of the house, and finally departs, again at night, when Micks, the new ground-floor servant, arrives. Watt then returns to the train station, endures a new round of battering, and is last seen traveling by train to "the end of the line." He may be seen as a terminal case—the pun is certainly relevant—but he has still to meet Sam at the asylum and tell his story. In earlier encounters with the Gothic we discovered encoded meanings amid the tracery and fretwork. If such accreted meanings appear in *Watt*, one can expect, in line with my main argument about Beckett, that they will be reductive, parodic, self-canceling.

Büttner's gnosiological account sees the opening (Part 1) as, analogically, Watt's birth, his journey from the station to the house as Watt's suffering the indignities of life, and Watt's discovering himself across the threshold of the house as his entering into death (Büttner, 125–26). That seems harmless as analogies go. There are, however, difficulties. If Watt is already in death at the house of Mr. Knott, he will have to come back to life before he can find a friend and confidant in Sam at the pavilions. This requirement would not phase Büttner, whose approving citations from the works of Rudolf Steiner, the Anthroposophist, suggest that he is, at least provisionally, a believer in reincarnation, like Steiner himself. One footnote in *Watt*, on page 82, hints at an incarnational scheme of things in which an individual moves from one "transitory refuge" to another before reaching the haven of a "last halt." Mr. Knott, described later on as "harbor . . . haven, calmly entered, freely ridden" *but also* "gladly left" (*Watt*, 135), could be such a halt for Watt, but he is not—at least not this time around. The scheme one makes out here, if it is in the book at all, needs to be differentiated from the Yeatsian phases of incarnation, where the subject, whether a man or a civilization, moves from "cradle" to cradle of rebirth, but then is shuttled back again, according to the regular waxing and waning of the moon, the endless shuttlings of the bobbins, cones, or gyres.

From another point of view, it is fairly easy to entertain the notion of Watt as a dead man, since he shares, with all the other main characters of Beckett's fiction, from Murphy to the Unnameable, so utter a separation and alienation from what passes for ordinary life. If, for the sake of argument, Watt is dead when he enters the house, one might surmise that he finds himself in Purgatory. One makes this out, first of all, from "the beautiful red floor [of the kitchen] . . . the floor burning up, from below" (*Watt*, 37), which suggests the Dantean Inferno underlying the Mount of Purgatory. Beckett, a strong Dante scholar, knew well Joyce's detailed parody of the *Purgatorio* in the *Dubliners* story "Grace." In *Watt*, the kitchen fire, which alternately glows and turns gray, seems modeled on the bedroom fire in "Grace" around which the cronies of the invalid Mr. Kernan gathered to exchange their wonderful bromides and bits of misinformation about the Roman Catholic Church and a purified life.

But Beckett dispenses with crowds, at least after Watt has left behind the choiring voices. Ascent up the Mount of Purgatory, level by level, to the "upper regions" is strictly by oneself and is experienced exclusively by Mr. Knott's manservants in sequence: Arsene going out and Erskine going up when Watt comes in; Arthur coming in and Watt going up when Erskine goes out; Arthur going up and Watt going out when Micks comes in. The other characters at the house—Mr. Graves the gardener, the Galls, father and son, who come to tune the pianos, and Mrs. Gorman—whatever they do or signify, do not function in the purgatorial design, such as it is. They do not move up from level to level, and they do not get ensnared in the hapless effort that Watt makes to grasp the nature and being of Mr. Knott. If the house is in any sense a purgatorium, what role does that open to its master? Not the God part, certainly. Beckett must have known enough Roman Catholic doctrine to realize that one of the chief pangs of Purgatory is that God does not show his face there. Mr. Knott shows many faces—and figures—but not the ineffable One.

When Watt leaves the house, revealing sadness and reluctance at the last, he walks off into a blaze of light cast by the full moon. We may surmise that this is a parodic version of the image of the multifoliate rose appearing at the end of the *Paradiso*, but that is difficult to square with earlier information that Watt most hates four things—earth and sky, sun and moon (*Watt*, 33). As he endures new contretemps and sufferings at the train station, we must conclude that no real purgation has taken place. The scheme of Purgatory in *Watt*, if it is there at all, turns out to be self-canceling.

A final sweep. Arthur's elaborated story of Ernest Louit's dissertation on "The Mathematical Intuitions of the Visicelts," Louit's discovery in the west of Ireland of the kilted Mr. Nackybal, a sufferer from *pruritus ani*, and his presentation of this ancient before the Trinity College grants committee are a travesty of the cult of the western peasant, in the works of Yeats, Lady Gregory, and Synge, which was so essential a feature of the Literary Revival. The cream of the jape is that Nackybal is an incompetent idiot savant whose mental calculations of square and cube roots are only correct an average of three times out of five, giving him a barely passing score of sixty percent. The introduction of the grants committee reveals a certain prescience on Beckett's part. When he was writing *Watt* in the French Vaucluse in 1943 and 1944, no one could have anticipated that the Literary Revival in Ireland and Irish Modernism would become a flourishing international academic industry a few decades later.

The starving dogs and the Lynch family who tend them bring into the picture the immemorial yet historical theme of Irish famine. The idle, indigent, sickly, stunted, and inbred Lynches, whose sole ambition is to reach a statistical plateau upon which the ages of all surviving Lynches will total one thousand years, an ambition comparable to Hitler's dream of a thousand-year German *Reich*, reduce the native Irish in their long suffering over the generations to a least common denominator of birth, procreation, and death. The Lynches appear to be a family of those "unintelligent classes" which Yeats, in a moment of spleen, hoped to limit through eugenical experiment. Actually, they practice eugenics on themselves, exhibiting all the while a gusto and ingenuity that is virtually without limit.

Other forms of human degradation are treated comically in *Watt*, some proving to be funny indeed. As he departs, Arsene gives a little disquisition on laughter, on the laugh hollow, the laugh bitter, the laugh mirthless:

> But the mirthless laugh is the dianoetic laugh, down the snout—Haw!—so. It is the laugh of laughs, the *risus purus*, the laugh laughing at the laugh, the beholding, the saluting of the highest joke, in a word the laugh that laughs—silence please—at that which is unhappy. Personally of course I regret all. All, all, all. (*Watt*, 48)

This has to be Melmothian laughter, the self-gnawing cachinnation of someone who gambled his very soul for three hundred years of great wealth, power, and extended life, only to have all his projects fail in the end. It is one kind of epitaph on the tradition we have traced in this book, a kind Samuel Beckett was uniquely suited to provide.

Addendum

Catholic Ireland has two physical sites, both associated with St. Patrick, both surviving from remote antiquity, to which pilgrims still travel to undergo purgation. One is the conical mountain Croagh Patrick, in County Mayo, near Clew Bay. During the week before Easter and in the so-called praying season that begins around June 1, the penitents climb up and down in a long suffering line. Structurally then, Croagh Patrick as purgatorium resembles the up and down sequence of the male servants at Mr. Knott's house, while the shape of the mountain is close to the Mount of Purgatory described in Dante.

The other site is St. Patrick's Purgatory, the "holy" island in Lough Derg, South Donegal, about which William Carleton and many other Irish writers have written. It is called Station Island on maps. Here the penitents are transported from the mainland by a boat service and move from station to station on the island, reciting prayers, many going barefoot over rough ground, kneeling and prostrating themselves in barren stony places, and going without sleep or nourishment for long periods of time. Sometimes groups are brought into the main chapel to hear sermons and exhortations and to pray. In former times the chapel cellarage was decorated to resemble hell, with painted demons, flames, and depictions of lost souls in torment.

Watt's trials going and coming outside the house of Mr. Knott, his sufferings at the railway station and on the road and in the ditch, and what he may be expected further to suffer as he resumes his journey to the last station on the line, resemble, in a rough way, the penitential round typically followed by pilgrims to Station Island in Lough Derg.[15]

AFTERWORD

ANGLO-IRISH LITERATURE, then, has a beginning, a middle, and an end, its richly untidy postmortem phase simply providing haunting evidence of the pain of giving up and letting go. A current view is that literary traditions, canons, periodizations, and the like are constructed, not found, and usually serve some partisan advantage. The not very partisan advantage of the tradition constructed here is that it puts some excellent to very great writers—both women and men, one is happy to say—back in touch with the local conditions that fostered them, with Ireland, and with each other. According to another construction, Irish writers who use English over the years between Maria Edgeworth and Beckett's last English-language novel *Watt*, may be sorted into a jejune phase,[1] followed by a Revival phase[2] (revival precisely of what?), followed by a Modern Greats phase (YeatsJoyceBeckett) much looked into by an international consortium of exegetes, critics, and bibliographers. It is a familiar construction but taken as a whole has never been a coherent one.

My version of a tradition shows more continuity. There is dialogue and conversation going on in it: the exchange of compliments and literary influence between Maria Edgeworth and William Carleton; or Charles Lever's odd anticipation of Samuel Beckett, not only in the comparability of their social origins, but also in their common aversion to literary London, leading both to pen their home thoughts from abroad on the Continent.

Other continuities and genealogical relations may be discerned. There is J. S. LeFanu's dilation of the footnote in *Castle Rackrent* describing Miss Cathcart's close confinement by Colonel M'Guire into an entire *Chapter in the History of a Tyrone Family*; and there is the decision of Edith Somerville and Martin Ross to begin their careers as serious novelists by rewriting the essential plot of *Uncle Silas* as a West Cork, rather than a Northumbrian, family scandal. In the late 1940s, at the height of her reputation as an important modernist writer, Elizabeth Bowen told Charles Ritchie, "Now that Virginia [Woolf] is dead Edith Somerville and Colette and Edith Sitwell are the only living writers whom I really admire" (Glendinning, 177). Sometimes in a strong tradition one is claimed by a heritage without one's knowing it. When Yeats in *Purgatory* has the gothic Old Man pray to God for the release of his mother's soul, he probably does not realize how closely he follows the words, cadences, and mood of the old Prior at the end of Maturin's Gothic verse play *Bertram*, when that ecclesiastic prays over the crazed expiring mother, the Lady Imogine.

The stoutest thread connecting the Anglo-Irish writers—apart from a sense of conflicted social and personal identity, which is in all of them but always differently felt—is probably the fascination with the expressive possibilities of a distinctive "Anglo-Irish" or "Hiberno-English" idiom. Beginning with the ventriloquism of *Castle Rackrent* and the panoply of linguistic research provided in that book's original notes and Glossary, and in its close sequel, *An Essay on Irish Bulls*, it may be followed through writer after writer until stopped dead by *Watt*'s repeated, wicked, and occasionally hilarious parody of Irish verbosity in narration. Servants telling long, untidy stories not only carry the reader back to Maria Edgeworth but also to *Melmoth the Wanderer*, that convoluted and verbose work in which characters narrated about routinely become narrators and scribes themselves, so that even a Biddy Brannigan, one of the lowly gathered in the Wicklow manor house kitchen to drink and eat up the dying proprietor's provisions, gets to speak her piece in the multistoried structure of the whole.

James Joyce, who is outside the family of Anglo-Irish writers strictly speaking, was nevertheless a significant and remarkably uninhibited borrower from that tradition. For example, he ransacks Sheridan LeFanu's *The House by the Churchyard* (1863) for the central images of river and elm in the Anna Livia Pluribelle section of *Finnegans Wake* (196–216), and he echoes, probably undesignedly, *The Essay on Irish Bulls* in the Aeolus episode of *Ulysses* (Gabler ed., 96–123), for both pieces of writing purport to demystify Hibernian eloquence and bombast by exposing the rhetorical tricks and figures deployed in a generous sample of specimen speeches.

As far back as John Banim's *Anglo-Irish of the Nineteenth Century* the reader encounters a fictional motif that might be called the Dublin Walkabout. It emerges as the youthful hero takes a long musing walk through the middle of the city, inventorying its architectural and civic distinctions, and claiming these as his own and the reviving nation's rightful heritage. A demoralized, even despairing version of the walk appears in George Moore's *A Drama in Muslin*, when the little Marquis Kilcarney slips through Dublin late at night and concludes fearfully that the city, monument by monument and feature by feature, is passing from control of the class to which he belongs and into the clutches of Parnell and his Land Leaguers. However, the fullest development of Dublin Walkabout comes in Joyce, in the fifth chapter of *A Portrait* (174–84) when Stephen Dedalus, on his way to classes at the National University, crosses inner Dublin from north to south, "reading" the city's features and appropriating it as a subject for future artistic recreation; and in *Ulysses*, where a long series of Dublin walks undertaken by Bloom, Dedalus, and others brings a complete urban culture to light and makes it available to the literary imagination.

If James Joyce in a certain sense was the epic poet not only of early-twentieth-century Dublin but also of a new Ireland that was taking political form amid shot and shell and bitter internecine conflict during the very year—1922—in which the complete *Ulysses* was published, it was appropriate that his work should incorporate aspects of an older literary phase which had had its day, just as Virgil's *Aeneid* looked back to Homer and Dante's *Divine Comedy* brought Virgil into view as a guiding light. Yeats had something different in mind when he hoped that Anglo-Irish values and styles would survive and be transmitted to sweeten the thought of the children of the new Ireland. Yet Yeats would also have realized that in the permutations and transmissions of a rich tradition no one is privileged to utter the final word.

That does not mean one cannot try. The key to the tradition traced is reconciliation. Maria Edgeworth began it by breaching the towering wall the penal century had built to silence communication between the two kinds, to put it flatly, of Irish people. That is what Thady Quirk's sweet talk of *his* Rackrent family accomplishes. William Carleton, pretending to inform on his native group, "invented" so much truth about them, reaching far back in time to the silenced, invisible generations, that they henceforth become known and therefore indismissible to the "great stock" once presuming to rule over them without knowing who or what they were.

Though the Irish Gothic writers may seem preoccupied with fantasy explorations of the fears and historic guilts of the Anglo-Irish, they also express a longing to change and be changed. Something awful ends when Melmoth the Wanderer leaps or is hurled from his stormy eminence. Something better may begin as Alonzo Monçada and young John Melmoth, both violently disinherited from a heritage of violence, try to go on together.

For all his diplomatic evasions, Lever's final move was to show Ireland both in intimate local detail and in a Pan-European conspectus of great powers promoting and exploiting the troubles of small nations. Though it meant biting the imperial hand which had appointed and partially maintained him in his series of British consular posts, it also meant claiming a "real part" in an Irish *patria* transcending the old divisions. Moore's "a pox o' both your houses!" directed at his fellow landlords, along with their revolted tenants, presumed that in future Ireland would be controlled either by English armies of occupation or by a dictatorship of Irish-American terrorists, unless, that is, there was a reconciling, if not an actual commingling of the two kinds, as indeed had happened in his own parental family.

When Yeats pronounced "tradition is kindred," he meant still to assert Anglo-Irish difference, though his final thoughtful position on the two communities envisioned mutual accommodation, the best of each kind becoming one. Within the space of Yeats's lifetime, Edith Somerville and Martin Ross were uncovering something rather different, the hidden truth that Irish of the two kinds were already akin. Over the generations there had been a good deal of visiting back and forth between "half-door" and "hall-door," the most fruitful of these contacts occurring after dark. Grasping this hypothesis—it is really a metaphor of the reconciliation process, though it wears the mask of a scandalous allegation—they launched a double literary career.

The tradition, then, before it dies out or is absorbed, is about making amends and reconciling, not about attempts to hold or grab power. The Irish of all conditions have never liked grabbers, though they have known a few in their day. Power only enters negatively as something the Anglo-Irish are steadily losing, along with proportionate numbers, beginning with the great Maria, ending where we do and as we must.

NOTES

PREFACE

1. "Yeats and Decolonization," in *Nationalism, Colonialism and Literature*, pamphlets by Terry Eagleton, Frederic Jameson, and Edward W. Said, 69–95 (1990). *Culture and Imperialism* (1993).

CHAPTER I

1. In the *Irish Times* for January 9, 1975, the Irish historian and Trinity Provost F.S.L. Lyons summed up the Protestant position in Ireland over the centuries as follows: "You can detect, I think, four main phases . . . first of settlement, second of ascendancy, third of contraction, and finally of siege" (12). His scheme is helpful for the group this study calls the Anglo-Irish, though the two groups are not identical.

CHAPTER II

1. In 1782, under pressure from the Irish parliament, the British parliament repealed Poynings' Law which, since 1495, gave the British government veto power over all Irish legislation.

2. Selections from these family archives were published in *The Black Book of Edgeworthstown and Other Edgeworth Memories, 1585–1817* (1927).

3. A passage in Edgeworth's published correspondence shows her interest in mimicry and ties it to her working methods as a novelist. Writing to the last Mrs. Edgeworth from England on December 3, 1821, she says: "Lady Morley was amazingly entertaining. She is one of the best mimics I ever saw. . . . We will give you at secondhand some time or other her Lady Cholmondeley and her conversation on coincidences—the tone exactly like my own idea of Lady Clonbrony [in *The Absentee*]—lisp and all to perfection" (*Letters*, 1971, 283).

4. An Irishism meaning to quarrel. Still current.

5. Hiberno-English is "the Irish-influenced English spoken by native Irish and long assimilated settlers" (Bliss, 11). The term is often preferable to "Anglo-Irish" when the topic is how English is spoken in Ireland.

6. We can see that the Edgeworths were doing something quite new in praising and documenting Irish eloquence and skill in using English by considering Jonathan Swift's fragments of a monologue, "Irish Eloquence," and "A Dialogue in Hybernian Style Between A. and B.," both found among his papers at his death in 1745. The latter begins—"A. Is not them Apples 'is' very good? B. I am *again* you in that"—continuing in a vein of pidgin English Swift attributes to a "planter" from the country and a town merchant. "Irish Eloquence" uses more expressions taken over from the other language ("His neighbor Squire Dolt is a meer buddough . . . He keeps none but garrawns and he rides on a soogawn with nothing for his bridle but gadd") yet is nearly as inept in handling English usage. See Swift, *A Dialogue*, 61–99.

7. Edgeworth published three plays as *Comic Dramas in Three Acts* (1817). Two of these, *Love and Law* and *The Rose,* are set in Ireland. R. L. Edgeworth's brief preface, dated May 1, 1817, describes how the late Thomas Sheridan invited his daughter to write a play on commission for Drury Lane. However, "in the Comedy, the characters must be shewn by strong and sudden lights, the sentiments must be condensed; and nothing that requires slow reflection can be admitted.—The audience must see, hear, feel, and understand at once. Overawed by these considerations, Miss Edgeworth has declined to risk a bolder flight. But encouraged by her father, without venturing on the stage, she publishes the following little Comic Dramas, to feel her way in this new career" (*Comic Dramas*, vi–vii).

CHAPTER III

1. Carleton did consider that his main subject was the northern peasant and his speech habits, only "generalized." He wrote in the Preface to the first edition of *Traits and Stories*: "The Author assumes that in the ground he has taken, he stands in great measure without a competitor; particularly as to certain sketches, peculiar, in the habits and manners delineated in them, to the Northern Irish. . . . In the language and expressions of the Northern peasantry he has studiously avoided local idiom, and that intolerable Scoto-Hibernic jargon which pierces the ear so unmercifully; but he has preserved everything Irish and generalized the phraseology" (v).

2. Part of a threat note sent by a Ribbon Lodge to a substantial farmer who was also a magistrate: "Buddha Bee—You 'ave wan iv our boys for abjiction an rubbry—an it seems is resolved to parsequte." By "abjiction" is probably meant "abduction." *Fardorougha the Miser* (*Works*, 2:306).

3. The expression "Irishism" dates from 1725–35, when the Penal Laws were in full force and the "Protestant Nation" was most eager to distinguish itself from the native or mere Irish majority (*Random House Dictionary*, 2d ed.).

4. Completing the inventory, the narrator says, "This catalogue of cottage furniture may appear to our English readers very unserviceable. We beg them to believe, however, that if every cabin in Ireland were equally comfortable, the country would be comparatively happy" (*Traits*, 2:224).

5. In nineteenth-century Ireland any scheme of truthful storytelling would run into taboos and mental reservations, and the deep-seated fear of giving scandal. At Ned M'Keown's it would be difficult to tell truthful stories about the foibles of the Roman clergy, owing to the constant presence in the fireside audience of Andy Morrow, a Protestant. Similar constraints might operate in stories where Whiteboys and other rural conspirators have a role to play.

6. Unusually dark, stormy, and cold weather contributed to spreading the potato blight during the summers of 1846 and 1847 (Woodham-Smith, 94–187).

CHAPTER IV

1. Adler, *The Practice and Theory of Individual Psychology*; Wilson, *The Wound and the Bow.*

2. She used the pen name "Mrs. Martin-Bell" and was generally called "Mrs. Bell Martin" following her marriage. She was also known as "the Princess of Connemara" (Stephen J. Brown, 202).

CHAPTER V

1. *The Novels of Charles Lever. Edited by His Daughter.* 37 vols. London: Downey, 1899.

2. For the makeup of the British army during the Napoleonic wars see Elie Halevy, *England in 1815* (New York: Barnes and Noble, 1961), especially 77–107.

3. Eighteenth-century and early-nineteenth-century landlords and estate agents sometimes carried large whips with hollow handles into which melted lead had been poured or "loaded," thus converting the whip handle into a formidable club.

4. Sir Jonah Barrington's *Personal Sketches of His Own Times* (1827), filled with candid indiscretions about Irish life around 1800, and written from the shelter of French exile, describes the common people's threefold classification of the country gentry into "1. Half-mounted gentlemen; 2. Gentlemen every inch of them; 3. Gentlemen to the backbone" (Barrington, 101). The first group, also called "half-sirs," is the one to which Mr. Burke belongs.

5. *On the Study of Celtic Literature* (London: Smith, Elder, 1867).

6. Faction fights, which faded out after the 1840s, were fought with heavy cudgels and sometimes involved as many as several hundred combatants. These battles were so productive of severe head trauma that Sylvester O'Halloran, an early-nineteenth-century surgeon of Limerick, made an international reputation in medicine through treating the victims and writing up his cases.

7. The expression "real Irish" is not used by Banim, but it is used by Thomas Moore in a fictional work of the same period, *Memoirs of Captain Rock, the Celebrated Irish Chieftain* (1824).

CHAPTER VI

1. See no. 43, from Francisco de Goya's series of etchings *Los Caprichos* (1799), entitled *El sueño de la razón produce monstruos.*

2. See Harry T. Levin, *The Power of Blackness: Hawthorne, Poe and Melville* (New York: Knopf, 1958).

3. Michael Sadleir in "The Northanger Novels" (1927) argued that Gothic fiction was politically and philosophically subversive. Montagu Summers in *The Gothic Quest* (1939) found that the Gothic was "not a revolutionary genre" (399). Geraldine Murphy's "Romancing the Center: Cold War Politics and Classic American Literature" (1988), argues that old Gothic romances, at least American ones, provide a neutral ideological ground on which modern critics, especially those of the Lionel Trilling–Richard Chase New York school, have staged ideological exercises and parades generally involving movement from the left to the center of the political spectrum.

4. In his preface to *The Castle of Otranto,* an important early document for

laying out some generic rules of Gothic prose fiction, Horace Walpole says that comic treatment of the lower orders—servants, peasants, and the like—may be allowed. His warrant comes from the plays of Shakespeare. In Irish Gothic servants and masters often come into more prolonged and friendly contact than in most English Gothic books. This incipient democracy complicates the problem of generic rules.

5. French Huguenots newly arrived in Ireland fought on the Williamite side at the Battle of the Boyne in 1690. As a reward, in 1692, the Irish parliament "approved a law granting freedom of worship to the Huguenots and other 'Protestant strangers.'" See "Historic Church in Ireland Still Used by Huguenots," *New York Times*, May 31, 1981, 81.

6. "Ugo, or Hugues, was a baron of Lanquedoc, who favored the Albigeois, and from whom the French Protestants of a later period derived the name of Huguenots. The superstition of the age represented him as a necromancer, who, after death, continued to haunt the castle and the neighborhood with a band of infernal aristocrats" *The Albigenses* (4:34). This derivation is fanciful.

7. In the very decade of the climactic struggle for Catholic Emancipation, Maturin's *Five Sermons on the Errors of the Catholic Church* were delivered to packed congregations at Saint Peter's, Dublin. Appearing as a book in 1824, it was Maturin's last published work and so successful that a second edition was issued in 1826.

8. Maturin's preface to *Women: or, Pour et Contre* (1818) luxuriates in a sense of failure from its opening—"None of my former prose works have been popular" to remarks such as: "the characters, situations, and language, are drawn merely from imagination; my limited acquaintance with life denied me any other resource."

9. "The candles burn blue and the air smells of brimstone at the approach of the Evil One" (LeFanu, *Best Ghost Stories*, 71).

10. Cf. Maud Vernon's ordeal in the madhouse disguised as a stately home where she has been placed by her wicked mother in J. S. LeFanu's *The Rose and the Key* (1871). Like the fantasy of premature burial, this stock situation reveals certain haunting anxieties of nineteenth-century middle- and upper-class society.

11. Perhaps only a writer domiciled in Ireland would put politics and religion on an equal footing with alcohol abuse as common causes of mental breakdown.

12. In his anti-Catholic sermons, Maturin calls the Catholic custom of displaying statues and paintings in church a form of idolatry. He is rather inconsistent on this point, for he also praises St. Peter's Rome, for the splendor of its art and architecture. See *Five Sermons*, especially no. 2 and no. 5.

13. Alonzo finally agreed to take his vows, after successfully holding out against every argument and blandishment of the Director, when he found out that his mother, like Volumnia in *Coriolanus*, had prostrated herself upon the threshold of the very room in which the Director held conference with him.

14. At some level the author himself is pleading to be remembered. With his cult of failure and habit of self-isolation, the problem was a real one. In a rather terrible summing up of Maturin, the poet James Clarence Mangan said: "He—in his own dark way—understood many people; but nobody understood him in

any way. And therefore it was that he, this man of the highest genius, Charles Robert Maturin, lived unappreciated—and died unsympathized with, uncared for, unenquired after—and not only forgotten, because he had never been thought about" (O'Donoghue, 229).

15. A paradigmatic LeFanu ghost story relatively free of political implications is "Authentic Narrative of a Haunted House," which appeared in the *Dublin University Magazine* during 1862. There is so much ghostly visiting, knocking, turning of door handles, and hammering sounds from beams above the ceilings that the servants come to believe that smugglers who had used the building before it was modernized continue to have access through secret entries and passages. See *Best Ghost Stories* (419–30). This fantasy of *co-inhabitation* without direct or regular communication between the two sets of inhabitants is also basic to many of the accounts of fairy folk provided by Yeats, Lady Gregory, and other Literary Revival writers beginning a generation or so later.

16. Clontarf, on Dublin Bay, where the native leader Brian Boru expelled the Danes from Ireland in a famous battle in 1069, was exactly the wrong place for Anglo-Irish Captain Barton to attempt a last stand.

17. After quoting Bowen on *Uncle Silas*, McCormack adds that the novel "indirectly reveals an Anglo-Irish provenance. Geographical isolation and denominational minority reproduce in the Ruthyns an approximate model of the ascendancy's position" (204).

CHAPTER VII

1. The Wesleys (later Wellesleys) were split on this question. The older brother, Richard Colley, First Marquess of Wellesley, supported Catholic Emancipation from early on. Wellington as a Tory opposed it but assented to passage of the actual bill during his brief term as prime minister (1828–30).

2. Along with the Lyons biography, Paul Bew's *C. S. Parnell* (1980), and "Chronology of Irish History " in Moody and Martin, eds., have been consulted for this chapter.

3. The law mandated a standard rent reduction of 20%. Unluckily for the proprietors, mortgage interest rates did not move down correspondingly. Moreover, many tenants were inclined to hold out for reductions in the 25 to 30 percent range.

4. "Once an Irishman has been in prison for a political offence . . . he becomes an immortal" (Moore, *Parnell and His Island*, 140)

5. For Self and Anti-Self, see Yeats's *Per Amica Silentia Lunae* (*Mythologies*, 318–69).

CHAPTER VIII

1. After the Treaty of Independence the Provisional and Free State governments continued these arrangements and assumed the burden of debt they entailed. The Irish government also paid compensation and claims for damages to the owners of big houses damaged or destroyed during the Civil War of 1922–24.

2. Viz. *Ann Veronica* (1909), by H. G. Wells; *Mrs. Warren's Profession* (written 1893, produced 1902); and *Major Barbara* (1905), by G. B. Shaw.

3. During his long, feuding relationship with Moore, the poet Yeats was not above charging that Moore was of "coarse-blooded" Mayo peasant stock on his mother's side (*Autobiography*, 269).

4. Much of this cultural journalism was gathered into two books: *Impressions and Opinions* (1891) and *Modern Painting* (1893).

5. After 1886 Moore suspended annual visits to Ireland. According to his biographer, "one reason was the offence which his Irish novel was reported to have given" (Hone, 123).

6. "T— 'Couldn't they blow up that horrible island with dynamite and carry it off in pieces—a long way off?'" (Allingham, *Diary*, 297). The conversation with Tennyson took place in 1880.

7. A likely source for the image of the poison tree was William Ewart Gladstone. During a widely reported and long remembered political speech at Wigan in 1867 he called the Irish Protestant ascendancy "a tall tree of noxious growth, lifting its head to heaven and poisoning the atmosphere of the land as far as its shadow can extend" (quoted in Deane, *Celtic Revivals*, 23). For Moore, transferring the tenor of this metaphorical vehicle to the Castle was a simple matter.

8. See "Introduction" by A. Norman Jeffares (*A Drama in Muslin*, viii).

9. "*A Drama in Muslin* is perhaps the best subject I have ever had excepting *Esther Waters*, and the book is unfortunately the worst written of all my books." Letter to Urwin, Jan. 14, 1902 (*Moore in Transition*, 245).

CHAPTER IX

1. *Some Experiences of an Irish R. M.*, containing twelve stories; *Further Experiences of an Irish R. M.*, containing twelve; *In Mr. Knox's Country*, containing eleven.

2. In David Thomson's *Woodbrook* (1974), an autobiographical account of life on a County Roscommon estate just before, during, and after World War II, local families remember confiscation and claim property rights after three hundred years (Thomson, 286–87).

3. *An Incorruptible Irishman.*

4. Both Edith and Violet kept diaries and made brief entries daily. The complete run of diaries for both writers are in the Somerville and Ross Manuscripts Collection at Queens University, Belfast, Northern Ireland.

5. Martin made contributions to *Irish Memories* before she died. The most important of these is "An Account of Robert Jasper Martin, of Ross," which takes up most of Chapter One (3–40).

6. He achieved passing fame as the lyricist for such popular songs of the period as "Ballyhooly" and "The Vagrants of Erin" (*Irish Memories*, 36).

7. About their revision in 1903 of their first novel, *An Irish Cousin* (1889), Edith wrote: "We combed out youthful redundancies and intensities. . . . We gave it a handling that scared it back to London as purged and chastened as a small boy after his first term at a public school" (*Irish Memories*, 299).

8. Violet Martin did not make a permanent home at Drishane until after the death of her mother late in 1905.

9. Somerville and Ross Collection, Queens University, Belfast.

10. In *Irish Memories* Edith writes, "For most boys and girls the varying, yet invariable, flirtations, and emotional episodes of youth, are resolved and composed by marriage. To Martin and me was opened another way, and the flowering of both our lives was when we met each other" (125). Neither cousin would ever go further than this in publicly acknowledging the homosexual component of their relationship. Maurice Collis remarks that while Edith could only have loved another woman, Martin could have loved a man and married. He does not bring out his evidence for this view (Collis, 32).

11. See "Children of the Captivity," *Some Irish Yesterdays*, 237–49.

12. Notebook pages of hand-lettered grammar exercises appear among the Somerville and Ross papers at Queen's University, Belfast. Some of the exercises are in a notebook containing a handwritten draft of a story called "Slide Number 42," which both authors signed and dated August 1889. This Irish-language material, while extensive, appears to be at the elementary level of language acquisition.

13. Why should I blame her that she filled my days
With misery, or that she would of late
Have taught to ignorant men most violent ways,
Or hurled the little streets upon the great,
Had they but courage equal to desire?

(Yeats, *The Poems*, 91)

14. Edith Somerville's thirty-four illustrations for *Stray-Aways* includes one of the delegate's daughter as she speaks these words.

15. "Gombeen-man": "*Irish-English*: a usurer or money-lender" (*Random House Dictionary*). This dictionary gives the usage from the period 1880–1885. The term is still current in Ireland, with or without the hyphen.

16. *The Real Charlotte* was begun in 1889 and completed, after interruptions, in 1893 (Robinson, 46).

17. In *The Absentee* the Raffartys moved to Bray to embark on a career of social climbing and conspicuous consumption. In *The Real Charlotte*, eighty years later, Francie's father moves the family from Dublin to Bray when he is financially pinched and needs to cut living expenses. There is less to this difference than meets the eye, since the Raffarties at Bray soon become bankrupt and must make a "moonlight flit" into the countryside to escape their creditors.

18. One reason Edith gave for continuing to put Martin Ross's name on the title page of her books after Martin died was: "An established firm does not change its style and title when, for any reason, one of its partners may be compelled to leave it" (*Inver*,5).

19. In *Naboth's Vineyard*, Mrs. Donovan lets her husband cross a river in flood over a bridge she knows to be dangerously undermined without warning him. He is swept to his death when the bridge falls. Later on, in a tacit admission of guilt, she joins a nunnery.

20. The lecture first saw print in *The Revival of Irish Literature* (1894), ed-

ited by Charles Gavan Duffy, George Sigerson, and Douglas Hyde. For Moran see Lyons, *Ireland Since the Famine* 230–33.

21. Yeates's very first items of information about himself are: "I am short-sighted. I am also of Irish extraction." A little later he says: "I don't profess to be a hunting man, but I am an Irish man" (*Some Experiences*, 2, 22).

22. The words (quoted in Robinson, 43) are Edith's and originally appeared in her late compilation of fugitive pieces *Happy Days!* (1946).

23. The essay in *Stray-Aways* is called "The Anglo-Irish Language." It first appeared in *Times Literary Supplement*, May 5, 1910, as a review of Patrick W. Joyce's *English as We Speak It in Ireland.*

CHAPTER X

1. Yeats's special sense of "subjective," deriving from his esoteric philosophy of lunar phases and objective and subjective gyres or "tinctures," broadly means such things as standing out against the common herd, being original, creative, and unaccountable. It has nothing to do with introversion or self-concern. The Nietzschean basis of Yeats's attributing value to "solitude" may be located in a passage of *The Will to Power* on "the great Man": "There is a solitude within him that is inaccessible to praise or blame, his own justice that is beyond appeal." Nietzsche also says of the great man that "he knows he is incommunicable: he finds it tasteless to be familiar. . . . He rather lies than tells the truth; it requires more spirit and will" (Nietzsche, 505).

2. See Terence Brown, esp. Chap. 1: "After the Revolution: Conservatism and Continuity: and Chap. 5: "The 1930s: A Self-Sufficient Ireland."

3. Quoted in Connolly, ed., *Literature and the Changing Ireland*, 18.

4. Article 4 of the treaty adopted between the two countries required an oath swearing by members of the Free State legislative body, which included the following language: "I . . . solemnly swear . . . that I will be faithful to H. M. King George V, his heirs and successors by law, in virtue of the common citizenship of Ireland with Great Britain and her adherence to and membership of the group of nations forming the British Commonwealth of Nations" (Hickey and Doherty, eds., "Treaty," 567).

5. See *Lady Gregory's Journals, 1916–1930*, 165–97.

6. See Yeats's untitled dedicatory poem to his 1914 volume, *Responsibilities*, where the speaker, expressing pride of ancestry, claims he derives from "Merchant and scholar who have left me blood / That has not passed through any huckster's loin" (*Poems*, 101).

7. "We were merchant people of the town. No matter how rich we grew . . . we could never be 'county,' nor indeed had we any desire to be so. We would meet on grand juries those people of the great houses . . . and we would speak no malicious gossip and knew ourselves respected in turn, but the long-settled habit of Irish life set up a wall" (*Memoirs*, 77).

8. In this context, Yeats's highest claim for his family was that they were "small gentry"—nothing more but nothing less either (*Explorations*, 347).

9. The humility of great ones and its paradoxes are taken up in the account

of Phase 24 in *A Vision.* Yeats's exemplars are Queen Victoria and Lady Gregory. "There is great humility . . . and an impersonal pride, as though one were to sign 'servant of servants'" (170).

10. For O'Duffy see Lyons, 529–31.

11. Yeats's swerve toward fascism may begin with the essay of 1919 called "If I were Four and Twenty," where he claims that the Irish "Nation" might achieve "unity of being" by integrating its economics, its nationalism, and its religion. At one point the poet sounds dismayingly like D. H. Lawrence at his metapolitical worst:

> Did some perception . . . create among primitive people the conviction that ordinary men had no immortality but obtained it through a magical bond with some chief or king? . . . Perhaps we are restless because we approach a realisation that our general will must surrender itself to another will within it, interpreted by certain men, at once economists, patriots and inquisitors. (*Explorations*, 279–80)

12. See Yeats's obituary essay of July 11, 1911 (*Essays and Introductions*, 343–45) where Shawe-Taylor is described as a "moral genius" and Anglo-Irish Galahad whose early death is as great a loss to Ireland as Synge's was two years earlier.

13. "It is perhaps because nature made me a gregarious man, going hither and thither looking for conversation and ready to deny for fear or favour his dearest conviction, that I love proud and lonely things" (*Autobiography*, 115).

14. In 1930, after examining a portrait Augustus John had painted of him, Yeats thought that for once he could claim possession of this quality: "Always particular about my clothes, never dissipated, never unshaven except during illness, I saw myself there an unshaven, drunken bar-tender, and then I began to feel John had found something he liked in me, something closer than character, and by that very transformation made it visible. He had found Anglo-Irish solitude, a solitude I have made for myself, an outlawed solitude" (*Explorations*, 308).

CHAPTER XI

1. Beckett has fanciful analogies of his own, once describing his writing as a type of "onto-speleology," that is, a report on explorations undertaken in the caverns of being (Büttner, 31).

2. See Yeats's "Certain Noble Plays of Japan," *Essays and Introductions*, 221–37.

3. See Yeats's "Swedenborg, Mediums, and the Desolate Places," *Explorations*, 30–72; also James Flannery, *W. B. Yeats and the Idea of a Theatre*; and Liam Miller, *The Noble Drama of W. B. Yeats.*

4. The opening line of *Purgatory*, spoken by the Boy, is "Half-door, hall-door." Though he does not yet know it, these metonymic spondees signify the side-by-side traditions of which he is the hybrid product.

5. Manuscripts of the second verse draft of the play carried the title *Souls in Purgatory* (Siegel, ed., 107). It raises the possibility that the Old Man and the

Boy also are already dead and are merely repeating or "dreaming back" the chief transgressive episode of their former lives. That does not, however, much affect the line of argument being pursued here.

6. In her introduction to the *Purgatory* manuscripts Siegel remarks that "eugenic reform" has been under discussion since classical times. She is wrong. Eugenics, defined as the "science" of selective breeding to improve human "racial" strains, dates only from 1883 (*OED*). It is one of the cruel half-sciences, like Lambrosan criminology, spawned by the false analogizing of late-nineteenth-century positivism and Darwinism. Yeats fought such trends of thought throughout his life, only to have the repressed return near the end.

7. Denis Donoghue, *W. B. Yeats*, 122.

8. The war diarist Charles Ritchie, in *The Siren Years*, notes the end of the Bowen-Cameron townhouse in the following entry dated July 20, 1944:

> Elizabeth's house in Clarence Terrace has been hit by a blast for the third time. She has at last decided to move out now. All the ceilings are down and all the windows are broken. She and Alan only escaped being killed by a chance. I hate the disappearance of Clarence Terrace—so will her other friends. It was the last house in London which still felt like a pre-war house. There was always good food, good talk and wine (as long as wine lasted) and a certain style. (176)

The couple did not leave London. They moved into a borrowed flat and Elizabeth continued writing.

9. Introduction, *The Collected Stories of Elizabeth Bowen*, 7.

10. In Bloom, ed., *Elizabeth Bowen: Critical Views*, 51–61.

11. Corkery, *The Hidden Ireland*.

12. *Samuel Beckett: A Biography* (1978). I rely on Ms. Bair's biography for all factual details about Beckett.

13. In the "Addenda" to *Watt*, Watt's world is referred to as a "soul-landscape" (249).

14. At a Christian Gauss Seminar on "Inderterminancy in Modern Fiction" presented at Princeton University in the mid-1970s. There is also Seamus Deane's remark in *Celtic Revivals*: "Everything which has a privileged position in Joyce—history, sexuality, hegemony over language, archetype, Ireland—is cancelled or humiliated in Beckett" (134).

15. Shane Leslie's compilation, *St. Patrick's Purgatory*, provides documentation of the island site since the Middle Ages. There are many popular accounts of visits to the island and some outstanding literary treatments, which include Carleton's "Lough Derg Pilgrim," Sean O'Faolain's "Lovers of the Lake," and long poems by Denis Devlin (1948) and Seamus Heaney (1984).

AFTERWORD

1. Thomas J. Flanagan's now classic study *The Irish Novelists 1800–1850* remains the best introduction to the subject. The Garland facsimile series called *Ireland: From the Act of Union . . . to the Death of Parnell*, a collection of seventy-seven novels and collections of shorter stories by twenty-two Irish and

Anglo-Irish novelists, selected and introduced by Robert Lee Wolff, is the other indispensable study aid.

2. Broad-based studies of the Irish Literary Revival include Ernest Boyd, *Ireland's Literary Renaissance*; and Richard Fallis, *The Irish Renaissance*. These accounts by American literary historians fall short in dealing with the complex relations between the Gaelic language and Gaelic culture revival spearheaded by Douglas Hyde and the literary movement proper that was dominated by Yeats, Synge, and Lady Gregory. Declan Kiberd's more recent "The Perils of Nostalgia: A Critique of the Revival" faults Hyde for failing to see Ireland's desperate need for modernization and industrialization to accompany a recovery of the old language, but praises him as "the most important scholar-in-waiting to the Irish Revival, supplying Yeats with folktales and themes, providing Synge and Lady Gregory with the basis of their dramatic dialect" (Connolly, ed., 16).

WORKS CITED

Adler, Alfred. *The Practice and Theory of Individual Psychology.* New York: Harcourt, 1929.

Aksakov, Sergei Timofeevich. *The Family Chronicle.* Translated by M. C. Beverley. New York: Dutton, 1961.

Allingham, William. *William Allingham's Diary.* Fontwell, Sussex: Centaur, 1967.

Arnold, Matthew. *On the Study of Celtic Literature.* London: Smith, Elder, 1867.

Auden. W. H. *Selected Poetry.* New York: Modern Library, 1958.

Austen, Jane. *Emma.* London: Dent Everyman, 1908.

———. *Northanger Abbey.* London: Dent Everyman, 1906.

Banim, John. *The Anglo-Irish of the Nineteenth Century.* 3 vols. New York: Garland, 1978. Facsimile of 1828 ed.

Barrington, Jonah. *Personal Sketches of His Own Times.* New York: Redfield, 1853.

Beckett, Samuel. *Endgame.* New York: Grove, 1958.

———. *Krapp's Last Tape and Other Dramatic Pieces.* New York: Grove, 1960.

———. *Watt.* New York: Grove, 1959.

Berkeley, George. *Philosophical Commentaries.* London: T. Nelson, 1944.

Bew, Paul. *C. S. Parnell.* Dublin: Gill and Macmillan, 1980.

Bliss, Alan, ed. *Spoken English in Ireland, 1600–1740: Twenty-seven Representative Texts Assembled and Analyzed.* Dublin: Cadenus, 1979.

Bloom, Harold, ed. *Elizabeth Bowen: Modern Critical Views.* New York: Chelsea House, 1981.

Blythe, Ernest. "Birth Pangs of a Nation." Dublin: *Irish Times*, Nov. 19, 1968, 1, 7.

Bowen, Elizabeth. *Bowen's Court.* 1st ed. New York: Knopf, 1942; 2d ed., 1964.

———. *Collected Impressions.* New York: Knopf, 1950.

———. *The Collected Stories of Elizabeth Bowen.* Introd. Angus Wilson. New York: Knopf, 1981.

———. *The Death of the Heart.* New York: Knopf, 1939.

———. *The Heat of the Day.* New York: Knopf, 1949.

———. *The House in Paris.* New York: Knopf, 1936.

———. *The Little Girls.* London: J. Cape, 1964.

———. *Look at All Those Roses: Short Stories.* London: Gollancz, 1941.

———. *Seven Winters: Memories of a Dublin Childhood and Afterthoughts: Pieces on Writing.* New York: Knopf, 1962.

———. *A World of Love.* London: J. Cape, 1955.

Boyd, Ernest. *Ireland's Literary Renaissance.* New York: Lane, 1916; rev. ed. Knopf, 1922.

Boyle, Mary. *Mary Boyle: Her Book.* Ed. C. Boyle. London: Dutton, 1902.

Brown, Stephen J. *Ireland in Fiction.* New ed. Dublin: Maunsel, 1919.

Brown, Terence. *Ireland: A Social and Cultural History, 1922 to the Present.* Ithaca: Cornell Univ. Press, 1985.

Butler, H. J. and H. E., eds. *The Black Book of Edgeworthstown and Other Edgeworth Memories, 1585–1817.* London: Faber and George, 1927.

Butler, Hubert. "The Country House—the Life of the Gentry." In *Social Life in Ireland, 1800–1845*, ed. R. B. MacDowell, 28–42. Dublin: Gill, 1947.

Butler, Marilyn. *Maria Edgeworth: A Literary Biography.* Oxford: Clarendon, 1972.

Büttner, Gottfried. *Samuel Beckett's Novel* Watt. Philadelphia: Univ. of Pennsylvania Press, 1984.

Carleton, William. *The Autobiography of William Carleton.* Rev. ed. London: Macgibbon and Kee, 1968.

———. *The Black Prophet: A Tale of the Irish Famine.* New York: Garland, 1979. Facsimile of 1847 ed.

———. *Father Butler* [and] *The Lough Dearg Pilgrim: Being Sketches of Irish Manners.* New York: Garland, 1979. Facsimile of 1829 ed.

———. *The Irish Agent; or, The Chronicles of Castle Cumber.* Illus. by Phiz. Dublin: James Duffy, 1847.

———. *Tales and Stories of the Irish Peasantry.* Illus. by Phiz. Dublin: James Duffy, 1845.

———. *Tales of Ireland.* New York: Garland, 1979. Facsimile of 1834 ed.

———. *Traits and Stories of the Irish Peasantry.* 1st ed. Dublin: William Curry, 1830; 2d series, 1833.

———. *Traits and Stories of the Irish Peasantry.* 2 vols. New ed. Illus. by Phiz, et al. Dublin: William Curry; London: William Orr, 1843–44.

———. *Willie Reilly and His Dear Cooleen Bawn.* New York: Lovell, 1856.

———. *The Works of William Carleton in Two Volumes.* 2 vols. Unabridged ed. New York: P. F. Collier, 1881.

Collis, Maurice. *Somerville and Ross: A Biography.* London: Faber and Faber, 1968.

Colum, Padraic. *Ourselves Alone!: The Story of Arthur Griffith and the Origin of the Irish Free State.* New York: Crown, 1959.

Connolly, Peter, ed. *Literature and the Changing Ireland.* Gerrard's Cross, Bucks.: Colin Smythe, 1982.

Conrad, Joseph. *The Secret Agent: A Simple Tale.* London: Methuen, 1907.

Corkery, Daniel. *The Hidden Ireland: A Study of Gaelic Munster in the Eighteenth Century.* Dublin: Gill, 1941.

Cronin, Anthony. *Heritage Now: Irish Literature in the English Language.* New York: St. Martin's Press, 1982.

Curtis, E., and R. B. Macdowell, eds. *Irish Historical Documents, 1172–1922.* London: Methuen, 1943.

Curtis, Edmund. *A History of Medieval Ireland.* Enlarged ed. London: Methuen, 1938.

Deane, S., A. Carpenter, and J. Williams, eds. *The Field Day Anthology of Irish Writing.* 3 vols. Derry: Field Day Publications, 1991.

Deane, Seamus. *Celtic Revivals: Essays in Modern Irish Literature, 1880–1980.* London: Faber and Faber, 1985.

———. *A Short History of Anglo-Irish Literature.* London: Hutchinson, 1986.

Devlin, Denis. *Lough Derg and Other Poems.* New York: Reynal, 1946.

Donleavy, J. P. *Leila.* New York: Delacorte/Seymour Lawrence, 1983.

Donoghue, Denis. *W. B. Yeats.* New York: Viking, 1971.

Downey, Edmund. *Charles Lever: His Life in His Letters.* 2 vols. Edinburgh and London: Blackwood, 1906.

Duffy, Charles Gavan, George Sigerson and Douglas Hyde, eds. *The Revival of Irish Literature.* London: T. F. Unwin, 1894.

Edgeworth, Henry Essex (the Abbé Edgeworth de Firmont). *Memoirs of the Abbé Edgeworth, Containing His Narrative of the Last Hours of Louis XVI.* London: Rowland Hunter, 1815.

Edgeworth, Maria. *The Absentee.* Ed. W. J. MacCormack and K. Walker. New York: Oxford Univ. Press, 1988.

———. *Belinda.* 3 vols. London, 1801.

———. *Castle Rackrent: An Hibernian Tale Taken from Facts, and from the Manners of the Irish Squires Before . . . 1782.* Ed. G. Watson. London: Oxford Univ. Press, 1964.

———. *Comic Dramas in Three Acts.* London: R. Hunter, 1817.

———. *Helen: A Tale.* London, 1834.

———. *Letters from England, 1813–1844.* Ed. Christina Colvin. Oxford: Clarendon, 1971.

———. *Maria Edgeworth in France and Switzerland: Selections from the Edgeworth Family Letters.* Oxford: Clarendon, 1979.

———. *Memoirs of R. L. Edgeworth . . . by Himself and Concluded by His Daughter, Maria Edgeworth.* 2 vols. Boston: Wells and Lilly, 1821.

———. *Tales of Fashionable Life.* 3 vols. Vol. 1: *Ennui.* London, 1809.

———. *A Tour in Connemara and The Martins of Ballinahinch.* Ed. H. E. Butler. London: Constable, 1950.

Edgeworth, Richard Lovell, and Maria Edgeworth. *Essay on Irish Bulls.* 3d ed. London: J. Johnson, 1808.

Fallis, Richard. *The Irish Renaissance.* Syracuse: Syracuse Univ. Press, 1977.

Farrell, J[ames] G[ordon]. *Troubles.* New York: Knopf, 1971.

Flanagan, Thomas J. *The Irish Novelists 1800–1850.* New York: Columbia Univ. Press, 1959.

Flannery, James. *W. B. Yeats and the Idea of a Theatre.* New Haven: Yale Univ. Press, 1976.

Gill, Richard. "The Country House in a Time of Trouble." In *Elizabeth Bowen: Modern Critical Views,* ed. H. Bloom, 51–61. New York: Chelsea House, 1981.

Glendinning, Victoria. *Elizabeth Bowen: Portrait of a Writer.* London: Weidenfeld, 1977.

Goya, Francisco de. *Los Caprichos.* Madrid, 1799.

Gregory, Augusta Persse. *Lady Gregory's Journals, 1916–1930.* Ed. Lennox Robinson. London: Putnam, 1946.

Gregory, Augusta Persse, and W. B. Yeats. *Visions and Beliefs in the West of Ireland.* 2 vols. New York and London: Putnam, 1920.

Halevy, Elie. *England in 1815.* New York: Barnes and Noble, 1961.

Hall, Wayne E. *Shadowy Heroes: Irish Literature of the 1890s.* Syracuse: Syracuse Univ. Press, 1980.

Hardy, Florence Emily. *The Life of Thomas Hardy, 1840–1928.* London: Macmillan, 1962.

Hardy, Thomas. *Notebooks.* Ed. F. E. Hardy. London: Hogarth, 1955.

Harris, Daniel. *Yeats: Coole Park and Ballylee.* Baltimore: Johns Hopkins Univ. Press, 1974.

Hayley, Barbara. *Carleton's* Traits and Stories *and the 19th Century Anglo-Irish Tradition.* Gerrard's Cross, Bucks.: Colin Smythe, 1983.

Heaney, Seamus. *Station Island.* New York: Farrar, Straus, 1985.

Henn, T. R. *The Lonely Tower: Studies on the Poetry of W. B. Yeats.* London: Methuen, 1950.

Hickey, D. J., and J. E. Doherty, eds. *A Dictionary of Irish History, 1800–1980.* Dublin: Gill and Macmillan, 1987.

Higgins, Aidan. *Langrishe Go Down.* New York: Grove, 1966.

"Historic Church in Ireland Still Used by Huguenots." *New York Times,* May 31, 1981, 8L.

Hone, Joseph. *The Life of George Moore.* New York: Macmillan, 1936.

Hughes, D. A., ed. *The Man of Wax: Critical Essays on George Moore.* New York: New York Univ. Press, 1971.

Hyde, Douglas, ed. and trans. *Love Songs of Connacht.* Dundrum: Dun Emer, 1904.

Joyce, James. *Dubliners.* New York: Viking, 1968.

———. *Finnegans Wake.* New York: Penguin , 1976.

———. *A Portrait of the Artist as a Young Man.* Definitive text. Ed. C. G. Anderson. New York: Random House, 1964.

———. *Ulysses.* Corrected text. New York: Random House, 1961.

———. *Ulysses.* Corrrected text. Ed. H. W. Gabler. New York: Random House Vintage, 1986.

Joyce, Patrick W. *English as We Speak It in Ireland.* Dublin: Talbot; London: Longmans, 1911.

Kiberd, Declan. "The Perils of Nostalgia: A Critique of the Revival." In *Literature and the Changing Ireland.* Ed. P. Connolly. Gerrard's Cross, Bucks.: Colin Smythe, 1982.

Kiely, Benedict. *Poor Scholar: A Study of William Carleton.* Dublin: Talbot, 1971.

Lawrence, D. H. *Studies in Classic American Literature.* New York: Viking, 1964.

Lecky, William Edward Hartpole. *A History of Ireland in the Eighteenth Century.* Abridged by L. P. Curtis. Chicago: Univ. of Chicago Press, 1972.

LeFanu, Joseph Sheridan. *Best Ghost Stories.* Ed. E. F. Bleiler. New York: Dover, 1964.

———. *The Cock and Anchor: Being a Chronicle of Old Dublin City.* 3 vols. Dublin: W. Curry, 1845.

———. *Ghost Stories and Mysteries*. Ed. E. F. Bleiler. New York: Dover, 1975.

———. *The House by the Churchyard*. Introd. E. Bowen. London: A. Blond, 1968.

———. *The Rose and the Key*. 3 vols. London: Chapman and Hall, 1871.

———. *The Watcher and Other Weird Stories*. London: Downey, 1894.

———. *Wylder's Hand*. New York: Carleton, 1865.

Lemon, Lee T., and Marion J. Reis, eds. *Russian Formalist Criticism: Four Essays*. Lincoln: Univ. of Nebraska Press, 1965.

Leslie, Shane, ed. and compiler. *St. Patrick's Purgatory: A Record from History and Literature*. London: Burns, Oates, 1932.

Lever, Charles James. *The Knight of Gwynne: A Tale of the Time of the Union*. 2 vols. Boston: Little, Brown, 1894.

———. *Lord Kilgobbin: A Tale of Ireland in Our Own Time*. 2 vols. London: Downey, 1899.

———. *The Martins of Cro-Martin*. Illus. by Phiz. London: Chapman and Hall, 1853.

———. *The Novels, Edited by his Daughter*. 37 vols. Copyright ed. London: Downey, 1899.

———. *The O'Donoghue: A Tale of Ireland Fifty Years Ago*. 2 vols. Boston: Little, Brown, 1894.

———. *St. Patrick's Eve*. London: Downey, 1899.

———. *Tom Burke of "Ours."* 2 vols. Boston: Little, Brown, 1892.

Lyons, F.S.L. *Charles Stewart Parnell*. London: Hutchinson, 1977.

———. *Ireland Since the Famine*. London: Collins, 1967.

———. "A Question of Identity: A Protestant View." *Irish Times*, Jan. 9, 1975.

MacCormack, William J. *Ascendancy and Tradition in Anglo-Irish Literary History from 1789 to 1939*. Oxford: Clarendon, 1985.

———. *Sheridan LeFanu and Victorian Ireland*. Oxford: Clarendon, 1980.

MacLysaght, Edward. *The Surnames of Ireland*. 3d ed. Dublin: Irish Academic Press, 1978.

Malton, James. *Dublin Views*. Dublin, 1799.

Martin, [Harriet] Mary Letitia. *Julia Howard*. 2d ed. London: Bentley, 1850.

Maturin, Charles Robert. *The Albigenses*. 4 vols. London: Hurst, 1824.

———. *Bertram; or, The Castle of St. Aldobrand: A Tragedy*. London: Murray, 1816.

———. *Fatal Revenge; or, The Family of Montorio: A Romance*. 4th ed. London, 1840.

———. *Five Sermons on the Errors of the Roman Catholic Church, Preached in St. Peter's Church, Dublin*. 2d ed. Dublin: Curry; London: Hamilton, Adams, 1826.

———. *Melmoth the Wanderer: A Tale*. Lincoln: Univ. of Nebraska Press, 1972. First published in 1820.

———. *The Milesian Chief: A Romance*. 4 vols. London: Colburn, 1812.

———. *The Wild Irish Boy*. 3 vols. London: Longman, 1808.

———. *Women; or,* Pour et Contre. 3 vols. London: Longman; Edinburgh: Constable, 1818.

Maxwell, Constantia. *Dublin under the Georges, 1714–1830.* 2d rev. ed. London: Faber, 1957.

McCarthy, Justin. *Reminiscences: In Two Volumes.* New York: Harper, 1899.

Miller, Liam. *The Noble Drama of W. B. Yeats.* Dublin: Dolmen Press; Atlantic Highlands, N.J.: Humanities Press, 1977.

Moody, T., and F. X. Martin, eds. *The Course of Irish History.* Cork: Mercier, 1967.

Moore, George. *Confessions of a Young Man.* New York: Brentano's, 1901.

———. *A Drama in Muslin: A Realistic Novel:.* Gerrard's Cross, Bucks.: Colin Smythe, 1981.

———. *George Moore in Transition: Letters to T. Fisher Unwin and Lena Milman, 1894–1910.* Ed. Helmut Garber. Detroit: Wayne State Univ. Press, 1968.

———. *Hail and Farewell.* 3 vols. (Vol. 1, *Ave*; Vol. 2, *Salve*; Vol. 3, *Vale*). London: Heinemann, 1947.

———. *Impressions and Opinions.* London: David Nutt, 1891.

———. *Letters to John Eglinton.* Ed. John Eglinton. Bournemouth: Sydenham, 1942.

———. *A Modern Lover.* 3 vols. London: Tinsley, 1883.

———. *Modern Painting.* London: Walter Scott, 1893.

———. *A Mummer's Wife.* London: Vizetelly, 1885.

———. *Parnell and His Island.* London: Swann, Sonnenschein, 1887.

———. *Terre d'Irelande.* Paris: Charpentier, 1887.

Moore, Thomas. *Memoirs of Captain Rock, the Celebrated Irish Chieftain.* Philadelphia: Carey and Lea, 1824.

Murphy, Geraldine. "Romancing the Center: Cold War Politics and Classic American Literature." *Poetics Today* 9, no. 4 (1988): 737–47.

Murphy, William. *Prodigal Father: The Life of John Butler Yeats (1839–1932).* Ithaca: Cornell Univ. Press, 1978.

Nietzsche, Friedrich. *The Will to Power.* Trans. W. Kaufmann and R. J. Hollingdale. New York: Random House, 1967.

O'Brien, Conor Cruise. *Writers and Politics.* New York: Pantheon, 1965.

O'Donoghue, D. J. *The Life and Writings of James Clarence Mangan.* Dublin: Gill, 1897.

O'Faolain, Sean. "Lovers of the Lake." In *The Stories of Sean O'Faolain.* London: Rupert Hart-Davis, 1958: 355–85.

O'Grady, Standish James. *Finn and His Companions.* London: Methuen, 1892.

———. *History of Ireland: The Heroic Period.* 2 vols. London: Methuen, 1878–81.

O'Sullivan, D. *The Irish Free State and Its Senate.* London, 1949.

Otway, The Reverend Cesar. *Sketches in Ireland: Descriptive of Interesting Portions of Donegal, Cork, and Kerry.* Dublin: Curry, 1827. Some copies subtitled *Descriptive of Interesting and Hitherto Unnoticed Districts in the North and South.*

Owen, Graham, ed. *George Moore's Mind and Art.* New York: Barnes and Noble, 1970.

Owenson, Sydney [Lady Morgan]. *The Wild Irish Girl.* London, 1806.

Powell, Violet. *The Irish Cousins.* London: Heinemann, 1970.

Random House Dictionary of the English Language. 2d ed. Unabridged. New York: Random House, 1987.

Ratchford, Fannie E., and William H. McCarthy, eds. *The Correspondence of Sir Walter Scott and Charles Robert Maturin.* Austin: Univ. of Texas Press, 1937.

Ritchie, Charles. *The Siren Years: Undiplomatic Diaries.* London: Macmillan, 1974.

Robinson, Hilary. *Somerville and Ross: A Critical Appreciation.* New York: St. Martin's, 1980.

Sadleir, Michael. "The Northanger Novels." *English Association Pamphlet 68.* London: Oxford Univ. Press, 1927.

Said, Edward W. *Culture and Imperialism.* New York: Knopf, 1993.

———"Yeats and Decolonization." In *Nationalism, Colonialism, and Literature.* Introd. Seamus Deane. Minneapolis: Univ. of Minnesota Press, 1990. 69–95.

Schroyer, Frederick. "Introduction." In *Uncle Silas.* New York: Dover, 1966. v–xiii.

Scott, Sir Walter. *Waverley.* 2 vols. Edinburgh: Constable, 1901.

Smith, Sydney. *The Works of the Reverend Sydney Smith.* 3 vols. London: Longman, Orme, 1840.

Somerville, Edith Oenone. *The Big House of Inver.* London: Zodiac, 1973.

———. *French Leave.* London: Longmans, Green, 1928.

———. *Happy Days!: Essays of Sorts.* London: Longmans, Green, 1946.

———. *An Incorruptible Irishman: Being an Account of Chief Justice Charles Kendal Bushe and of His Wife, Nancy Crampton, and Their Times, 1767–1843.* London: Ivor Nicholson and Watson, 1932.

———. *Maria and Some Other Dogs.* Illus E. Somerville. London: Methuen, 1949.

———. *Mount Music.* London: Longmans, Green, 1919.

Somerville, Edith Oenone, compiler. *Notes of the Horn: Hunting Verse, Old and New.* London: Peter Davies, 1934.

Somerville, Edith Oenone, and Martin Ross. *Further Experiences of an Irish R. M.* Illus. E. Somerville. London: Longmans, Green, 1908.

———. *In Mr. Knox's Country.* Illus. E. Somerville. London: Longmans, Green, 1915.

———. *An Irish Cousin.* London: Richard Bentley, 1889.

———. *Irish Memories.* London: Longmans, Green, 1918.

———. *Naboth's Vineyard.* London: Spencer Blackett, 1891.

———. *The Real Charlotte.* Ed. Virginia Beards. New Brunswick: Rutgers Univ. Press, 1986.

———. *Some Experiences of an Irish R. M.* Illus. E. Somerville. London: Longmans, Green, 1899.

———. *Some Irish Yesterdays.* Illus. E. Somerville. London: Longmans, Green, 1906.

———. *Stray-Aways.* Illus. E. Somerville. London: Longmans, Green, 1920.

———. *Through Connemara in a Governess Cart.* Illus. W. W. Russell and E. Somerville. London: W. H. Allen, 1893.

Spenser, Edmund. *A View of the Present State of Ireland.* 1596. In *Spenser's Prose Works.* Variorum ed., ed. R. Gotfried. Baltimore: Johns Hopkins Univ. Press, 1949: 39–231.

Stevenson, Lionel. *Dr. Quicksilver: The Life of Charles Lever.* London: Chapman and Hall, 1939.

Summers, Montague. *The Gothic Quest.* London: Fortune Press, 1939.

Swift, Jonathan. *A Dialogue in Hybernian Style Between A. and B. And Irish Eloquence.* Ed. A. Bliss. Dublin: Cadenus, 1977.

———. *The Drapier's Letters to the People of Ireland against Receiving Wood's Halfpence.* Ed. H. Davis. Oxford: Clarendon, 1935.

———. *A Modest Proposal for Preventing the Children of Poor People from Being a Burden to Their Parents, or the Country, and for Making Them Beneficial to the Publick.* Dublin: S. Harding, 1729.

Synge, John Millington. *Collected Works.* 4 vols. Ed. A. Saddlemyer. London: Oxford Univ. Press, 1968.

Thomson, David. *Woodbrook.* London: Barrie and Jenkins, 1974.

Toqueville, Alexis de. *Journeys to England and Ireland.* Ed. J. P. Mayer. New Haven: Yale Univ. Press, 1958.

Torchiana, Donald T. *W. B. Yeats and Georgian Ireland.* Evanston: Northwestern Univ. Press, 1966.

Trevor, William. *Fools of Fortune.* New York: Viking, 1983.

———. *The Silence in the Garden.* New York: Viking, 1989.

Ure, Peter. *Yeats and Anglo-Irish Literature: Critical Essays by Peter Ure.* Ed. C. J. Rawson. New York: Barnes and Noble, 1974.

Varma, Devendra P., ed. "General Introduction." In *The Collected Works of Joseph Sheridan LeFanu.* New York: Arno Press, 1977.

Walpole, Horace. *The Castle of Otranto: A Gothic Story.* 2d ed. London, 1765.

Webster's New World Dictionary of the American Language. College ed. Cleveland: World, 1964.

Wilde, Oscar. *The Artist as Critic: Critical Writings of Oscar Wilde.* Ed. R. Ellmann. New York: Random House Vintage, 1968.

Wilson, Edmund. *The Wound and the Bow.* Boston: Houghton, Mifflin, 1941.

Wilt, Judith. *Ghosts of the Gothic.* Princeton: Princeton Univ. Press, 1980.

Wolff, Robert Lee. *Ireland: From the Act of Union, 1800, to the Death of Parnell, 1891.* Publisher's brochure for Nineteenth Century Fiction Series, no. 2. New York: Garland, 1978.

———. *William Carleton: Irish Peasant Novelist.* New York: Garland, 1980.

Woodham-Smith, Cecil. *The Great Hunger: Ireland 1845–9.* London: H. Hamilton, 1962.

Wordsworth, William, and Samuel Taylor Coleridge. *Lyrical Ballads.* 2d ed. London, 1800.

Yeats, John Butler. *Letters to His Son W. B Yeats and Others, 1869–1922.* Ed J. Hone. New York: Dutton, 1946.

Yeats, William Butler. *The Autobiography.* New York: Collier Macmillan, 1965.

———. *The Celtic Twilight.* London: Lawrence and Bullen, 1893.

———. *The Collected Plays of W. B. Yeats.* New ed. New York: Macmillan, 1963.

———. *Essays and Introductions.* London: Macmillan, 1961.

———. *Explorations.* London: Macmillan, 1962.
———. "Fighting the Waves." In *Wheels and Butterflies.* London: Macmillan, 1934: 65–95.
———. *The Letters of W. B. Yeats.* Ed. Allan Wade. London: Rupert Hart-Davis, 1954.
———. *Memoirs: Autobiography First Draft and Journal.* Ed. Denis Donoghue. News York: Macmillan, 1972.
———. *Mythologies.* London: Macmillan, 1962.
———. *Purgatory: Manuscript Materials Including the Author's Final Text.* Ed. S. F. Siegel. Ithaca: Cornell Univ. Press, 1986.
———. *The Senate Speeches of W. B. Yeats.* Ed. D. R. Pearse. Bloomington: Indiana Univ. Press, 1960.
———. *A Vision: With Author's Final Revisions.* New York: Macmillan Collier, 1966.
———. *W. B. Yeats: The Poems.* Ed. R. J. Finneran. Rev. ed. New York: Macmillan, 1989.

INDEX

EAST BATON ROUGE PARISH LIBRARY
3 1659 01651 7688
DISCARD